IN A NUTSHELL

A Collection of Popular English Phrases

RICHARD LAWSON SINGLEY

Authored by a high school classmate
of mine who inspires me with his
search for knowledge.

Dad

PROMETHEUS EDUCATIONAL AND BUSINESS CONSULTANTS

IN A NUTSHELL

Published by Prometheus Educational and Business Consultants, Germantown, MD, 20876

ISBN   978-1-7321844-0-4

Amazon: https://www.amazon.com/Richard-Singley/e/B07FC71R87?ref=sr_ntt_srch_lnk_fkmr0_1&qid=1563812520&sr=8-1-fkmr0

Medium.com: https://medium.com/@richardsingley

Email: rich.singley5234@gmail.com

LinkedIn: https://www.linkedin.com/in/richard-singley-a7218332

Cover design by Adrian Christopher Singley and Richard Lawson Singley

Cover Image Library of Congress Reading Room [Public Domain]

Dedication: To my classmates and teachers at Abraham Clark High School in Roselle, NJ (Class of 1972) and Drexel University (Class of 1977) celebrating our 45th and 40th Anniversaries respectively. (See the Appendix for a list of the Class of 1972)

Special thanks to my good friend, Glenn Yanis, for his help in constructing and reviewing this book and Mabel Singletary, a fellow author, for her insight into the publishing world

Author's note:
Many have asked why I include my middle name, Lawson, on everything that I write. It is to honor my father Lawson Singley. He told me once that he didn't want to name any of his kids after him, but since I was born just before Father's Day, he decided to give me his name as a middle name. I am thankful to have been so honored and so blessed to have had a father like him

Contents

"I could be bounded in a nutshell, and count myself a king of infinite space"

William Shakespeare

Hamlet (Act II, Scene II)

Terms and Phrases

The following is an explanation of the terms and phrases used in this book:

1. **Adage** - A proverb or short statement expressing a general truth
2. **Aphorism** - A sharp observation that contains a general truth, such as, "if it ain't broke, don't fix it"
3. **Axiom** - A statement or proposition that is regarded as being established, accepted, or self-evidently true
4. **Catchphrase** - A well-known phrase, or expression typically one that is associated with a famous person, event or product
5. **Cliché** - A phrase or opinion that is overused so much that it betrays a lack of original thought
6. **Colloquialism** - A word or phrase that is not formal or literary, typically one used in ordinary or familiar conversation
7. **Definition** - A statement of the exact meaning of a word, especially in a dictionary
8. **Epigram** - A concise saying or remark expressing an idea in a clever and amusing way
9. **Euphemism** - A mild or indirect word or expression substituted for one considered to be too harsh or blunt when referring to something unpleasant or embarrassing
10. **Epithet** - An adjective or descriptive phrase expressing a quality characteristic of the person or thing mentioned
11. **Eponym** - A person after whom a discovery, invention, place, etc., is named or thought to be named
12. **Expression** - The process of making known one's thoughts or feelings
13. **Folklore** - Traditional beliefs, customs, and stories of a community, passed through the generations by word of mouth
14. **Foreign term** - Of, from, in, or characteristic of a country or language other than one's own
15. **Idiom** - A group of words established by usage as having a meaning not deducible from those of the individual words (e.g., raining cats and dogs, see the light)
16. **Lexicon** - The vocabulary of a person, language, or branch of knowledge
17. **Maxim** - A short, sharp statement expressing a general truth or rule of conduct
18. **Phrase** - A small group of words standing together as a conceptual unit, typically forming a component of a clause
19. **Proverb** - A short concise saying in general use, stating a general truth or piece of advice
20. **Pun** - A joke exploiting the different possible meanings of a word or the fact that there are words that sound alike but have different meanings

21. **Quotation** - A group of words taken from a text or speech and repeated by someone other than the original author or speaker
22. **Saying** - A short, terse expression that generally contains advice or wisdom
23. **Slang** - A type of language that consists of words and phrases that are regarded as very informal, are more common in speech than writing, and are typically restricted to a particular context or group of people
24. **Term** - A word or phrase used to describe a thing or to express a concept, especially in a particular kind of language or branch of study
25. **Vernacular** - The language or dialect spoken by the ordinary people in a particular country or region

Source: OxfordDictionaries© Oxford University Press

Introduction

Humans are the only species on earth capable of intelligent speech. Although every language is unique, each language has its own set of metaphorical terms, proverbs and phrases which are constantly used in formal and informal speech. In fact, it is difficult to go a day without using at least one. I have always been fascinated by them, and over the years I kept a log of such expressions. As a result, it has become second nature for me to listen to what people are saying and to extract conversational expressions. The average person familiar with English will recognize thousands of metaphorical sayings and intuitively know what they mean. For example: If a person says that "someone is not dealing with a full deck," most people will know what he or she means and how it applied to the situation. Such expressions paint a picture of a given situation that is more enduring and insightful than if it were said literally. They tend to be rich in wisdom and range from the simple to the sublime. It is safe to assume, that for an expression to last throughout the ages, and in some cases to transcend languages, it must strike at the heart of what it is for us to be human.

The art of communication lies not in its terms or its phrases but in the metaphors that they evoke. "The mystic chords of memory" and "the better angels of our nature:" enduring words spoken by America's 16th president, clearly illustrate that "the whole is much greater than the sum of its parts."[1] Such expressions not only identify the times; but stand as a testimony to the character and intellect of the person that uttered them. Aristotle in the *Poetics* (330 BC) stated: "The greatest thing by far, is to have a command of metaphor. This alone cannot be imparted by another; it is the mark of genius, for to make good metaphors implies an eye for resemblance." Metaphors are like chameleons and depending on the background in which they are spoken, they can change or enrich the content of the conversation. In this regard, metaphors are often used to emphasize a point or to provide a unique perspective. Take the phrase: "the meeting was a three-ring circus." The word circus has been transformed from the realm of entertainment to the domain of business and thus the listener forms a picture of how the meeting progressed; replete with its share of clowns, ringside seats, as well as a kaleidoscope of strange sights to behold.

---

[1] From Abraham Lincoln's First Inaugural Address: We are not enemies, but friends. We must not be enemies. Though passion may have strained it must not break our bonds of affection. The mystic chords of memory, stretching from every battlefield and patriot grave to every living heart and hearthstone all over this broad land, will yet swell the chorus of the Union, when again touched, as surely they will be, by the better angels of our nature.

IN A NUTSHELL

We speak words with our mouths and hear them with our ears, but our brains interpret the world in images often formed by metaphorical terms and phrases. Our minds are wired pictorially and even when we dream of things, real or imaginary, we cognitively paint pictures of those experiences in metaphors. It is interesting to note, that although we hear words and phrases, when we understand what is articulated we often say I "see" what you mean. In the final analysis, everything is a metaphor for something else. If, therefore, we are to imbue our machines to emulate human behavior we must be conscious of this universal fact. In other words, if our machines are to communicate effectively and emotionally with us in the future, they must be taught how to speak to us metaphorically. Instead of saying "hello" or "goodbye" in a non-human way; perhaps they would say: "what's happening?" or "see you later alligator, in a while crocodile."

This is not a book about how to speak English directly but rather, one about how to communicate better by using the hidden power of metaphor. So often, in traditional English classes, grammar, vocabulary and spelling are emphasized to the exclusion of other elements that are germane to communication. More often, it is the figurative and not the literal speech that is used to explain a given situation and sometimes the reader must read between the lines to interpret what was said. With the advent of automatic grammar and spell checkers, we should revisit how English is taught and perhaps place a greater emphasis on how people speak figuratively. Our conversational styles and the phrases we choose to use are often invisible to us. But like our body language, they tell the listener much about how we view the world. Moreover, they often leave impressions that are not easy to erase or change. As the saying goes: "You never get a second chance to make a first impression." How you use your words and phrases is crucial to how you will be remembered.

There are expressions in this book for the white-collar and blue-collar worker; the prince and the pauper, the well-read and the under-read. It contains a wide range of sayings: from antiquity to modern times; from intellectuals such as Homer and Shakespeare to comic figures such as Snagglepuss and Homey D. Clown. Non-English-speakers or people new to the English language, often have a tough time understanding terms and phrases that are unique to the English language and its culture which cannot be taken literally. When learning English formally, one would learn to ask: Where is the restroom? However, informally one may say: where is the John or I need to take a crap. These are English eponyms associated with the invention of the toilet. Knowledge of such expressions will not only increase their understanding and fluency of English; but will also open up new windows of self-expression and conventions of social homogeneity. Even those familiar with the English language can use this book to enhance their knowledge of phrases and terms used in conversational English. The more accurate the metaphor, the more concise the idea or thought that is exchanged-- hence the expression "a picture is worth a thousand words."

A COLLECTION OF POPULAR ENGLISH PHRASES

Although many sayings have their origins in Great Britain, America has a set of colloquialisms uniquely their own such as Benedict Arnold. Furthermore, like American vocabulary, there are some expressions originating in England that were later Americanized. As George Bernard Shaw once said: "England and America are two countries separated by a common language." But there are many common threads, as Shakespeare and the King James Bible, the legacy of Britain's Elizabethan and Jacobean eras, have been great resources of such expressions. It is no accident that the works of Shakespeare and the Bible are both rich in metaphor. [2] Both seem to encompass the full multiplicity of human experiences which is the essence of metaphor. Shakespeare contributed over 1,700 words and numerous phrases to the English language. The King James Bible historically has been one of the most read and quoted books. In fact, Abraham Lincoln, a person known for his sayings, read both judiciously and perhaps this is why his figurative speech is so enduring.

It was from this island off the coast of the European continent, or as Shakespeare referred to it: "the precious stone set in the silver sea" that enriched the world through its culture and language. Through conquest and culture, the stone which has now become its language, has been polished but not removed. So often we forget, that the Founding Fathers of America were born Englishmen and not Americans and although America has been the melting pot of the world, it is the English language that unites its people and serves as an emblem of its greatness.

Phrases tend to resonate because there is a common source from which people can identify. In addition to expressions that have English origins, Greco-Roman mythology and philosophy also serve as a foundation of many English expressions.[3] Famous lines from books and novels have been a source for popular phrases. With the emergence of film, radio and television in the 20th century, various catchphrases also entered the English vernacular. This book is an earnest attempt to catalogue, and in some cases, explain English phrases used in daily speech. Two different versions of the book will be released (but not necessarily at the same time). The hard copy will contain over 1,500 explained expressions (volume I), and the electronic version will contain those explained expressions plus 7,500 unexplained expressions (volume II). In this case, the Internet could be used on some devices to reference or search unexplained expressions (newer versions of the Kindle are equipped with this feature). Furthermore, the electronic version is linked to websites, to help in the pronunciation of terms, e.g., (As Rich as Croesus) and to provide additional historical clarification via YouTube. To this end, over 750 video and external links are included in the electronic book. This feature allows the reader to venture down the rabbit hole of the expression and to engage in the rich history and cinematic features contained within.

---

[2] To familiarize the reader with these enduring and seminal works, the Appendix of this book includes a list of Shakespeare's work along with a list of Biblical chapters. For the Shakespearean lover, I highly recommend Shakespeare, The invention of the Human, by Harold Bloom
[3] See Appendix for a list of Greek and Roman gods and goddesses

IN A NUTSHELL

In the first volume, the origins and the meaning of some of the more elaborate sayings are provided. Although many of them are idiomatic in nature, it also contains proverbs, aphorisms, unique terms and sources of wisdom. I have found that knowing the origin of prevalent sayings to be intriguing and helpful in understanding the context of the saying, the times from which it originated along with its importance to posterity. We are not only passing the expression itself, but its history and significance. We must be remindful that "language is the archive of history." Many things that once had practical meanings have become metaphors for something else. For instance, when we say "rocket science" or "to drop a dime on someone," or "straight from the horse's mouth;" or to tape something instead of to record it; they speak of the times from which they emerged. To some extent, this book is as much about history as it is about language.

The second volume is dedicated to those expressions that are more generic in use and idiomatic in nature. Quite often, these expressions are self-explanatory. For example, most people may not know or understand what it means "to cross the Rubicon" or "to cut the Gordian knot" or what a "Hobson's choice" is without knowing something about the origin of the phrase. Such phrases are part of the first volume. Whereas phrases such as "not dealing with a full deck" are more self-explanatory and therefore are included in the second volume. But if such phrases have an interesting origin, or if I feel that a popular phrase can be enriched or elaborated on, they appear in the first volume.

Because of the dynamic nature of colloquial expressions, there is no such thing as a complete book on idioms, slang, proverbs, terms, etc., regardless how large or how small. A term or phrase such as *Google* or *Xerox* can emerge tomorrow and reverberate for a thousand years as some in this book have resonated. I was fortunate enough to have lived in a household that was rich in sayings and metaphors. Although my forefathers and foremothers were not exemplars of the English language; they were masters of the art of metaphor. I was raised on the richness of their verse and nurtured from the fruits of their wisdom. Hardly a day passed without someone saying: "you know what those old folks used to say." As I got older, I found myself repeating those phrases to my children. I have realized that knowing metaphorical expressions enhances my knowledge of the English language and provides me with additional ways to express myself both orally and in written form. Perhaps this was the genesis of this book. In addition to metaphors, I also wanted to expose the reader to the history of unique terms that have become an integral part of our daily lives.

Tracing the origins of a phrase could be difficult and every so often unknown or unclear. Quite often, it is difficult to discern the originator from the person that popularized it. Occasionally, expressions are related to each other; sometimes because they articulate the same or similar idea in different words, or the opposite of the idea or because they come from the same time period or source. For example: straight from the horse's mouth, long in the tooth and don't look a gift horse in the mouth are all derived from the fact that one could determine the age of a horse by looking in its mouth. Similarly, vale of years and salad days are opposite to each other. In such cases, I have placed the related saying in bold letters as part of the explanation of the saying. I have also taken the opportunity in this volume to teach about the history or the times of the phrase or to add philosophical comments when appropriate.

Because of the influence of the English-speaking people on the world over the last several centuries, English is the Lingua Franca of the emerging global world. Nearly two billion people worldwide speak the English language. All the more reason for people to be familiar with its expressions, idiosyncrasies and usage. The volumes of this book are particularly helpful to high school and college students that desire to attain a better command of the English language or to broaden the scope of their oral and written skills. To this end, as an exercise, students should try to use the expressions, especially those delineated in the first volume, in sentences. It is my hope that the reader will not only learn to speak better conversational English but learn from the wisdom and life experiences contained within. Also included are over 100 internet and texting terms; such as LOL (Laughing Out Loud) that are becoming an increasing part of communication.

Finally, I have tried to give an accurate quotation of the expression. For example, my parents would always say "an owl's mind is a devil's work pit" when the saying actually states: "an idle mind is a devil's workshop." In most cases, I try to represent the expression in its most popular form. For instance, instead of listing skin a cat, I have listed, there is more than one way to skin a cat. Above all, it is my sincerest wish that this book will give the reader an appreciation of the wide scope, beauty and richness of the English language.

The format of the first volume of this book is as follows:
1. The phrase or term is introduced
2. The origin of the phrase is explained
3. Historical content, videos and external links are added when appropriate
4. An explanation of its current usage is given
5. Similar phrases or terms as well as other idiomatic expressions are highlighted in bold
6. Bold underlined text represents external links to videos or other sources (applicable only in the electronic version)

IN A NUTSHELL

Volume I

Explained Terms and Phrases

Stands for:

Ambrosia from the gods

IN A NUTSHELL

A Benedict Arnold - This term originated from the name of an American general during the American Revolutionary War. Arnold switched from the American side to the British side of the war after being passed over by Congress for a promotion. He fled behind British lines and lived the rest of his life in Britain. In an ironic historical twist, the fort that he was given command of by George Washington at West Point, became the home of the United States Military Academy established by Thomas Jefferson and headed by a grandnephew of Ben Franklin. Furthermore, America's second most notorious traitor, Aaron Burr, once served under Arnold. Because of his treasonous acts, during America's war of Independence, Arnold's name became synonymous in America with "traitor." **A turncoat** essentially means the same thing and is a person who deserts one group or cause to join an opposing one. This term, however, has its origin in trading one's uniform for another

A bird doesn't sing because it has an answer, it sings because it has a song - This quote is widely attributed to Marguerite Ann Johnson better known as: Maya Angelou and even appears on a United States postage stamp honoring her. However, further investigation attributes it to Joan Walsh Anglund. This is just one of many cases where a saying is attributed to the person that popularized it and not the person that originated it. Nevertheless, the quote speaks to the innate power of the human spirit that dares to show us the nature of its being. We are all, in essence, caged birds confined to our version of reality interpreted by our senses and **sense of being**. Yet we dare to sing, not because we have all of the answers, but because we have a song and we want it to be heard. On a similar note, **a bird in a gilded cage** means: to live a life of wealth and luxury but to be without true freedom, joy or pleasure

A blessing in disguise - Like so many sayings that have **stood the test of time**, the origin of the phrase is unknown. However, it is believed to have come into use in the mid-1700s. The earliest occurrence of the term in print was a work by the English clergyman and writer, James Hervey, in his book entitled: Reflections on a Flower-Garden, In A Letter To A Lady. published in 1746 and some have attributed it to him. So often in life, we cannot determine if something is good or bad without the benefit of retrospect. The common interpretation is: an apparent misfortune that eventually has good results or consequences. **Unintended consequences**

A booty call - This is a term that has resurfaced during the 1990s along with other sexual euphemisms such as **to hook up**. The term booty has been around for some time and is regularly associated with a person's behind(butt), e.g., **shake that booty; loose booty**. The term refers to: an invitation, rendezvous or tryst in which both parties agree to have sex often **without any strings attached** or long-term commitment. Additionally, **Netflix and chill** is a term that emerged in the early 21st century and means virtually the same thing. The following expressions are also similar in connotation: **A one-night stand;** like **two ships passing in the night**

A brave new world - This is a phrase that was made famous by the book of the same name written by Aldous Huxley and published in 1932. The title comes from Shakespeare's play The Tempest (Act V, Scene I) although it was used in a different context. It is a **dystopian** book **in the vein of** Capek's earlier RUR, about a future world in which humans are reliant on technology. The popular interpretation is: a world or environment that is drastically transformed (especially by science and technology) featuring positive or negative consequences. An imaginary futuristic world

A bridge to far - The source of this expression has its roots in the World War II Operation Market Garden initiative (September 1944) that was popularized by the book by Cornelius Ryan (1974) and the subsequent film (1977). It has migrated to mean: a step or act that is regarded as being too drastic to take. **A bridge to nowhere** is similar but means: a bridge with at least one end open. The common usage of this phrase is: a step or act that is regarded as being too drastic to take; going nowhere. Similar expressions include: **don't cross the bridge till you come to it; praise the bridge that carries you over**

A calculated risk - The origin of this term comes from the calculations made during World War II about the chances of losing bombers on a particular bombing mission. It now means: a chance of failure, the probability of which is estimated before some action is undertaken. **Risk versus reward**

A carbon copy - This term originated from the use of carbon paper to make a copy of a document. This was before the advent of modern-day copying machines. It now means: a copy of something or someone, an exact duplicate. **Xerox copy**

A Cassandra - In Greek mythology, Cassandra was the daughter of Priam and Hecuba, endowed with the gift of prophecy but fated never to be believed. It now refers to one that predicts misfortune or disaster especially if it is discarded. **A bad omen**

A Casanova - The origin of this term comes from Giacomo Casanova. He was an Italian writer known for his sexual exploits and erotic writings. The term now designates: a person known to habitually seduce or attract women. **A Don Juan** is used similarly. This term, however, originated from the legendary Spanish nobleman Don Juan Tenorio who was famous for his many seductions and self-indulgent lifestyle. It now means: a ladies' man; a womanizer

A chain is only as strong as its weakest link - This expression is credited to the Scottish philosopher Thomas Reid in his essays entitled: The Intellectual Powers of Man, 1786. It means that the total strength of something is dependent upon its individual parts

A chameleon - This term, when used as a metaphor, has its origins in a type of lizard with a highly developed capability to change color to match its background as a means of avoiding predators. It is often used to describe a person that changes his opinion, attitude or beliefs to match the situation. Something that changes in order to blend in with its surroundings

A chicken in every pot and a car in every garage - This was the 1928 campaign slogan of Herbert Hoover. Ironically, it did not prove to be prophetic, instead just the opposite. During his term as president, the Great Depression started and it lasted throughout his presidency; rendering Hoover near the bottom of the list of American presidents. The phrase now means that everyone will be prosperous in America and thus live **the American dream. Streets are paved with gold**

IN A NUTSHELL

A Cinderella story - This saying is attributed to a young female in various traditional European fairy tales. In the version by the French author, Charles Perrault noted for his Mother Goose Tales and his contributions to the fairy tale genre. She is exploited as a servant by her family but enabled by **a fairy godmother** to attend a royal ball. The common usage is: someone who is unjustly neglected or treated unfair, yet finds temporary or lasting happiness. **A fairytale ending. A fairy godmother,** common in many fairytales, has migrated to mean; someone that is helpful to or serves as a mentor or benefactor to someone; especially in times of need

A clear and present danger - The origin of this expression is from the Supreme Court's assessment regarding the conditions of which restrictions can be placed on the rights guaranteed by the First Amendment of the Constitution (Freedom of Speech). For example: words which by their very utterance inflict injury or tend to incite an immediate breach of the peace are not protected by the First Amendment. The phrase itself may have been propagated by the popular book and subsequent 1994 movie of the same name which moved it into the public view not as a legal matter but of a figure of speech. It now refers to: any immediate threat to the welfare or well-being of a nation, individual or group. **Represents a clear and present danger; existential threat**

A contented mind is a perpetual feast - The source of this saying appears to be the Bible (Proverbs 15:15) "he who is of a merry heart has a continual feast." Although the exact words are not used, it echoes the same sentiment. The phrase is generally interpreted to mean: if a person is happy and satisfied, they are at peace with themselves and therefore happy with what they have and who they are

A coward dies a thousand deaths a hero dies but one - This phrase, like so many, is ascribed to the renowned English playwright William Shakespeare and is from his play Julius Caesar (Act I, Scene I). It means: fears and anxieties beset a coward who lives in constant fear; whereas the hero will only die once and not by the many imagined ways a coward will envision his death. It also speaks to the nobility of doing the right thing and accepting responsibility along with the willingness to sacrifice. Similar expressions are: **Virtue is its own reward, a guilty conscience needs no accuser**

A crystal ball - This expression has its origins in fortunetellers and mystics that proclaimed they could peer into the future by using a crystal (glass) ball. It has since, by extension, migrated to mean: to predict the future. **Crystal clear**

A cup of hemlock - The source of this expression is from Plato's Phaedo. In this dialogue, Plato's mentor Socrates was convicted of heresy and of corruption of the youth and thus forced to drink hemlock (poison). It is now used in the vein of **walk the plank** or **to fall on your sword.** It means" to be forced to do something that is detrimental to you even when your cause or intent was just. **Nail Jesus to the cross**

A Daniel come to judgement - The roots of this phrase is undoubtably the Bible (Dan. 5:14), however, the phrase itself was coined by Shakespeare in his play a Merchant of Venice (Act IV, Scene I). "A Daniel come to judgment, yea, a Daniel! O wise young judge, how I do honor thee!" Daniel was known for his wise judgement and his ability to interpret dreams. The phrase now denotes: a person that wisely settles a difficult matter or resolves a problematic situation. **To cut the Gordian knot; wisdom of Solomon**

6

A COLLECTION OF POPULAR ENGLISH PHRASES

A Delilah - This term is from the Bible, (Judges 16: 4-22). She is the woman who betrayed Samson to the Philistines by revealing to them that the secret of his strength lay in his long hair. The common usage is: a treacherous and seductive woman, especially a wife or mistress who brings ruin upon her lovers. **A Jezebel**; Samson and Delilah

A diamond in the rough - The first recorded use in print of this saying is in A Wife for a Month, 1624 by the English playwriter John Fletcher. It now designates: an object or a person with exceptional qualities that cannot be seen on the surface

A dinosaur - This term has its roots in the fact that the age of the dinosaur ended tens of millions of years ago and thus considered old and extinct. It has therefore come to be used as old or in some cases to mean: to become extinct, obsolete, old-fashioned, or no longer in common use; anachronistic. **Go the way of the dinosaur(s); old school**

A Don Quixote - The source of this term is from a novel of the same name written in the early 17th century by Miguel de Cervantes who is often regarded as the foremost Spanish writer. Cervantes lived an interesting life and was imprisoned on several occasions. Ironically, this Shakespeare of the Spanish language is reported to have died on April 23, 1616 the same day that William Shakespeare died. Don Quixote is a knight obsessed upon bringing justice to the world around him. The book is about him **fighting windmills** that he imagines are giants. The term now means: an impractical idealist bent on righting hopeless wrongs. Other terms or phrases associated with this book are: **Fighting (chasing) windmills** means: to chase or to fight something that is meaningless. **Quixotic**, means: something that is exceedingly idealistic; unrealistic and impractical. **Tilt at windmills** means: to attack imaginary enemies or evils. **To fling your cap over the windmill** means: to act in a deranged or reckless manner

A drowning man will clutch at a straw - The source of this proverb is unknown. The common interpretation is: someone who is desperate will try to use anything or anybody for help, even if it is really no help at all. In this case there are three choices: you pull him up; he pulls you down; or you let him go. **When your back is against the wall**

A faint heart never won a fair lady - The origin of this phrase goes back to the Renaissance period and the phrase: "A coward verely neuer obteyned the loue of a faire lady" recorded in R. Taverner tr. Erasmus' Adages written in 1545 and was refined to give us its current usage. Erasmus' Adagia contains more than 4,000 proverbs and maxims gathered and commented on by Erasmus, many of them from Greek and Latin sources. This expression is currently used to tell someone that they must make a lot of effort if they want to achieve something difficult. Similar phrases include: **the course of true love never runs smooth; if you want something, you have to work for it**

A fallen angel - The source of this term is from the Bible (Revelation 12: 7-12) although the term itself is not mentioned directly in the Bible. It refers to an angel that has been casted out of Heaven, chief among the so-called demons is Satan. So often we forget that "**the devil is an angel too**" and Shakespeare wrote in Macbeth (Act IV, Scene III): Angels are bright; still, though, the brightest fell. However, it is in John

Milton's Paradise Lost that we find perhaps the most iconoclastic view of Satan as the fallen angel best expressed by the phrase: **better to reign in Hell than to serve in Heaven**. The term has migrated to mean: a demon or evil person or sometimes a good person turned bad. **The devil can cite scripture for his own purpose.** On a similar note: **a guardian angel is** an angel assigned to protect a person, a group, or a nation and is antithetical to a fallen angel. **Lucifer; Prince of Darkness**

A fate worse than death - This phrase originally applied to rape or to lose one's virginity. It attested to the belief that a dishonored woman was better off dead. It has migrated to mean: any misfortune that would make life unbearable or agonizing

A fish rots from the head down - This is an ancient proverb that appears in several cultures although it is regularly associated with Italians. The popular interpretation is: when an organization, group or nation fails, it is usually caused by poor or incompetent leadership. **The buck stops here; pass the buck.** A **fish wrapped in paper** is another fish metaphor of Italian origin and is a sign that something or someone is dead or better yet has been murdered and is now **sleeping with the fishes** or that the body was dumped in the ocean. It normally contains an article of the deceased clothing or even a piece such as a finger of the deceased

A fool and his money are soon parted - The first recorded use of this expression was in a poem entitled: Five Hundred Points of Good Husbandry, written by the English poet Thomas Tusser in 1557. The common usage is: an irresponsible, naive or foolish person and his money are soon separated. **To the fool, he who speaks wisdom will sound foolish**

A fool may give a wise man counsel - The sentiment of this expression dates to at least the Middle Ages, however, it was first recorded in English in the 1600s. It means: on one hand, do not be overconfident in the advice of others, and on the other; someone who is intellectually inferior may, in some cases, offer good or sound advice

A foregone conclusion - The source of this expression is William Shakespeare's Othello (Act III, Scene III) and is one of many that comes from this **time-honored** play. It refers to: a result that can be predicted with certainty. An obvious result. **Forlorn hope** is somewhat similar and means: a persistent or desperate hope that is unlikely to be fulfilled or realized

A fortiori - This is a Latin term that has become part of the English language. In Latin it literally means: "from the stronger." It is normally used when making an argument that is stronger than the previous argument made or taking a position that is tougher or more robust than the previous one. **Argumentum a fortiori**

A friend in need is a friend indeed - This is a popular proverb that appears in several languages. It was first recorded by the Roman Quintus Ennius in the 3rd century BCE. It is sometimes erroneously ascribed to the

A COLLECTION OF POPULAR ENGLISH PHRASES

American polymath and Founding Father Ben Franklin. It means what it says: a person who helps at a difficult time is a truly reliable person

A geek - The origin of this term is a performer in a circus, and it emerged at the turn of the 20th century. It was originally used to describe a sideshow of freaks. The word **nerd** is similar; but, the origin of this word is uncertain. However, this term was popularized by the 1970s show Happy Days. Both terms now mean: a socially inept person, a technical person, scientist or engineer with a passion for technology. **Computer geek**

A gentleman and a scholar - The origin of this phrase is unclear. However, it appears to have been used in a poem entitled The Twa (Two) Dogs by Robert Burns (1759-1796). "His locked, lettered, lovely brass collar; Showed him the gentleman and scholar; But although he was of high degree; The fiend of pride, no pride had he." There are some men that are scholars and others that are gentlemen; but the preferred choice is to be a scholar and a gentleman. This term is frequently used to describe a person that is not only respected for his knowledge but the way he conducts himself as a member of the human race. **A lady and a scholar** means the same thing. They are normally used as compliments

A Hail Mary - This term has its origin in the Catholic Church specifically a prayer the "Hail Mary," *Ave Maria* in Latin, which is a plea for the Virgin Mary to intercede on your behalf or a cause. The saying became popular after a 1975 football game between the Dallas Cowboys and the Minnesota Vikings won by the Cowboys on a long pass from Roger Staubach to Drew Pearson. Since then, it has been known as a Hail Mary pass in football. However, outside of football, the term has migrated to generally mean: a desperate last effort to accomplish or achieve something. Something that is difficult to accomplish and thus needs the intervention of an outside spiritual source. **A long shot; A Hail Mary pass**

A ham - This term was first linked to the performance of white people dressed up in blackface to imitate black people in the late 1800s and early 1900s. This was a way of poking fun at African Americans and is a stain on American history. The term migrated to mean an inferior performer. The association of this term with black people comes from the Bible. Black people, according to the interpretation (exegesis) of the Bible, are the descendants of Noah's son Ham. Ham, according to the Table of Nations in the Book of Genesis (Genesis: Chapters 10-11), was a son of Noah and the father of Cush (Ethiopia), Mizraim (Egypt), Phut and Canaan. In an ironic twist, according to biblical history, the descendants of Ham were among the most prolific of all the races in antiquity. Moreover, modern science through DNA testing, (both mitochondrial and Y chromosome) has proven that the black race is the primogenitor of all races dating back at least 100,000 years. Consequently, the other races are the results of genetic mutations, in most cases, these mutations were induced to increase their chances of survival in various environments. The common interpretation is: any incomplete or unskilled actor and has also been extended to a person

A (Harry) Houdini (Pull a Houdini) - The origin of this term comes from the renowned American magician Ehrich Weisz, known as Harry Houdini. He took his stage name from another magician known for his fearless and dangerous feats. Known for escaping from unusual and strange circumstances, such as coffins, straightjackets and multiple handcuffs, he received universal acclaim for his daring stage and public acts. The phrase **to pull a Houdini** now designates: a person that performs amazing disappearing acts, illusions or escapes. Similarly, a Houdini is a person that displays magical or amazing acumen in any field especially in difficult situations. **Pull the rabbit out of the hat; to disappear (vanish) into thin air**

A house divided against itself cannot stand - This saying is attributed to Abraham Lincoln and was delivered in a speech given on June 16, 1858 in which he referred to the United States being divided between the North and the South. In fact, Lincoln is quoting the Bible (Mark 3:25) "And if a house be divided against itself, that house cannot stand." The common usage is: a group or organization weakened by internal dissensions will be unable to withstand external pressures

A house of cards - The origin of this term is unclear. However, it dates back to the 18th century. It originally applied to a structure that was build out of balanced playing cards. It is now used to describe: something that is innately fragile and thus can be easily broken or destroyed. Something that cannot stand the test of time and thus will eventually crumble. **And the walls came crumbling down**

A Humpty Dumpty - This saying originates from the egglike nursery rhyme character, Humpty Dumpty. The rhyme goes: "Humpty Dumpty sat on a wall; Humpty Dumpty had a great fall. **All the King's horses and all the King's men**; Couldn't put Humpty together again." The rhyme was first printed in 1810 and became famous through the novel: Alice Through the Looking Glass by the English writer Lewis Carroll. However, it is a very old English rhyme that precedes Carroll and goes back at least to the time of Charles I. In Carroll's novel, Humpty Dumpty is depicted as a large round egg. It has come to mean a fat, overweight person or a person or thing that once overthrown cannot be restored. Similar phrases include: **to knock Humpty Dumpty off the wall; Alice in Wonderland; what's done cannot be undone**

A Jezebel - This term comes from the biblical figure notorious for her wickedness. She was denounced by Elijah for introducing the worship of Baal into Israel (1 Kings 16:31, 21:5–15, 2 Kings 9:30–7). It means: a shameless, scheming or immoral woman. **A Delilah**

A Jonah - This term comes from the Bible (2 Kings 14:25), Jonah was called by God to preach in Nineveh, but disobeyed and attempted to escape by sea. In a storm, he was thrown overboard and swallowed by a great fish. He remained in its belly for three days before being cast up onto the shore unharmed. The term means: a person that brings bad luck or who spoils the plans of others. **Typhoid Mary; a Casandra**

A journey of a thousand miles begins with the first step - This proverb is often credited to the Chinese philosopher, Lao Tzu. He is traditionally regarded as the founder of Taoism and author of the Tao-te-Ching. The phrase means: in any endeavor, no matter how long or how short, the initial step must be taken before the journey or task can begin. **On arrival, the journey begins**

A Judas goat - So named after Judas Iscariot one of the original twelve disciples who betrayed Christ and is defined as: the stockyard goat that leads the unsuspecting animals to slaughter. **A Judas kiss** is also named after Judas Iscariot. In the New Testament, Judas identifies Jesus to the Roman soldiers with a kiss.

A COLLECTION OF POPULAR ENGLISH PHRASES

The latter means: an act of betrayal, especially one disguised as a gesture of friendship. Also, referred to as **a kiss of death. Thirty pieces of silver**

A la carte - This is a French expression that has worked its way into the English language. It literally means according to the card. When used in a restaurant setting, it denotes: a listing or serving of food that can be ordered as separate items, rather than as a set meal

A little knowledge is dangerous - This phrase is attributed to the 18th century English poet, Alexander Pope. From his Essays on Criticism. "A little learning is a dangerous thing; drink deep, or taste not the Pierian spring: there shallow draughts intoxicate the brain, and drinking largely sobers us again." The **Pierian spring** was a fountain in Pieria, sacred to the Muses and supposedly conferring inspiration or learning on anyone who drank from it. Hence, the phrase means that those that know a little about something may think that they are more expert than they are which could lead to overreach; knowing a little about something can tempt one to overestimate one's abilities or boundaries

A living dog is better than a dead lion - This saying comes from the Bible (Ecclesiastes, 9:4-5) "for to him that is joined to all the living there is hope: for a living dog is better than a dead lion. For the living know that they shall die: but the dead know not any thing, neither have they any more a reward." The saying in the context that it was written is a celebration of life and means that anything that is living is better than something that is dead

A lone wolf - This term takes its name from the behavior of wolves in the wild. Typically, wolves live and hunt in packs. Occasionally, for various reasons, a wolf will be excluded from or leave a pack and act independently. Wolves are known for their ferocity, ability to hunt and track their prey. Therefore, the term means: a person that prefers to live or act alone. Most recently, the term has been applied to a terrorist that acts alone and independent of a group

A man who is his own lawyer has a fool for a client - The origin of this phrase is uncertain. However, it dates back to at least the 19th century and appears in: The Flowers of Wit, or a Choice Collection of Bon Mots, by the English clergymen and writer Henry Kett, 1814. Its literal interpretation is the most palpable. But it could be applied to circumstances outside the legal profession such as hiring a professional or skilled person instead of doing it yourself or not seeking outside advice or counsel in a given situation. **Get a second opinion**

A man's reach should exceed his grasp [or what's a heaven for?] - This quote is accredited to the English poet Robert Browning. It is from his poem Andrea del Santo named after the Italian painter whose style he admired. It means: a person should always strive to go beyond what he or she knows or feels comfortable with, to reach new horizons and to achieve his or her potential. **Think outside of the box; reach for the stars**

A Mexican standoff - The source of this expression is unknown, but many believe that it originated as a derogatory term similar to terms that have the Dutch word attached to them, e.g., **Dutch uncle** and evolved into its current generic usage. The first known use was in the late 1800s. The common usage is: a dispute or argument that cannot be won; a situation in which no one emerges as a clear winner; a deadlock, a stalemate or impasse

A Mini-Me - The origin of this term comes from a series of Austin Powers movies in which a character played by Verne Troyer is a small version of Power's nemesis Doctor Evil. He first appeared in the movie The Spy Who Shagged Me. It is now used to describe: a smaller duplicate or clone of another person whether smaller in stature or any other deeming quality. A person who tries to emulate someone else especially if it is for personal gain or influence. **Mojo** is another term popularized by the Austin Powers series. This term is believed to have originated among African Americans and was used to designate a magical charm, amulet, tailspin or a spell. It later evolved to mean: a personal confidence in one's ability to achieve a goal particularly as it relates to sexual activities, music or dance. A charismatic feeling that **everything is going your way. Got my mojo back(working); you lost your mojo**

A moot point - This expression has its roots in old English law. Sometimes misspelled as its homonym "mute" point, it derives from the English word moot that has its etymology in a meeting or an assembly especially for legal or legislative purposes. The expression dates back to at least the late Middle Ages. The term moot is also used in the American legal field as in moot court which is a mock court where law students argue imaginary cases for practice. The expression denotes: a fact or something that does not matter (particularly in a debate) because it is not relevant to the point being made. Something that is pointless. **The point is moot**

A more perfect Union - This phrase comes from the preamble of the United States Constitution. At the time, it referred to the union of the thirteen original colonies(states) and it states: "We the People of the United States, in Order to form a more perfect Union, establish Justice, insure domestic Tranquility, provide for the common defence, promote the general Welfare, and secure the Blessings of Liberty to ourselves and our Posterity, do ordain and establish this Constitution for the United States of America." This phrase was further popularized in speeches by Abraham Lincoln and Barack Obama. It generally refers to the union of the United States and its attempts to become better over time. But it can also refer to the unity of any state, government or group

A nod's as good as a wink [to a blind horse] - This is an old English proverb that has been in existence since the 18th century. It now means: to take action or to attain approval based on the slightest indication or hint. It is not always necessary to give written or oral approval of a desired action or position. **To turn a blind eye; silence gives consent; a okay**

A penny saved is a penny earned - This saying is often ascribed to Benjamin Franklin. While the American Founding Fathers have become famous over time, Franklin was the only one respected by Europeans at the time of the American Revolutionary War. However, there is evidence that the phrase, or at least one that conveys the same message, precedes Franklin. Nonetheless, the common interpretation is: saving money is just as important as making money. Similar phrases include: **it's not how much you make, it's how much you spend; broken piggybank**

A perfect storm - The origin of this term comes from a ferocious storm (often at sea) resulting from a rare combination of severe or hostile weather influences. It is now used to describe: a combination of rare factors or circumstances that ultimately lead to an adverse or unexpected result

A photo finish - The origin of this term comes from a sporting event such as horseracing or track and field when the winner can only be determined by a photo taken at the finish line. The common usage is: something that is not easily determined in real time or is so close that the output is not easily determined. **Down to the wire** is another phrase that has its source in horseracing **A close shave**

A picture is worth a thousand words - This saying is thought to be a Chinese proverb (although the origins have been disputed). Many believe that it is much later and attributed to Chinese or Japanese origins to enhance its validity. Nonetheless, it is regularly interpreted to mean: an illustration can take the place of many words

A piñata - This term is commonly believed to have Mexican origins and there is some truth to this belief. However, further research reveals that the source of this tradition is Chinese. It is believed that the tradition entered Europe because of Marco Polo's trip to China. It is now the consensus that the etymology of the word piñata comes from the Italian word *pignatta* meaning clay pot. The tradition migrated from Italy to Spain and became part of the celebration of Lent. When the Spanish conquered Mexico, they noticed that the Aztecs and other Mesoamerican cultures had a similar tradition. They used this similarity to evangelize and convert the Aztecs to Christianity by associating this tradition with Christmas celebrations. The tradition consisted of a decorated container often made of papier-mache, clay or cloth and is filled with candy, toys or other items. This container is beaten with a stick until broken. As time progressed, this celebration migrated from the religious realm to birthday parties particularly in Mexico. As a figurative term, it has taken on several connotations. The most common is a person or thing that is beaten relentlessly with a stick or other object. But as a slang, it is sometimes used to describe a fat woman with money. **Beaten like a piñata; I'll beat you like a piñata; I'll beat you so bad your momma wouldn't know you**

A plague on both your houses - The source of this saying is from Shakespeare's play Romeo and Juliet (Act III, Scene I). It is interpreted to mean: a frustrated curse or displeasure on both sides of the argument

A posteriori - This is a Latin term that has worked its way into the English language. It is frequently used in conjunction with *a priori.* The terms "a priori" and "a posteriori" are used primarily to signify the conditions upon which a proposition is known. *A posteriori* means what comes after and *a priori* means: what comes before. A given proposition is *a priori,* if it can be known independent of any experience. However, a proposition that is *a posteriori,* is based on experience. For example, the proposition that only women bear children is *a priori,* and the proposition that it is snowing outside now is *a posteriori*

IN A NUTSHELL

A pound of flesh - This expression was coined by William Shakespeare in his play <u>The Merchant of Venice</u> (Act IV, Scene I). It was a demand made by **Shylock** for a debt that was owed to him. The common usage is: a harsh demand for something that is owed. **Draconian**

A riddle wrapped up in an enigma -This expression is attributed to the Prime Minister of Great Britain and historian <u>Winston Churchill</u> regarding comments that he made about the Soviet Union in 1939. Known for his insight and witticisms, Churchill was one of the seminal figures of the 20th century. It is regularly interpreted to mean: a mysterious puzzle that is difficult to solve; a puzzle within a puzzle. **A riddle wrapped in a mystery inside an enigma; the Sphinx; to cut the Gordian knot**

A rising tide lifts all boats - This phrase is often attributed to President John Kennedy, who used the phrase on several occasions. However, according to his speech writer, Ted Sorensen, the phrase was taken from a slogan from the New England Council. Whether or not it originated with the council is uncertain and therefore, may have been used previously as the area is known for sailing. In the context used by Kennedy it means: a general improvement in the economy helps all participants. In this regard, however, a rising tide may lift all boats, but not necessarily in the same proportion. Generally speaking, it means: by improving the overall condition of a group, the individual condition is also improved

A Robin Hood - According to <u>English legend, Robin Hood</u> was a medieval outlaw (around 1160) whose base was located in Sherwood Forest. In this forest, he and his **band of merry men** reportedly **robbed the rich to give to the poor.** His nemesis was the **Sheriff of Nottingham.** The term therefore means: a person that acts as a benefactor or guardian of the poor and an enemy of the rich. **A reverse Robin Hood** is the opposite or the rich stealing from the poor. **All around Robin Hood's barn** is an expression that means to go somewhere by an indirect route or to attain the desired results in an indirect or **roundabout way**

A rolling stone [gathers no moss] - This notion was known to the ancient world and Greek and Latin versions of the phrase are cited by Erasmus in the third volume of his collection of Latin proverbs <u>Adagia,</u> 1508. It has also been attributed to Pubilius Syrus (85-43 BCE). Moss normally grows in dark areas and is common on the north side of a house or building because it is the area that gets the least amount of sunshine. The phrase has two connotations. It refers to keep moving or what can happen if you don't move, e.g., **I'd rather wear out than rust out.** It also refers to a person that keeps changing jobs or locations or someone that has difficulty sticking to one thing, e.g., **Poppa was a rolling stone, wherever he laid his hat was his home.** On a side note, the popular British band, <u>The Rolling Stones,</u> took its name from the title of a <u>Muddy Waters</u> song. Muddy Waters and other American Blues singers greatly influence both <u>Rock and Roll and Rock.</u>

A rose by any other name would smell as sweet - The source of this expression is from Shakespeare's <u>Romeo and Juliet</u> (Act II, Scene II). It is often interpreted to mean: the nature or essence of a thing is more important than what it is called. **What's in a name? Call me anything you like, but don't call me late for dinner. A rose is a rose is a rose** is a similar saying. The source of this saying, however, is from a poem by the American novelist <u>Gertrude Stein</u> entitled: <u>Sacred Emily.</u> It means that if you love a name, saying it

14

over and over only makes you love it more. It has also been interpreted to mean: **when all is said and done**, a thing is what it is

A sacred cow - In some religions, particularly Hinduism, the cow is considered sacred or the incarnation of a deity. Notwithstanding, the widespread interpretation of this term is: an idea, custom, or institution held, to be above criticism; someone or something that has been accepted or respected for a long time and that people are afraid or unwilling to criticize or question. **Golden calf** means: to worship false ideals, especially wealth

A Scrooge - Scrooge was the chief character in A Christmas Carol, by Charles Dickens. Published in 1843, the book has endured the ages and the movie is shown just about every year around Christmas time in the United States. Scrooge is a miserable miser who hates Christmas and **does not have a charitable bone in his body** until he is visited by three ghosts. The common usage is: a mean-spirited and miserable person; who in many cases, doesn't like giving or spending money. A **Silas Marner; Bah humbug**

A sleeping beauty - The source of this term comes from a fairytale by the French writer Charles Perrault (author of Cinderella and Mother Goose) about a princess that is charmed into a 100-year long sleep only to be awaken by a brave prince. Popularized in various movies, it has become a metaphor for a woman whose full potential has not been realized. Similar expressions include: **a Cinderella story; a fairytale ending; a diamond in the rough**

A soap opera - This term originated from the early days of radio and like so many terms, migrated to television. It was so named because the early sponsors were often soap manufactures. It is a drama series (often followed by housewives) dealing with daily events in the lives of the same group of characters that included many aspects of the human experience, i.e., love, hate, jealousy, sickness, betrayal, etc., each with its own storyline, cast of unique characters and interwoven themes, e.g., The Days of Our Lives. It is currently used as an idiom to describe a person's life that resembles the life and events depicted in a soap opera. **My life is one big soap opera. Drama queen** is a similar term and is a person who routinely responds to situations in an overdramatic way

A thing of beauty is a joy forever - The source of this saying is a poem written by the English poet John Keats. He lost both of his parents at an early age and although he died young at the age of 25, he left an indelible impression on English poetry. The phrase can be interpreted to mean: Beauty is everlasting. **Beauty is in the eye of the beholder**

A thorn in the flesh - This expression is from the Bible, (2 Corinthians 12:7). The thorn in the flesh refers to Paul and not Jesus and has been a source of different interpretations as to what the thorn was. The expression can be interpreted to mean: a persistent difficulty or annoyance. **To be a thorn in someone's side; a stone in someone's shoe**

IN A NUTSHELL

A three-ring circus - This phrase has its origin in the circus where simultaneous events were performed in each ring or arena. The phrase has migrated to mean: a very confusing situation normally characterized by bewilderment, amazement or bizarre and shocking sights. Life is a three-ring circus

A Walter Mitty - The source of this term is from a character in the short story entitled: The Secret Life of Walter Mitty by the American humorists James Thurber. It has migrated to mean: a person who indulges in extravagant daydreams of his own triumphs

A watched pot never boils - This saying is attributed to Benjamin Franklin, however, Franklin used slowly *boils* instead of never. The saying speaks to the relativistic nature of time and how it seems to pass. Although time moves at a constant rate (except for Einstein's theory of relativity); time seems to go by faster when you are doing something that you enjoy. However, when you are doing something that you dislike or anxiously waiting for something to end, time seems to pass by slowly. This is the essence of the saying. **Time waits for no man**

A whipping boy - The source of this saying is from the English court in which whipping boys were assigned to take the punishment of the prince. Quite often, the prince in later life, would reward his whipping boy. The expression is interpreted to mean: a person who is blamed or punished for the faults or incompetence of others. **A scapegoat**

A wolf in sheep's clothing - This saying is from an Aesop fable and the Bible (Matt. 7:15). Aesop was a 6th century BCE Greek storyteller. The ethical and often anthropomorphic animals in his fables were collected from many sources and initially communicated orally. The New Testament version is much later but more popular. Regardless, the saying has come to mean: someone who hides malicious intent under the guise of kindliness

A word to the wise [is sufficient] - Even though this expression is sometimes ascribed to the Bible, it is a Latin proverb that dates back to the time of the Romans. Like many others, it has worked its way into the English vernacular. Often quoted in its abbreviated form, **a word to the wise,** the phrase now means: wisdom normally comes with experience and good judgement. Therefore, wise people are quick to understand a given situation and act appropriately. Similar phrases include: **a wise man can act like a fool, but a fool cannot act like a wise man; 'the heart of a fool is in his mouth, but the mouth of the wise man is in his heart**

Ab Ovo **-** One of the twin eggs of Leda and Zeus, disguised as a swan, from which Helen was born. It means from the very beginning. **From time immemorial**

Abracadabra! - The origin of this phrase is unclear, although many believe that a similar phrase dates back to the Roman Empire, being first recorded in a 2nd century poem by the Roman scholar, Q. Serenus Sammonicus,. from his Liber Medicinalis. Yet, others believe that it has Hebrew, or Arabic origins. During the late Middle Ages, it was inscribed on charms and amulets and was believed to have magical powers.

A COLLECTION OF POPULAR ENGLISH PHRASES

Often, it was written out in a triangle shape and worn around the neck to ward off sickness. It now means: a word said by magicians when performing a magic trick. **Hocus Pocus**

Abraham's bosom - This term relates to the Abraham of the Bible and is from the story of the rich man and Lazarus (Luke 16:19-31) In this parable, Jesus taught about the reality of heaven and hell. It refers to the sleeping place of the blessed in death or paradise given as a reward to the righteous

Absalom, my son - The source of this saying is from the Bible (2 Samuel 13-18). Absalom was the third son of David, King of Israel. He rebelled against his father and was killed by Joab (2 Samuel 18:33). "And the king was much moved, and went up to the chamber over the gate, and wept: and as he went, thus he said, O my son Absalom, my son, my son Absalom! would God I had died for thee, O Absalom, my son, my son!" We all would like to think that we love all of our children equally. However, because we are human and by definition frail, and because love is a nebulous and sacred thing; we sometimes love one more than the other. Sometimes we even love the one that we struggle with the most, more than the one that cost us the least pain. The expression can be interpreted to mean: a parent's enduring love for their child(ren), even when the child has done something terribly wrong

Absence makes the heart grow fonder - This is an old proverb and is attributed to the Roman poet, Sextus Propertius, one of the many writers that emerged during the Augustan Age. It means: you feel more affection for those you love when separated from them. People, places, or things become dearer to us when they are no longer around. **You never miss your water till the well runs dry**

Absence of evidence is not evidence of absence - The source of this saying is unclear. Nevertheless, it is often interpreted to mean: just because there is no current evidence that something exist, does not validate the possibility that it does, did or can exist

According to Cocker - So named after the 17th century English mathematician Edward Cocker. It has migrated to mean: in a manner that is correct, accurate and reliable. **According to Gunter** is the Americanized version of this phrase

According to Hoyle - The source of this saying comes from the English writer, Edmond Hoyle, who was well known for writing rules for card games. The expression has evolved to mean: in agreement with the highest standards and a strict set of rules

Achilles' heel - The source of this term is from the Greek hero Achilles whose mother held him by the heels while dipping the rest of his body into a solution that made him impregnable. It has migrated to mean: a deadly weakness despite an overall strength, that can actually or potentially lead to a downfall. It is generally used to indicate a weakness. **Chink in the armor** or **feet of clay** are similar terms

Acknowledge the corn- The origin of this expression is unclear. Early usage of the expression, however, related to admitting to the participation in a crime or some type of plea bargain. In this context, it meant to plea guilty to a lesser crime to avoid being charged with a more serious crime. Common usage of the expression: is to admit to a fault. **Come clean; Mea Culpa**

Across the pond - The exact origin of this idiomatic expression is unclear. It refers to the distance between the United States or Canada and the United Kingdom, and in some cases, Europe. Chances are that the expression originated in the United Kingdom as it seems to be British and not American in sentiment. The phrase is an understatement as the distance between them is over 3,000 miles of water; hardly considered a pond. It therefore could be interpreted as: although the distance of water is great, the relationship remains close and **just a stone's throw away**. George Bernard Shaw is quoted as saying: **England and America are two nations divided by a common language**

Acid test - The source of this saying comes from the practice of using nitric acid to determine gold content. It was used by prospectors to give a rough estimate of the purity or percentage of gold. It now denotes: a conclusive test of the success or value of something. **Litmus test** has the same connotation

Actions speak louder than word - This is an ancient proverb recorded first in English in <u>Colonial Currency</u> (1736). It means: what you do is more important than what you say; Similar phrases include: **put your money where your mouth is; put up or shut up; all show and no dough; all talk and no action; easier said than done**

Ad Hominem - This is a Latin term "for the man" that has worked its way into the English language. It means: something or an argument that is directed against a person rather than against his arguments or position. **Ad Hominem argument (attack)**

Ad Nauseam - This is another Latin term that has worked its way into the English language. It means: something that has been done or repeated so often that it has become annoying or tiresome

Adam's rib - The source of this term comes from the Bible (Genesis 2:21-23) which describes that a woman, Eve, was made from the rib of Adam. This passage has been interpreted many ways. One interpretation is that God took the rib from Adam thus opening up a space for his heart to be open to receive the love of Eve. Sometimes this term is used as a euphemism for a woman or when guys want to get away from women. For example, there was a story told about why guys hang out at fraternities, sporting events, etc.. It is because they are going in search of their rib; and they want to put it back. **Bone of my bones**

Add a cubit to his stature - The source of this term is from the Bible (Matt.6:27). "Which of you by worrying can add <u>one cubit to his stature</u>?" A similar saying is also found in (Luke 12:25). A cubit was an ancient measurement equivalent to about 18 inches. It is often interpreted to mean: to go beyond one's natural limitations

A COLLECTION OF POPULAR ENGLISH PHRASES

Add fuel to the fire - This saying is accredited to the Roman historian, Livy and it means: to cause a situation or conflict to become more intense, especially by provocative comments; to keep something going

Adonis - In Greek mythology, Adonis was a beautiful youth loved by both Aphrodite and Persephone. According to legend, he was killed by a boar, but Zeus allowed him to spend the winter of each year in the underworld with Persephone and the summer months with Aphrodite. The term now means: an extremely handsome young man. **Tall, dark and handsome**

Aegis **Shield** - In Greek mythology, this was the shield of Zeus or Athena. The expression has evolved to mean: the protection, backing, or support of a particular person or organization. **Under the aegis of** someone or something (a shield of protection normally provided by the powerful)

Affinity group - This term has been around since the turn of the 20th century, however, it did not become popular until a century later. As a means of coping with diversity in the workplace, employers began to embrace the concept of multiple social groups within their company that coalesced around a common goal or sense of identity. These groups provide support for employees while opening an avenue for management to reach out to segments of their organization

Affirmative Action - This term describes a set of policies initiated with an Executive Order by President Kennedy but not implemented in mass until the late 1960s to support members of a disadvantaged group through education, employment or business initiatives. The intent was to **level the playing field** between such groups and the general white male population. This action was the result of **study after study** that uncovered discrimination in the workplace, particularly against women and members of the **African American** community

African American - The origin of this term is from the 1960s, when black people in the United States rejected the term *Negro* that whites had used to identify them. At first, the term was Afro-American but later migrated to African American. It was during the decade of the 1960s that the cauldron of racism ignited a series of riots across America. In cities such as Los Angeles, Detroit and Newark the cry of **burn baby burn** could be heard. Today, black people in America find the term Negro or colored offensive; a relic of the past that reminds them of slavery and **Jim Crow** eras. Black and **people of color** are also acceptable although the latter extends beyond the black race. Some whites are confused regarding the use of African American and black. African American is always the safer and **politically correct** choice. Other races of color have identified themselves likewise such as **Native American, Asian American,** etc.

After me the deluge - This phrase *"au reste, après nous, le Déluge"* is attributed to the French king Louis XV. Some have also attributed it to Madame de Pompadour. It is often suggested that this saying was a portent of the French Revolution in which Louis XVI was executed and the French monarchy abolished. It is sometimes interpreted to mean that a person does not care what happens after they are gone or removed. Other times it is used as a warning of impending doom resulting from an abrupt or sudden change

IN A NUTSHELL

After the feast comes the reckoning - This is an old proverb of unclear or unknown origin which means; sooner or later you got to pay for what you get. **You got to pay the piper, there are no free lunches**

After you, my dear Alphonse - This phrase derives from Happy Hooligan, the 1920s comic strip by Frederick Burr Opper, which featured two bumbling Frenchmen, Alphonse and Gaston. The phrase is commonly used when two people want or try to do the same thing at once

Aid and abet - The origin of this phrase is unclear. Nevertheless, it dates back centuries and was used by George Washington in a letter regarding the French. While it is regularly used regarding legal matters, (such as being an accomplice to a crime). it is also used generally to mean: to help someone often in an illegal or ill-behaved act or to encourage unlawful or immoral actions

Ain't nothing going on but the rent - This is a saying that became popular in the 1960s and was part of the lyrics of a James Brown song. It was very popular in the African American community and was a frequent response to **What's happening**. It has come to mean that you are just **trying to make ends meet** and pay your rent. Similar phrases are: **Keep your head above water; keep some food on the table; bring home the bacon.** Whereas: <u>Well, raise my rent!</u> Is a phrase that is often used as a sign of amazement or sarcasm. **You got to have J-O-B if you want to be with me**

Aladdin's cave - The origin of this saying is from the story of Aladdin in <u>The Arabian Nights</u>. He finds gold, jewels, and other valuable things in a secret place. It has evolved to mean: a place that contains many interesting or valuable objects. **Treasure trove; Aladdin's lamp**

Albatross around your neck - The origin of this saying comes from a poem written by the English poet <u>Samuel Taylor Coleridge</u> entitled: <u>The Rime of the Ancient Mariner</u>. It tells of a sailor that killed a large bird called an Albatross which was considered very unlucky. Bad things happened to the ship and they hung the bird around his neck. It means: A psychological burden that feels like a curse or a heavy burden of guilt. **Pain in the neck; weight on your shoulders**

Alice in Wonderland - This phrase comes from the title of a novel by the English writer, Charles Lutwidge Dodgson better known by the pseudonym of <u>Lewis Carrol</u>. The common interpretation is: a strange and fantastic world in which the normal laws of logical reasoning have been suspended. Similar phrases from this **time-honored** classic include: **through the looking glass; go down a rabbit hole mad hatter;** <u>Chimerical</u>

All animals are equal, but some animals are more equal than others - The source of this saying is <u>Animal Farm</u> by the British novelist <u>George Orwell</u> (pseudonym of Eric Arthur Blair). Published in 1945, it is a satirical look at the Russian Revolution and the evolution of the Communist state under Joseph Stalin. The statement is a comment on the hypocrisy of governments that proclaim the absolute equality of their citizens but give power and privileges to a small elite. Additionally, **Orwellian** means: pertaining to or characteristic of the writings of George Orwell, particularly his dystopian version of future totalitarian states as depicted in <u>Nineteen Eighty-Four</u> and <u>Animal Farm.</u> **The proletarians have nothing to lose but their chains**

A COLLECTION OF POPULAR ENGLISH PHRASES

All dressed up with no place to go - The source of this term is unclear and perhaps unknown. It is one of those colloquialisms that pop up in conversations often when someone is disappointed or lonely. It means: to be in a position to go somewhere or to do something and not be able to do it **for one reason or another**. To be prepared for something and not have it happen. Similar phrases include: **a bummer; a letdown; don't get your hopes up too high; always the bridesmaid, never the bride**

All for one and one for all - This saying is from The Three Musketeers written by Alexander Dumas, the black French novelist and author of The Count of Monte Cristo and other novels. Dumas' father, Thomas Alexander Dumas, was a general of Haitian descent in the French Revolutionary Army and a close friend of Napoleon. He was one of the youngest generals in Napoleon's army and was renowned for his swordsmanship and equestrian abilities. Known as, the Black Devil, he commanded tens of thousands of troops in the field. The phrase means literally what it says: all the members of a group support each of the individual members, and the individual members pledge to support the group. **If we don't hang together, we will hang separately**

All good things must come to an end - The expression has been traced back to the English poet Geoffrey Chaucer's Troilus and Criseyde written in the 1380s and later turned into a tragic play by William Shakespeare. Chaucer is often referred to as the father of English literature. Although this phrase could be taken literally, it really speaks to the temporal nature of life. **Nothing lasts forever**

All politics is local – This phrase is often credited to the legendary Speaker of the House Tip O'Neil, although it is not certain that he originated it. Notwithstanding, it has become a political axiom. It generally means: to understand the factors and interests that motivate and ultimately influence the people that you represent. To know what is most important to your constituents. **Vote with your feet**

All quiet on the Western Front – The source of this phrase is the Western Front of World War I. It was also the title of a 1929 novel by Erich Maria Remarque and the subsequent 1930 movie. The Western Front was an area that traversed part of France and was the major battlefield of the First World War. It was a type of **no man's land; a** result of **trench warfare**, replete with mustard gas and horrors which defined the war. At times, one could fly across the battlefield and not see a single soldier, and at others, the graveyard littered with dead soldiers that marked the tombstone of modern warfare. The phrase has migrated to mean: nothing is happening right now. **The war to end all wars**

All roads lead to Rome - The Romans left an indelible impression on the European continent and Western Civilization. They were famous for building roads throughout Europe which led to Rome. This network of roads was critical to the interconnectivity of the European continent and like the phrase still resonates today. The common interpretation is: there are many different ways of reaching the same goal or conclusion

All systems go - This phrase is a product of the early days of the **Space Age.** It referred to everything being approved for the launch. It now means: all the steps have met the approval processes and have been checked off. Other idioms of this period include: Blast off or lift off referring to the launching of a rocket or spacecraft and Splash down referring to the landing of a returning spacecraft on the sea with the assistance of parachutes. **Rocket science,** another space age idiom, refers to a complex and intellectually demanding activity. **This isn't rocket science**

All that glitters is not gold - This phrase originated from Shakespeare's <u>The Merchant of Venice</u> (Act II, Scene VII). "<u>All that glitters is not gold</u>. Often have you heard that told. Many a man his life hath sold. But my outside to behold." It means: just because something looks attractive, does not mean it is genuine or valuable. The beautiful external appearance of something is not a dependable indication of its true nature or value. Things that have an outward appeal are often not as beautiful or valuable as they seem. Similar sentiment is also present in two fables by Aesop. **Wolf in sheep's clothing; fool's gold; you can't judge a book by its cover**

All the way to Timbuktu - Timbuktu was known during the late Middle Ages as a faraway place in Africa full of gold and educational institutions. It was a major trading center located in Mali West Africa and part of the Islamic Empire. Mali was made famous by <u>Mansa Musa,</u> perhaps the foremost richest person in the world, who during his pilgrimage to Mecca, flooded the Cairo market with gold. Thereby causing such a decline in its value that the market took 12 years to fully recover. It now refers to: a faraway place. **Never-never land**

All the world's a stage - The origin of this phrase is from Shakespeare's: <u>As You Like It</u> (Act II, Scene VII). "<u>All the world's a stage;</u> and all the men and women merely players; they have their exits and their entrances; and **one man in his time plays many parts.**" It means: life is like a play, we merely go through the stages of our life acting it out

All things to all people - The origin of the phrase is from the Bible (I Corinthians 9:22). The common interpretation is: to be everything that someone wants or desires. Similar expressions include: **you cannot be all things to all people; I don't know the key to success, but I know the key to failure is trying to please everybody**

All's well that ends well - This phrase was made popular by the title of one of <u>Shakespeare's plays</u>. Similar in connotation to **the ends justifies the means**, it could imply that whatever means, and methods used to achieve a desired goal are justified. Most people, however, interpret this phrase from a positive prospective, meaning that bad things could be overcome by good things. Yet others contend that for something to end well it must start and continue until it ends in a state of wellness. In this regard, an evil or dishonest act cannot justify a good outcome

<u>Aloha</u> - This is a Hawaiian word that has worked its way into the English language. It is used when greeting or parting from someone, i.e., hello or goodbye. Because it means both, it has also been used sarcastically: as in meeting someone very briefly. Similar phrases include: **Arrivederci; Au revoir; see you later alligator, in a while crocodile**

A COLLECTION OF POPULAR ENGLISH PHRASES

Alpha and omega - This expression is based on the first and last letters of the Greek alphabet and is used in the Bible (Revelations 1: 8). It means: from the beginning to the end. **From A to Z; from soup to nuts**

Alter ego - This is a Latin term that means "other self" and is often attributed to the Roman orator and statesman Cicero in a letter to his friend and adviser, Atticus: "You are a second brother to me, an alter ego to whom I can tell everything." Used by psychiatrists and plebeians alike, it now designates: a person's secondary personality; a second self. **Jekyll and Hyde**

Am I my brother's keeper? - The source of this saying is the Bible (Genesis 4:9) and it was Cain's response to God after he killed his younger brother Abel. The frequent interpretation is: to be responsible for the welfare of another person or the human race. **Cain and Abel**

Amazon - The origin of this term is a member of a legendary race of female warriors believed by the ancient Greeks to exist in Scythia (near the Black Sea in modern Russia) or elsewhere on the edge of the known world. It is also the name of a river in South America that flows more than 4,150 miles (6,683 km) through Peru, Colombia and Brazil into the Atlantic Ocean. It drains two-fifths of the continent and, in terms of water-flow, is the largest river in the world. The term is now used to describe: a tall strong often masculine woman; a powerful woman and, most recently, was made famous by one of the largest Internet companies in the world

Ambrosia from the gods - In Greek mythology, ambrosia was a honey-flavored food eaten by the gods that allowed them to remain immortal. The phrase means: something especially delicious to taste or smell or anything so fragrant, so delicious that it seems divine. Similarly, **nectar** is the drink of the gods and has an analogous connotation. Shakespeare wrote in <u>Julius Caesar</u> (Act II, Scene I) **A dish fit for the gods**

An ambulance chaser - This is an old term that emerged in the 19th century from lawyers that attended accidents and encourage victims to sue. So designated because he or she normally represents victims of accidents or those seeking damages for personal injury. It now means: a lawyer who specializes in bringing cases seeking damages for personal injury. The term has also been applied to others that seek personal profit or publicity from people that are personally harmed

An Annie Oakley - The source of this term is the legendary female sharpshooter Annie Oakley. This eponym is an allusion to her penchant for filling playing cards with bullet holes that resembled tickets that had been punched to prevent resale. The term now means: a ticket to a movie, sporting event or one required for entry

An Archie Bunker (type) - Archie, played by Carroll O' Connor, was a fictional character on the popular 1970 sitcom <u>All in the Family</u>. Archie was the stereotypical white male conservative, with disdain for liberals and a lack of empathy for others outside of his race. He was a product of previous times, when **white privilege** was **an unalienable right**. He was a bigot that was unaware at times of his bigotry and prejudice, even though he was reminded of it by his liberal daughter and son-in-law who he regularly

23

referred to as "meathead." George Jefferson, his successful black neighbor, was in many ways his antagonist and in others his nemesis. Archie routinely looked back to a nostalgic America; "those were the days;" one in which television was "in black and white and so was everything else." A time and a place where the lines of demarcation between races were clearly drawn and everyone knew their place. The term is associated with: a person that exhibits the traits and exalts the ideals of those portrayed by this fictional character. Albert Einstein once said: It is harder to crack a prejudice than an atom. Redneck; white privilege

An eagle doesn't catch flies - This is an old Latin proverb. It means that someone who is important shouldn't be concerned with unimportant questions or things but leave those things to lesser people. Don't punch down

An Evel Knievel - The source of this term is the American daredevil Evel Knievel known for engaging in dangerous motorcycle stunts. The term now applies to a daring person willing to take on unusual challenges. A Harry Houdini

An explanation of cause is not a justification by reason - This saying is attributed to the Irish novelist C. S. Lewis. His full name was Clive Staples Lewis. He was a prolific writer of religious and moral issues. The phrase is often interpreted to mean: the cause of something happening does not justify or excuse the reason why it happened

An eye for an eye and a tooth for a tooth - The source of this saying is the Bible, (Matt. 5:38). The phrase means: if you believe that someone has done something wrong to you, the person should be punished by having the same thing done to them. Revenge is a dish that is best served cold

An eye for an eye makes the whole world blind - This quote is regularly attributed to the Indian sage Gandhi, although it is uncertain if he ever said it. Quite often, a popular quote is attributed to a popular person whose life story echoes the sentiment of the quote. Based on the biblical phrase, an eye for an eye and a tooth for a tooth (Exodus 21:24), it addresses vengeance and the need for us, in the words of Dr. Martin Luther King: to live together as brothers, rather than perish as fools. Similar expressions include: vengeance is mine saith the Lord; turn the other cheek

An idle mind is a devil's workshop - There are several sources that may have contributed to this saying. The first is the Bible (Proverbs 16:27) "Idle hands are the devil's workshop" and the second is: "Idle brains are the devil's workhouses" attributed to Thomas Fuller, 1732. It has come to mean that when a person's mind is not occupied with other thoughts, it tends to think about negative thoughts or actions. Having too much time on your hands

An ounce of prevention is worth a pound of cure - This saying is ascribed to the American author, inventor and Founding Father Ben Franklin. The phrase is often interpreted to mean: it's easier to stop something from happening in the first place than it is to repair the damage after it is done

A COLLECTION OF POPULAR ENGLISH PHRASES

Anal retentive - The source of this phrase comes from Sigmund Freud and is one of the stages of development that he outlined. It means: a person excessively orderly and fussy (supposedly owing to conflict over toilet-training in infancy)

And yet it moves - This is a phrase attributed to the famous Italian scientist and polymath Galileo Galilei (1564 - 1642). It was the response that he gave to the Catholic Church after it refused to accept his theory of a heliocentric universe. Even though it was supported by empirical observations of the moons revolving around Jupiter that he viewed through his telescope. The phrase is often interpreted to mean: it doesn't matter what you believe, the facts are the facts. **Facts do not cease to exist because they are ignored**

Ante/Post meridian - These terms are related to the movement of the sun as it reaches its peak height on the meridian at noon. Ante meridian means: relating to or taking place in the morning, occurring before noon. Post meridian is after noon. AM and PM are abbreviations for ante meridian and post meridian

Antebellum - This is a Latin term that means "before the war." In the United States, it means: the period before the Civil War, e.g., Antebellum America, This period includes the Revolutionary War and of course the legacy of slavery. But, in some cases, it denotes the immediate period from the Compromise of1820 up to the Civil War

Any emotion, if it is sincere, is involuntary - This quote is credited to the American author Mark Twain. It strikes at the core of what it means to be human. While other animals have emotions, they do not have the mental capacity to display the range of emotions expressed by humans. For example, other animals shed tears, however, they do not cry out of sadness which is very common among humans. Furthermore, there are times when we expect people to be emotional such as at the death of someone special in their lives. Love is perhaps our greatest emotion and it cannot be bought or sold. It must be involuntarily given, like all sincere emotions. One should beg another for forgiveness if so inclined; but one should never beg another for love

Apples and oranges - This saying has its roots in John Ray's 1670 Proverbs Collection as "apples and oysters" but was later changed to apples and oranges. The phrase is frequently interpreted to mean: two things that are fundamentally different and therefore not suited to comparison. **Mutually exclusive**

Apple of my eye - This is a very old saying and appears in two places in the King James Bible (Deuteronomy 32:10 and Zechariah 2:8) "He found him in a desert land and in the waste howling wilderness; He led him about, He instructed him, He kept him as the apple of His eye." It also appears in Shakespeare's A Midsummer Night's Dream (Act III, Scene II). "Flower of this purple dye; "Hit with Cupid's archery; Sink in apple of his eye." The King James version and Shakespeare's play were written around the same time which implies an earlier English source. It referred to the eye pupil. The apple used as a metaphor for a delicious piece of fruit can be found throughout antiquity. The saying is often used to denote: something that is cherished above all others; a person or a thing that you love more than anything else. **Apple of discord (Golden apple)**

Arcadia - So named after a mountainous district in the Peloponnese of southern Greece. In poetic fantasy, it represents a pastoral paradise, and in Greek mythology it is the home of Pan, the god of Nature. It now means: a place in which people are imagined or believed to enjoy a perfect life of rustic simplicity

Argus-eyed - The origin of this term is the Greek mythological figure Argos the watchman with a hundred eyes. The term has migrated to mean: someone who is vigilant or extremely alert. **On the lookout, hawk-eyed**

Armageddon - The source of this term is from the New Testament (Rev. 16:16) and it is only referenced once in the Bible. Revelations is the last book in the Bible and forecasts the conditions that lead to the end of the world. According to the New Testament, Armageddon is the place where the forces of evil led by the **Antichrist** make their stand. It is the last battle **between good and evil** before the **Day of Judgment**. It now designates: a final destructive battle such as **Nuclear War**; a war fought on earth of unparalleled scale, force and destruction leading to an Apocalypse which is the complete and final destruction of the world. According to this narrative, the **Four Horsemen of the Apocalypse** are four symbolic mounted figures, each of a difference color, commonly acknowledged as: Pestilence (or Conquest), War, Famine, and Death. Their arrival announces the end of the world. The **Antichrist** is a personal opponent of Christ expected to appear before the end of the world. **The Second Coming of Christ** is the expected time when Jesus Christ will return to the earth to establish His reign of justice and peace. It has often been associated with millenniums. **Number of the beast 666.** The aforementioned events and figures are all part of the scenario associated with **the end of days; Doomsday**

Arrivederci - This is an Italian word that literally means "till seeing again" that has become part of the English vernacular. It means: goodbye for now. Similar phrases include: **Au revoir; ciao**

Arrow of Acestes - In Greek and Roman legend, Acestes was an unrivaled archer. The phrase now means: an oratorical point made with fiery brilliance

Art is long, life is short - This expression is credited to Hippocrates' Aphorisms. He was a foremost Greek physician, renowned for his **Hippocratic Oath** that still endures today. The expression is frequently interpreted to mean: the work of an artist endures although the life of the artist is fleeting. The **Hippocratic Oath** serves as a testament of this aphorism

Artificial Intelligence (AI) - The concept of AI has been around since antiquity. Some will argue that the concept of a computing machine put forth by Charles Babbage, Ada Lovelace and Alan Turing meets the criteria of an AI machine. Yet, the term as it is used today wasn't formally used until 1956, at a conference at Dartmouth College. It was coined by MIT's Marvin Minsky and others that attended the conference. The term means: a machine or a device that can perform anthropomorphic tasks such as speaking, reading, language translation or cognitive skills normally attributed to humans

As cool as a cucumber - The origin of this phrase appears to be a poem by John Gay entitled: A New Songs of New Similes written in 1732. It is a common belief that cucumbers often appear to be cool. In this regard however, cool means unchanged. The phrase means: unfazed by events, to remain **calm and collected** in stressful situations. **Keep your cool**

As dead as a doornail - The origin of this popular English idiom dates back to at least the 14th century as it appears in a William Langland poem. Often, it is attributed to William Shakespeare who may have helped to popularize the phrase. It appears in (Act IV, Scene X) of Henry IV Part 2 written between 1596 and 1599."I have eat no meat these five days; yet, come thou and thy five men, and if I do not leave you all as dead as a doornail, I pray God I may never eat grass more." It is frequently used to describe something that is dead or does not function properly

As merry as the day is long - This phrase dates to Elizabethan England and was attributed to William Shakespeare who used it twice in his writings: Much Ado About Nothing, 1599, (Act II, Scene I) "I up my apes, and away to Saint Peter for the heavens; he shows me where the bachelors sit, and there live we as merry as the day is long" and in King John, 1595, (Act IV, Scene I)"So I were out of prison and kept sheep, I should be as merry as the day is long; And so I would be here, but that I doubt." The phrase generally means: lively and full of fun, happy. **As happy as a lark; as happy as a clam**

As old as Methuselah - Methuselah was a Hebrew patriarch and grandfather of Noah who was supposed to have lived for 969 years. He is the oldest living person in the Bible (Genesis 5:27). It has migrated to mean: very old or to be very old in origin. **Old school, a dinosaur**

As pure as the driven snow - This saying is sometimes credited to Shakespeare from his play The Winter's Tale (Act IV, Scene IV) but it may have been in use before his play. The exact words do not appear in this play but rather. "Lawn as white as driven snow." It is defined as: something that is completely pure and untainted

As rich as Croesus - The ancient Greeks thought that Croesus was the richest man on earth from a story told by Herodotus about Solon. Hence, to be as rich as Croesus is to be very wealthy indeed. The Greeks would say that we all have a choice: to be as rich as Croesus or as wise as Solon. The phrase now refers to a very wealthy person

As the crow flies –The exact origin of this phrase is not known, however, some have accredited it to William Kenrick who used the phrase in 1767. The phrase is based on the belief that crows fly in a direct straight line (which is not necessarily true), or **the shortest distance between two points**. Nonetheless, the phrase now means: a direct route or the shortest distance between two points or the path with the least obstacles. **A beeline** is similar in connotation. It has also been sarcastically said that the longest distance between two points is a shortcut LOL

As thick as [two] thieves - The source of this expression is unknown, although it has been around since the 18th century. It is based on the relationship between two people or a group that have a common objective or commitment. The term is generally used to describe two close friends particularly if they are involved in a common endeavor. Two people that hang around together so much so that they are considered as one group and **can finish each other's sentence.** David and Jonathan; Achilles and Patroclus; Fred and Barney; Rocky and Bullwinkle

As ugly as sin - The source of this popular saying remains a mystery. Historically, sin has been associated with something that is detestable or ugly. Hence, the saying often denotes: something, particularly a person, that is hideously ugly or detestable

Ask me no questions and I'll tell you no lies - This expression is attributed to the Irish playwright Oliver Goldsmith. It is often given as a response to a question that the person does not want to answer for a variety of reasons. The common usage is: If you ask me that, my answer might not be the truth. Similar expressions include: **if I tell you, I'll have to kill you; take the fifth**

Ask not what your country can do for you -- ask what you can do for your country - The source of this saying is the 1961 inaugural address given by President Kennedy. As the **leader of the free world** in which **nuclear holocaust** loomed over the heads of nations like the **sword of Damocles**, he sent not only a message to his fellow Americans but to his fellow denizens of the world. A declaration much needed in the aftermath of a world war that brought **Armageddon** to the doorsteps of humanity. The statement is one of a greater commitment and the willingness to sacrifice yourself for **a cause greater than yourself**

Athanasian wench - The source of this term appears to be taken from the Athanasian Creed (*quicumque vult*) a Christian statement dating back to the 6th century. While this term is seldom used today, it means a woman that would have sex with anyone willing. A **nymphomaniac** means the same thing with nymph coming from the Latin "nympha" which was a mythological spirit of nature believed to be a beautiful young woman and "mania" refers to a preoccupation or obsession

Atlantis - The source of this term comes from Plato's Timaeus and Critias. It was a continent west of the **Rock of Gibraltar** which according to legend had an advanced civilization about 9,000 years before the Greeks and was believed to have been destroyed by an earthquake and sank into the sea. Throughout the ages, this myth has been embraced perhaps because it extends the antiquity of the Greeks beyond other civilizations, although there is no historical or scientific basis for such beliefs. It is frequently used to designate: a mysterious or enchanted place. The Mysteries of Atlantis

Atlas - In Greek mythology, Atlas was one of the Titans who was punished for his part in their revolt against Zeus by being made to support the burden of the heavens on his shoulders. The term now means: a collection of maps and charts depicting various parts of the earth or the earth in total. A person that bears the weight of the world or a great burden on his shoulders

Attila the Hun - Often referred to as "the scourge of God," he was the king of the Huns that ravaged parts of Europe in the 5th century CE which accelerated the fall of the Roman Empire. His armies were feared because of their violence and cruelty. He was finally defeated by the joint forces of the Roman army and the Visigoths at Châlons in 451 which saved the European continent from his wrath. His name is now associated with anyone of extreme brutality, violence or cruelty especially in leadership. Mayor Frank Rizzo, the controversial mayor of Philadelphia in the 1970s, once said about himself and his crime policies: "I'm going to make Attila the Hun look like a faggot." **Hannibal at the gates**

A COLLECTION OF POPULAR ENGLISH PHRASES

Augustan era - This is the era of Roman history under the leadership of <u>Augustus Caesar</u> the nephew of <u>Julius Caesar</u> previously known as Octavian. He transformed Rome from a Republic to an Empire. This was one of the most prosperous eras of Roman history and was the **harbinger** of the <u>Pax Romana</u> or the age of peace after decades of Roman civil war. The Pax Romana is normally designated as the time between the reign of Augustus Caesar to the reign of <u>Marcus Aurelius</u> (27 BCE-180 CE) Both Paul and Jesus were born during the Augustan era (27 BCE -14 CE). It was during this era that Rome developed its literary voice and produced such authors as Virgil, Horace and <u>Ovid</u> among others. It was succeeded by the <u>Julio-Claudian period</u> which produced corrupt and decadent leaders such as Nero and Caligula and it was this era that gave birth to Christianity

Au revoir - This is a French term that literally means "till seeing again" that has become part of the English vernacular. It means: goodbye or till we meet again

Aunt Sally - The origin of this term is an effigy of a pipe smoking woman that was popular as an amusement attraction in British fairs. It was setup for patrons to throw objects at. It has since migrated to mean: an object of criticism, particularly one that is set to invite condemnation

Avant garde - This is a French term that literally means "advanced culture." It was part of a movement in Europe particularly in France that embraced new and daring things. There was a movement in jazz that was labeled the *avant garde*. It now means: anything that pushes the boundaries of accepted taste

AWOL - This is an acronym for *Absent Without Official Leave*. It was a term that originated in the United States military and has since been adopted by the general public. It pertained to a soldier or other military member who has left their post without permission or someone that did not return from leave. This term generally means: any person that leaves a situation for a longer period than expected or does not return

Stands for:

Be careful what you wish for,

you just may get it

IN A NUTSHELL

B Movie - The origin of this term comes from a film originally made in Hollywood in the 1940s and 50s as a supporting film. The term means: a low-budget movie, one made for use as a companion to the main attraction in a double feature. B Movies are considered in many cases to be subpar to other movies made in Hollywood and **B movie actors** are sometimes likewise associated. The term is often used to describe something that is **second-rate. I've seen this movie before** is another movie related phrase and means that you have been through a particular situation or experience before and you are somewhat skeptical because you can predict the outcome. **Second banana; second fiddle; a ham**

Bah humbug - The origin of this expression is unclear; however, it was made famous by Charles Dicken's popular novel: A Christmas Carol. It was uttered by the chief character Ebenezer Scrooge. In this novel, published in 1843, Scrooge is a cold-hearted miser who hates Christmas. The term, humbug, was **in vogue** during Dicken's day and was used to designate a hoax or a deception. Because of Dicken's book, bah humbug, is often used to denote a hatred or dislike of Christmas but is sometimes extended to other dislikes as well. It is regularly used as an expression when someone does not approve or enjoy something that other people abundantly enjoy. **A Scrooge**

Baker's dozen - This term originated from bakers in England that cheated their customers by baking bread with less weight which led to a law that punished bakers that did so. To assure that they complied with the law, some bakers started to give thirteen loaves instead of twelve. It means: a set of thirteen items

Balm in Gilead - The source of this expression is from the Bible (Jeremiah 8 :22). Balm was a rare herb that was used in medicine. "Is there no balm in Gilead; is there no physician there? why then is not the health of the daughter of my people recovered?" The phrase is now associated with any kind of healing or solace

Banana Republic - This was the name originally given to a group of Central American countries by members of American fruit industries. The term now means: a small country, especially in Central or Latin America, that is politically unstable and has an economy dominated by foreign interest, usually dependent on one export, such as bananas or tourism. **Third world**

Bandwidth - This is a term that was taken from the engineering realm. In electrical engineering, the bandwidth is defined as: the range of frequencies within a given band or a rate of data flow. It has since been used generically to define a range or a level of activity, capacity or capability

Baptism by fire - The origin of this saying is the Bible (Matt. 3:11) and relates to the story of John the Baptist and his baptism of Jesus. The common usage is: a difficult or painful new undertaking or experience. **Trial by fire**

Barking up the wrong tree - The source of this expression comes from the practice of using hunting dogs to chase game. Many times, the dog would be tricked into thinking that an animal was up one tree when in fact it was up another. The expression now means: to make a mistake or a bad assumption about something

A COLLECTION OF POPULAR ENGLISH PHRASES

Barmacide feast - The derivation of this phrase is from the Arabian Nights about a member of a Persian family that gave a beggar a pretended feast with empty dishes. The common interpretation is: something that is illusory or imaginary and therefore disappointing. A **barmecide meal** is one that looks good but doesn't live up to expectations. **Potemkin village; can't judge a book by its cover**

Barometer - This is a science term that has also become a colloquial expression. A barometer is an instrument used to measure atmospheric pressure and thus is used to help forecast the weather. Currently, it is also used as an indicator of fluctuations or changes in other things such as public opinion, stock market changes, etc.. It is a way of assessing current conditions or prognosticating the future based on past experiences or what is considered normal. A **thermometer** is often used in an equivalent manner. Similar expressions include: **take the temperature of something; measure the heartbeat**

Basket case - The origin of this phrase is from the practice of carrying wounded or physically impaired people in baskets. The term gained popularity during World War I, **(the war to end all wars)** and originally denoted a soldier who had lost all four limbs, thus unable to move independently. Since that time, the term has migrated to mean: a person or thing that is regarded as useless or unable to cope with something. **Nutcase; basket of nerves**

Bated breath - This expression appears in Shakespeare's The Merchant of Venice (Act I, Scene III) but this may not be the first time it was used. This phrase is repeatedly misspelled baited breath. Bated means to modulate or restrict. Thus, it means: breathing that is subdued because of some emotion or difficulty. **You take my breath away**

Be careful what you wish for, you just may get it - The source of this saying appears to be unknown despite its popularity. The phrase is often interpreted to mean: when people wish for something, they often think of the good things that come with the wish and not the unintended negative consequences of that wish. **Unintended consequences**

Be nice to people on your way up because you'll meet them on your way down - This saying is attributed to the American playwright Wilson Minzer. The common interpretation is: life is unpredictable, therefore, it is important to be nice to people that you meet. Or to quote Reverend Ike: **Always make your words sweet, because you never know when you will have to eat them**

Bear/Bull market - The term appears to stem from the bearskin trading market in the 18th century. Because bull and bear fighting was once a popular sport, bulls were considered the opposite of bears. Some believe a bull market is like a bull charging thus an aggressive market, and likewise a bear market is like a bear in hibernation or a dormant market. Nonetheless, a bear market is: a market in which prices are falling, encouraging selling. Conversely, **a bull market** is a market in which share prices are rising, encouraging buying

Beat a dead horse - The source of this saying is a Roman play written in 195 BCE by, Plautus, one of the earliest Latin playwrights. in which a dead horse was beaten to get him to get up and carry the load. It now means: to waste energy on a lost cause or unalterable situation

Beat around the bush - The origin of this term lies in the practice of hunters, particularly bird hunters, to beat bushes in order to get the game to come out. The common usage is: to discuss a matter without coming to the point; to be vague about something or someone. **Don't beat around the bush; tell it like it is; get to the point**

Beauty and the beast - Some scholars trace the source of this motif to the **time-honored** classic The Golden Ass written by the Roman author Apuleius in which he tells the story of **Cupid and Psyche**. It, like so many stories, is one of contrast that alludes to **beauty is only skin deep,** whereas love is internal. Other scholars point to a more recent source mainly Charles Perrault included the story *Riquet a la Houppe* in his *Histoires ou Contes du Temps Passé* (1697). Nonetheless, the expression has come to mean: two physically contrasting people (often of different sexes) that are attracted to each other by forces outside of the physical. Sometimes the expression is used to denote two contrasting things such as **good and evil.** Perhaps, the **overarching theme** is that every beast has a beauty within, and likewise, every beauty has a beast inside. **Beauty is in the eye of the beholder**

Beauty is in the eye of the beholder - The origin of this phrase is believed to be William Shakespeare although he did not use it in its direct form. The Irish novelist Margaret Wolfe Hungerford in the late 19th century used it in the form it is known today. The phrase is frequently interpreted to mean: beauty is subjective and therefore, exists in the mind of the observer. This expression is often used to describe a person or thing whose appearance does not match the commonly accepted standards of beauty. Beauty cannot be judged objectively, for what one person finds beautiful or admirable may not appeal to another. **Beauty is only skin deep; you can't judge a book by its cover**

Beck and call - The origin of this phrase is unclear. It means to be always ready to obey someone's wishes or demands. To be freely available to comply or ready to do something for a person at any time or place. **At the drop of a hat** is similar and comes from 1800s when it was common to signal the beginning of a fight or race by either dropping a hat or sweeping it in a rapid downward motion. It now means: without delay, immediately; instantly; on the slightest signal or urging. **Wait on someone hand and foot** is also similar and means: to attend to all of someone's needs, requests or wishes, especially when they are considered unreasonable. The French term tout de suite is also used in such situations and means at once, straight away

Bed of roses - The origin of this phrase comes from a poem written by the English author and Shakespeare's contemporary Christopher Marlowe entitled: The Passionate Shepherd To His Love. It was published posthumously in 1599, six years after his death. "And I will make thee beds of roses; And a thousand fragrant posies, A cap of flowers, and a kirtle; Embroidered all with leaves of myrtle." It is regularly used to refer to something that is easy or a very comfortable situation. **A piece of cake. No bed of roses** is also often used and means the opposite and is synonymous to a **bed of nails** meaning something that is very uncomfortable

A COLLECTION OF POPULAR ENGLISH PHRASES

Beef to the hoof(heel) - This phrase appears to have its origin in the cattle industry especially in Ireland. It comes from the phrase "beef to the heel like a Mullingar heifer," referring to cattle bred in Mullingar, Ireland. The phrase is used to define: a fat or chubby woman particularly one that is fat in the legs. **Tub of lard** is similar. **All hat and no cattle** is a phrase that also emanates from the cattle culture and was originally used to refer to a person that wore a cowboy hat but did not experience the life of a cattle rancher. It later migrated to mean: **all talk and no action**

Bejesus - This term seems to be of Irish origin and was used as an alteration of oath by Jesus. The term is at least a century old. It has come to be used as an expression of surprise, fear, anger, pleasure or like. **You scared the bejesus out of me!**

Bells and whistles - This term has been around for some time with its origins unknown, but its use was more practical, i.e., containing bells or whistles. The current context emerged in the 20th century with television and advertisements geared to push **the next shiny thing** particularly automobiles replete with all the features. It is currently used to denote: extra or non-essential features that are appealing or in some cases **above the top**. In marketing, such features are regularly used as a discriminator or to **separate the men from the boys. All the bells and whistles**, therefore, can be used to describe everything possible or available

Bellwether - The origin of this term comes from shepherds that would attach a bell to the lead castrated male sheep called a *wether* that would lead the flock. The term now means: a leader or a trendsetter. An indicator or portend of the way that things are trending or changing. Other related terms are: **Head honcho; Mr. Big, Chief banana; Judas goat; like a lamb to the slaughter**

Benjamin's mess - The source of this phrase comes from the Bible (Genesis 43: 34) and alludes to the banquet given by Joseph, viceroy of Egypt, to his brethren. "Benjamin's mess was five times so much as any of theirs." It is defined as: the largest share

Beta test - This term has its origin in the Greek letter *Beta* which is the second letter in the Greek Alphabet. It is the second level of testing or development after **Alpha testing** (which normally applies to software development). It is now used to describe: a trial run of machinery, software, or other products, in the final stages of its development, carried out by a party unconnected with its development. **Smoke test**

Bête noire - This is a French term that has become part of the English lexicon. It means: something or someone particularly disliked

Better angels of our nature - This popular phrase is from Abraham Lincoln's first inaugural address. However, in 1841, Charles Dickens had used "our better angels" in his novel Barnaby Rudge. William Seward, Lincoln's Secretary of State, suggested that Lincoln use the term guardian angels in his address. Furthermore, Shakespeare used the words "better angel" in Othello, (Act V, Scene II) and Lincoln was familiar with most of the Shakespearean classics and undoubtedly read Othello. The phrase is an appeal

35

for people to seek the good that is inherent in us as human beings. **Salt of the earth; on the side of the angels**

Better half - This term has its origin in the Puritan belief that a person is made up of two halves; one half body and one-half soul. It was later applied to a marriage and then later just the wife of the marriage although it could apply to both. It is now used to describe: a person's wife, husband, or partner, but usually the wife that is the best part of the relationship and the part that makes it work. **Significant other** is similar and means: a person with whom someone has an established romantic or sexual relationship

Better the devil you know than the devil you don't know - The source of this adage was first recorded In Erasmus' Adages by R. Taverner tr. The phrase is often interpreted to mean: it is better to deal with someone or something familiar, although you may not like him, her or it than to deal with someone or something you do not know that might be much worse. **Lesser of two evils**

Better to be an old man's darling than a young man's slave - The source of this saying is from the English writer John Heywood's proverbs first published in 1546. This saying means what it literally says, that it is better to be married to someone that appreciates you than to someone that doesn't, regardless of age. **Trophy wife; sugar daddy**

Better to beg for forgiveness than to ask for permission - This saying, **in its various incarnations,** is attributed to Grace Murray Hopper also known as "Amazing Grace." A graduate of Harvard University, she was a pioneer in the early days of computing and became one of the first women to reach the rank of Rear Admiral in the United States Navy. The phrase is often interpreted to mean: if you see something that absolutely needs to be done, don't wait around for someone to approve or to **rubber stamp** your actions, but **go with the flow** and be willing to **suffer the consequences** of your actions. In other words, **take the initiative.** The reverse of this phrase: **it is better to ask for permission than to seek forgiveness** has also been used as a cautionary note. **He who hesitates is lost**

Better to have, and not need, than to need, and not have - This phrase is regularly attributed to Franz Kafka. However, it has also been attributed to others. The phrase means literally what it says, it is merely a statement about survival. It can be viewed as an axiom when it comes to money and the essentials of life. It has been used in recent times by some as a justification for gun ownership **Kafkaesque**

Better to remain silent and be thought a fool than to speak and to remove all doubt - This saying has been ascribed to Abraham Lincoln and sometimes to the American author and humorist Mark Twain. But the true source may be the Bible (Proverbs 17:28) (although the exact wording is not used). The verse states: "Even fools are thought wise if they keep silent, and discerning if they hold their tongues." The saying has also been credited to Maurice Switzer who may have been inspired by the biblical verse. Nonetheless, the common interpretation is: even a fool can be thought of as wise if he is silent. Similar phrases include: **silence is golden; speak when you are spoken to; keep your mouth shut and your eyes open**

Between Scylla and Charybdis - In Greek mythology, they were two immortal monsters who beset the narrow waters navigated by the hero Odysseus. To be caught between Scylla and Charybdis means to be

36

caught in a situation with no good way out; caught in a dilemma. Similar phrases include: **between the devil and the deep blue sea; a rock and a hard place**

Beware of Greeks bearing gifts - This phrase comes from the Trojan War, where the Greeks presented the Trojans with a gift in the form of a wooden horse. The Trojans brought the horse inside where the Greeks emerged from the hollow horse at night to surprise and thus conquer the Trojans. The common interpretation is: to beware of any gift or offer given under dubious circumstances. **Trojan horse**

Beware the Ides of March - The Ides of March (*Eidus Martiae* in Latin) is a day on the traditional Roman calendar that corresponds to the date of March 15th. It is most commonly associated with the assassination of Julius Caesar, on the Ides of March in the year 44 BC. Beware the Ides of March' is the soothsayer's message to Julius Caesar, warning of his death. It often alludes to: a warning of something bad. **A Cassandra**

Beyond the pale - The origin of the saying is not known. Yet, most people think that pale refers to a fence made of pale. It is often used to describe: something that is outside the bounds of acceptable behavior. Similar phrases include: **over the top; off limits**

Big Brother - The source of this saying is from the name of the head of state in George Orwell's Nineteen Eighty-Four (1949). It is a story of a frightening dystopia that has become a symbol of such a society in mainstream culture particularly as the society becomes more technical. It has given rise to the expression that "**Big Brother is watching you.**" It now describes: a person, organization or government that exercises total control over the lives of people, **A brave new world; Room 101**

Bigfoot - The origin of this term is a North American folklore in which a large ape-like creature(s) roams the wilderness leaving large footprints and unconfirmed sporadic sightings. Also referred to as Sasquatch, it is akin to the **Lock Ness Monster** in its sightings and believability, the latter folklore of Scottish origin. Both Bigfoot and the Lock Ness Monster have been used to describe something that is unbelievable or strange. Something that may exist, but there is no indisputable proof of its existence similar to **UFOs** and aliens; unexplainable or strange phenomena. **Abdominal snowman**

Bite off more than you can chew - The origin of this phrase appears to come from the days when chewing tobacco was quite popular. In those days, someone would offer another person a bite off their tobacco and in some cases, they bit off more than they could chew. Thus, the warning: **don't bite off more than you can chew**. The common interpretation is: to attempt something that is too hard to do. Similar phrases include: **in over your head; eyes are bigger than your stomach; to have too much on your plate**

Bite the bullet - This phrase appears to have its origin in the practice of wounded soldiers biting down on a bullet to help them endure the pain of a wound or to help in such extreme cases as amputations. It means: to decide to do something difficult or unpleasant that one has been putting off or hesitating to do; to commit oneself to a course of action about which one is apprehensive or worried. **Go for it** and **take the plunge** are similar expressions

IN A NUTSHELL

Bits and bytes - These two terms emerged with the computer age, more specifically with the advent of microprocessors in the 1970s. A bit is a binary digit either a zero or a one, a byte is a collection of eight bits and a nibble, which is rarely used, is four bits. Hence the geek joke: it takes two nibbles to make one byte. (Ha ha) By combining bits into bytes, computers can generate any number although they fundamentally only understand two digits. Bytes lie at the core of characters and memory is normally designated as bytes, e.g., megabytes, gigabytes, etc.. Using this system of logic, a one and a zero are complements (or opposites) of each other. A **binary choice** has been used to express a choice between one extreme or the other. For example, hot or cold, black or white, up or down, etc.

Bitter end- The term has its origin in sailing. The bitter end is the end of an anchor rope or chain that is tied to the ship. When the rope reaches this point, there is no more slack in the rope, and you have **come to the end of the rope.** This meant that the water was too deep to set anchor. The common usage is: a final or disastrous end

Black don't crack - This is a phrase that originated in the African American community and refers to the skin of African Americans. It is believed by many that since people of color have more melanin in their skin, it has a tendency not to wrinkle as fast once they become older. It therefore has become a term for the reason why some African Americans, in good health, rarely look their age

Black Friday - This term seems to have its origins in the fact that people wanted to take the day after **Thanksgiving** (which in America traditionally falls on a Thursday) off and would repeatedly call in sick or take vacation to extend their weekend. It now represents: the day after Thanksgiving and is regarded as the first day of the traditional Christmas shopping season, on which retailers offer special reduced prices. Similarly, **Cyber Monday** is the Monday following Thanksgiving, promoted by online retailers as a day for exceptional bargains

Black hole - This is a term that was borrowed from the science realm. A black hole is a region of space having a gravitational field so intense that no material or radiation, such as light, can escape. Once only a theory, along with Dark Matter and Dark Energy, science has confirmed that black holes do exist and could be found at the center of galaxies. It now represents: a place or situation in which nothing can escape. **Being sucked into a black hole. Big bang** is another closely related scientific term that is sometimes used as an expression of a large explosion are the start of something big. In science, it is the belief that the universe started from a very small **cosmic egg**, that eventually created the stars and all forms of matter and energy that we observe in the universe. **Black box** is another black term that is also used in the scientific realm and has migrated to the general public. In science, it is an electronic device, e.g., a flight recorder of which the inner workings are unknown or not relevant. It generally means: something that operates in a hidden or mysterious way; an opaque thing or situation

Black is beautiful - This was a popular phrase of the 1960s along with: **Say it loud, I'm black and I'm proud.** It was an era when black people in America were in search of a new identity. One that sharply contrasted from those labels bestowed upon them by whites. Even though the phrase emerged during these turbulent times, it dates back to slavery and was first articulated by the black polymath Dr. John S. Rock. A seminal figure of the abolitionist movement, he was a medical doctor and a lawyer that exemplified the potential of the black race, at a time when the intelligence of black people and their God-ordained right to be free was repeatedly called into question. The phrase now means: there is no shame in being black as long as you view yourself as beautiful. **African American; soul brother; brothers and sisters**

Black sheep of the family - This term seems to have its origin it the fact that occasionally a black sheep would be born in the flock. Since white wool could be easily dyed, the value of black wool was less desirable. The metaphor was easily extended to members of a family, because of the negative connotation associated with dark color or black (e.g., devil's food cake is chocolate, whereas angel food cake is white). Similarly, a white sheep is often identified as a good person within a group that has been designated as bad. Unfortunately, in some cases, this metaphor was extended to the human family, with black people being viewed, at least subliminally, as the black sheep. As the theory of evolution became more prominent, scientific justification of this paradigm became mainstream. The widespread interpretation is: a member of a family or group who is regarded as shameful. Any person who is different in a way which others disapprove of, find odd, or does not meet the expectations or standards of the group. **Like a red-headed stepchild** is similar in connotation. **Can an Ethiopian change his skin?**

Blind as a bat - This phrase originated from the belief that bats are blind which is untrue. Although bats navigate in the dark using echolocation, (self-generated echoes) they are not blind. There are over 1,000 species of bats with varying degrees of sight. The term, however, has migrated to mean: incapable of seeing something. On a similar note; **like a bat out of Hell** means: very wild and fast

Blockbuster - The origin of this term seems to come from a large aerial bomb used during World War II that could level an entire block. Soldiers returning home began to use the term to describe other big things. It soon was used to describe something big and now refers to: a motion picture, novel, etc., especially one lavishly produced, that has or is expected to have widespread popular appeal or financial success. Something large and spectacular

Blood brothers - Although this term became popular by the numerous westerns depicting Native Americans and white men mixing their blood as a sign of agreement or **to seal the deal**, it is a ritual that was performed by many ethnic groups around the globe. It now refers to two different things. First, a brother by birth that shares at least one parent. Second, a male who has pledged to be loyal to another male usually in a ceremony in which they mix their blood, i.e., a deep bond of friendship. **Brother from another mother; homeboys**

Bloody Mary - Queen Mary I, was the daughter of Henry the VIII and the sister of Queen Elizabeth. She was a Catholic and instituted a reign of terror against non-Catholics mostly Protestants. The English called her "Bloody Mary" and named an alcoholic drink after her. She should not be confused with Mary Queen of Scots who was the mother of King James (author of the English version of the Bible). She was murdered by her cousin, Queen Elizabeth. Next time you order this drink, you may want to think about the bloody rein of Queen Mary I and the circumstances from which it is named

IN A NUTSHELL

Blow my high - This term dates back at least to the drug culture of the 1960s when marijuana, LSD and other forms of mind-altering drugs became prevalent. It has since come to mean: to interfere with a person's happy state or bliss; to pull someone down and even make them depressed at a time when they were feeling good and optimistic about someone or something. Similar expressions include: **you're bumming me out; don't blow my high**

Blown to smithereens - This expression seems to have Irish origins and dates back to the early part of the 19ᵗʰ century. This phrase was often uttered (and perhaps popularized) by the cartoon character Yosemite Sam. It means: to disintegrate into very small pieces. **I'll blow you to smithereens**

Blue bloods – This term originated in Spain and was later transferred to other parts of Europe. Spain was conquered and occupied by the dark skin Moors for centuries. During this time, many Spaniards married darker skin Moors and their progeny were darker. When the Spaniards finally expelled the Moors in 1492, those that were lighter in complexion and claimed to be pure of Moorish blood designated themselves as *blue bloods*. So light they you could see the blood in their veins (which is blue when not exposed to the air). As time progressed, blood blue became a symbol of the aristocracy and royalty

Blue chip - This term dates to the early 1900s and takes its name from the blue chips used in gambling which typically have high value. It now refers to: companies or their shares considered to be a reliable investment, although less secure than gilt-edged stock. **Blue chip stock**

Blue/Red State - While the Democratic and Republican parties have been around for over a century, the terms Blue State and Red State are relatively new and only emerged at the turn of the 21ˢᵗ century as a sign of a much-divided America. Blue States are associated with states that predominately vote Democratic and Red States those that predominately vote Republican. A **Purple State** is the same as a **swing state** that could vote either Democratic or Republican

Blue/White collar worker - The exact origin of this term is unclear. However, historically, factory and manual workers wore uniforms often blue and office workers wore dress clothes often with white shirts. Hence, blue collar is defined as: of or relating to manual work or workers, particularly in industry contrasted with **white collar workers** who were usually college graduates or professionals, e.g., doctors, lawyers, engineers, etc. Similarly, **pink collar** is used to designate a job traditionally held by women. **Green collar** is an emerging term and refers to a person that is employed in products or services that improve the quality of the environment

Bon appetit - This is a French term meaning good appetite that has become part of the English lexicon. It is used as a salutation to a person about to eat and in this context, means enjoy your meal

Bon voyage - This again is one of many French expressions that has worked its way into the English language. It is used to express good wishes to someone about to go on a journey meaning: "I hope you have a safe and pleasant trip." **Maiden Voyage**

A COLLECTION OF POPULAR ENGLISH PHRASES

Bone of contention - The origin of this phrase seems to come from two dogs fighting over the last or same bone. It is now used to describe: the source or subject of a dispute, problem or dilemma; a dispute over something that does not have an apparent solution. **Pet peeve**

Bone of my bones - The source of this saying is from the Bible (Genesis 2:23) "And Adam said; This is now bone of my bones, and **flesh of my flesh:** she shall be called Woman, because she was taken out of Man." The common usage is: any close relationship as between parent and child

Bootleg - This term has its origin in the smuggling of liquor in boots around the turn of the 20th century and popularized during the days of prohibition in the United States. Though it originally applied to alcohol, it is currently used to designate something that is sold illegally or given without the proper consent. Something that is not the original. Similar phrases include: **a bootleg copy; sold under the table**

Born with a silver spoon in your mouth - This phrase is believed to have been used in Cervantes' popular book, **Don Quixote,** in the early 1600s and translated into English later. However, it is not clear that the term was not already familiar. Since silver spoons were expensive; only wealthy people could afford them. It is therefore highly probable that the idiom developed by its association with people that could afford such spoons. This is particularly true for the apostle spoon or christening spoon given to babies at their baptism by their godparents. It now refers to: someone who is born into wealth and privilege. **Woke up on third base and thought you hit a triple** is similar and means that someone else gave you an enormous advantage

Bourgeois - This is another French term incorporated into the English language that originally designated the French middle class. It was ridiculed by the French playwright Molière and redefined later by Karl Marx, the founder of modern Communism along with Friedrich Engels. It now connotes: materialism, and a striving concern for "respectability." It can involve, but not limited to, driving the right car, eating the right (healthy or gourmet) foods, going to expensive restaurants, having a professional/**white-collar** job or being part of a particular social group or club. **Stuck up; status symbol; white shoe lawyer. Bohemian** is a term that also has its roots in a French movement and means socially unconventional particularly as it relates to living outside of the bourgeoisie

Boy wonder - This term has its origins in the Batman series, appearing first in 1940, and was the moniker ascribed to Robin the young sidekick of Batman. It now denotes: a young man that has achieved more than what is expected for his age, a protégé. **Whiz kid. The Dynamic Duo** (a nickname for Batman and Robin) is another Batman metaphor that is often used to describe a dynamic or interesting pair of people. **Green Hornet and Kato; Lone Ranger and Tonto**

Boycott - The origin of this eponym comes from a dispute between the Irish Land League and Charles Boycott in Ireland in the 1880s. This practice of public ostracism against Boycott was so popular and effective that it was quickly emulated by other to settle similar disputes. It is now defined to mean: to withdraw from commercial, social or private relations with a country, organization, or person as a form of punishment, protest or retribution. **To go on strike** is one form of a boycott

IN A NUTSHELL

Brainstorming - This phrase was coined by Alex Faickney Osborn in his book entitled: <u>Your Creative Power</u> published in 1948. As so conceived, it was a process of using multiple brains to storm or attack a specific problem or dilemma. Brainstorming sessions vary in scope and in content. Some consist of **throwing it up against the wall and seeing if it sticks.** Others use detail **mind maps** or **flow charts**, yet others use sticky notes posted together. The term generally means: A group discussion used to generate new ideas or to find solutions to difficult problems. Sometimes, the room that is used for serious brainstorming to combat a difficult or urgent problem is called a **war room. Round table**; **think tank**

Bread and circus - The origin of this phrase comes from the Romans, specifically the Roman author Juvenal. They believed that all you needed to do to control the people was to give them cheap food and entertainment. The phrase is regularly interpreted to mean: a diet of entertainment or political policies on which the masses are fed to keep them happy and docile. **Smoke and mirrors**

Break a leg - The source of this term appears to come from the belief that one should not utter "good luck" to an actor before a performance. Instead, they should wish the opposite. It now means: good luck. Similar expressions include: **bonne chance; keep your fingers crossed; knock on wood**

Break the ice - This phrase has been around for several centuries. However, it was popularized by ships that were specifically made to break up ice which allowed other ships to pass. It has been used in its current colloquial form since the 1800s. The term is often used: to do or say something that relieves tension, or to get things going particularly at a party or other social gathering. **An icebreaker; to break the ice**

Brevity is the soul of wit - This expression is from William Shakespeare's play <u>Hamlet</u> (Act II, Scene II). It generally means: the quality or ability of expressing much in few words or the essence of a witty statement lies in its concise wording and delivery. **In a nutshell**

Bring home the bacon - The origin of this expression is not clear and possibly unknown. Notwithstanding, by the turn of the 20th century it was popular. It has a duel meaning the first is to bring home money that you have earned. In this case, the **breadwinner** is the primary source of income. The second is related to winning a prize or a contest

Broken reed - The origin of this term is unclear, although it has been used since the mid-15th century. Often misunderstood as something or someone that cannot be fixed, its true meaning is: an unreliable or unsupportive person

Brown paper bag test - This is a term that has its origin in intra-racial discrimination based on skin color. It is well known within the African American community that the lighter skinned blacks were more privileged than their brethren of a darker hue. This phenomenon could be traced back to the days of slavery, in which some mulatto blacks were the progeny of the slave master. In many colleges, fraternities and social organizations, particularly post-Reconstruction up to <u>the Civil Rights movement</u>, the brown paper bag test was used as a criterion for admission and inclusion giving lighter skinned black people an advantage. If you were lighter than a brown paper bag, you were admitted. So ingrained was this belief that iconoclastic organizations such as The Nation of Islam considered skin color in the selection of its ministers and it is no accident that most of the elite African Americans of the pre-Civil Rights era were light skinned. Say it loud, I'm black and I'm proud, a song by James Brown was instrumental in the destruction of this barrier within the African American community. The term is used (but seldom implemented) within the African American community today. As in most cases involving race, non-blacks should use discretion in using this term because some blacks find it offensive depending on its connotation. **They keep the green olives in a jar, but they keep the black olives in a can**

Brownie points - The origin of this term appears not to be the famed dessert, but rather junior members of the Girl Scouts known as Brownies who earned merits or points based on achievements. This term has been in use since the 1940s. It means: an imaginary reward or form of **social currency** awarded or used by someone who performs a good act or tries to please

Bull in a China shop - The source of this expression is an Aesop fable about a donkey in a potter shop which was later changed to a bull in a China shop. It means: a very clumsy or angry person in a delicate situation

Bully pulpit - This was a term that was coined by Theodore (Teddy) Roosevelt. It is now used to describe: a public office or position of authority that provides its occupant with an outstanding opportunity to speak out on any issue. Also, the term **Teddy Bear** comes from Teddy Roosevelt who was a fervent bear hunter

Buridan's donkey (Ass) **-** This expression refers to a Medieval paradox concerning the logic of rationality and freewill. It demonstrates the strain between formal and informal ways of thinking and the sometimes-paradoxical consequences when this tension is ignored. The concept is illustrated in the following example. Imagine a hungry donkey standing equidistant from two identical piles of hay. The donkey tries to decide which pile he should eat first and finding no reason to choose one over another, starves to death. It is regularly used to describe: the perils of indecisiveness. **He who hesitates is lost; he who considers too much will perform little**

Bury the hatchet - The origin of this popular idiom comes from Native Americans. The chief of a tribe would bury a hatchet or tomahawk as a sign of peace. The common usage is: to make peace with a person or a group. **Let's bury the hatchet**

Butterfly effect - The source of this expression is from a 1972 presentation by Edward Norton Lorenz who highlighted the possibilities that small changes may have momentous effects or consequences. The question proposed by Lorenz was: does the flap of a butterfly's wings in Brazil set a tornado in Texas? The expression is often used to demonstrate how small permutations in the initial conditions can have long-term and irreversible consequences. Any small change that yields a large result, particularly as it pertains to weather. **Snowball effect**

IN A NUTSHELL

By and large - This was a maritime phrase that became popular. As far back as the 16th century, the term *large* referred to a ship that was sailing with the wind. Conversely, the term *by* meant sailing into or against the wind. Thus, *by and large* meant sailing in all directions relative to the wind. The term migrated to mean: all things considered; on the whole; overall

By any means necessary - The origin of this phrase is attributed to the French playwright Jean Paul Sartre from his play <u>Dirty Hands.</u> It was made popular in America during the 1960s by the Civil Rights leader <u>Malcolm X</u> and is often, at least in the African American community, associated with his movement. Particularly, once he separated from the Black Muslim (Nation of Islam) organization. The common interpretation is: to leave open all available options necessary to achieve a particular goal. **Don't rule anything out; praise the Lord and pass the ammunition**

Bye, Felicia - The origin of this expression comes from the 1995 movie <u>Friday</u> starring Chris Tucker and Ice Cube. It was uttered by Craig played by Ice Cube after his neighbor, Felicia, tried to borrow several items from him and the character, Smokey, played by Chris Tucker. An Internet and Twitter sensation, it means: **I'm done with you, it's all over**, or "I'm not interested in you or what you have to say. **See ya wouldn't wanna be ya** and **don't let the door hit ya, where the good Lord split ya** are similarly used

Stands for:

Cross the Rubicon

IN A NUTSHELL

C'est la vie - This is a French term for "that's life" that has worked its way into the English vernacular. In fact, it is used far more in English than it is in French. It means: that's how things happen or an acceptance of circumstances as they unfold. It is normally a response to an unfavorable occurrence in life or an expression used to play down some minor disappointment. **That's the way the cookie crumples**

Cabal - Legend has it that the origin of this term comes from an acronym of the five chief political figures (Clifford, Arlington, Buckingham, Ashley, and Lauderdale) in the court of Charles II. However, further research indicates that the term preceded Charles II and may have its roots in the Jewish word Kabbalah. Nonetheless, the term has migrated to mean: a clandestine or secret political group often united by some underlying or common cause. Jacobins

Cabin fever - This term originated in the American West as a result of staying in a cabin for long periods of time due to snow or **inclement weather**. It had a tendency to drive someone **stir crazy**. The term now means: irritability, anxiety, and similar symptoms resulting from long confinement or isolation indoors during the winter

Caesar's wife must be above suspicion - Julius Caesar is supposed to have said this when asked why he divorced his wife, Pompeii. Because she was suspected of some wrongdoing, he could not associate with her anymore. It normally refers to: the associates of public figures must not even be suspected of wrongdoing; they must be clear and honest in morals. **Above suspicion; no one is above the law**

Call no man happy until he dies - This phrase is attributed to the Greek historian Herodotus and could be found in Book I of his Histories. "But call no man happy before he dies; but rather call him fortunate." It is a story told about the sage Solon and the king of Lydia Croesus who was reported to be the richest man alive. He was conquered by the Persian King Cyrus the Great and died penniless. The phrase is frequently interpreted to mean: happiness is a nebulous and often fleeting thing, therefore it cannot be defined by wealth alone. **As rich as Croesus**

Calm before the storm - This expression dates to the 1700s, but its origin is unclear. The phrase is often used to express a quiet or peaceful period before a period of great difficulty or high activity. **A storm is brewing; when it rains it pours; come rain or shine. The eye of the storm** is another storm metaphor. It has its origin in hurricanes, and it means: the center of turmoil or conflict or the calm region of a storm

Can an Ethiopian change his skin? - This saying is from the Bible (Jeremiah 13:23) "Can the Ethiopian change his skin, or the leopard his spots?" It simply means: you are what you are. **The wolf may change his coat, but not his character**

Can't hold a candle to - In ancient times, there was a person whose job was to hold a candle for someone to provide them with light. This was considered an inferior job or secondary to the person that needed the light. It now means: second rate in certain skills or someone that is inferior to another; not equal to someone; unable to measure up to someone. **Playing second fiddle; second banana**

46

A COLLECTION OF POPULAR ENGLISH PHRASES

Canary in a [coal] mine - This phrase has its origins in coal mining. A singing caged canary would be used as a warning to detect poisonous gases such as carbon monoxide or methane in the mine. In such cases, the canary would stop singing and die before they reached levels toxic to humans. The phrase migrated to a generic use to mean: an advanced warning of some impending danger or in the case of the canary as **a sacrificial lamb** which means: a person or an animal sacrificed for the common good. **A singing canary** is sometimes used to denote someone who informs on another person or a group

Canonical scripture - Relating to or belonging to the biblical canon; those New Testament scriptures that made it into the Bible. In 367 CE, Athanasius of Alexandria published a list of 27 New Testament books which were accepted in his time, and these are the same 27 which are recognized today. The term frequently refers to: something that is sacred and absolute. **The gospel truth.** Notwithstanding, in the 20th century, noncanonical scripture has gain prominence among biblical scholars particularly The Nag Hammadi library also known as the "Gnostic Gospels" discovered near the Upper Egyptian town of Nag Hammadi in 1945

Carnal knowledge - This expression is from Latin *carnalis* for "fleshly:" Copulation is the act of a man having sexual relations with a woman. Penetration is an essential element of sexual intercourse, and there is carnal knowledge if even the slightest penetration of the female by the male organ takes place. It is frequently used as: a euphemism for sexual intercourse Likewise, **do the deed** is slang for to have sex with someone

Carolingian - The period in European history that relates to the Frankish dynasty, founded by Pepin III, son of Charles Martel and father of Charlemagne (also known as Charles the Great), that ruled in western Europe from 750 to 987. On Christmas Day 800, as Charlemagne knelt in prayer in Saint Peter's Basilica in Rome, Pope Leo III placed an Emperor's crown upon his head making him emperor of the Holy Roman Empire. The name derives from the large number of family members who bore the name Charles, most notably Charlemagne

Carthaginian peace - The origin of this term is from the treaty by which Rome reduced Carthage to the status of **a puppet state** in 201 BCE. In 219 BCE, Hannibal of Carthage led an attack on Rome, which sparked the outbreak of the Second Punic War. The Romans ultimately defeated the Carthaginians. The term now means: any brutal peace treaty demanding total subjugation of the defeated side. **Unconditional Surrender. On a similar note,** Hannibal at the gates is a saying that emerged in Rome as a means of frightening someone, particularly children, into doing what you want them to do

Cast aspersions - The exact origin of this popular phrase appears to be unknown or unclear. But it seems to have originated in the 1700s. The earliest usage of this phrase is from Henry Fielding's novel Tom Jones published in 1749. Like wet your appetite, bated breath and other malapropisms, this phrase is often used incorrectly as cast "dispersion." The word aspersion originally referred to the sprinkling of someone with water or another liquid substance. The phrase is now defined as: to doubt or disparage someone; to call something into question. **To cast aspersions**; Doubting Thomas

Cast pearls before swine - This expression comes from the Bible (Matt. 7:6). It was also used by Shakespeare and Charles Dickens. The phrase means: to waste something good on someone who doesn't care about it. **Don't give holy things to hounds (dogs)**

Cast the first stone - The source of this expression is the Bible (John 8:7) and refers to a statement made by Jesus: "So when they continued asking him, he lifted up himself, and said unto them, **He that is without sin among you, let him first cast a stone**." The phrase is frequently used to designate: the first to make an accusation or is used to emphasize that a potential critic is not wholly blameless

Castor and Pollux - In Greek and Roman mythology, Castor and Pollux (known as Polydeuces to the Greeks) were twin brothers who appeared in several prominent myths. The constellation Gemini, represents the two brothers. It has migrated to mean: two friends or brothers that are faithful to each other. Similar expressions include: **David and Jonathan; Achilles and Patroclus; Fred and Barney; Rocky and Bullwinkle**

Cat got your tongue – The origin of this popular idiom is unclear or unknown. But some believe that its origin lies in the medieval superstition that if you saw a witch with her cat that she would use magic to get her cat to steal your tongue so that you could not tell anyone that you saw her. Yet, another comes from Ancient Egypt where it is believed that the tongues of liars were cut out and fed to the cats. Nonetheless, the popular interpretation is: unexplained or unusual silence in a situation where a person is expected to speak. **What's wrong, cat got your tongue?**

Cat on a hot tin roof - Although this phrase was popularized by the title of a 1955 play by Tennessee Williams and the subsequent 1958 movie, the source is much older and dates back to the 17th century. It is often credited to the English theologian John Ray. In the earlier version of this idiom, *hot bricks* was used instead of hot tin roof (which seems to be the more Americanized version of the saying). The phrase means to be extremely anxious and unable to relax. **Like a cat on a hot tin roof**

Catalyst - This is a scientific term that has migrated to other parts of the English vernacular. In science, it is used to describe: a substance that increases the rate of a chemical reaction without itself undergoing any permanent chemical change. It has also been used generically as something that aids in the production or development of something else

Catch 22 - The source of this term is from the novel Catch 22 by the American writer Joseph Heller. It is now defined as: a dilemma that is difficult to solve or a situation or predicament from which it is impossible to extricate yourself from. Similar phrases include: **caught between a rock and a hard place; damned if you do, damned if you don't**

Catch as catch can - The origin of this term appears to be an old style of wrestling that did not adhere to standard rules. Instead, any conceivable means or advantage could be used to achieve victory (**by any means necessary**). It has migrated out of the wrestling arena and is now generally used to denote: to take advantage of any opportunity using any means or methods. **No holds barred** also emanates from wresting and essentially means the same thing

Catch some Zs - The origin of this phrase comes from the "Z" representation for sleeping or snoring often seen in comic strip and other illustrations. Consequently, the phrase now denotes: to get some sleep. **Cop some Zs; get some shut eye; hit the sack; hit the hay** mean the same thing. Additionally, imagining that you are **counting sheep**, jumping over a fence one by one, is an expression often used to indicate that you are trying to fall asleep. **Catch some rays** means to spend some time in the sun

Caught red-handed - The source of this popular phrase appears to be Scottish and dates back to the 15th century. It was used by the Scottish writer Sir Walter Scott in his renowned novel Ivanhoe (1819). How the phrase originated is uncertain as *red- handed* could have been a sign of having blood on one's hands. Regardless of origin, the phrase now means: to be caught in the act of committing a crime particularly when the evidence of the crime is readily available. **Smoking gun**

Cause and effect - The origin of this concept can be traced to antiquity. For example, Aristotle wrote in his treatise on Rhetoric: "If you prove the cause, you at once prove the effect; and conversely nothing can exist without its cause." It is also an integral part of **the Scientific Method** and religions such as Buddhism. The diagnosis of an illness based on its symptoms is a classic example of cause and effect. It means: to note a relationship between actions or events such that one or more are the result of the other or others. **Domino effect. Root cause** is the initiating cause of the condition or an effect. Often, as part of the problem resolution process, a **Root Cause Analysis** (RCA) is conducted

Cavalier - This is an interesting word that dates back centuries. During the English Civil Wars (1642–1651), it designated a supporter of King Charles I. When used as a noun, it has one connotation and a completely different one when used as an adjective. As a noun, it means: a gallant or chivalrous man, especially one serving as an escort to a lady of high social standings: attributes associated with knighthood, e.g., the American basketball team the Cleveland Cavaliers. Though, as an adjective, it means: marked by or given to offhand and often disdainful disregard of important things or matters, e.g., a **cavalier attitude** toward the rights and welfare of others. In most languages, however, the same connotation is transferred from the noun to adjective and **vice versa** and it is rare that the two are antithetical to each other. The source of this ambiguity may lie in the difference between how the Cavaliers acted and how their overall actions were perceived by others. Particularly by their opponents, the victorious Parliamentary forces (or Roundheads) led by Oliver Cromwell

Caveat emptor - This is an old Latin term that means: **"let the buyer beware."** Similar to the phrase "**sold as is**," this term means the buyer assumes the risk that the product may fail to meet expectations or have defects. The principle that the buyer alone is responsible for checking the quality and suitability of goods before a purchase is made

Caviar to the general - This expression is from Shakespeare's Hamlet (Act II, Scene II) and it has migrated to mean: something of an exceptionally high quality or intelligence not befitting or appreciated by those who consume, see, or partake in it. A good thing unappreciated by the ignorant. This phrase can be misleading. "general" here refers to the general population, not a military general

Chain reaction - This term seems to have its origin in the science or chemistry fields when one action triggers another, and another and so forth. For example, a nuclear bomb (explosion) is a result of a chain reaction. The term means: a series of events in which each event causes the next one; a series of events caused by one single event, e.g., **domino effect**

Chairman of the board - The origin of this phrase is uncertain. However, many believe that it dates back to the Middle Ages. In this regard, it referred to a board that was used for eating. The central person at the table, usually the man of the house, was the *'chair man'* and hence the saying chairmen of the board. Even though the term board used as an eating table goes back to the 1200s, it only became popular in the 1600s to designate a business group. The term is now defined as: the head of the board of a company or corporation or group. **Ranking member**

Chance favors the prepared mind - This is a quotation from Louis Pasteur, the French chemist and bacteriologist. He introduced pasteurization and made pioneering studies in vaccination techniques. The common usage is: the way to increase your chances of success is to be prepared beforehand. **Forewarned is forearmed**

Chapter and verse - This term alludes to the Bible as the central authority. It is often used as an authoritative ending to something that is to be considered an undisputable fact or to go through something in great detail; an exact reference or authority. **Root and branch**

Charity begins at home - The source of this expression is unclear; however, the sentiments are echoed in the Bible 1 Timothy 5:8. "But if any provide not for his own, and specially for those of his own house, he hath denied the faith, and is worse than an infidel." Different versions of this expression have been around for centuries before it converged on its current usage. It is generally interpreted to mean: a person should help their family and close friends before helping others

Checks and balances - The source of this saying is the formation of the United States governmental system and the Constitution. It means: a system that limits the power of a particular group as a means of maintaining the operation and integrity of the systems, i.e., **balance of power**

Cherchez la femme - This is a French expression, which literally means: "to chase women" that has worked its way into the English vernacular. It is often associated with men that seek sex or companionship from women. **A playboy; ladies' man**

Cheshire Cat - This term originates from the smiling cat in Lewis Carrol's Alice in Wonderland known for its distinctive mischievous grin. The term has evolved to mean: someone that grins or smiles very broadly, particularly during mischievous of self-gratifying situations. **Smile from ear to ear; Cheshire Cat grin**

A COLLECTION OF POPULAR ENGLISH PHRASES

Chicken Little - The source of this term is from a common folktale of the same name also known as <u>Henny Penny</u>. In this tale, <u>Chicken Little</u> mistakes a falling acorn for a piece of the sky that is falling. It also gave rise to the popular idiom **the sky is falling**. Both expressions are synonymous with **impending doom** or a pessimistic view of life

Chickens coming home to roost - In 1810, the English poet <u>Robert Southey</u> included a sentence in his poem about chickens coming home to roost. Chickens normally come home to rest and sleep. This phrase received notoriety in the 1960s, when Malcolm X used it to describe the assassination of President Kennedy. It has migrated to mean that bad things done in the past will eventually **come back to haunt you**. Similar expression are: **you reap what you sow; what goes around comes around**

Children should be seen and not heard - This is an old adage that dates back at lease to the early Middle Ages. A relic of its times, it applied to children and young women. In recent times, however, many are of the opinion that we should listen more to our children as there are many outside influences that adults should be aware of. The literal interpretation is the best. **Out of the mouth of babes** is another children's related phrase that is somewhat antithetical to the previously mentioned adage and means: sometimes children or an unexperienced person can have great insight because they are not tainted by bias or prejudice; perhaps best exemplified by the children's story: **The Emperor has no clothes** in which the truth is spoken by a child while the adults remain silent. **Deep meaning often lie in childish play; kids say the darndest things**

Chink - The origin of this derogatory term is uncertain. Notwithstanding, some believe that it was derived from ching-ching, or even perhaps from the <u>Ching Manchu dynasty</u> which was the last imperial dynasty in China and ruled from 1644–1912. Another potential explanation comes from the English word chink or a slit and refers to their eyes. While the term originally applied to Chinese as far back as the mid-1800s, it has also been used as a derogatory term to designate people of Pacific Asian ancestry in general. **Ching chong and ching chang chong** are also used in the same derogatory manner. Needless to say, like all derogatory terms, these terms should not be used when referring to people of Pacific Asian ancestry

Chomping (Champing) at the bit - This phrase has its origins in horseracing where a horse would bite on the mouthpiece as a sign of nervousness or excitement. Champing at the bit is much older, however in recent years, chomping has become more popular. The phrase has migrated to generally mean: to be restless or excited especially before an event or activity. **Butterflies in the stomach** is similar in connotation

Chutzpah(hutzpah) - This term has its origins in the Hebrew or Yiddish language. Yiddish is a language comprised of German and Hebrew dialects, originally spoken by Jews in central and eastern Europe. The term now means: audacity, nerve or flagrant boldness. **You've got some nerve!**

Clarion call - This expression seems to have originated from the battlefield as clarion is a small high pitch trumpet used on the field as a call to battle. The general usage is: a strong demand or request for action;

a very clear message or instruction about what action is required. **To sound (hear) a clarion call; call to arms**

Clean someone's clock - The earliest mention of this phrase is from the Trenton Evening Times newspaper in July of 1908. It was made in a reference to a local sporting event. But it may have been used earlier as the term clock is British slang for face. The common interpretation is: to give someone a severe beating; to defeat someone decisively in a physical fight or other opposition such as a negotiation or sporting event. Similar expressions are: **knock someone out [cold]; dust someone off; beat the living daylights out of; open up a can of whoop-ass; knock your block off**

Clean the Augean stables - Hercules had to clean out the horse stables of King Aegeus, which hadn't been cleaned in 30 years. One of Hercules' tasks was to clean them in one day, which he achieved by diverting two rivers through them. This was one of the twelve labors of Hercules. The last and the most difficult was the removal of **Cerberus** from Hades. The phrase has migrated to mean: the task of removing the accumulation of different sorts of corruption. **Herculean task; a hard row to hoe; expel the money changers from the temple**

Cleanliness is next to Godliness - The proverb is popularly credited to the English Anglican theologian John Wesley's 1778 sermon, as well as to writings in the Jewish holy scripts the Talmud. Contrary to popular opinion, it is not contained in the Bible. It now means that being in a state of spiritual cleanliness is the next best thing to being righteous with God

Clickbait - Although this term has been popularized in recent times, the concept dates back to the turn of the 20th century and has its roots in **yellow journalism** that emerged during this period. What we observe today on the Internet is a more **weaponized version** of a much older technique of grabbing the reader's attention. In an era in which the **attention span** of the average reader is diminishing, and competition for that attention expanding; clickbait has become an integral part of the online experience. The term means: content on the Internet with the sole purpose of getting someone to select the link

Cloak and dagger - The source of this expression is unclear as it appears in French and Spanish as well as English. The general consensus is that it was in use as early as the 18th century and may have been derived independently as the phrase implies something that his hidden, i.e., the dagger by the cloak, a common occurrence in its day. Charles Dickens used the phrase In Barnaby Rudge, (1841) and is somewhat credited with its popularization in the English language. The expression usually denotes: a situation that often involves secrecy, espionage, intrigue or mystery. **What's up your sleeve?**

Close but no cigar - The origin of this phrase appears to be American fairs where cigars were given out as prizes. It has migrated to mean: almost, but not quite successful or a narrowly avoided collision or other accident. **A near miss. On a similar note, "Missed it by that much"** replete with a hand gesture denoting small is similar and was made famous by the secret agent Maxwell Smart on the show Get Smart popular in the late 1960s. **Close only counts in horseshoes and hand grenades** literally means the same thing

Close your eyes and think of England - The root of this phrase is a British belief (probably dating back to the Victorian era) that it was the responsibility of a married woman to have sex with her husband whenever and however he wanted it. In this regard, she should just lay back and think of more pleasant thoughts until the act was over. It harps back to those days when women had few rights, and their privileges were left to the discretion of their husband. When **the rule of thumb** dictated that a man could beat his wife with a stick if it was not thicker than his thumb. **Barefoot and pregnant**; **speak when spoken to**

Clothes make the man - This expression is from Shakespeare's Hamlet (Act I, Scene III). The phrase is often interpreted to mean: you can judge a man's character based on his clothing and appearance. This saying also has it opposite expression: **clothes do not make the man. You never get a second chance to make a first impression, dress for success. Can't judge a book by its cover**

Cognitive dissonance - This term and identification of the condition is credited to the American psychologist Leon Festinger. It is used to describe: the state of having inconsistent or conflicting thoughts, beliefs, or attitudes, resulting from when beliefs do not match behaviors. Cognitive dissonance can also be described as a feefefling of uncomfortable stress emanating from holding two conflicting views in the mind at the same time. An example would be living the life of a slave or a second-class citizen in a country that espouses freedom, justice and equality for all. In such as system, those oppressed could unknowingly exhibit symptoms consistent with this term

Cold turkey - In America, the term turkey has been used to describe talking and the term "cold turkey" once meant **straight talk**. In the early 20th century, it migrated to its current meaning. It now means: the abrupt and complete end of taking drugs, alcohol or smoking to which one is addicted; to quit something in a sudden and abrupt manner. It is important to note, that some addictive drugs (including alcohol) cannot be quit abruptly without professional help if the person is addicted to them. **To go cold turkey; fall off the wagon; to talk turkey**

Cold War - This term has its origin in the aftermath of World War II when the United States and the Soviet Union were fighting for global superiority. It was deemed as a battle between ideologies, pitting Democracy against Communism which gave rise to terms such as the Red Scare and McCarthyism. The common usage is: a state of political hostility between countries characterized by threats, propaganda, and other measures short of open warfare

Come rain or shine - The source of this phrase is uncertain however; it was popularized by a song written for a 1946 Broadway show entitled: St. Louis Women. The song was also recorded by Frank Sinatra and Ray Charles which furthered its popularity. The phrase means: no matter what the circumstances

Come to Jesus moment(meeting) - The origin of this phrase lies in the Christian belief that there is a moment of conversion when one accepts Jesus Christ as their lord and savior. This is a moment of epiphany similar to the one experienced by the Apostle Paul on **the road to Damascus**. In some Christian denominations, the person is **born again** in reference to (John 3:3) "Jesus answered and said unto him, Verily, verily, I say unto thee; Except a man be born again, he cannot see **the kingdom of God**." Over time, the phrase "come to Jesus" developed a secular connotation which means: a dawning, epiphany or agreement following a disagreement or misunderstanding of something or someone. Any moment or meeting in which a candid, unpleasant, or critical conversation is held to resolve an issue or to confront a lingering problem. **What would Jesus do (WWJD)**

Coming events cast their shadow before - The saying is from a quotation from Thomas Campbell's Loichiel's Warning. The common usage is: certain signs precede certain events. Similarly, the **calm before the storm** is the tranquil period before something chaotic or destructive begins

Coming out of the woodwork - Although the exact origins of this term is unclear, it is a popular belief that it originated with insects, primarily cockroaches, coming out of woodwork, e.g., wood cabinets, baseboards, etc.. It has migrated to mean: to appear unexpectedly or to be caught by surprise; to be everywhere

Conflict of interest (COI) - The origin of this term is unclear. However, it may have emanated from the legal profession. It is now used to describe: a situation in which the concerns or aims of two different parties are incompatible. A situation that has the potential to undermine the impartiality of a person because of the possibility of a clash between the person's self-interest and professional or public interest. **Full disclosure** which is the requirement of those involved in a transaction to reveal all the facts relating to it, is one way of mitigating conflicts of interests

Confucius say - So named after the Chinese philosopher Confucius. (551–479 BCE). It is the Latinized name of Kongfuzi (K'ung Fu-tzu) "Kong the master." His ideas about the importance of practical moral values was collected by his disciples in the Analects and forms the basis of Confucianism. The term is a tribute to his wisdom and has come to mean: a humorous expression often used to introduce a maxim or thought that is considered wise

Conspicuous by (his) absence - This phrase is attributed to the Roman historian Tacitus and comes from The Annals of Imperial Rome, Book 3. It means: glaringly obvious by the fact of not being there. Suspect because of not being present

Conspiracy of silence - This expression was first used by the Victorian poet Sir Lewis Morris. It means: the behavior of a group that by unspoken consensus does not mention, discuss or acknowledge a given subject. **A gentleman's agreement**

Conspiracy theory - This term came of age in the mid-1960s with the assassination of President Kennedy and the subsequent investigation that culminated with the Warren Report. Many believed that the report was inaccurate and that his death was the result of some coordinated conspiracy that may have involved the government or organized crime. It has since moved to mean: the belief that some covert but influential organization is responsible for a circumstance or event. **Manchurian candidate**

Constant dripping hollows out a stone - This saying is attributed to the Roman poet Lucretius. It is a statement about persistence and time. It has migrated to mean: we do not see the small changes in things or life. But nothing stays the same and **change is inevitable**. For the most part, we look the same from day to day. However, it is the cumulative effect of small things that bring about great things

Conventional wisdom - This term was coined by Canadian economist John Kenneth Galbraith in his book entitled: The Affluent Society to describe economic ideas and principles. The common usage is: a generally accepted theory or belief. **Defies conventional wisdom**

Copious notes - The origin of this popular expression is unclear. The word copious means abundant or large in number. The phrase, therefore, means abundant notes; detailed notes. **To take copious notes**

Cornerstone: - This term has been around for centuries and has its origin in the building of monuments, edifices and temples. The cornerstone is normally the first stone placed and is often accompanied by ceremonies as in the placing of the cornerstones of the White House, Capitol and Washington Monument. In the Masonic tradition, the cornerstone is the Northeast stone placed and is symbolic of the place where the darkness of the North meets the sunlight of the East. The term is regularly used as a metaphor for setting a foundation or the groundwork of something and is often the point in which other things revolve. For example, Jesus Christ is the cornerstone of the Christian religion, Washington DC, is the cornerstone of the United States. **Lay the cornerstone; ground zero**

Cornucopia - Also known as the horn of plenty, in Greek mythology it was the horn of the goat that suckled the infant Zeus. According to folklore, it broke off and was filled with whatever the owner desired. It evolved into a horn shaped basket that was filled with, flowers, fruits and vegetables and used as a symbol of abundance. It is now defined as: a store of abundance; an inexhaustible supply

Cost an arm and a leg - The origin of this phrase is unknown. However, a popular rumor is that it originated with painters charging more to paint arms and legs but there is no evidence to support such a claim. It appears that the phrase is much more recent and seems to have emerged in the 20th century. The expression has migrated to mean: something that is very expensive or achieved at great personal costs. **It cost me an arm and a leg**

Coup de grâce - This is a French term meaning "stroke of grace" that has worked its way into the English vocabulary. It is defined as: a deathblow or death shot administered to end the suffering of a mortally wounded person; a decisive finishing blow, act, or event. Any decision to swiftly terminate an act, contract or agreement. A **knockout punch** is a boxing metaphor that essentially means the same thing. **Put the [final] nail in the coffin** is also used in a similar context

Court jester - The source of this term is the medieval practice of monarchs and noblemen employing a professional clown to entertain them or their guests. It has given rise to the idiom: **wear the cap and bells** the typical headwear of court jesters. The term is frequently applied to a person that acts like a fool, particularly in front of a crowd or a group. **Play the court jester or to wear the cap and bells**

IN A NUTSHELL

Courtly love - The origin of this term was a medieval European conception of nobility and chivalrously expressing love and admiration. Generally, courtly love was secret. It is an idealized and often illicit form of love renowned in the literature of the Middle Ages and the Renaissance. In this case, a knight or courtier devotes himself to a noblewoman who is usually married and pretends indifference to preserve her reputation. The common usage is: a type of love that obeys a set of rules and obligation sometimes kept secret between the two parties involved

Covenant of salt - The source of this phrase is the Bible as it appears several times: Leviticus 2:13, 2 Chronicles 13:5 and Numbers 18:19. Salt is referenced over thirty times in the Old Testament and ten times in the New Testament, e.g., "Ye are **the salt of the earth**" (Matt. 5:13). In ancient times, salt was a valuable commodity used to preserve meat. Whether or not it was used in ancient times as a means of currency is debatable. Because of its essential nature and its ability to preserve, salt was used as a metaphor for both. The phrase has come to mean: an enduring agreement between two people or groups. **Above the salt** is another salt idiom and means: of or in a high position; of high rank or repute; elite

Cover a multitude of sins - This saying is from the Bible (I Peter 4:8). "Above all, love each other deeply, because love covers over a multitude of sins." It now means: to conceal or gloss over many problems or defects in order to prevent people from seeing or discovering something bad or evil. **Charity covers a multitude of sins**

CP time - This term which stands for: Colored People time has its roots in the stereotype that black people are notoriously late. A common joke is that if you have a party attended by white and black people that in effect you have three parties. The first attended only by white people that come on time or early, the second attended by white and black people, the latter coming late, and the third by only black people after the white people have left. It refers to: to arrive late for a party or an event often causing the event to run later. While this term is quite common in the African American community, those outside of the community should use it with caution or not at all because some blacks find the term offensive. **On CP Time**

Creatio ex nihilo - This is a Latin term that is sometimes used in the English language particularly concerning issues of Creation and Science. **Ex nihilo** means from nothing. Historically, Christians hold firm to the doctrine of ex nihilo creation. Whereas other religions and denominations, e.g., Mormonism dispute this doctrine. Modern scientific cosmology has also challenged this doctrine in favor of the **Anthropic Principle.** The common interpretation is: God created the universe out of nothing

Crème de la crème - This is a French expression meaning "cream of the cream" that has worked its way into the English language. It is now used to describe: the best person or thing of a particular kind. **Cream of the crop**

Crescendo - This term originated from music. It comes from the Latin word *crēscere*, meaning "to grow." In music, it is a passage of music during which the volume is gradually increased. It has migrated to mean:

something that increases gradually until it reaches a climax or comes to a climactic end. For example: a crescendo of errors and **faux pas** led to his resignation. Other musical terms and phrases that have become popular are: **end on the same note; strike a [familiar] chord; sing from the same hymnbook; it's music to my ears; tone and tenor**

Crickets - The exact origin of this term is unclear. Nevertheless, it is believed to have originated from the sound of crickets at night when nothing else is heard. The term is often used to describe: absolute silence, no communication or no response; especially when one is expected. **White noise; deafening silence**

Critical mass - This term appears to have its origin in the scientific field. In science, it is frequently used to denote the amount of something needed to start **a chain reaction**. It now means: the minimum size or quantity of something required to start or maintain an endeavor; the size, number, or amount that is large enough to produce a particular result

Crocodile tears - The source of this saying is from the belief that crocodiles shed tears while they are devouring their prey. Though, this belief is entirely anecdotal, recent scientific research has given some biological reasons as to why it may in fact be true. Nonetheless, the widespread interpretation is: a hypocritical or insincere show of grief; tears or expressions of sorrow that are insincere

Cross the Rubicon - The Rubicon was a river in northern Italy that Julius Caesar crossed with his army, in violation of the orders of the leaders in Rome, who feared his power. When he crossed the river, Caesar said that **"the die was cast"** referring to a die, one part of a pair of dice, had been thrown. Which has since become another idiom which means the same as to cross the Rubicon. The common interpretation is: to do something that inevitably commits one to following a certain course of action. Similar phrases include: **point of no return; crossed a redline; line in the sand**

Cross to bear - The origin of this saying is from the cross that Jesus had to bear before his crucifixion. The crucifixion of Jesus is recorded in all four gospels: Matthew 27:23-44; Mark 15:22-32; Luke 23:33-43; John 19:17-30 and is a central theme in the New Testament. "And they spat on Him, and took the reed and began to beat Him on the head. And after they had mocked Him, they took His robe off and put His garments on Him, and led Him away to crucify Him," (Matt. 27:30-31). "And after weaving a **crown of thorns,** they put it on His head, and a reed in His right hand; and they kneeled down before Him and mocked Him, saying, "Hail, King of the Jews!" (Matt. 27:29). It is interesting to note that Paul could not be crucified like Jesus and Peter because he was a Roman citizen. Instead he was beheaded. The phrase now means: an unpleasant situation or responsibility that you must accept because you cannot change it. **We all have our cross to bear; nailed to the cross**

Crusade - This term has its origin in the medieval military expeditions, made by European Christians to recover the **Holy Land** from the Muslims in the 11th, 12th, and 13th centuries. The first of a series of Crusades was initiated by Pope Urban II in the year 1095. Contrary to popular opinion, most of the Crusades were unsuccessful with the last Crusade directed against fellow Christians. A point that is seldom mentioned is that the Crusades exposed Europeans to the scientific and architectural prowess of the Islamic world which was also implemented on the Iberian Peninsula under Muslim (Moorish) control for centuries. In fact, **it is no accident** that Spain and Portugal, the European powers which first emerged from the **Dark Ages**, were both located on the Iberian Peninsula. Furthermore, the term **Jihad** has become one of the most controversial terms used today and, in some circles, has become synonymous with terrorism. The term means "struggle." Yet, inside and outside of the Muslim community, the term is ambiguously applied to mean an inward or external struggle. It has often been mentioned that Islam was spread by the sword. However, as the Crusades and subsequent colonization of the globe by Christians illustrate; the spread of Christianity could also be viewed as a **Jihad** by another name replete with its own incidents of terrorism directed against the indigenous people of the Americas, Africa and Asia. Yet people in the West consistently use the word crusade without any negative connotations attached. The term has migrated to mean: any vigorous, aggressive movement for the defense or advancement of an idea, cause, etc.. For example, a crusade against drugs. Regarding Islam, *Al Salaam a' alaykum* - Also *Assalamu alaikum* (as-salam-u-alay-koom) is an Arabic expression that is used by Muslims as a greeting. It literally means "peace upon you." This universal Islamic greeting has its roots in the Quran. As-Salaam is one of the Names of Allah, meaning "The Source of Peace." In the Quran, Allah instructs the believers to greet one another with words of peace. Because our interactions are expanding as we become a closer global community and the misguided view of Islam as a bellicose religion, I have included this important Islamic phrase with the hope that we will better understand and appreciate each other as humans and work toward world peace. Non-Muslims should be careful in its usage or not use it at all. **King's ransom**

Cuckhold - The source of this term is from the cuckoo's habit of laying its egg in another bird's nest. The common usage is: the husband of an adulteress, often regarded as an object of ridicule. Similar expression include: **pussy whipped**: a **henpecked** man and to **wear the horns** (the cuckhold is traditionally associated with horns)

Cupid's arrow - In Roman mythology, Cupid was the god of love often depicted as a boy with wings, a bow and arrow. The myth of Cupid and Psyche was recorded by Lucius Apuleius in The Golden Ass about how Cupid accidently struck himself with his arrow and fell in love with **Psyche**, the most beautiful woman on earth. So much so that his mother Venus was jealous of her beauty. Although their story is not well known, her name has entered the English language as psyche which means the human faculty for thought, judgment, and emotion; including both the conscious and unconscious mind. It also denotes the human soul, mind, or spirit: To be **struck by Cupid's arrow** is to be struck by love

Custer's last stand - Was a battle between George Armstrong Custer and Native Americans at the Battle of the Little Bighorn in which he was soundly defeated. Custer was once a flamboyant Civil War general, known for his long hair and flashy uniform and fought on the side of the Union. Even though he graduated last in his class of 1861 at West Point, he was the only soldier to achieve the rank of general in his class; and became one of the youngest soldiers to reach the rank of general. The Battle of the Little Bighorn was fought on June 25, 1876, a couple of days before the American Centennial celebration. It was a seminal battle fought between the U.S. Army's 7th Cavalry and Native Americans; in one of the last armed efforts to preserve their way of life and independence. It was here that 263 U.S. soldiers died

58

fighting several thousand Lakota, Sioux and Cheyenne warriors. It often refers to a heroic effort that ends in defeat. The battle of Thermopylae is similar and was the scene of the Greek defense against the Persian army of Xerxes I. There were 6,000 Greeks; among them were **300 Spartans**, all of whom, including their king Leonidas, were killed - **Remember the Alamo**

Cut from the same cloth - This saying has its origins in the textile and clothing industries and relates to when different sets of fabric varied slightly in texture or color. When making something like a suit, it is important that both pieces match without deviation. Same is true of other endeavors. For example, the Washington Monument in Washington DC is made of two sets of stones from different stone quarries. If you look closely at it, you can plainly see where one set stops and the other begins. This is because construction on the monument was halted during the American Civil War and when resumed stone from the original quarry was unavailable. The phrase now means: to be comprised of the same nature or content; very similar so much to be indistinguishable. **Not cut from the same cloth**; cut from the same fabric

Cut to the chase - This phrase dates to the early days of Hollywood when the climactic scene in silent movies was often a chase scene. It is also worthy to note that this was during a time when the automobile came into prominence. Like in a novel, how and when you approach the climactic scene was important to the theme of the movie. But in film, time was all the more important which led to this expression. The expression has migrated to mean: **to get to the point** without wasting time or adding extraneous or unnecessary information. **Get to the bottom of it**

Cutting edge - This term undoubtedly has its origins in the sharpest of an axe, knife or other cutting object. However, it wasn't until the early 20th century with the rise of technology that it was applied to its current usage. It means: the latest or most advance technology or development. The **bleeding edge** is similar in connotation and means the very forefront of technological development. It has been said that **there is a thin line** between being on the cutting edge and being cut by the edge. **State of the art**

Cyberbullying – This term emerged in the late 1990s as social media platforms and cellphones became more prevalent. Although bullying has been around for centuries, the Internet provides a new conduit. As a result of several suicides, many states have passed cyberbullying laws. The term simply means: to intimidate or threaten someone using an electronic source or means

Cybersex - This term came of age in the late 20th century with the advent of computer chatrooms where people engage in virtual sex (masturbation). It is basically a form of **phone sex** using the computer as a conduit. In some cases, pictures and videos are exchanged. The term means: sexual arousal using computer technology, especially by wearing virtual reality equipment or by exchanging messages, pictures, etc. with another person via the Internet. **Sexting** is similar and means: to send (someone) sexually explicit photographs, videos or messages via mobile phone

Stands for:

Don't count your chickens before they hatch

IN A NUTSHELL

D-Day - The source of this term is the June 6, 1944 Normandy landing of the Allied forces codename Operation Neptune. Its mission was to liberate France from Germany during World War II and it was the largest seaborne invasion in history. It is considered by many historians to be the **turning of the tide** in the European theatre. The term often refers to the day of a forthcoming operation or initiative

Daisy chain - Originally used to describe a string of daisies with stems linked to form a chain. It has migrated to mean: a group of individual things linked together. Today, the term has also been used to describe a certain sexual act. **To string along**

Damn the torpedoes full speed ahead - This phrase is attributed to <u>Admiral David Farragut</u> during an American Civil War naval battle. The common usage is: sometimes in the face of danger, the risks of failure should be secondary to the chances of success. **Failure is not an option**

Damn with faint praise - This expression is ascribed to the 18th century English poet <u>Alexander Pope</u> from his <u>Epistle to Doctor Arbuthnot</u>. The common usage is: a compliment so feeble that it amounts to no compliment at all and may even imply the opposite. **Left-handed compliment; backhanded compliment**

Damsel in distress - Even though the term damsel goes back to the Middle Ages and evokes thoughts of knights or princes saving beautiful young maidens from the towers of castles, the motif is quite ancient. Part of this motif is after the maiden is saved, the two are married and live **happily ever after.** For example, in Greek mythology, we have the story of Andromeda the Ethiopian princess who was fastened to a rock and later rescued by Perseus. The two are married and according to Greek legend, all Greeks are the progeny of Andromeda and Perseus. The term has migrated to mean: a young woman in trouble that needs to be rescued. **Prince Charming; sleeping beauty**

Dance with the girl you came with - The phrase was coined by Darrell Royal. A song <u>"I'm Going to Dance with the One Who Brung Me"</u> was popular in the 1920s. The expression has evolved to mean: to continue the things that got you to the point that you are

Danger, Will Robinson [danger] - This saying is from the 1960s TV series <u>"Lost in Space."</u> It is a phrase spoken by the Robot B9 to Will Robinson one of the children of the Robinson family, a group of colonists sent from earth. It is currently used as a phrase to warn someone about making a pending mistake, impending danger; or to stop them from doing something stupid or outrageous. **Danger cannot be avoided without danger**

Daniel in the lion's den - The source of this phrase is from the Bible (Daniel, 6:16-17), where he was place in the lion's den. It now refers to someone in a place that exposes them to intense danger

Dark horse - This term originally comes from horse racing in the early 1800s and was popularized during the presidential campaign of <u>John K. Polk</u>. He was the last strong president up until the Civil War and under his leadership the United States was extended **from sea to shining sea.** The term has since been defined as: a candidate or competitor about whom little is known or is given little chance but who unexpectedly wins or succeeds. **Back the wrong horse**

Data mining - This is a term that originated in the late 1990s to describe a process of finding variances, patterns and associations within large amounts of data to predict results. It is often used to increase profits, manage risks, improve customer service or in advertisement

David and Goliath - This phrase comes from the biblical story of David (1 Samuel 16-18). In this story, Goliath is a giant that seems to have an overwhelming advantage over the young David armed with only a slingshot. But he does not kill Goliath with the slingshot, he only wounds him. Then he cuts the head off Goliath using Goliath's sword. The lesson here is that giants often bear the seeds of their own destruction in their hands and that overconfidence could be used as a weakness against a much stronger foe. Sometimes a weakness is nothing more than a strength overplayed. The common usage is: a contest between someone who is apparently weak and someone who seems to have an overwhelming advantage, particularly one in which the underdog wins

David and Jonathan - The source of this phrase is from the biblical story of King David and his relationship with Jonathan (1 Samuel 18:1). It regularly refers to a close relationship between friends especially two male friends. Damon and Pythias is similar. In Greek legend, they are a celebrated pair of friends who came to signify the willingness to sacrifice oneself for the sake of a friend. It now refers to unwavering and true friendship

Day of infamy - This phrase originated from a speech by President Franklin Delano Roosevelt after the Japanese bombed Pearl Harbor on December 7, 1941. It now means: a time or state of being known for something bad happening; a troublesome time

Days are numbered - This expression comes from the Bible (Daniel 5:26, Psalm 90:12). "So teach us to number our days, that we may apply our hearts unto wisdom." It has migrated to mean: the end is near. **Your days are numbered**

De facto - This is a Latin term that has become part of the English vernacular. It literally means "of fact." It is sometimes contrasted with its antonym **de jure**. The term means: something that is taken to be a fact although it is not formally recognized as one. For example, de facto segregation is segregation that occurs without any official or government approval and was often practiced in most of the United States before the Civil Rights movement. Whereas **de jure segregation** was practice in the southern states and was sanctioned by law

Dead man walking - The exact origin of this term is uncertain, but Thomas Harding used it as the title of a poem. In recent times, however, the term has been associated with a prisoner that is about to be executed or someone whose demise is imminent. **Death row** is similar in connotation

IN A NUTSHELL

Dead on arrival (DOA) - This is a medical term used by doctors to indicate that a person was dead before they arrived at the hospital. It migrated to generally mean: something that is ineffective or something that is not a viable option or alternative to be considered. **Forgone conclusion**

Dead presidents - The origin of this term is unclear, but it dates back to 1944. Popularized in the late 20th century by the Hip Hop and Rap culture, it has come to mean: money, dollar bills; because many, but not all, of the people on U.S. currency are dead presidents. Other terms used for money are: **Cheddar, Lettuce, Dough, Bread** and **Benjamins.** The latter applies only to 100-dollar bills (Ben Franklin's face who, by the way, is not a dead president). Similar expressions include: it**'s all about the Benjamins; all mighty dollar; for the love of money**

Dead ringer - It has been widely reported that the origin of this phrase dates back to the Middle Ages. In this context, it referred to a person that was buried without direct confirmation that the person was dead. Before modern medicine, the criteria for dead or alive was in many cases subjective and in some cases a person that was pronounced dead by such primitive methods would come back alive. Some were buried with a rope in the coffin that was attached to a bell that could be rung if the person reached a state of consciousness after being pronounced dead. Other terms such as **graveyard shift** and **saved by the bell** were also incorrectly attributed to this phenomenon. Yet, further investigation suggests that this story was not the source of this phrase. Instead, dead ringer is attributed to horse racing where a substitute horse was substituted for a horse that strongly resembled it in order to deceive bookies or those that bet on a particular horse. Furthermore, the term dead is often used to mean something that is accurate or precise as in dead on. Hence, dead ringer refers to: something or someone that looks exactly like something or someone else. **Saved by the bell** is another sports analogy and refers to boxing. **Chip off the old block**

Deadline - The origin of this term seems to be the American Civil War. During this war, a deadline was a line drawn around a prison that prisoners of war were forbidden to cross under penalty of death. It has migrated to mean: the latest time or date that something should be delivered or done. **Make or meet a deadline**

Deafening silence - The origin of this phrase appears to be unknown. While at first it appears to be an oxymoron, there are cases, particularly when complete silence is proceeded by extreme noise that things seem unusually quiet. This is because our ears, and more specifically, our brains have a difficult time going from one extreme to another. The phrase refers to: the presence of silence when you expect some type of response or outrage to an action, event or phenomena. Dr. Martin Luther King, Jr. once said, "In the end, we will remember not the words of our enemies, but the silence of our friends. **Silence gives consent; speak truth to power; see no evil, hear no evil, speak no evil. White noise** is another term with a similar connotation that is often used. It has its origin in the science realm and is a group of ambient frequencies perhaps best described, in the old days, before cable as the sound made when turning from one TV station to another. It is often visually described as snow. The sound of rain without thunder or the roaring of cars on a highway are also examples of white noise. White noise generators are used to mask other sounds. It can best be described as a constant sound or display that contains no intelligible information and can be used as a metaphor to describe such speech. **It's all white noise**

Death by one thousand cuts - The source of this expression seems to have originated from the Chinese practice of execution by many cuts and was westernized to be a thousand cuts. This extreme punishment known as "lingchi" was only instituted for extreme crimes and ended in 1904. The phrase has migrated to mean: a slow and painful death or destruction of something

Deer in the headlights - Like so many colloquial phrases, this phrase is of unknown or unclear origins (but does not predate the automobile). It is based on the premise that a deer will freeze out of fear at night when approached head-on by a vehicle with its lights on. Consequently, deer crossing signs are often posted in areas heavily populated by deer. While in this paralyzed state, one wonders what goes through a deer's mind; perhaps, "**oh dear.**" Whether this is due to the deer's nocturnal nature or some other factor at work is not readily clear. It is often used to describe: to be in a state of paralyzing shock or bewilderment; to be in a confused state of mind. **Like a deer in the headlights**

Deliver the message to Garcia - The source of this expression is a well-known essay entitled: A Message to Garcia written by Elbert Hubbard in 1899. The essay is about a letter from President McKinley to the Cuban General Garcia seeking his help prior to the Spanish-American War. Since no one knew exactly where Garcia was located, the delivery of the letter required **undaunted courage** and perseverance over **treacherous territory** by its carrier. The saying now means: to take the initiative in executing an important task without specific instructions on how to do so. **Get the job done; Doctor Livingston, I presume**

Delusions of grandeur - This term became popular in the 19th century but has been applied to many people in history that predate that date. It infers: a false impression of one's own importance or the fixed, false or misguided belief that one possesses superior qualities such as genius, fame, omnipotence, or wealth. It is habitually associated with mental illness and is a form of narcissism or paranoia. **A legend in his own mind** is similar and means: someone who thinks that their contributions, importance or capability is greater than it actually is

Demigod - The source of this term is from a mythological being with more power than a mortal but less than a god or a being with partial or lesser divine status, such as a minor deity, the offspring of a god and a mortal, or a mortal raised to divine rank. It means: a person that acts like he is a god. Many demigods suffer from **delusions of grandeur** and are truly **legends in their own minds**

Deus ex machina - The term owes its origin to Greek drama. *'Deus ex machina'*, literally 'god from the machina'* refers to the *machina,* a device by which gods were suspended above the stage in the Greek theatre. It now refers to: an unexpected power or event saving a seemingly hopeless situation, especially as a contrived plot device in a play or novel

Devil's advocate - This term has its roots in the Latin expression *'advocatus diaboli'*. This expression can be traced back to the Roman Catholic Church under the leadership of Pope Sixtus V (not to be confused with

IN A NUTSHELL

Sixtus IV from whom the famous Sistine Chapel is named after). In this capacity, it was an official appointed person that presented arguments against a proposed canonization or beatification. It refers to: a person who expresses a contentious view in order to provoke discussion or test the strength of the opposing arguments. It also has the negative connotation of a person that wants **to stir up the pot** in a given situation. **Angel's advocate** has the opposite connotation. **Play the devil's advocate.** Other popular terms that mention the devil are as follows: **Devil incarnate** comes from Shakespeare's King Henry V, and Titus Andronicus, and means: the devil in human form. Another similar term is **Prince of darkness** and has its origin in John Milton's classic poem Paradise Lost, first published in 1667. It refers to Satan or the devil as the embodiment or incarnation of evil. **Speak of the devil** is an old phrase that has its origin in the belief or superstition that if you speak of the devil, he will appear or that evil things would happen. This phrase is often used when a person appears just after being mentioned. **Talk behind someone's back**

Diehard - The source of this term dates to the 18th century. It was associated with men that were executed by hanging and struggled for a long time before dying. It has migrated to mean: a person who strongly opposes change; someone who feels strongly about something

Diligence is the mother of good luck - This phrase is attributed to the American author, inventor and Founding Father Ben Franklin. The common usage is: the harder you work at something the greater the chance that you will be successful. **Chance favors the prepared mind**

Dionysian - This term relates to Dionysus the god of the grape harvest, wine and fertility, theatre and religious ecstasy in Greek mythology. It means: recklessly uninhibited; unrestrained; undisciplined or frenzied behavior

Dire straits - This term is believed to have its origin in the navigation of narrow straits around the world which at times could be difficult and perilous and dates back to the Age of Exploration. Often confused with straight, a strait is a narrow passage of land connecting two larger bodies of water. It was also the name of a popular British band of the late 1970s and early 1980s. The term in its current context means: a bad or difficult situation. **In dire straits; between Scylla and Charybdis**

Discretion is the better part of valor - This phrase originates from Shakespeare's Henry IV, Part I, (Act V, Scene IV) 1596. The common usage is: it is good to be brave, but it is also good to be prudent; it is better to avoid a dangerous situation than to confront it

Distance lends enchantment to the view - This expression is accredited to the Scottish poet Thomas Campbell. "Tis distance lends enchantment to the view, and robes the mountain in its azure hue." While Campbell wrote these words with Nature as his reference, it is really about perspective. For example, when we think of things from a nostalgic perspective, we tend to think only about the good times and not the bad. There is something about having the luxury of retrospect. The expression can be interpreted to mean: things that are far away from you often appear to be better than they are. **The devil is in the details; hindsight is 20/20**

A COLLECTION OF POPULAR ENGLISH PHRASES

Divide and conquer - This saying is repeatedly ascribed to Julius Caesar. Caesar was a brilliant military leader who conquered most of western Europe. The common usage is: the policy of maintaining control over one's subordinates, enemies or subjects by encouraging dissent between them

Do a Devon Loch - The origin of this expression comes from a 1956 British Grand National horserace when the horse Devon Loch collapsed just short of the finish line. Ironically, the horse was owned by the young Queen Elizabeth II. The phrase has migrated to mean: to fail when you are very close to winning. **It ain't over until the fat lady sings**

Do unto others as you would have them do unto you - The source of the saying is the Bible (Matt. 7:12) and the Sermon on the Mount. It is also known as the **golden rule.** It is important to note that in one form or the other, the theme appears in many writings of the ancient world. The phrase is often interpreted to mean: to treat others the way you expect or want to be treated. **Love your neighbor as yourself**

Doctor Livingston, I presume - These were the words spoken by the American Journalist Morton Stanley when he finally found Doctor Livingston who was in Africa in search of the source of the Nile River. The common usage is: a greeting between two people that have never met especially if one is famous

Dog days of summer - The origin of this phrase relates to the heliacal rising of Sirius (the dog star) which was once around the end of June and signaled the beginning of summer. It now means: the hot days of summer

Dog eat dog - This term has been around for some time; however, its exact origins are unclear. So long that its eggcorn, *doggy dog*, has also become popular. Often, dog has been associated with bad behavior such as a man being **put in the doghouse** by his wife or a bad female being associated with a female dog. The term means: a fierce competition between two people or groups. **It's a dog eat dog (doggy dog) world; who let the dogs out**; drastic (desperate) times call for drastic (desperate) measures

Dog whistle - The origin of this term comes from the fact that the hearing range of dogs is above that of humans. **As a consequence**, dogs can hear sounds that humans cannot. Whistles were made to call dogs without humans knowing that they were summoned. This term has migrated to mean: code language used to appeal or attract a particular group. In most cases, the general public will interpret the message one way and the targeted group another way. **Call off the dogs**; red meat

Dollars to doughnuts - This term comes from betting and was first used in the late 19th century. It was recorded in 1920 in a story by the American writer Ellery Queen being willing to bet dollars against doughnuts. It meant that you were pretty sure you were right. It is normally used to emphasize one's certainty. Such as **"I'll bet you dollars to doughnuts"**

Domino effect - The term was first coined by President Dwight D. Eisenhower in a news conference he made on April 7th, 1954, when he referred to the possible effect of Indochina falling under communist rule. It has migrated to mean: the cumulative effect that results when one event precipitates a series of like events. **One thing after another**

Don't count your chickens before they hatch - This saying comes from an Aesop's fable about a woman who was carrying a basket of eggs thinking about how much she would get when they hatched. She got so excited that she dropped the basket and all the eggs cracked. The common usage is: you should not make plans that depend on something good happening before you know that it has actually happened. The following expression echo similar sentiment: **Don't put all of your eggs in one basket; first catch your rabbit then make your stew; don't cross the bridge till you come to it**

Don't cry over spilled milk - The exact origin of this phrase is unknown, but it has been around for centuries in one form or another. Also known as *don't cry over spilt milk* it generally means: not to dwell on something that you cannot change. **Let bygones be bygones** is similar in connotation

Don't give holy things to hounds (dogs) - The source of this expression is from the Bible (Matthew 7:6). "Give not that which is holy unto the dogs, neither **cast ye your pearls before swine**, lest they trample them under their feet, and turn again and rend you. It is often interpreted to mean: do not take something that was given to you by God or that is sacred and defile it. Or don't waste the gift that God has given you. **Cast pearls before swine**

Don't give up the ship - This expression is attributed to American Captain James Lawrence who uttered these words aboard the USS Chesapeake during a naval battle in the War of 1812. He died an American hero. It has since become an American rallying cry, particularly in the navy, and as a sign to keep fighting on despite the obstacles before you. Related expressions include: **I have not yet begun to fight; don't make (any) waves**

Don't know him from Adam - This phrase refers to the fact that Adam had no navel and thus was distinguishable from all other men. It now refers to: not known or to be completely unable to recognize the person in question

Don't let the door hit ya, where the good Lord split ya - This expression appears to have its origin in the African American community during the 1970s and is similar to: **See ya, wouldn't wanna be ya.** "Split you" refers to the crack in your ass. It means: get out or leave, the person making the response does not care if you stay, so you can just get out now. It is usually used as a response to someone that has given you an ultimatum to yield to their demands. **Get the hell out; pack your bags and leave; good riddance to bad rubbish; take it or leave it**

Don't let the perfect be the enemy of the good - The origin of this popular phrase is unknown or unclear. However, most people attribute it to a variant of a saying by the French author Voltaire. Nonetheless, it means: perfection is something that is very difficult to achieve and even masterpieces have their flaws. Although we should all strive for perfection, we must also recognize that true perfection is unachievable. Yet, sometimes a weakness is nothing more than a strength overplayed. The trick is to know when something is good enough to serve its purpose. Similar expressions include: **polishing the bowling ball;**

68

the point of diminishing returns; added value. A similar phrase, **close enough for government work** means: suitably close; done just well enough to meet the needs or the standards

Don't look a gift horse in the mouth - The source of this saying comes from the practice of judging the age of a horse by looking at its teeth. The phrase is apparently quite old because a Latin version of it appeared in a work by St. Jerome in 420 CE. This practice is also the source of the phrases **long in the tooth** and **straight from the horse's mouth** as the gums of the horse tend to recede as they get older and the teeth continues to grow. If the horse is a gift you may not want to know its age when it is given to you as it may make the giver feel uncomfortable. The common interpretation is: not to be ungracious when you receive a gift by calling into question the gift itself. **Never (Don't) change horses in the middle of a stream** is another popular horse metaphor

Don't look back, someone might be gaining on you - The origin of this phrase is from the African American baseball player Satchel Paige. He was a pitcher for the Negro Leagues (1924–1947) and briefly in the major leagues. He threw 55 career no-hitters. For decades, Paige was not allowed to play in the major leagues because of racial discrimination, but he never looked back. It has migrated to mean: to focus on the task before you and to not let something else get in the way. To keep moving toward a goal and not to be distracted from it by others or past events. **Keep your eyes on the prize**

Don't piss down my back and tell me it's raining - The source of this saying is unclear, but it was popularized by the character Josey Wales played by Clint Eastwood in the movie The Outlaw Josey Wales. It can be interpreted to mean: to tell a lie in such a way as to be shamefully transparent; doing one thing and saying another to mislead someone or playing them for a fool. **Janus-faced**

Don't shoot the messenger - The origin of this phrase is the Greek philosopher Sophocles in his play Antigone around 440 BCE. "No one loves the messenger who brings bad news." Similar sentiments were expressed by Shakespeare in Henry IV, part 2 and in Antony and Cleopatra. The common usage is: not to be angry or revengeful to the person bearing bad news

Don't sweat the small stuff - While this phrase may have been around beforehand, it was popularized by the book of the same name by Richard Carlson in the 1990s. It means: to focus on the things in life that you can control and not to get caught up in extraneous things that in the end really don't matter. An expression found in Erasmus' book on Proverbs and Adages echoes similar sentiments: **It is foolish to distress ourselves over what cannot be prevented**

Don't worry, be happy - This phrase was made popular during the 1980s and it comes from the title of a song by Bobby McFerrin. The song's title is taken from a famous quotation by the Indian spiritualist Meher Baba. It means exactly what it says, despite all the things that can go wrong for you in life, don't worry be happy. "In every life, we have some trouble; When you worry, you make it double; Don't worry, be happy." **Breathe a sigh of relief**

IN A NUTSHELL

Dot-com - This is a term that came of age during the nascent days of the Internet. It is used mostly as a designation for companies doing business over the Internet. In some areas, Dot-com companies have virtually eliminated **brick and mortar shops** perhaps best exemplified by the rise of companies such as Amazon. Today, practically every physical store has its online twin. Other designations such as **.gov** and **.org** are used to designate government agencies and organizations respectively. Dot-com is also generally used to designate the era in which companies emerged using the Internet as a conduit

Double cross - The origin of this term is obscure as the cross was used in several instances. References to double cross have been found as early as the 1700s. However, it seems to have been popularized in its current form in the 1800s from horseracing. More specifically, the word cross meant to fix a horse race. Double cross was used to describe a horse race that had been fixed, in which the horse that was supposed to lose actually won. It was also used to designate a boxer that was supposed to lose and later won. In both cases, the second cross nullifies the first. It means: to deceive or betray a person with whom one is supposedly cooperating. **Double agent** has a similar connotation and means: an agent or person who pretends to act on the behalf of one country, organization or group while in fact is acting on behalf of an enemy or another. In both cases, it is an act of betrayal or deceit. **Turncoat; a Judas**

Double entendre - This is a term that comes from the French meaning "double understanding" that has worked its way into the English language. It means: a word or phrase open to two interpretations, one of which is usually rude or indecent and often includes a pun. William Shakespeare was famous for his clever use of double entendre

Double whammy - The origin of this term is unclear. However, it appears to date back to at least the 1940s. A whammy was first used to designate something that was evil or bad. A double whammy has evolved to mean: something twice as bad or a situation in which two negative things happen at the same time or one immediately after the other

Doubt is the beginning, not the end of wisdom - The origin of this saying is attributed to the science writer George Iles (1852–1942). Some have also ascribed a similar saying to Aristotle. It can be interpreted to mean: in order to understand something, you must first have doubts and then come to a conclusion. Similarly, the Lebanese American writer, Khalil Gibran wrote: "Perplexity is the beginning of knowledge"

Doubting Thomas - This expression is from the Bible (John 20:24-31).and is named after Saint Thomas who doubted Jesus' resurrection until he had proof of it. The common usage is: one who is habitually doubtful; a person who is skeptical and refuses to believe something without proof

Doves and hawks - The exact origin of this expression is uncertain, however, the use of doves as a sign of peace and tranquility can be traced back to the biblical narrative of Noah and the Great Flood as delineated in Genesis. Hawks, on the other hand, are antithetical to doves because of their **killer instincts** and aggressive nature. The term **war hawk** or hawk dates back to at least the War of 1812 and was used to describe Henry Clay and John C. Calhoun. The expression doves and hawks was applied during the Kennedy administration in reference to the policy toward Cuba and extended to the Vietnam War era. Doves, therefore, oppose war or conflict as the first action in the resolution of a problem and thus favor diplomatic solutions. This approach is normally associated with **soft power**. Hawks, in contrast, favor martial actions to resolve a problem. The synthesis of these two opposing paradigms is perhaps best illustrated on the back of the dollar bill with the American eagle holding an **olive branch** in one hand, as a symbol of peace, and arrows in the other, as a symbol of war. **War hawks; peace doves**

Draconian - This term derives from Draco, an Athenian law scribe under whom small offenses had heavy punishment. Before Draco, the Athenian laws were oral, and he was given the tasks of writing them. His laws were so extreme that Aristotle said, perhaps metaphorically, that they were written in blood. But **out of the shadows of** such severe laws emerged Solon known as the wise lawgiver. He rescinded most of the laws established by Draco and put Greece on the road toward Periclean democracy. The term means: excessively harsh and severe laws or the applications or methods used to implement them. Similar phrases include: **Draconian measures; Machiavellian; out Herod, Herod**

Drastic (desperate) times call for drastic (desperate) measures - This is an old English saying that is a derivative of the proverb "Desperate diseases must have desperate remedies." The common usage is: extreme and undesirable circumstances or situations can only be resolved by resorting to equally extreme and radical actions. **Extreme times call for extreme measures**

Drink (Drunk) the Kool-Aid - The origin of this phrase is the 1978 Jamestown, Guyana massacre in which 918 members of the Peoples Temple, headed by the charismatic leader Jim Jones, died from drinking a cyanide-laced soft drink. The phrase has migrated to mean: to unconditionally accept the dictates of a person or a group. To blindly follow someone. **Blind leading the blind**

Drop a dime (on someone) - Before cellphones, there were phonebooths everywhere. If you wanted to call someone, it cost you a dime. The call could be traced to a phonebooth but not to a person. From these origins emerged this term which means: to call up someone and squeal on a person. The person that drops the dime is often called **a stool pigeon** or a **whistle blower** particularly if the call is made to the police or the authorities. **Dimed him out; you've done a dime's worth of talking** means **it's time to shut up; rat out**

Drop in the bucket - This saying originated from the Bible, (Isaiah 40: 15). It means: a very small proportion of the whole; something small or insignificant. **A small piece of the pie**

Due diligence - This is an old English expression that first migrated to the legal profession before entering general usage. Often misstated as "do" diligence, it is now used to describe: a detailed or comprehensive examination of something before a decision is made or reached. To investigate something thoroughly. **Do your homework**

Dumb blonde - The origin of this derogatory term is uncertain. There are some that contend that it dates back to ancient times and others that believe that it is a product of the early 20th century and the rise of motion pictures. There is no doubt that the popular novel by Anita Loos entitled: Gentlemen Prefer Blondes helped to proliferate the fascination with blondes during this era. Notwithstanding, the popularity of this term seems to stem from Marilyn Monroe who was the stereotypical 'dumb blonde" (although she was not a natural blonde). The fascination with blondes has led many women who were not born blonde to color their hair in search of its mystique and allure. There are some women, however, who view the dumb blonde stereotype as a figment of the male misogynistic imagination which finds an intelligent woman (attractive or otherwise) threatening. Such men regress to those days when women were **kept barefoot and pregnant, seen but not heard** and **closed their eyes and thought of England.** The term frequently refers to a beautiful woman that is known for her beauty and not her intelligence. **Gentleman prefer blondes; just another pretty face**

Dutch courage - This was a term that worked its way into the English language because Englishmen noticed that Dutchmen took a drink before battle. It has migrated to mean: strength or confidence gained from drinking alcohol; or an alcoholic beverage had before an unpleasant task

Dutch treat (To go Dutch) - The phrase probably originates from Dutch etiquette. In the Netherlands, it is not unusual to pay separately when dating. The Dutch were already internationally known as **scrooges,** and England's rivalry with The Netherlands, especially during the period of the <u>Anglo-Dutch Wars,</u> gave rise to several phrases including: **Dutch uncle** and **Dutch courage** that promoted certain negative stereotypes. It means: each person pays for their food or entertainment. **Let's go fifty-fifty (half and half).** **Dutch uncle** is a particular English stereotype associated with the idea of Dutch people as unsociable and selfish. As result, it is sometimes viewed as offensive. The common interpretation is: a person that gives strict but caring advice or a person who criticizes or scolds with harsh severity and bluntness

Stands for:

Eight hundred (800) pound gorilla

IN A NUTSHELL

E pluribus unum - This expression that is often associated with the inception of the United States has its origin in the Moretum by the Roman author Virgil. A seminal writer of the Augustan era, he was to the Romans what Homer was to the Greeks. It means "out of many one" and is a 13-letter motto that appears on the US one-dollar bill along with the Latin phrase *Nouvus ordo seclorum* (New order of the ages). It is part of the Great Seal of the United States. The reference in Virgil is not related to forging a group of states into one nation, but rather to the blending of several vegetables into one salad

Each of us bears his own Hell - This saying is also attributed to Vergil. It is frequently interpreted to mean: we all have **our crosses to bear**. We often look at others, wishing that their fortunes are bestowed upon us, not knowing the internal strife, pain or misfortunes associated with their perceived success. As Dante so aptly put, there are several levels of hell, each with their torments. It is not so much that we all experience hell, but how we choose to go through it. **When you're going through hell, keep going**

Easter bunny and eggs - The source of both of these terms seems to stem from the fact that Easter is linked to the spring equinox and fertility. Celebrations of the coming of spring date back to antiquity and was an integral part of many pagan rituals. In fact, in ancient times there are several stories regarding death and resurrection during spring festivals. For example, the Egyptian god Horus and the story of Mithras are just two examples that adhere to this motif. Many of them were born around the winter solstice and resurrected or conceived in the spring. As far as the Christian religion is concern, Jesus was born around the winter solstice. **Christmas**, the celebration of his birth, is on December 25th. He was resurrected around the spring equinox and thus the celebration of Easter. Moreover, if it takes nine months for a baby to be born, his conception also happened at the spring equinox. Hence, completing the cycle of conception, birth and resurrection. Many of these figures, including Jesus, are part of what the esteemed scholar of myths Joseph Campbell called a monomyth. Easter bunnies and eggs share a common factor of fertility and that is why they were chosen as symbols of Easter and are thus aligned with the fertility of spring. Accordingly, in 325CE, the Council of Nicaea established that Easter would be held on the first Sunday after the first full moon occurring on or after the spring equinox. In fact, the Egyptian obelisk at the center of the Vatican with a cross at its top casts a shadow that marks the spring equinox **as a harbinger** of the coming Easter festival. **Saint Nick**

Eat your heart out - The source of this expression is Iliad Book 6 attributed to the Greek orator and sage Homer. It also appears in the 1539 Richard Taverner translation of Erasmus. The common usage is: when one person thinks that they are better at something than another or has something that the other person wants, needs or envies

Echo chamber - This expression has its roots in the recording industry. Even though the use of echoes and reverberation in singing and music has been known and used since antiquity, the use of a recording studio or chamber to utilize or minimized this effect in a chamber is something that emerged in the 20th century. The term has migrated to mean: a group of media outlets that tend to repeat a narrative or opinion that is consistent with a view or perspective centered around a common goal

Eddington's monkeys - This expression is from the physicist Sir Arthur Eddington who stated: if an army of monkeys were strumming on typewriters, they might write all the books in the British Museum. It is also known as the **infinite monkey theorem.** The common usage is: although something is highly improbable it is not impossible

Eight hundred (800) pound gorilla - This phrase is believed to have originated with the joke (riddle) first documented in the 1970s that generally has the form of the question: Where does an 800-pound gorilla sleep or sit? Anywhere he wants to. It is now used to describe: a person or organization so powerful that it can act without regard to the rights of others or the law. It can also describe a dominant player

Elementary, my dear Watson - The source of this catchphrase is from a novel by the British author Sir Arthur Conan Doyle and his character the <u>detective Sherlock Holmes</u>. Watson was the assistant of Sherlock Homes. Even though Doyle used "elementary" a few times in the Sherlock Holmes stories, and "my dear Watson" many times, he never combined them into the phrase that has become a famous quote. It has come to be used as a catchphrase for something that is simple or something that should be obvious or easily deduced or understood

Elephant in the room - The origin of this expression is not clear, but it dates back to the 1950s. The common usage is: an important and obvious subject, which everyone present is aware of, but will not discuss; an obvious truth that no one is addressing. **Open secret**

Elizabethan and Jacobean - These two consecutive periods in English history are named after <u>Queen Elizabeth I and King James I</u> (VI of Scotland) respectively. They were defining moments in English history, a period where England defeated the mighty <u>Spanish Armada</u> (1588) and gave us the literary works of Shakespeare and the King James Bible

Elvis has left the building - This phrase originates from the late Rock and Roll Singer <u>Elvis Presley</u>. He was the dominant personality of early Rock and Roll with songs such as "<u>Heartbreak Hotel</u>," "<u>Don't Be Cruel</u>," and "<u>Hound Dog</u>" and was noted for the frank sexuality of his performances. The saying now means the show or the act is over

Elysian [Fields] - This term comes to us from Greek mythology. The Elysian Fields were the final resting place for Greek heroes or those mortals that were related to the gods and their version of paradise. It now denotes: any place or state of perfect happiness; paradise

Embarrassment of riches - This term originated from a translation by John Ozell's of the title of a French play. It means: plentiful; to have more options or resources than one knows what to do with

Emotional intelligence (EI) - This term and phenomena, sometimes referred to as emotional quotient (EQ), is credited to psychologist Dr. Daniel Goleman as outlined in his 1995 book entitled: <u>Emotional Intelligence</u>. The term is defined as: the ability to manage and control your feelings so that the correct emotion is expressed at the appropriate time. A person's capability to recognize their emotions and the emotions of others. It is an essential tool in the management and leadership of others. **To be able to read someone**

IN A NUTSHELL

Enough to choke Caligula's horse - The origin of this phrase comes from the Roman emperor Caligula who was known for his decadence and his fondness of horses. So much so, according to the Roman historian Suetonius, he planned to make his favorite horse, Incitatus, a consul to the Roman Senate; a move that brought his sanity into question. The reigns of Caligula and Nero are **prime examples** of the madness and pervasive decadence of the Julio-Claudian emperors that succeeded Caesar Augustus. This phrase now denotes: a lot of something, to do something in excess. **Enough is enough; I've had it up to here; I'm sick and tired of being sick and tired**

Epicurean - The source of this term comes from the Greek philosopher Epicurus. He was one of the major philosophers in the Hellenistic period. He put forth a wide range of philosophies concerning the nature of human existence. Regarding science, Epicurus taught that the basic elements of the world are atoms, indivisible pieces of matter, moving through empty space. He tried to explain natural phenomena in atomic terms. In this regard, he was a luminary ahead of his time. For example, he was an early proponent of chaos theory and much of his work was revitalized during the 17th century and carried forward into modern times. The term means: a person that is devoted to the enjoyment of **the best things in life. The best things in life are free**

Esprit de corps - This is a French term that has become part of the English language. It literally means "group spirit." It means: a common spirit of camaraderie, commitment and sense of cooperation within a group. A sense of unity based on a common interest or goal

Et tu, Brute - This is a Latin phrase meaning "and you, Brutus?" or "you too, Brutus?" It supposedly was the words spoken by Julius Caesar when he was attacked and killed. But this is from the Shakespearean version and not history in which it is rumored that he uttered the phrase in Greek and not Latin. It is important to note that there were two famous Brutus' in Roman history. The Brutus that most of us are familiar with, the assassin of Julius Caesar, was a descendent of Brutus the founder of the Roman Republic. **In an ironic twist,** the defense of the second Brutus in the killing of Julius Caesar was that he was saving the Republic from a dictator or king in which the Romans despised dating back to the Etruscan kings. This expression has come down in history to mean: the ultimate betrayal by one's closest friend. **A Judas**

Etch-a-sketch - The origin of this term comes from a mechanical toy used to make drawings by using two knobs. The drawing could be easily erased by shaking the device. It was popularized during the 1960s, particularly in the United States. The term has since come to mean three things: to draw up a preliminary plan to be formalized at a later date. To erase a memory or an event, or to change something very easily; sometimes as if it never took place. **You can't etch-a-sketch your way out of this one**

Ethnic cleansing - The term ethnic cleansing, a literal translation of the Serbo-Croatian phrase *etnicko ciscenje,* was widely employed in the 1990s (though the term first appeared earlier). It now means: the systematic elimination of an ethnic group or groups from a region or society, as by deportation, forced emigration, or genocide

76

A COLLECTION OF POPULAR ENGLISH PHRASES

Ethos, pathos, logos - These are three Greek terms that are the pillars of argument and persuasion. They date back to ancient Greece and are essential to public speaking and rhetoric. Ethos addresses character, pathos addresses emotion and logos addresses logic. Today, most arguments contain at least one element and often the three are combined to form an overarching argument. There is an old legal adage that perhaps best exemplifies the use of these terms. **First you argue the facts, then the law and if both fail; then you pound the table**

Eureka moment (The level of Archimedes) - The origin of this expression dates back to the Greek philosopher and scientist Archimedes. While taking a bath, he noticed that the level of the water in the tub rose as he got in. He then realized that this effect could be used to determine the volume of the crown. This phenomenon was later called **Archimedes' principle.** Upon finding the solution, he yelled Eureka! This was his **"eureka moment"** and is now used to denote a great idea, feat; or an epiphany or the moment of a sudden unexpected discovery. Additionally, the **level of Archimedes** can be used to denote balance, stability or equilibrium. **Road to Damascus (moment)** is similar

Even a broken (stopped) clock is right twice a day - The source of this often-quoted proverb is unknown or unclear. Because a clock has two hours that repeat each day, e.g., 4 am and 4 pm and since time is continuous, it will be right twice a day. It means: success or reward obtained by chance or luck. **Potluck** is similar and means: a chance that whatever is available will prove to be good or satisfactory. **Roll the dice; the luck of the draw; dumb luck** are also similar expressions

Every cloud has a silver lining - The origin of this phrase goes back to John Milton's reference of clouds with silver linings and has since been used by many other writers. The phrase is often interpreted to mean: every difficult or sad situation has a comforting or more hopeful aspect even though this may not be immediately apparent. **It is always darkest before the dawn** has a similar meaning

Every dog has its day - The source of this expression goes back to the Renaissance era and was recorded in R. Taverner tr. Erasmus' Adages. It was also used by Shakespeare in his play, Hamlet (Act V, Scene I) "Let Hercules himself do what he may, the cat will mew, and dog will have his day." It has migrated to mean: everyone gets a chance eventually; or that everyone is successful or fails during some period in their life. **Fifteen minutes of fame**

Everyone is entitled to his own opinion, but not to his own facts - This quote is ascribed to the U.S. Senator Daniel Patrick Moynihan. It can be interpreted as: although opinions may vary from person to person; facts are like the truth and therefore remain constant. Often, opinions are formed based on the interpretation of facts. **Facts do not cease to exist because they are ignored**

Everything has its limit [iron ore cannot be educated into gold] - This expression is accredited to Mark Twain. A friend of Grant and Tesla, Twain was not only an iconic figure in his day, but a spokesman for the human race. The common interpretation is: it is important in any endeavor or situation to know where the boundaries lie and not to overreach those boundaries. **Nothing lasts forever** and **everything has its season**. For example: a person could have faith in another person or a leader, but few people have unbridled or unlimited faith in anyone. It is important to know what can be achieved and what cannot, given the amount of resources and time available. As Dirty Harry once said: **a man's got to know his limitations. I'm at my limits**

Exception proves the rule - The origin of this saying is not clear. Some believe that it comes from the early days of English law, others say it dates back to the Romans. The common usage is: something that does not follow a rule but proves that the rule exists. Or, in other words, **every rule needs an exception to prove it. Rule of thumb**

Existential threat - This is a term that arose in the 20th century and has become popular, particularly regarding Israel's right to exist, but has also been used to describe things such as **global warming**. Some believe that the term has its roots in existentialism. It means that someone's or something's existence is in jeopardy

Existentialism - This term originated with the 19th century philosophers Søren Kierkegaard and Friedrich Nietzsche. It means: a philosophical theory or approach that emphasizes the existence of the individual person as a free and responsible agent determining their own development through acts of will. **By virtue of the absurd**

Exit stage left - The source of this expression comes from the directions in theater, indicating when, where and how an actor should exit the stage from a scene. It was popularized by the Hanna Barbera cartoon character, Snagglepuss, in the early 1960s. Snagglepuss was a pink mountain lion with strong desires to be an actor. His famous line was: *Heavens to Murgatroyd! Exit stage left (right)*. This series ran as part of The Yogi Bear Show. It has migrated to mean: to leave in a timely and inconspicuous manner, so as not to make a scene or attract attention to oneself. **Vanish into thin air**

Expel the money changers from the temple - This expression is from the Bible New Testament (Matthew 21:12-13). "When Jesus cleared the money changers from the Temple, he drove them out by overturning their tables". The general interpretation is: the cleansing of corruption. **Den of thieves** (Matthew 21:13) is a similar saying from the Bible "And said unto them; It is written; My house shall be called the house of prayer; but ye have made it a den of thieves." **Clean the Augean stables**

Extrasensory perception (ESP) - This phenomenon has been around since antiquity, with its share of soothsayers, oracles and mystics. In fact, the belief in such phenomenon is central to most ancient myths and religions that transverse the globe. The term extrasensory perception was apparently coined by the British explorer and polymath Sir Richard Burton in the late 1800s. At the turn of the 20th century, it was popularized by the French researcher Dr. Paul Joire, who used the term ESP to describe the ability of a person under hypnosis to sense things without using the five known senses. In the 1930s, Duke University psychologist J.B. Rhine popularized the term to denote psychic abilities. In the early years of the 20th century, **psychic phenomena** was more than a scientific curiosity, it was also the rage of certain social groups. Sometimes referred to as the **sixth sense**, the term means: the ability to perceive things by means other than the five known senses, e.g., by telepathy or clairvoyance. The term **mental telepathy** is similar and is often used synonymously with ESP. Both of these terms are used jokingly, e.g., **you must have ESP** or **you have mental telepathy**. Whether such abilities are part of the human faculty or limited to a selected few such as the renowned Edgar Cayce or if they exist at all, continues to be a subject of debate. Cayce, known as the "Sleeping Prophet," is reported to have correctly predicted the stock market crash of 1929, the subsequent **Great Depression**, the beginning of World War II and other events of the future. Oracle

Eye candy - This term first appeared in the mid-1980s. But it did not become popular until around the turn of the 21st century when it was used by the rap culture to designate a very attractive woman. Such women were repeatedly featured in music videos (with tight clothing and in some cases, scarcely nothing at all). It is perhaps a derivative of the earlier term "**ear candy**", the latter referring to music that is aesthetically pleasing. The term refers to: someone or something that is visually attractive or pleasing but is usually considered to lack worth or merit. Similar phrases include: **just another pretty face; sexy momma; a brickhouse**

Eye of Providence - The source of this iconic symbol and phrase (also referred to as **The All-Seeing Eye** of God) can be traced to Ancient Egypt and the Eye of Horus which sat atop of some obelisk. It was later adopted by Christians with the triangle representing the **Trinity**. It was also espoused by the Freemasons and is represented on the back of the dollar bill. This symbol was placed on the dollar bill during the presidency of Franklin Roosevelt an avid Freemason at the suggestion of his vice president Henry Wallace. During the French Revolution, it was also used as a sign that God was looking or guiding the revolution. As a phrase it is used to represent the presence or watchful eye of God

Stands for:

Fortune favors the bold (brave)

IN A NUTSHELL

Facts do not cease to exist because they are ignored - This axiom is attributed to the English writer Aldous Huxley. There are two different kinds of ignorance, general ignorance and willful ignorance. In the first case, people are ignorant simply because they do not know. However, in the latter case, there is a downright disregard for the facts; a refusal to accept the evidence on the grounds that it disagrees with a predetermined belief and lastly; a total disregard for the opinions of others that don't agree with you. In such cases there is no argument or **method of persuasion** that can rehabilitate such ignorance and the facts simply do not matter. Yet, in the end facts do matter and the truth is restored. Sophocles wrote: "no lie ever reaches old age." Similar phrases include: **get your facts first, [and then you can distort them as much as you please]; see no evil, hear no evil, speak no evil; turn a blind eye to**

Failure is not an option - The origin of this expression is from the Apollo 13 Moon Mission. During the Apollo 13 mission, it was famously said, "We've never lost an American in space and we're sure as hell not going to lose one now. Failure is not an option!" It has migrated to mean: in times of crisis, we must persevere, and try to **think out of the box** to develop alternative solutions

Fair is foul and foul is fair - This saying is attributed to William Shakespeare's Macbeth (Act I, Scene I). "Fair is foul and fouls is fair: Hover through the fog and filthy air." In this play, Macbeth outwardly appears to be a man of honor, but inwardly he is a coward that takes advice from witches. Sometimes, **the world seems upside down.** We often wonder why sometimes **the wicked prosper** and **no good deed goes unpunished.** What is fake is real and what is real is fake. **The end justifies the means**; and sometimes evil is invoked in the name of good. The phrase is regularly interpreted to mean: appearances are often deceptive. My dad would always say to me. Life is like a baseball game. Every ball you hit, try to hit it fair. Similar phrases include: **all that glitters is not gold; first appearance deceives many; perception is reality**

Fair-weather friend – The origin of this expression is unknow, however, it has been around since the mid-eighteenth century. Fair weather means good weather and thus the phrase means a friend that is around when things are going good but abandons you when things are unfavorable. Someone that is not loyal

Fait accompli - A French term that means an "accomplished fact" that is, presumably irreversible or a thing that has already happened or been decided before those affected hear about it, leaving them with no option but to accept

Faith can move mountains - The origin of this expression comes from the Bible (Mat. 21:21). Jesus said: "Verily I say unto you; If ye have faith, and doubt not, ye shall not only do this which is done to the fig tree, but also if ye shall say unto this mountain; Be thou removed, and be thou cast into the sea; it shall be done." While this idea was articulated in the Christian religion, faith lies at the **cornerstone** of all religions. It can be interpreted to mean: faith is one of the most powerful attributes of the human experience. It is essential to one's self esteem and the ability to conquer all including things that once seemed to be impossible

Fall off the wagon - During the late 19th century, water carts drawn by horses went down dusty roads in the summer. During the Prohibition crusade in the 1890s and early 1900s, men who promised to stop drinking would say that they were thirsty but would rather climb aboard the water cart to get a drink than break their pledges. It means: to start drinking again after you have pledged not to

False as Cressida - The expression has its roots in Greek mythology as Cressida was a Trojan woman who pledged herself to Troilus only to forsake him for Diomedes. Shakespeare wrote a play entitled <u>Troilus and Cressida</u> in which the vertex of their love was explored. However, unlike his <u>Romeo and Juliet,</u> one lover is unfaithful. "The will is infinite, and the execution confined" (Act III, Scene II). describes the dilemma in which the scales of: true as Troilus or false as Cressida are weighed in Shakespeare's play. The expression means: unfaithful or to forsake someone for another; a betrayal of love or trust. **A Delilah; a Jezebel**

False equivalence - The origins of this term is unclear. Notwithstanding, it is frequently used to denote when two things have common or similar aspects but are not necessarily equal in scope, meaning or application. Often when making such an equivalence, key factors are ignored. **Moral equivalence** could be considered a special case of false equivalence. It is regularly used to indicate that both sides are equally guilty when in fact only one side is to blame. In both cases, the perception of the events is skewed or biased **in one direction or the other**

False face must hide what the false heart doth know - This saying is attributed to William Shakespeare's <u>Macbeth</u> (Act I, Scene II). One of Shakespeare's greatest attributes was his ability to identify **the human condition** and the **frailties of life.** In this scene, Macbeth claims to be innocent, although he knows in his heart that he is guilty. Many of us put on a face to hide the truth, but you cannot lie to yourself, and in our **heart of hearts** lies the unaltered truth that sears itself in the internal soul, regardless of how sincere the face may appear. The face knows the face, but the heart knows whether the truth is seen on the face or masked by a lie. Shakespeare also wrote: **To thine own self be true; oh, liars they can look so honest; fair is foul and foul is fair.** Homer conveyed a similar sentiment: "Hateful to me as the gates of Hades is that man who hides one thing in his heart and speaks another." V.S. Naipaul wrote in his book entitled: <u>In a Free State</u> **"The only lies for which we are truly punished are those we tell ourselves**

<u>Falstaffian</u> - <u>Sir John Falstaff,</u> was a central character in several Shakespearean plays: <u>Henry IV, Part 1</u> and <u>Part 2</u> and <u>The Merry Wives of Windsor</u> and is especially known for his robust, bawdy humor, good-natured rascality, and brazen braggadocio. The term means: of, relating to, or having the qualities of this Shakespearean character. **Falstaffian wit**

Familiarity breeds contempt – One of the first noted use of this expression was in Chaucer's <u>Tale of Melibee</u> (c. 1386) but also appears in Erasmus' book on <u>Proverbs and Adages</u> so it may have been used earlier. The phrase is often interpreted to mean: extensive knowledge of or close association with someone or something leads to a loss of respect for them or it. In other words, the better we know people, the more likely we are to find fault with them

Far from (off) the beaten path - This phrase was used by the famous psychiatrist Carl Jung, but it is not clear if it originated with him. Nonetheless, it means: something that is not well known or common to people; something that is different than the norm; in or into an isolated place. **The beaten path, the beaten track**

Far from the madding crowd - The source of this expression is from a poem written by the English poet Thomas Gray entitle: Elegy Written in a Country Churchyard. It was popularized, however, by the title of a book by the British author, Thomas Hardy, written in 1874. Long recognized as a classic and perhaps the **Magnum Opus** of Hardy's work, it tells the story of the young farmer Gabriel Oak and his love for and pursuit of an elusive woman, Bathsheba, that leads her to both true love and tragedy. It is regularly interpreted to mean: to be secluded or removed from public notice. A quiet and pastoral place

Fata morgana – The origin of this term is the legendary court of King Arthur. The term is an Italian translation of the sorceress, Morgan le Fay, the sister of King Arthur. Among the powers alleged to her was the ability to change shapes and to cause mirage's particularly at sea. Today, the term is often used synonymously with a mirage. On a similar note, **Flying Dutchman** is a ghostly phantom ship alleged to sail around the Cape of Good Hope forever, and reportedly seen by sailors

Fatigue makes cowards of us all - This saying is attributed to General George S. Patton. Memorialized in the 1970 film Patton, starring George C. Scott as Patton. He was instrumental in the Allied victory over Hitler in World War II. Like Custer, he was a flamboyant general that designed his own uniform. Furthermore, he believed that he was a reincarnated warrior with a destiny to do something great. The quote is an excellent metaphor for war and sports and was used by former Green Bay Packers coach Vince Lombardi and others. The phrase is often interpreted to mean: rest is essential to the human endeavor and none of us can go without it. It is therefore difficult to be motivated or **be in the right state of mind** when you are tired and hence much easier **to call the quits** or **give up. Run out of gas, throw in the towel; the spirit is willing, but the flesh is weak.** A similar phrase, **conscience does make cowards of us all** is from Shakespeare's Hamlet (Act III, Scene I) and it means: conscience often averts one from doing things that they would regret in the future

Fault line - This term has its origin in science, more specifically in geology. In geological terms, a fault line is a line on a rock surface or the ground that traces a geological fault or fissure. The term has migrated to other areas and now means: a situation that often separates a person or a thing from some type of danger, collapse or calamity. **Line of demarcation** is similar and means: a line defining the boundary or limits of a buffer zone, area of restriction or situation

Fauna and flora - The origin of fauna and flora is from Carl Linnaeus, often referred to as the Father of Taxonomy. His system for naming, ranking, and classifying organisms is still in wide use today. Fauna is a term for animals, flora is a term for plants. This term now refers to the animal and plant life of a region. **Megafauna** refers to the large mammals of a particular region, habitat, or geological period. Likewise, **Megaflora** refers to large plants

A COLLECTION OF POPULAR ENGLISH PHRASES

Faustian bargain - Faust in the legend, traded his soul to the devil in exchange for knowledge. Although fictional in literature, the legend is based on an actual magician who lived in the area of northern Germany in the 15th century. It has since migrated to mean: **a deal with the devil.** To "strike a Faustian bargain" is to be willing to sacrifice anything to satisfy a limitless desire for knowledge or power. Similarly, Mephistophelean is a term that comes from the evil spirit to whom Faust sold his soul and means: someone who is diabolical or evil in a **sinister** persuasive manner. **To sell your soul**

Faux pas - This is a French term which means "false step" that has worked its way into the English language. It means: a social blunder; an embarrassing or tactless act or remark in a social situation

Feasts must be solemn and rare, or else they cease to be feasts - This expression is credited to the British author Aldous Huxley. This statement speaks to the complacency of human nature. What makes something special or valuable is its rareness. When things become commonplace, they become mundane. For instance, if diamonds or gold were everywhere, they would be virtually worthless. **Everyday can't be Christmas**

Feedback loop - This term appears to have its origin in the engineering realm specifically control theory in which the output of a system is fed back into the input to decrease error or to help stabilize the system. It has recently migrated to other areas and it now mean: a cycle of behavior in which two people or groups each act to continuously strengthen or support the other's action. **Cause and effect; close the loop**

Feet of clay - The source of this saying is from the Bible (Daniel 2:30-33) and the interpretation of the king's dream. It now means: a fundamental flaw or weakness in a person otherwise revered; or a hidden flaw in the character of a greatly admired or respected person or a failing or feebleness in a person's character. **Legs of iron, feet of clay; Achilles' heel; chink in the armor**

Fell swoop - The origin of the expression comes from Shakespeare's Macbeth (Act IV, Scene III). "What, all my pretty chickens and their dam, at one fell swoop?" It is often used to describe: in a single action; suddenly

Ferret out - This term has its origin in the practice of using ferrets to drive rabbits and rats from burrows. It means: to force somebody or something out of a hiding place by persistent searching

Fiddled while Rome burned - The source of this phrase is the story that Nero played the fiddle (violin) while Rome burned, during the great fire in 64 CE. It has migrated to mean: to pay attention to something small while larger things are happening; to ignore a large problem

Fifteen minutes of fame - This famous quote is often credited to the American artist Andy Warhol. However, recent doubts have been casted regarding its origins. Nonetheless, he is the one that popularized it. It is frequently used as: a commentary on the amount of time anyone is really in the spotlight; a brief period of celebrity or notoriety

IN A NUTSHELL

Fifty million Frenchmen can't all be wrong - The source of this phrase is uncertain. But it was popular in the late 1920s. In 1927, there was a hit song with the same title. I heard a similar saying during my youth: a billion Chinese can't all be wrong. It is often interpreted to mean: when a large group thinks that something is wrong or right, it needs to be taken seriously or at least investigated. **Where there is smoke, there is fire** is somewhat similar but means: an indication that something is wrong

Figment of imagination - The source of this expression is unclear. However, imagination is one of those sacred gifts bestowed upon humans by a benevolent Creator. It is one of those things that separates our species from the other beasts of this earth. It can be interpreted to mean: a thing that someone believes to be real but that exists only in their imagination. **A Don Quixote; a figment of your imagination**

Finger licking good - The origin of this expression is from a slogan made popular by Kentucky Fried Chicken (KFC). Since their chicken is normally eaten without utensils, the add suggests that it is so good it would have you licking your fingers. Subsequently, the expression has been applied to anything that is very good especially eaten in the manner depicted in the KFC advertisements. **Down to the bone. Good to the last drop** is a similar phrase coined by Maxwell House (they ascribed the phrase to Teddy Roosevelt after he tasted their coffee)

First come first served - Like so many popular expressions, the exact origin of this phrase is unknown although it was in general use before the turn of the 20th century. The common belief is that it emerged in stores and markets as a service protocol. Often used incorrectly as: first come first serve, it is frequently used: to indicate that people will be served in the order in which they arrive or apply (first come first served basis). Similarly, the term **FIFO, (First In First Out)** and **LIFO, Last In Frist Out** are also used but not as frequent

Flash in the pan - The source of this expression is unclear as there are two compelling theories. The first refers to the firing of muskets when you would get a flash, but the shot was not fired. The second refers to gold prospecting when a shining object would appear in a pan used to sort gold but was not gold. Nonetheless, the phrase has migrated to mean: something or someone that experiences a short-lived success; or. something that is disappointing because it fails to live up to its expectation. **One hit wonder**

Flip side - This term has its origins in the music recording industry. In the days of phonographs, records (LPs) and vinyl, there were two sides to each record with different songs on each side. In most cases, the flip side was the least important side or the B-side. But sometimes, they would become hits also. The term now means: the reverse or opposite side of an argument, opinion or situation. It could also refer to the bad or opposite side of something

Florence Nightingale effect - So named after the famous British nurse of the Crimean War (1853 – 1856). A war virtually lost to posterity apart from Nightingale and the **Charge of the Light Brigade**. Often called *the mother of modern nursing*, she was known for her tender care of wounded soldiers, much like Clara Barton who would emerge years later during the American Civil War at the battle of Antietam in 1862. The effect is associated with a caregiver that develops romantic or sexual feeling for someone under their care. Sometimes a caring or kind person is referred to as **a Florence Nightingale**

A COLLECTION OF POPULAR ENGLISH PHRASES

Flow chart - This term has been in existence since the 1920s, however, it did not become popular until it was widely applied to the development of software. Flow charts are used to express the step by step flow of functions or processes required to achieve a desired result. Traditional symbols are used to denote functions or operations. **Block diagrams** may be considered a special type of flow chart in which blocks are used to represent major components, functions or operations. **A mind map** is a more open type of mapping depicting the relationship of ideas or concepts. It is a useful tool for brainstorming

Fire and brimstone - This expression is from the Bible (Genesis 19:24), when God destroyed **Sodom and Gomorrah**. It has since come to mean: a sign of God's wrath, the torments of hell; or in some cases a style of preaching

Five O - The origin of this phrase comes from the popular TV series Hawaii Five O and has since become a term used to denote the police particularly in urban neighborhoods. **Book em Danno**

Flotsam and jetsam - This saying refers to the floating wreckage of a ship and its cargo, or floating cargo deliberately cast overboard to stabilize a ship in a rough sea. Specifically, flotsam is the wreckage of a ship or its cargo found floating on or washed up by the sea. Jetsam is unwanted material or goods that have been thrown overboard from a ship and washed ashore, especially material that has been discarded to lighten the vessel. The two terms are frequently used together and normally mean: something that is useless or discharged

Fly in the ointment - The origin of this phrase comes from the Bible (Ecclesiastes 10:1). "As is dead flies give perfume a bad smell, so a little folly outweighs wisdom and honor." It can be interpreted to mean: a small but irritating flaw that spoils its value

Fly the coop – The origin of this phrase is from chickens flying (leaving) the coop, which is an enclosure used to house them. The phrase migrated to inmates that escaped prison before resolving on its current usage which means: to leave or escape something. **Chickens coming home to roost**

Fly the flag at half-mast - This practice originated as a sign of respect after a person died at sea. It has since migrated to occasions when a person, usually an important or famous person, dies

Foaming at the mouth - The source of this expression is the observation that animals afflicted with rabies often foam at the mouth as a sign of their illness. The expression has migrated to mean: to be in a state of rage; to be extremely angered or troubled by something or someone. **Rabid dog**

Follow the money - Although similar expressions may have been used before, the source of this saying appears to be from the 1976 documentary All the Presidents Men. Specifically, it is ascribed to the government informant, Mark Felt, pseudonymously known as **Deep Throat** a name taken from the title of a popular pornographic movie of its day starring Linda Lovelace. Felt was deputy associate director of the FBI in 1972 when he began supplying information to Bob Woodward and Carl Bernstein of the Washington Post. It has come to mean: in cases of corruption of illegal activities, the trail of money is often a clue to the initial crime or misdoing. Similar phrases include: **Watergate; it's the coverup and not the crime**

Food chain - This is a term that has been borrowed from the science realm. In science, it is a hierarchical series of plants and animals each dependent on the next as a source of food or energy required to survive. At the bottom of the food chain are plants that get their energy from the sun through a process known as photosynthesis. These plants are eaten by animals which in turn are eaten (typically) by larger animals. Humans are at the top of the food chain. The term food chain is often used as a metaphor for a hierarchical system in which the higher you are, the more important you are and the more benefits you are allotted. **Move up(down) the food chain**

Food for thought - The origin of this term is unknown. Yet, it has been around since the 1800s. It implies that the brain, like the body, needs to be nourished. It is regularly interpreted to mean: something that warrants serious consideration or thought; something that provides mental stimulus for future thought or ideas. **Train of thought** is similar and means: the process in which someone reaches a conclusion or a line of reasoning

Fools rush in where angels dare to tread - This line was first written by the 18th century English poet Alexander Pope in his poem: An Essay on Criticism. The phrase is often interpreted to mean: the rash or inexperienced will attempt things that wiser people are more cautious of. **A fool flatters himself, a wise man flatters the fool**

For all intents and purposes - The origin of this phrase appears to be English law and dates back to the 16th century. It was originally stated as "to all intents, constructions, and purposes before it migrated to its current form. It means: in every practical sense; in almost every respect

For all the marbles - This phrase has its origins in the **time-honored** game of marbles. Although several versions of this game have been in existence since antiquity, in a popular version, one can play more than one marble in the game and risk all of his marbles. It has migrated to mean: to risk everything at once; **to go all in, the whole nine yards, the whole shebang**. While **to lose your marbles** is another idiom that contains marbles, it is unclear if it has the same source. It means to go mad or crazy. However, **to knuckle down** does appear to have the same origin. In the game of marbles, a person puts his knuckles to the ground as part of the shooting position. This phrase can be interpreted to mean: to become serious about something or to begin to work hard at something particularly as it relates to studying. **You better knuckle down**

For every action, there is an equal and opposite reaction - The origin of this term comes from the Physics realm. Specifically, Newton's Third Law of Motion. It has migrated to mean: things often come in pairs, similar to **cause and effect**. It speaks to the symmetrical nature of Nature. The bigger the push, the bigger the push back. In this regard, we must be aware of the negative reflections of our positive attributes

A COLLECTION OF POPULAR ENGLISH PHRASES

For the birds - The origin of this expression comes from the tendency of some birds to search horse droppings for seeds. The expression evolved to mean: not worthy of consideration; something that is unimportant

For want of a nail the kingdom was lost - The source of this phrase is unclear, and its connotation has been used by several writers in various forms since the 13th century including: William Shakespeare, Ben Franklin and James Baldwin. Franklin wrote: "For the want of a nail the shoe was lost, For the want of a shoe the horse was lost, For the want of a horse the rider was lost, For the want of a rider the battle was lost, For the want of a battle the kingdom was lost, And all for the want of a horseshoe-nail. "It can be interpreted to mean that even the smallest detail is important to something big. Shakespeare wrote in Richard III (Act V, Scene IV) the final play in his series on the War of the Roses: **A horse, a horse! My kingdom for a horse!**

For whom the bell tolls - The origin of this expression is from the English poet John Donne's (1572 - 1631) poem Devotions upon emergent occasions and several steps in my sickness - Meditation XVII. It used the lines **"ask not for whom the bell tolls, it tolls for thee."** The bells refer to the church bells that are rung when a person dies. Hence the author is suggesting that we should not be curious as to for whom the church bell is tolling for. It is for all of us. It was also a title of a book by Ernest Hemmingway. The expression can be interpreted to mean: because we are all part of humankind, any person's death is a loss to all of us. Similar phrases include **no man is an island; there but for the grace of God go I**

Forbidden fruit - This saying is a reference to Adam and Eve and the Garden of Eden (Genesis chapters 2 and 3) where **Adam and Eve** lived before the fall. Yet, there is no mention in the Bible that it was an apple, just that it was a fruit from the **Tree of the Knowledge of Good and Evil** that they were forbidden to eat. It has evolved to mean: unlawful pleasure or enjoyment; illicit love, a tempting but forbidden thing; a thing that is desired all the more because it is not allowed. **A taste of forbidden fruit; jam made of forbidden fruits; a second bite of the apple; fruit of the poison tree forbidden fruit is the sweetest.** Garden of Eden has come to be synonymous with a paradise. **A fig leaf** is also a related metaphor and has its origin in what Adam and Eve used to cover their **private parts** after the ate the forbidden fruit (Genesis 3:7). Frequently, it is used to depict the concealing of genitals in art. *A fig leaf* has come to mean: the covering up of an act, object or situation that could be embarrassing, unpleasant or distasteful

Forever is composed of nows - This quote is attributed to the American poet Emily Dickinson. A recluse and unique person, most of her work was published after her death by the abolitionist and Civil War officer Thomas Wentworth Higginson. "Forever – is composed of Nows –'Tis not a different time –Except for Infiniteness –And Latitude of Home." The phrase could be interpreted as: although we all should **plan for the future; tomorrow isn't promised to anyone**. We should therefore cherish each day and be thankful for **each and every moment.** Each now is like a rose in an infinite garden called forever; and we should yearn to smell its fragrance without the fear of being cut by its thorns

IN A NUTSHELL

Forewarned is forearmed - The source of this phrase is often attributed to a translation from the Latins "*praemonitus, praemunitus.*" It is frequently interpreted to mean: prior knowledge of possible dangers or problems gives one a tactical advantage. **To be forewarned is to be forearmed**

Fort Knox - The origin of this term comes from a fort in Kentucky built in 1936 during the **Great Depression**. It holds the bulk of the United States' gold bullion locked in its secured vaults. Because of its immense value, the term has come to be known as: something or someone that has a large monetary value. **What do you think I am, Fort Knox?**

Fortune favors the bold (brave) - *Fortes Fortuna adjuvat.* The source of this saying is the Roman playwright Terence in Phormio and it also appears at the end of Virgil's The Aeneid. The phrase was intended to mean that the goddess of luck, Fortuna would reward and help those that took risks. It is often interpreted to mean: if you are willing to be bold you will eventually reap rewards. Similar phrases include: **courageous action is often rewarded; chance favors the prepared mind**

Forty acres and a mule - This phrase originates from a promise made by General Sherman in his Special Field Order No. 15, issued on Jan. 16, 1865 near the end of the Civil War. It gave former black slaves 40 acres and a mule. It is now used, mostly by African Americans, as a symbol of the numerous promises made by whites to them that were later denied

Founding Father(s) - Although the term has been in use before the American Revolutionary War, the term as we know it, did not become popular until the 20th century. It is often credited to Warren G. Harding, a president who consistently ranks at the bottom of presidential listings. Today the term is used to indicate: the men that helped to form the foundations of the United States before and immediately after the Revolutionary War

Fountain of youth - This term has been around since antiquity and was mention by Herodotus to be in Ethiopia. Similarly, during the Middle Ages, many believed that such a fountain or spring rested in Prester John's kingdom which was also alleged to have been in Ethiopia. It was made famous, however, by the legend of Ponce de Leon and his search for such a fountain in America. The term now means: something that restores the vitality, health or youthfulness of an individual

Four-leaf clover - The exact origin of this term is unclear; however, it is widely assumed to be Ireland and the three-leaf clover (known as the shamrock) which is used as a national symbol of that country. The three-leaf clover is associated with Saint Patrick's Day celebrations as the three leaves represent the Trinity. For leaf clovers, on the other hand, are extremely rare as the standard clover has three leaves. Because of their rarity, four-leaf clovers are considered a sign of good luck and therefore are often used as a good luck charm. **The luck of the Irish; pot of gold at the end of the rainbow**

Freak out - The origin of this popular term is unclear. It dates back to the wild 1960s and the drug scene when people were **freaking out or tripping out** off of dropping acid (LSD). It usually referred to a bad

90

psychedelic trip. Today, it means: to be or caused to be in a heightened emotional state, such as that of fear, anger, or excitement. During the late 1970s the was a popular song by Chic entitled: Le Freak which feature the lyrics "Freak out." Similar terms are as follows: **You're freaking me out; don't freak out on me; to go berserk; to hit the ceiling; to go bananas; to start tripping; to blow my high**

French shower (bath) - The origin of this expression is unclear. However, the French were known for their products and etiquette such as French perfume, French wine, French cuisine, etc. As a result, several things common in the French culture migrated to the English language. **As a matter of fact**, Thomas Jefferson, a true Francophile, sent James Hemmings (his chef and brother of his black mistress Sally Hemmings) to France to learn French cooking. Jefferson also became a wine connoisseur while in France. The expression now means: to clean yourself quickly without taking a shower or a bath. In some cases, it is merely to put on perfume or body spray to give the appearance of cleanliness and in others to clean areas of the body such as genitals or under the arms. **French leave** is another expression assigned to the French. This expression comes from an 18th century French custom of leaving a reception without informing the host or hostess. It has come to mean: an unauthorized, unexpected or unexcused departure; an absence without permission. **(AWOL). French kiss** is yet another expression of French designation and means: an exotic kiss with contact between tongues

Freedom of speech - The source of this term, as used in the United States, is the Bill of Rights outlined in the Constitution. Proposed by James Madison, along with eleven other amendments, its roots may lie in the English **Magna Carta** put forth in 1215. The Founding Fathers, being Englishmen, often looked to the governing laws of England for inspiration or, in some cases, to propose laws that the new nation would rest. The Bill of Rights was not part of the original Constitution and some Founding Fathers refused to sign the Constitution because it did not include provisions for individual rights. It did not become part of the Constitution until 1791. *Freedom of speech* is sometimes referred to as **The First Amendment**. It is a **Civil Right** that guarantees that the federal government shall not interfere unnecessarily or arbitrarily with an individual's speech (if it is not used maliciously, e.g., as in yelling fire in a building that is not on fire.) The First Amendment is also extended to free expression as in the right to peacefully assemble. For over two centuries, this amendment, which also includes freedom of religion and the press, has been a **cornerstone of the American ideal**

Freudian slip - So named after Sigmund Freud. He was the first to emphasize the significance of unconscious processes in normal and neurotic behavior and was the founder of psychoanalysis as both a theory of personality and a therapeutic practice. It is used to describe: an unintentional error regarded as revealing subconscious feelings. A **slip of the tongue** that is motivated by some unconscious aspect of the mind

From Dan to Beersheba - The origin of this saying is from the Bible (2 Samuel 17:11). "Dan" was the northern boundary of Palestine, while "Beersheba" was its southern border. The common interpretation is: from one end to the other. **From Alpha to Omega; from soup to nuts**

IN A NUTSHELL

From each according to his abilities, to each according to his needs - This is a quote made famous by Karl Marx. He was the founder of modern communism along with Friedrich Engels and they collaborated in the writing of the Communist Manifesto. It is regularly interpreted to mean that each person produces in accordance with their ability but receives in accordance to their needs

From soup to nuts - The source of this saying comes from the Muslim Moor Ziryab, who developed a number of cultural practices in Muslim Spain that eventually would work their way into Western Civilization. He also introduced new culinary recipes, new tableware, toothpaste, new sartorial fashions and even the games of chess and polo. It refers to the order of meals that he established and has come to mean: everything, **from A to Z** or **to run the gamut**

From the cradle to the grave - This is a popular proverb of unknown origin. So often we forget that ours lives is nothing more than a dash between two dates. It literally means: from the beginning until the end or from the **start to the finish. From A to Z**

From (out)the mouths of babes [comes words of wisdom] - This saying is a derivative of the expression in the Bible (Psalms 8). Often, children say the most interesting and most insightful things because they see the truth as it is perhaps best exemplified by the story of The Emperor's New Clothes. It has migrated to mean: the young or inexperience at times can exhibit wisdom. **Deep meaning often lies in childish play**

From the sublime to the ridiculous [is but a step] - This saying has been linked to people such as Napoleon and Thomas Paine. However, it first appeared in France in 1777 in the writing of Bernard Le Bovier de Fontenelle. The phrase is regularly interpreted to mean: from the beautiful to the silly, from great to weak

Frozen in amber - The source of this phrase is that phenomena of insects and other objects that were enclosed in amber. Amber is a yellow/orange translucent fossilized tree resin. The notion was perhaps popularized by the movie Jurassic Park in which dinosaurs were cloned using their DNA that was preserved in ticks enclosed in amber. **To be frozen in amber** is to be locked in a static or unchanged state. **Locked in a time warp**

Full court press - This term originated from basketball. In this sport, it is an aggressive defensive strategy in which multiple players apply pressure to the ball handler and other players from one end of the court to the other. The term has migrated to other areas and has migrated to mean: a **concerted effort** by a group to achieve a goal that they deem imperative or important. **All hands on deck. Ball is in your court** can also apply to basketball or tennis and means: it is up to you to **take the initiative.** Other basketball expressions include: **a jump ball** which means: something that is undecided and could go either way; **pass the ball** meaning to give something up and the proverbial **slam dunk** meaning something that is easy, **a cakewalk** or **a foregone conclusion**

Stands for:

Gordian knot

G2 - This term comes from the intelligence community and denotes: information about a person or situation. **411** (information) is replacing G2 in some circles but refers more to gossip, Similarly, **911** is used in cases of emergencies

Gallous humor - Though the phenomenon has been around since **time immemorial**, this term is believed to have its origin in the German language. Specifically, the European revolutions of 1848. It referred to sarcastic or cynical humor derived from, painful, stressful or traumatic situations. For instance, the Roman Emperor Vespasian last words were reported to be: "Oh dear, I think I'm becoming a god," an allusion to the Roman belief that emperors become gods when they die. It means: grim and ironic humor in a desperate or disastrous situation. Humor that pokes fun of a life-threatening, catastrophic, or terrifying situation. For example, the comedian Steve Martin once said: "First the doctor told me the good news: I was going to have a disease named after me"

Garrison finish – The origin of this phrase is a US jockey Edward Garrison who was known for his come from behind finishes. It now refers to a come from behind victory

Gaslighting - The origin of the term is a 1938 play entitled: Gas Light by Patrick Hamilton and the subsequent 1940 and 1944 films. It is interesting to note that the term, along with the play and movies, emerged during the rise of Hitler in Germany and the subsequent effects on Europe. His rhetoric, propaganda and use of "alternative facts" were viewed by many as gaslighting. The term refers to: the psychological manipulation of a person or a group in such a way as to make the victim question their sanity or reason for believing something to be true or false

Genie in the bottle - The source of this expression comes from Arabian folklore depicting an imprisoned or trapped genie (spirit) in a bottle or oil lamp and capable of granting wishes (often three wishes) when released from the bottle. **Letting the genie out of the bottle** is similar to opening up Pandora's box. The expression can be interpreted to mean: to initiate something which can change your life for the good or the bad depending on your wishes or circumstances. A situation once started with unintended or unknown consequences. **Aladdin's lamp** is similar and is a charm enabling its holder to satisfy any wish. **Be careful what you wish for you just may get it. Open up a can of worms** is sometimes used similarly with a negative outcome. **Open sesame**

Gentlemen's agreement - Throughout history, there have been various agreements among men. However, the term itself is of recent times. Perhaps the most prominent was the agreement made between Teddy Roosevelt and the Japanese government regarding the immigration of Japanese to America in the early 1900s. Other gentlemen agreements include: the ban on African American in professional sports and other aspects of American life. It has migrated to mean: an agreement secured only by the honor and trust of the participants, in most cases, the condition is oral and therefore not legally binding. Similar phrases include: **glass ceiling; good old boy network; buddy system**

Geronimo! - So named after the Native American Apache leader Geronimo who was fearless. He reportedly said on his deathbed: "I should never have surrendered. I should have fought until I was the last man alive." The term was first used by the 82nd Airborne paratroopers as they jumped from planes during World War II. Now often used as a yell before a daring act

Gerrymandering - The source of this term comes from the name of a Massachusetts governor, Eldridge Gerry, and salamander, the rough shape of the election district he created in 1812. It was designed to keep political control of that area. The term means: to manipulate a district or area to favor one party or one class

Get down to brass tacks - The source of this popular phrase is uncertain; however, brass tacks were used as decretive items in furniture dating back to the **Elizabethan era** and perhaps beyond. Often misstated as *brass tax*, the phrase means: to discuss the essentials of a situation; **get down to the nitty gritty; get down to the nuts and bolts**

Get [the hell] out of Dodge - The origin of this phrase comes from Dodge City, Kansas, a town known for its lawlessness and typical of many western (Wild, Wild West) towns after the American Civil War replete with gunfights. It was popularized by Western movies and TV shows that appeared at the dawn of Television. Most noted was the TV show Gunsmoke, starring James Arness (the older brother of Mission Impossible's Peter Graves) as Marshal Matt Dillion. It ran from 1955-1975. The common usage is: to get out in a hurry. **grab your stuff and leave. It's time to get the hell out of Dodge**

Get your facts first, [and then you can distort them as much as you please] - This quote is attributed to Mark Twain. Also stated as: you must first learn the facts before you can distort them. People that lie, often know the truth. The lie, in many cases, is nothing more than a distortion of the truth; by omitting certain facts or playing on the ignorance or lack of knowledge of the listener(s). It is frequently interpreted to mean: in any endeavor, it is important to know what the facts are before you discuss or argue the situation with others. In any legal proceeding, the facts along with how they related to the law is the central part of the defense and the prosecution of the crime. We must be forever mindful that **"the most dangerous untruths are truths slightly distorted"**

Get your walking papers - The source of this term appears to be the release papers given to prisoners after they have served their time. It generally means: to be released or to be fired from a job

Ghetto - The origin of this term is Italian. Specifically, from an island that forms part of Venice, where in 1516 the Venetians restricted Jewish residence. Afterwards, it migrated to other European countries as a restricted area for Jews. For instance, during World War II, the Nazis established more than 400 ghettos in order to isolate Jews from the non-Jewish population. The term now means: a part of a metropolis, especially a slum area, occupied by a minority group(s); or an impoverished, underdeveloped area, usually troubled by a disproportionate level of crime and other social impediments such as drug and alcohol abuse, or a type of behavior usually associated with residents of this area. **Inner city** is sometimes euphemistically used to designate someone, or a behavior associated with the ghetto

IN A NUTSHELL

Ghost town - This term has its roots in the American west and mid-west and has been around since the early 1900s. It means: a deserted town with few or no remaining inhabitants. **This place looks like a ghost town**

Ghostwriter - The origin of this term is unclear, but the first known usage of the term was in 1927. It means: a person whose job it is to write material for someone else who is the named author

Gild the lily - This saying is often ascribed to Shakespeare who used similar words in his play King John, (Act IV, Scene II) 1595. It has migrated to mean: to try to improve what is already beautiful or excellent

Gilgamesh's Monster - The Epic of Gilgamesh is often viewed as the longest and greatest literary composition of Mesopotamia and is often cited as the first great work of literature in world history. It narrates a quest for fame and immortality lived by, Gilgamesh, the king of the city of Uruk. In this epic, Gilgamesh and Enkidu overcome the fierce monster Humbaba. It frequently refers to: overcoming a monstrous task with wit

Girl Friday - The origin of this term comes from the book Robinson Crusoe by the English novelist, Daniel Defoe. who gave the name Friday to the native who became his companion. It was also the title of a 1940 movie His Girl Friday starring Cary Grant. The term now refers to: a female helper, especially a junior office worker or a personal assistant to a business executive. **Man Friday**, is the male version. However, in recent times, these terms may have negative connotations in some circles

Give me five or high five - These expressions have their origins in the African American culture and refers to the fingers on the hand exchanged between two people not as a handshake but on the palms. It may go back to American slavery or even parts of west Africa as a greeting gesture. Give me five on the black hand side is also used. In this case, instead of using the palms, it is done on the back of the hand, i.e., the black side. It is used as: a greeting or as a sign of accomplishment or agreement

Give someone the finger - To give someone the finger means to extend **the middle finger** with the other fingers curled together as in a fist. This is one of the oldest gestures and goes back at least to antiquity and perhaps beyond. Many people feel that it has its origin in **a phallic symbol** with the middle finger representing the phallus and the closed fingers representing the testicles, thus meaning **screw you**. In many cultures throughout time it has been viewed as a highly offensive gesture. It has come to mean: to show someone, in an offensive way that you are angry with that person. **Flip someone the bird** is much more modern and means the same thing

Give someone the thumbs up/down - The general consensus of this gesture is that it comes from the Romans as it was used to give approval or disapproval of a gladiator in the Colosseum. Yet, there is some confusion if a thumbs up was used as it is currently used. Nonetheless, it has migrated to mean: an indication of satisfaction or approval and **a thumbs down** is used to show disapproval or dissatisfaction

A COLLECTION OF POPULAR ENGLISH PHRASES

Glass ceiling - This is a term that became popular during the 1980s. It means: an unofficially acknowledged barrier to the advancement in a profession, especially affecting women and members of minorities. Although laws have been enacted to eliminate glass ceilings, many remain in place as the result of **gentlemen agreements. To break the glass ceiling**

Go against the grain - This phrase was used by William Shakespeare in Coriolanus, 1607 but it may have been in use before. "Preoccupied with what you rather must do; Than what you should, made you against the grain" The common usage is: to go contrary to someone's natural disposition. Against one's inclination or natural tendency or to do something that is the opposite of what is usually done. Also, **to cut against the grain**

Go down a rabbit hole - The origin of this phrase comes from Alice in Wonderland by Lewis Carroll and is one of many sayings that have emerged from this **time-honored** classic. It is now used to describe: to embark upon a journey, situation or progression that is particularly problematic, difficult, complex, or sometimes chaotic. Specifically, one that becomes increasingly so as it progresses or unfolds. To investigate or explore something in greater detail. **Dig deep into**

Go for the jugular - This expression originated in the late Middle Ages when the word jugular was introduced into the English language from Latin. In this context, it meant throat. Hence, going for the jugular meant going for someone's throat. It now means: to be very aggressive or uninhibited in making an attack. **Go for the throat; go for it; to be all in (out)**

Go postal - This term originated in America during the 1990s as a result of several shooting at Post Offices. It now refers to: someone who becomes crazed and violent, especially as the result of stress

Go (going) viral - This is a term that became popular in the first decade of the 21st century with the rise of several online social media and video platforms. Viral is a derivative of the word virus and thus means to spread rapidly. It also denotes: to create content that will be shared exponentially via the Internet

God helps those that help themselves - This is a popular saying that many think is contained in the Bible but it is not. The first appearance of a similar phrase appears in ancient Greece. For example: Sophocles wrote "Heaven ne'er helps the men who will not act." The English version is attributed to the English statesman Algernon Sidney (1622-1683) in his Discourses on Government. But may have been popularized, at least in America, by Benjamin Franklin in Poor Richard's Almanac of 1757. The phrase is often interpreted to mean: Many times in life, people say: Lord please help me and expect God to do all of the work. However, this is like your kids coming to you all the time for help, but **not lifting a finger** to help themselves. Many argue that God will not come to the aid of those who refuse to try; therefore, we must exert ourselves and use the tools that God gave us if we want to prosper. **God give me strength**

God is a comedian playing to an audience too afraid to laugh - This quote is credited to the French author Voltaire a pseudonym of François-Marie Arouet. He was a leading figure of the Enlightenment period. Like so many people of the Enlightenment, Voltaire was a deist and not an atheist or a Christian. The phrase has many interpretations; some see it as a statement against religion. Others as a statement about the power of God and the feebleness of man. God can joke because he knows the beginning and the end, the good and the bad. Man fears because he does not and is therefore at the mercy of God's will. **If you want to make God laugh, tell him about your plans**

God of the gaps - This term emerged in the 20th century as a result of the increase in science and technology. It refers to a view of God as existing in the "gaps" or aspects of reality that are currently unexplained by scientific knowledge, or that we otherwise lack knowledge of. **Intelligent design**

God (The Lord) moves in mysterious ways [His wonders to perform] - The origin of this popular phrase is from a Christian Hymn written by the English poet William Cowper in 1773. It is often misquoted as a biblical verse, but it does not appear in the Bible, although the sentiments are echoed throughout this sacred book (most noted Romans 11:33). The phrase is habitually interpreted to mean: the wisdom, purposes and actions of God are incomprehensible to humankind and that we are mere vassals of his inerrant will. **The judgments of the Lord are true and righteous altogether**

God(s) on Mount Olympus - Mount Olympus was the home of the Olympian gods and the supreme court for human offenses. To be a god on Mount Olympus, is to be placed above others. The phrase is regularly interpreted to mean: a person or a group that is placed or viewed above others. **Above the law**

Gold digger - This term originated around the turn of the 20th century and was first popularized by two plays entitled: Gold Diggers (1919) and Gold Diggers of Broadway (1929). Most recently, it was popularized by a Kanye West song entitled: Gold Digger. The song includes the lyrics: She take my money when I'm in need; Yeah, she's a triflin' friend indeed; Oh, she's a gold digger; Way over town, that digs on me. The term is defined as: a person, usually a female, that dates or marries for money. Similar terms include: **Sugar Daddy, trophy wife**

Gold rush - The origin of this term, at least how it is applied in America, is the 1849 California gold rush in which gold was discovered in Northern California. In an ironic twist, the United States acquired California as a result of an 1848 treaty with Mexico which ended the Mexican-American War. As the saying goes, **God looks after fools, drunks and the United States**. Although the Bay Area was the chief beneficiary, Salt Lake City, Utah also prospered because of people traveling through this city on their way to the Bay Area. The term now denotes: a sudden movement of people to a newly discovered place in which money is easily made. **There's gold in them thar hills; seek your fortunes**

Gold of Tolosa - The Roman Caepio looted all the gold from the temple of Apollo at Tolosa only to have the gold stolen from him. It is now used to describe: that nothing is gained from **ill-gotten gains**

Golden Fleece - In Greek mythology, the fleece was made of pure gold and was kept in a sacred grove by King Aeëtes and guarded by an unsleeping dragon. It was pursued and stolen by Jason and the Argonauts with the help of Medea. It means: a goal that is highly desirable but difficult to achieve

A COLLECTION OF POPULAR ENGLISH PHRASES

Golden parachute - Firms began adopting golden parachute-style payout packages in the late 1970s. It is a large payment or other financial compensation guaranteed to a company executive should the executive be dismissed as a result of a merger, takeover or misconduct. Likewise, a **Golden handshake** is often a smaller incentive to leave. Lesser employees receive **Golden handcuffs** which is similar but antithetical. It means: a situation in which someone is offered a special inducement to stay such as a bonus to be awarded over a period of time. Velvet handcuffs means: an unenjoyable situation or condition often bounded or contained by financial restraints

Goldilocks - The source of this term comes from the children's story Goldilocks and the Three Bears. It is about a girl who wanted things to be a particular way or exactly right, saying, for example, that one bed was too hard, one too soft, and one just right. The term now means: a situation in which something is or must be exactly right without deviation. Additionally, the term goldilocks zone has been used in astronomy to designate a habitable zone around a star where life, as we know it, could exist on another planet. Goldilocks in general refers to: something that is just right

Gone to pot - One source of the phrase comes from the practice of when a chicken could no longer lay eggs or a cow to give milk, or when they have leftover meat; they took it to the pot or cooked it. The phrase is often interpreted to mean: something which is broken, defective or substandard

Gone with the wind - This saying was popularized by the title of the 1936 book by Margaret Mitchell and the subsequent 1939 movie starring Clark Cable. The title referred to the Southern slave-based lifestyle which was destroyed by the American Civil War. The phrase has migrated to mean: something that is gone forever, never to be seen again

Goody two shoes - The first to use the phrase was alleged to have been by Charles Cotton, in A Voyage to Ireland in Burlesque a 1694 poem. It applied to a bad-tempered housewife. Subsequently, it appears as the main character in a children's tale entitled: The History of Little Goody Two-Shoes, published around 1765 by John Newbery. The term now refers to: a female (presumably young) who tries to be as good and pure as humanly possible. **A boy scout** is sometimes used synonymously. **Vestal virgin, a goody- goody**

GOP - This is an acronym for the *Grand Old Party* and the term emerged around 1870 and is a moniker for the Republican Party. As the party of Lincoln and the victorious Union, it originally stood for the Gallant Old Party among other names that share the same acronym. Accused by the Democrats of wearing the blood of the martyred 16th president, this party was the dominant post-Civil War party which passed the Reconstruction amendments to the Constitution granting rights to former slaves. The GOP moniker, however, did not come into full prominence until later in the century and is still alive today. **The Party of Lincoln** is also sometimes used to designate the Republican Party

Gordian knot - In Greek and Roman mythology, the Gordian knot was an extremely complicated knot tied by Gordius. The knot came to symbolize a difficult problem that was almost impossible to solve. It was eventually solved by Alexander the Great simply by cutting it. The phrase is generally interpreted to mean: a problem for which it is very difficult to find a solution; an extremely difficult or involved problem. **To cut the Gordian knot**

Gorgon - In Greek mythology, a Gorgon was a monstrous feminine creature whose appearance would turn anyone who laid eyes upon it to stone. Each of three sisters, Stheno, Euryale, and Medusa, had snakes for hair and had the power to turn anyone who looked at them to stone. It is often used to describe: an ugly or repulsive woman

Got the shaft - This phrase seems to have its origin in the practice of burring people vertically on top of each other in Medieval cemeteries due to the scarcity of land. Like many other phrases, it migrated to other areas. In this case, to an aggressive male homosexual act performed on an unwilling recipient. The phrase was perhaps further popularized by a 1982 song by Jerry Reed entitled She got the goldmine. The song includes the lyrics: She got the gold mine! She got the gold mine! I got the shaft. I got the shaft. They split it right down the middle, And then they give her the better half. The term has come to mean. to be taken advantage of or exploited in a very unfair and sometimes hurtful manner. **I got shafted; got the wrong end of the stick**

Got to have enough green to cover your black - This is an expression that originated in the African American community. It means that if you have enough money, you can overcome racial discrimination to some degree. On the other hand, being poor and black is **a double-edged sword**

Government of the people, by the people and for the people - This phrase is habitually attributed to Abraham Lincoln's Gettysburg Address. However, it predates Lincoln and was also used by the English theologian John Wycliffe (1329- 1384) and the sentiment was first articulated by the Greek historian Thucydides as a quote from Pericles. Often quoted in many speeches, it embodies not only the belief of Lincoln but lies at the bedrock of a democratic system and America's creed of freedom, justice and equality for all

Grandfather clause - This is a term that emerged in the 1900s as a means of permitting whites to vote and prohibiting blacks from voting in Southern states. The descendants of those voting before 1867, in this case white folks, were permitted without meeting certain criteria targeted against the descendants of former slaves, thereby, circumventing the 15th Amendment of the Constitution. It is important to note, that during slavery, the South could count their slaves as three-fifths of a person thereby giving the South a political advantage over the North. So much so, that all the presidents that were elected president before Lincoln and served two terms came from the South. The term now means: a clause creating an exemption based on circumstances previously existing. **Grandfathered in; white privilege**

Grease monkey - The origin of this term appears to be the use of children during the Industrial Revolution in Great Britain when they were used in manufacturing facilities to grease machinery and other objects in the facility. They were given the moniker "monkey" because they were small and, in some cases, had to crawl into spaces too small for adult workers. The term now means: a mechanic or someone working in an area where grease or dirt gets over their hands and clothing or someone that likes to work on automobiles; bikes, etc.

Great divide - The exact origins of this term is unclear; however, the first known usage was in 1868. It is often used to describe: a significant point of division and at times death, the ultimate divide. The **Continental Divide,** a mountainous region of America, is sometimes referred to as the **Great Divide.** Related phrases are: **across the great divide; cross the Rubicon; point of no return**

Great minds think alike - This is an old English proverb. The common interpretation is: intelligent people normally share the same or similar perspective. **Poets(geniuses) are born not made**

Great white hope - This term is from the play of the same name about the life of the black boxer Jack Johnson, the first black heavyweight champion. There was also a 1970 movie of the same name about him that featured James Earl Jones. The term itself was a reference to the first white boxer that would defeat Johnson. Johnson's championship and flamboyant life style ignited the furry of many whites because like Muhammad Ali decades later, he refused to be **put in his place.** In 1912, he was convicted of violating the Mann Act for bringing his white girlfriend across state lines before their marriage and sentenced to prison. Some have said that the Rocky series is about a great white hope inspired by the fight between Chuck Wepner and Muhammad Ali. The phrase has since become a metaphor for the racism of Johnson's era and a white person, particularly in sports, that excels in a field dominated by blacks or other non-white races. It also serves as a reminder to many blacks, that every time they try to get ahead, racism raises its ugly head

Greatest thing since sliced bread - The origin of this phrase comes from the Wonder Bread Company that introduced sliced bread in the 1930s. Sliced bread is something that we take for granted today, but it was not always an option. Once it was introduced, people liked its convenience and it **sold like hot cakes.** It serves as a perfect example of something simple that **catches on fire.** The phrase frequently denotes: something new and innovative and of practical use. **The best thing since sliced bread. To know which side your bread is buttered (on)** is another bread idiom which means: to know who to be nice in order to gain favor or how to guarantee your success; to pick the right side

Green Beret - The source of this term is the green headgear that members of the army special forces adorned as part of their designation of an elite fighting force. Although special forces were part of previous wars, such distinction did not come into effect until 1953. It wasn't, however, until President Kennedy visited Fort Bragg North Carolina (home of the special forces) in 1962 that the wearing of the Green Beret became official. These soldiers are normally employed as the **tip of the spear** or the first to initiate combat. The main mission of the special forces is to train and lead unconventional warfare or to conduct clandestine operations. Today, the term is also applied to any elite person or group. *Crème de la crème*

Green with envy - This expression is from Shakespeare's Othello (Act III, Scene III). It means: to be jealous or envious of someone. **Green-eyed Monster** is from the same origin. The key to both phrases is the color green used by Shakespeare to denote jealousy. He also wrote in <u>As You like It</u> (Act V, Scene I): How bitter a thing it is to look into happiness through another man's eyes!

Greenhouse effect - While this effect has been known for quite some time, it was not coined until the turn of the 20th century. <u>Global warming</u> is related to this effect, and at the turn of the 21st century, it became a **political football** and a source of heated debates. The term means: the trapping of the sun's warmth in a planet's lower atmosphere due to the presence of certain gases in the atmosphere. Over time it causes temperatures to rise which impact the environment

<u>Gregorian Calendar</u> - This calendar was introduced by Pope Gregory XIII in 1582 to replace the Julian calendar. <u>The Julian Calendar</u> is the calendar introduced by Julius Caesar in 46 B.C. to replace the Roman calendar. In the Julian calendar a common year is defined to comprise 365 days, and every fourth year is a leap year comprising 366 days. The Gregorian calendar replaced the Julian calendar and is now used as the civil calendar in most countries. In the Gregorian calendar, every year that is exactly divisible by four is a leap year, except for centurial years, which must be exactly divisible by 400 to be leap years. Thus, 2000 was a leap year, but 1900 and 2100 are not leap years

<u>Gresham's Law</u> - This is an economic principle proposed by an English financier, Sir Thomas Gresham. It is a monetary principle stating that "bad money drives out good." Often interpreted that bad things drive out good things

Grey Eminence or *éminence grise* (French pronunciation) - It originally referred to François Leclerc du Tremblay, the right-hand man of Cardinal Richelieu who was a powerful man behind the scenes in France. It means: a powerful person that pulls the strings of the leader. **Power behind the throne**; kingmaker

Grim Reaper - The exact origin of this skeleton-like figure cloaked in a dark robe is uncertain, however. it is believed to have emerged in Europe during the Black (Death)Plague (1347-1351). This was a time of widespread death, that indiscriminately struck plebeians and aristocrats regardless of social or economic standing. In such a horrific milieu, with death knocking on everyone's door, it is easy to imagine such a grim symbol of death emerging to grimly reap the bodies of those inflicted with this uncurable illness. Today the term and the image is symbolic of death. **Angel of death** is similar and is associated with the **plagues of Egypt** as delineated in the biblical Book of Exodus. **Valley and the shadow of death**

Ground zero - The origin of this expression is the Trinity nuclear (atomic bomb) tests conducted in the deserts of New Mexico in 1945. Since that time, it has been applied to other situations most noted: the September 11, 2001 attacks on the World Trade Center Twin Towers in New York City. It now commonly designates: the starting point, center or base for some major event or activity. **Epicenter**

Groundhog Day - This term was originally used to designate February 2, when the groundhog, <u>Punxsutawney Phil</u>, is said to come out of its hole at the end of hibernation. February 2 is traditionally ascribed as **a cross quarter day,** which lies an equal distance between the **Winter solstice** and the **Spring equinox.** If the animal sees its shadow, i.e., if the weather is sunny, it is said to foreshadow six weeks more of winter weather. But recent reference is to the 1993 movie <u>Groundhog Day,</u> in which the central character finds himself repeatedly reliving the events of a particular Groundhog Day. It has migrated to mean: to repeat something over and over. In other words: **Deja vu all over again**, a phrase made famous by Yogi Berra

Grow (Grown) like Topsy - The source of this expression is from Harriet Beecher Stowe's Uncle Tom's Cabin. This book was extremely popular in the United States and Great Britain before the Civil War, so much so that Lincoln referred to Stowe as the lady that started the Civil War. Topsy is a minor character in the book. She is a little girl that declares herself to be grown. The common interpretation is: to grow very fast; to flourish and grow without tending. **Uncle Tom**

Gunfight at the O.K. corral - This expression takes its name from a famous wild west shootout between a gang of outlaws and law enforcement chiefly composed of the Earp brothers led by Wyatt Earp and assisted by Doc Holiday. The battle took place in Tombstone, Arizona Territory in 1881. Although etched in American folklore as an iconic shootout, the battle did not last that long. It was popularized by the 1957 movie of the same name starring Burt Lancaster as Wyatt Earp and Kirk Douglas as Doc Holiday. The term now means: a final showdown between two people or groups in which the dispute is **settled once and for all**; a shootout; wild wild west

Gung ho - In Chinese means "work together" and was later adopted by the United States Marine Corp during World War II. The phrase is often interpreted to mean: careless enthusiasm or eagerness, especially about taking part in fighting or warfare. **Up for the task**

Guru - This term comes from Hinduism and Buddhism. In these religions, it refers to a spiritual teacher, especially one who imparts initiation. A wise sage. The westernized version of the term means: one who is an acknowledged leader or chief authority; an expert or specialist at something: a person with specific knowledge or expertise. **Computer Guru**

Stands for:

Hell hath no fury like a woman scorned

IN A NUTSHELL

Hair of the dog that bit you - The ancient Romans believed that the best way to cure a wound of a dog bite was to wrap it in the hair of the dog. It now refers to: a remedy that contains a small amount of whatever caused the ailment

Halcyon - Is a bird identified with the kingfisher and held in ancient legend to nest at sea about the time of the winter solstice the shortest day of the year, about December 22 in the northern hemisphere, and to calm the waves. It now means: calm and peaceful; tranquil; prosperous; golden: as in **halcyon years. Vale of years; salad days**

Hale and hearty - This is an old saying that dates back to the mid-1800s. It some ways, it is redundant as both hale and hearty mean the same thing. The phrase is often interpreted to mean: to be in good or excellent health

Hallelujah - This is a derivative of a Hebrew word that literally means "to praise the Lord" that has worked its way into the English language and Christian circles. It is now used to mean: God be praised and is often used to express devotion to God or as a rejoicing expression or one of thankfulness. **Glory be to God**

Halloween - The origin of this occasion appears to be a Celtic tradition of *Samhain* that was adopted by the Romans after they conquered the region. The Celtics believed that on this day the dead would rise and walk among the living. It marked the summer/fall transition and just as the spring represented birth, the dying leaves of autumn and the coming of cold weather and shorter days represented death. It also coincided with the last harvest and **All Saints Eve.** It was in America during the 19th century that Halloween, as we know it today, emerged with its tradition of **trick or treat** and relics of the dead such as ghosts, zombies, tombstones and **the grim reaper** as well as **vampires**, werewolves, witches and pumpkins

Handle with kid gloves - The source of this saying comes from the fact that "kid gloves" were made from the skin of a young goat or lamb. Because they were softer and finer than leather gloves, they became a symbol of elegance, refinement and social status in the early 19th century. Since that time, such gloves have found other applications particularly when handling something delicate. The saying now means: to treat someone or something with extreme delicacy, care or gentleness. **Handle with care**

Hanky panky - The origin of this term dates to at least the mid-1800s and was first recorded in the London Charivari in 1841. Its first usage did not have a sexual connotation and referred to suspicious behavior or deceit. The term means: dubious or improper behavior whether sexual or otherwise. The feeling that something just isn't **kosher. Got some hanky panky going on**

Happy days are here again - The source of this expression is from a 1929 song of the same title. The song was also a part of a 1930 hit musical Chasing Rainbows. It was further popularized by Franklin Roosevelt and it was his 1932 campaign song. It was not the first song selected by his team. However, due to **unforeseen circumstances,** it was chosen, and **the rest is history**. The 1932 election was held amid the **Great Depression** and the song resonated because people were looking for those happy times of the Roaring Twenties again. The phrase is used to express the coming of good times and the end of discontent. **Now is the winter of our discontent**

A COLLECTION OF POPULAR ENGLISH PHRASES

Harbinger of spring - Originally from birds flying to a different location as a sign that spring was approaching. A harbinger is something that comes before and that shows what will follow in the future. The robin is a harbinger of spring- its presence means spring is coming soon. The saying is often taken to mean: a forewarning or foretelling of something. **Harbinger of things to come; John the Baptist figure**

Hard work never killed anyone, but why take the chance - The first part of this saying comes from an old proverb and the second part was added later and attributed to ventriloquist Edgar Bergen and his dummy "Charlie McCarthy who delivered the second part." It was made more famous when President Ronald Reagan used it in 1987. The saying is repeatedly interpreted to mean: even if something is believed by many to be a sure thing, why take the chance if you don't have to. Especially, if doing so can cause you some harm. History has proven that hard work can kill someone and **Karoshi** is a Japanese term that means death by overwork

Harmony in discord - The origin of this expression is attributed to the Roman writer Horace. It comes from his Epistles Book I. It basically means **to agree to disagree** and to part without anger or ill feelings toward each other

Harvest moon - This is the full moon that occurs around the autumn equinox, on or about September 22 in the northern hemisphere, and it rises at sunset and then will rise near sunset for several nights in a row because the difference is at a yearly minimum. It may almost seem as if there are full moons multiple nights in a row. This extra light is habitually used to do harvesting thus the name Harvest Moon. The **hunter's moon** is similar but occurs a month later and is used to designate a time to go hunting in preparation for winter. Similar expressions are: **blue moon; gibbous moon**

Have a monkey (gorilla) on your back – The origin of this expression is unclear. However, some believe that it is related to a mortgage and the expression to have a monkey on you roof meaning a burden. During the 1960s, having a monkey on your back was also used to denote a drug addiction. The expression now means: to bear some type of problem or burden either known or concealed. To stress out over something or to have a problem that you just can't get rid of. To have a gorilla on your back is to have a much larger problem or burden. **Get the monkey off your back**

Haymaker – The source of this term comes from the practice of making hay. Haymakers used a long sickle-like tool to cut hay. This tool required a broad sweeping swing to maximize its effectiveness. At the beginning of the 20th century, perhaps because of the emergence of boxing as a popular sport, this term became associated with a wide sweeping powerful punch. Similar boxing expressions are: **Roll with the punches** which means: to tolerate or endure something that is hard or difficult and **Knockout punch** which means: the final or decisive blow. Throwing haymakers

He that does not punish evil commands it to be done - This quote is accredited to Leonardo Da Vinci. A seminal figure of the Renaissance era and known for his famous paintings of the Mona Lisa and the Last Supper, he was more than just a painter; he was a polymath and a true **Renaissance man.** Da Vinci was also a foremost scientist, an engineer and a luminary that outlined devices that men of his era **dared to**

dream of. He dedicated himself to a wide range of subjects, ranging from anatomy and biology to mechanics and hydraulics. His many notebooks included studies of the human circulatory system as well as designs for airplanes and submarines. While there have been many people throughout history that have exhibited tremendous genius, it is rare to find a person that revealed genius on multiple levels. At the core of his genius, was his curiosity and relentless search for the truth. The phrase is construed to mean: evil is something that must be confronted and **if left unchecked** will **spread like a virus.** Over time, the failure to **deal with it** appropriately will destroy the integrity and **moral compass** of a society

He who excuses himself accuses himself - The source of this saying is unclear. But it is believed to have French origins in the phrase *qui s'excuse s'accuse.* The common usage is: to make an excuse that implies that you are guilty of the act

He who laughs last laughs longest - This is a saying that is believed to have its roots in Tudor England (1485-1603). However, several sources for its current form have been cited. It means: the person who has control of a situation in the end is most successful, even if other people had seemed originally to have an advantage. **Pyrrhic victory**

He who lives by the sword, dies by the sword - This phrase comes from the Bible (Matt. 26:52). It is frequently used to illustrate: those who commit violent acts must expect to suffer violence themselves. Similarly, Shakespeare wrote in Romeo and Juliet (Act II, Scene VI): **Violent delights have violent ends** and **the grave will fall in upon him who digs it,** have the same connotation. **You reap what you sow.**

He who must (shall) not be name - The source of this expression is from the fictional character Voldemort from the Harry Potter novels. Voldemort is often pronounced incorrectly, the t at the end is silent according to the author J.K. Rowling. The phrase is frequently used to denote a person known to two or more parties as the subject of the conversation whose name they will not mentioned out of secrecy

Hebbie-jebbies -This creepy term is attributed to William Morgan 'Billy' De Beck in his popular Barney Google strip in 1923. He was a famous American comic strip artist of the 1920's. There was even a dance by the same name that appeared during the **Roaring 20s.**The term has come to mean: something that makes you feel uncomfortable or even creepy, e.g., looking at worms **gives me the hebbie-jebbies**

Heir apparent - The source of this term is the succession of power among monarchs. Often the first-born male is the first in line to the inheritance or to rise to power. This system has been in place for millenniums and was the natural succession in antiquity. In recent times however the term has generally applied to: the next in line or a person who seems certain to take the place of someone else. **Pick of the mantle**

Helicopter parent - This is a term that emerged with the millennial generation and alludes to the parental guidance of some parents. It is so named because, like helicopters, these parents hover over every aspect of their children's lives particularly when it comes to education. In more recent times, however, another phenomenon has emerged known as **Bulldozer (snowplow) parents.** In addition to hovering over their children, these parents try to remove every obstacle that lies before them in a painstaking effort to assure their success

Hell hath no fury like a woman scorned - This expression is from a 1697 play by the English playwright William Congreve's The Mourning Bride. It means: there is nothing as bad as the revenge from a woman that has been hurt or rejected

Hell in a handbasket - The origin of this phrase is uncertain, however, many believe it dates to the French Revolution -- renowned for its mass execution of aristocrats and felons. The principle tool of execution was the guillotine in which the decapitated heads were collected in baskets. Since the victims were assumed to be bad people and thus sentenced to hell, their heads represented their impending destiny. **Hence, going to hell in a handbasket.** Others contend it is of American origins and still others believe that it predates America and the French Revolution. Notwithstanding, the phrase has migrated to mean. to be rapidly worsening or on a path toward disaster

Hell or high water - This phrase seems to have its origin in the cattle drives of the old West (United States). Cattle had to be moved in all types of weather and terrain. It was therefore common to move cattle in extremely hot or inclement weather and through high water, streams, rivers etc. The expression evolved to mean: to accomplish a task despite the difficulties that may occur. **Come hell or high water; no matter what; bring it on**

Hellenism - The Greek name for Greece after the time of the Homeric poems was Hellas. The word Greece comes from the Latin word *Graec'a* from the Roman name of the first tribe in Hellas that they met. Thus, Hellenism, Hellenic, Hellenophile and other words related to Greek culture are derivatives of the word Hellas. More specifically, Hellenism relates to the period between the death of Alexander the Great up until the inception of the Roman Empire during the reign of Augustus Caesar

Herculean effort - So named after the Greek hero Hercules who was known for his strength. It means: a great or near impossible effort; requiring great strength or effort; **Herculean task;** twelve labors of Hercules; **shirt of Nessus. Hercules's choice** is the reward of toil in preference to pleasure

Herding cats – The exact origins of this expression is unknown or unclear. Yet, it has frequently been used in the technical field. The expression has come to refer to a difficult or impossible task. A futile attempt to organize a group

High on the hog - The source of this expression is the practice of eating choice or the best cuts of meat. Those that could afford to do so were affluent, and thus **living high on the hog.** The term therefore has migrated to mean: to live the good life or **the life of Riley**

Hip, Hip, Hooray - The origin of this phrase is unclear, although some believe that it has anti-Semitic roots in the middle-age Latin battle-cry "*Hieroslyma est perdita'*, which means "Jerusalem is fallen" or "Jerusalem is lost." It is believed that it was also used in the Hep Hep riots against the Jews in Germany during 1819. In this case, it's not entirely known when, this now anti-Semitic rallying cry of "hep hep" became "hip hip" and the response cry of "hooray" became traditional. It should be noted that the aforementioned anti-Semitic links to the phrase have come under scrutiny in recent years with some challenges to its etymology. Today, it is used as a cheer to express joy or approval of somebody or something

Hip hop - The origin of this term comes from a type of music and culture first developed in New York City's African American community in the late seventies. Often used synonymously with Rap, it initially consisted of break dancing and Disc Jockeys (DJs) where rappers rapped to music as opposed to singers and bands. In the 1980s and 1990s, Hip hop became more prevalent, migrating out of the inner cities into the mainstream eventually becoming accepted around the world. However, Hip hop has been criticized for its vulgar language and explicit use of **the N word**. Like musical genres that preceded it such as Ragtime, Swing, Rock and Roll and Soul, Hip hop has also defined an era. **Old school** is a term that emerged during the Hip hop era and usually refers to something that predates Hip hop or something that is old fashion or traditional

Hippie - The origin of this term appears to be the term **hip** which was used first in the African American community in the early 20th century. In the post-World War II years, hip was associated with music and the term hippie emerged. During the 1960s and early 1970s, hippie was linked with a culture and lifestyle somewhat characterized by rock music, experimentation with drugs, and a burgeoning counterculture movement (particularly among white youth) that was antiestablishment and against the Vietnam War. It is now associated with the 1960s era and the aforementioned culture. **Hippie movement**

History doesn't repeat itself, but it rhymes - This quote is often attributed to Mark Twain however, where, when or if he even said it is **a matter of conjecture.** There is no doubt the quote is Twainish in nature, but others have said things with the same connotation, e.g., Karl Marx: History repeats itself, first as tragedy, second as farce. It could therefore be one of those cases where a quotation over time is attributed to a famous person who "could" have said it. Nonetheless it means: **the past is prologue** and although things do not manifest in the same way, there are stark similarities between what has happen and what will happen

Hit them where they ain't - The saying has been attributed to the baseball player named "Wee" Willie Keeler, although it has been used to refer to military operations and other sports. It has since come to mean: to attack something in a vacant, unsuspecting or weak area. A somewhat similar saying was echoed by Confederate General Nathan Bedford Forrest; "**Git thar fustest with the most moistest** meaning:" get there first(the open spot) with the most men

Hitch your wagon to [a star] - This popular phrase is attributed to the American writer Ralph Waldo Emerson. He was a leader of the **transcendentalist movement** in the mid-19th century and a liberal voice during the American Civil War. Along with Henry Thoreau, Herman Melville, Nathaniel Hawthorne, Edgar Allen Poe and Walt Whitman; he helped to define America's literary voice in a manner similar to Vergil,

A COLLECTION OF POPULAR ENGLISH PHRASES

Horace and Ovid during the Roman Augustan era. The quintessential optimist, his phrase means: to reach for your goals and to be inspired to be the best you can be; to reach your potential and to discover your purpose in life. **A man's reach should exceed his grasp, or what's a heaven for?**

Hobson's choice - This phrase is said to have had its roots in the name of one Thomas Hobson (1544-1631), at Cambridge, England, who kept a livery stable and required every customer to take either the horse nearest the stable door or none at all. Additionally, anytime you ask someone for a favor, you are, in effect, asking for a Hobson's choice. It now means: a choice between what is being offered or nothing at all. In a similar manner, Henry Ford once said: **You can have any color of a car you want, as long as it is black; beggars can't be choosers**

Hocus pocus - A possible origin of this phrase is from a play by the English playwright and contemporary of Shakespeare, Ben Johnson, entitled: Magnetic Lady in which a juggler *Hokos-Pokos* performed. It was uttered by performers during a trick. It has migrated to mean: a trick itself or meaningless talk or activity, often designed to draw attention away from and disguise what is actually happening. **Smoke and mirrors**

Hogan's goat - The origin of this expression is unclear. Some believe that it originated from a story about a goat farmer by the name of Hogan who raised a horrible goat that was not only ugly but had a terrible smell. Others believe that it is a reference to a newspaper comic strip entitled: Hogan's Alley. It was also the title of a 1965 play by William Alfred. Nonetheless, it now means: something that is completely messed up; something that is faulty

Hold your feet to the fire - This phrase appears to have its origins in the days of the Spanish Inquisition when the inquisitor was allowed to hold suspected subject's feet to the fire to extract a confession. **The Spanish Inquisition** was a court established in Roman Catholic Spain in 1478 at the direction of Ferdinand II of Aragon and Isabella I of Castile. It was originally directed against converts from Judaism and Islam (often accusing them of practicing their original religion in secret) but later also against Protestants and heretics. It operated overtly with great cruelty until suppressed in the early 19th century. The popular interpretation is: to subject someone to strong and painful persuasion or to hold someone accountable. **Spanish Inquisition** is often used a term to describe or suggest persecution, i.e., **a witch-hunt**

Holier than thou - The source of this term is the Bible (Isaiah 65:5). It means: characterized by an attitude of moral superiority. Other phrases with a similar connotation are: **High and mighty; on your high horse. The chosen few** originally referred to the Jews but has since been used by some in a similar way

Holocaust - The word "Holocaust," comes from the Greek words "holos" (whole) and "kaustos" (burned) and was historically used to describe a sacrificial offering burned on an altar. However, since the end of World War II, the word has taken on a different connotation. It is now associated with the horrific mass murder of some six million European Jews (the so-called **Final Solution**), as well as many Gypsies and homosexuals by German Nazis during the Second World War. Although this term is so often associated with the Jewish Holocaust that took place with the rise of Adolf Hitler, roughly between 1933 and 1945, there have been several holocausts in history. For example, many may argue that the mass genocide committed by Christopher Columbus and the Spanish Conquistadors could easily be described as a holocaust of a different name. Columbus was not just some blameless mariner; he became Viceroy and Governor of the Indies and directly ruled the territories from 1494 to 1500. He created work camps, established slavery and worked thousands of "Indians" to death in gold mines. History bears testimony to the fact that the crimes committed over several decades by the Spanish based exploratory triumvirate of Columbus, Cortes and Pizzaro against the indigenous people of the Americas and Caribbean, was a holocaust of unprecedented proportions. Through conquest and disease, they killed millions of people, took over their land and made those that survived slaves. Yet most history books paint them not as demons but as saints. Moreover, many contend that their activities were conducted under the shadow of a hideous cross casted by the avarice of the Roman Catholic Church. We so often view the Columbian Exchange from a **flora and fauna** perspective. We therefore seldom stop and think that the capitol of the United States lies in a district named after a person many believe to be a mass murder of whom Americans openly celebrate once a year. Even if his landing led to subsequent prosperity for people of European descent, it was **the opening salvo** of slavery, subjugation and exploitation for the rest of the world. If we are true to our **better angels**, we should **call a spade a spade** and **not turn a blind eye** to history or condemn one holocaust while singing praises to another. Shakespeare once wrote "the evil that men do lives on after them. The good is often buried with their bones." Yet, we can clearly see in the case of the aforementioned triumvirate, the opposite is true. The term holocaust now refers to: the mass slaughter of people, a genocide and does not specify any race, ethnic group or religion although these factors are often the causes of such devastation. **Nuclear holocaust**

Holy Grail - The origin of this saying, lies in the medieval legend of the cup or platter used by Jesus at the Last Supper, and in which Joseph of Arimathea received Christ's blood at the Cross. Quests for it was undertaken by medieval knights and are described in versions of the Arthurian legends written from the early 13th century and onward. It has evolved to mean: a thing that is being earnestly pursued or sought after; something that you want very much but that is very hard to get or achieve. In search of the Holy Grail, **golden fleece; round table**

Holy of Holies - The source of this saying is from the inner chamber of the sanctuary in the Jewish Temple in Jerusalem. It is separated by a veil from the outer chamber. It was reserved for the presence of God and could be entered only by the High Priest on the Day of Atonement. It frequently refers to: a very sacred or special place or sanctuary; the most sacred place. **The inner sanctum**

Holy Toledo - The origin of this term is uncertain; however, it is a widespread belief that it comes from Toledo, Spain (the namesake of Toledo, Ohio). After its liberation from the Moors in 1085, this Spanish city became a bastion of Christian faith known for its numerous churches (it contains one of the largest European Gothic churches). So much so that it earned the moniker: The Holy City of Toledo. Yet, others contend that it is more recent (20th century) and localized to Toledo, Ohio. Nonetheless, it was made popular by the Oakland, CA sportscaster Bill King, it is often used today as an explanation of astonishment or surprise. **Holy Cow** is used similarly

A COLLECTION OF POPULAR ENGLISH PHRASES

Home James (and don't spare the horses) - The origin of this phrase dates from the mid-1800s. It is said that it originated from the name of Queen Victoria's carriage driver, however, this is uncertain. Nonetheless, it has gained popularity and there was also a 1934 song with the same phrase as a title: "Home, James, and don't spare the horses" by Fred Hillebrand and recorded by Elsie Carlisle. It is now used as: an amusing command for a driver to take you home or someplace else without delay. **Step on it** means the same thing but refers to an automobile

Homer sometimes nods - This saying is from the Latin writer, Horace, a Roman poet of the **Augustan period** and his full name was Quintus Horatius Flaccus. He was a well-known satirist and literary critic. It has evolved to mean: even someone who is the best at what they do can turn in a subpar performance; even the most gifted person occasionally makes mistakes. **To err is human, to forgive is divine**

Homey don't play that - This is a saying made popular on the hit show In Living Color and repeatedly uttered by Homey D. Clown played by Damon Wayans. The show was popular in the early 1990s. It has since been used as a response when someone doesn't go along with something that someone else is proposing or doing

Homina, homina, homina - This expression was made famous by the Honeymooners television series of the 1950s. It was uttered by Ralph Kramden played by Jackie Gleason whenever his wife, Alice, caught him in a bind, a lie or when she demanded an explanation. It is often used to express shock, befuddlement, or general speechlessness. **Cat got your tongue**

Hood or cowl does not make the monk - This is a Latin proverb and is regularly interpreted to mean: it is a person's way of life not what he or she professes that really matters. **Clothes do not make the man; can't judge a book by its cover**

Hoodwink - This term dates b ack to the 16th century. Wink had been used before as a means of closing one's eyes, and it was joined by hood. It was used by thieves and others and became a part of the initiation process of the Freemasons. It has migrated to mean: to deceive someone, fool or **pull the wool over someone's eyes**. It is often used with the synonym, **bamboozled.** Jonathan Swift (1667-1745) disliked bamboozled and considered it to be one of the words that corrupted the English language. **I've been hoodwinked, bamboozled**

Hooker - This term, used in America, is normally credited to the American Civil War General "Fighting Joe" Hooker who reportedly supplied prostitutes to his men. But the term itself was used in Europe before the American Civil War. The usage in Europe referred to streetwalkers hooking men like fish and reeling them in. Nevertheless, it means: a prostitute, **Lady of the night** and **Call girl** are also used to refer to a prostitute

Hope springs eternal - The origin of this expression is from an essay by Alexander Pope entitled: An Essay on Man. "Hope springs eternal in the human breast; Man, never Is, but always to be blest. The soul, uneasy, and confin'd from home, Rests and expatiates in a life to come." Hope is one of those precious gifts that a benevolent Creator has bestowed upon humanity. It is the fresh stream that runs through the wilderness of our despair and flows into the river of our wishes and our dreams. Amid the evils of the world, hope was the last thing to emerge from **Pandora's box**. The phrase is repeatedly interpreted to mean: people should always **hope for the best**, even in the face of overwhelming adversity and despair. The phrase is often said when a person continues to hope that something better or good will happen, although at the time the odds are that it will not happen

Horatius at the bridge - The source of this phrase is from the Roman legend of the hero Horatius Cocles who defended the Romans against the Etruscans, which led to the establishment of the Roman Republic and ultimately to the Roman Empire. The English poet Thomas Babington McAulay immortalized this legend in his poem entitled: Horatius at the Bridge. The term has migrated to mean: to stand up against formidable odds and to successfully endure

Horse feathers (horsefeathers) - The origin of this term comes from the American comic strip artist William Morgan Billy De Beck popularized in the 1920s. Since only birds have feathers, the term has no practical meaning and is therefore utter nonsense. There was a 1932 movie starring the renowned Marx Brothers of the same name. The term has migrated to mean: nonsense; baloney; something that is completely fictional

Hot dog - The source of this term seems to have come from Frankfurt, Germany a town famous for its seasoned sausage that often bears its name, franks of frankfurter. The term itself is of American origin and was popularized around the turn of the 20th century. Some attribute its initial popularity to the Columbian Exposition in Chicago in 1893, others to baseball in Saint Louis and still others to Coney Island in New York. Nonetheless, the term has become synonymous with American baseball. It is also used to denote: enthusiasm, excitement or delight as in **hot diggity dog**. It is also used to denote a person the loves to show off

Houston, we have a problem - The foundation of this phrase is from the Apollo 13 mission, April 11, 1970, in which there was a problem aboard the spacecraft. Although the astronauts did not reach the moon, their ability **to think outside of the box** and to return to earth safely serves as an exemplary example of how to **overcome adversity** and how to **think outside of the box**. It is now used humorously to report any kind of problem. **Failure is not an option; splash down; lift off**

How long? Not long, because no lie can live forever - The source of this phrase is from a speech given by Martin Luther King Jr., entitled: Our God is Marching On given on March 25, 1965. It was delivered during the apex of the Civil Rights era, when many urged Dr. King not to move to fast and to be patient. Instead, he proceeded **with all deliberate speed** which alienated his Southern opponents that vowed to let the **Jim Crow** system of "**separate but equal**" stand. The phrase is repeatedly interpreted to mean: the truth will eventually prevail over any lie because all lies ultimately converge on the truth. Similar phrases include: **to speak truth to power; he that does not punish evil commands it to be done**

How the mighty have fallen - The source of this saying is from the Bible. (2 Samuel 1:25). It is now used in a humorous way, to mock someone who was once on top and has now lost their position, prestige or dignity. Oh, how the mighty have fallen; be nice to those you meet on the way up because you will meet them on the way down

Hypocrisy is the compliment vice pays to virtue - This saying is accredited to the French author, Francois La Rochefoucau. It is often interpreted as: a person realizes that virtue is the preferred option to vice and therefore hypocritically disguises his or her vice as virtue. **Imitation is the sincerest form of flattery**

I

Stands for:

If you want to make God laugh,
tell him about your plans

IN A NUTSHELL

I am the state - This phrase is ascribed to <u>Louis XIV of France.</u> He ruled France for over 70 years from 1643 to 1715. Known as the Sun King, he was the quintessential Absolute Ruler. Whether he actually said: *"'L'etat c'est moi'"* (I am the state) has been disputed. The phrase has been associated with a dictator or someone that has absolute power or a person who thinks that all things revolve around him

I am (yam) what I am (yam) - This saying is from the popular <u>Popeye the Sailor cartoon series</u> and was frequently quoted by him. It is often used to express a person's individualism or to justify one's actions. **Accept me as I am; when someone shows you who they are, believe them the first time.** Another popular line from this cartoon series was uttered by Wimpy the character with an insatiable appetite for hamburgers: **I will gladly pay you on Tuesday for a hamburger today.** It infers that the person will keep asking for something but will never pay you in full for it and moreover, that you will never see him/her on Tuesday

I came, I saw, I conquered, (<u>veni, vidi, vici</u>**)** - This saying is attributed to Julius Caesar when addressing the senate in Rome after conquering King Pharnaces II of Pontus in the battle of Zela in 47 BCE. Taken literally, in modern times, this phrase is often used after a victory

I don't know the key to success, but I know the key to failure is trying to please everybody - This quote is credited to the comedian and actor Bill Cosby. It is regularly interpreted to mean: there is no **secret formula** or guarantee for success because of **the law of unintended consequences** and **the luck of the draw.** Furthermore, **you cannot please all of the people all of the time,** regardless how much you try. All you can do is to try to **do your best** and **let the chips fall where they may.** When you try to please others, at the expense of **being true to yourself,** you are embarking on **the slippery slope** toward failure and not success. **"They who are all things to their neighbors cease to be anything to themselves"**

I have not yet begun to fight - These were the words of <u>John Paul Jones</u> often called the Father of the American Navy. It was a response to a request to surrender to the British Navy during the Revolutionary War. He and his crew then captured the British ship. His own ship, the <u>Bonhomme Richard</u> later sank. Like: **Don't give up the ship, Remember the Alamo** and **Custer's last stand,** this expression is often used as an American rallying cry. It is also used colloquially to demonstrate that the fight is not over, although it appears to be lost

I pity the fool - This phrase was a title of a 1961 song by Bobby Blue Bland. However, the catchphrase was made popular by the actor Mr. T who played the villain in the Rocky movie series and B.A. Baracus on the hit T.V. series the A Team. Although <u>uttered by Mr. T</u> on several occasions, it was not spoken by B.A. on the A Team **contrary to popular opinion.** The phrase has come to mean: to have empathy (however real) for someone who is about to make a big mistake or to partake in a great or daring endeavor. **See ya wouldn't wanna be ya**

I rather be here than in Philadelphia - This quote is supposedly from a joke made by comedian/actor <u>W.C. Fields</u> and refers to the fact that he rather be in his grave than in his hometown of Philadelphia. Fields

118

was notorious for making jokes about "the city of brotherly love." Contrary to the belief of many, this is not written on his tombstone and he never said it. When asked about his epitaph, he said he rather be living in Philadelphia. Neither saying is written on his tombstone. The misquoted phrase is often used by a person to indicate that although they do not like the place that they are currently in, they rather be there than in a place that they dread even more

I shall return - This saying is habitually attributed to General Douglas MacArthur after he was forced by the Japanese to retreat from the Philippine Islands during World War II. He later returned to drive the Japanese from the Philippines. Consequently, it has come to be a saying that someone uses when they are forced to leave but vows to come back. To quote the Cyborg in the Terminator movie: **I'll be back!**

I think, therefore I am - The origin of this phrase "*Cogito, ergo sum*" (I think, therefore I am) is the French philosopher and mathematician Rene' Descartes. Subsequently, it has been interpreted as: thinking is the one thing that cannot be faked. It is the one way that individuals know they exist. **To live is to think**

I was adored once too - The origin of this phrase is William Shakespeare's Twelfth Night (Act II, Scene III). It speaks to the transient and fleeting nature of life. We all have our **fifteen minutes of fame**, a time when we **basked in the sun** and were **the apple of someone's eye**. However, **nothing lasts forever**, not even time because forever is the absence of time. Yet it is the passing of time that makes us **yearn for yesterday** and the time when we were once young, adored and perhaps loved. We often forget the elderly, the old folks that made our lives possible. Sadly, we often view them as a burden forgetting that we were once a burden to them. We put them **out to pasture**, in adult daycare centers or homes forgetting that if we are lucky, the fate of old age will also beset us. The phrase could be interpreted to mean: to nostalgically reflect with the benefit of retrospect and **the remembrance of things past**

I would never join a club that would have me as a member - This saying is credited to Groucho Marx of the famous Marx Brothers. It has been interpreted many ways. One way is that the people in the club that are accepting him do not exercise good judgment or character, therefore, the club is not worthy of joining. Another interpretation is to think that you are inferior and that any club that would accept you as a member is also inferior. Yet another interpretation is based on your independence and dislike for clubs in general

I'll be a monkey's uncle - The root of this popular phrase is from the famous Tennessee Scopes trial in 1925. This trial centered around the battle between evolution and creationism and the right to teach the Theory of Evolution in school. Dubbed the Monkey Trial, the state was represented by William Jennings Bryan a national figure in his day. At the time, many Americans had never heard of the possibility that humans and apes shared a common ancestry and the current theory suggested that humans evolved from apes. Scopes was found guilty of teaching evolution in violation of Tennessee laws. At the core of the outrage was that such a theory was being taught in school instead of creationism. It is currently used to show surprise or astonishment. **Survival of the fittest**

IN A NUTSHELL

I'm mad as hell, and I'm not going to take it anymore! - While this phrase may have been used before, it was popularized by the longtime news anchor Howard Beale in the 1975 film classic Network. It was one of those phrases that resonated and became a catchphrase for many frustrations that defined the post-1960s era. It is currently used as a statement of extreme frustration or disappointment. **To be mad as hell**

I'm sick and tired of being sick and tired - The origin of this quotation is from a speech given by Fannie Lou Hamer on August 22, 1964. In this speech, the poor Mississippi sharecropper and Civil Rights activist described a severe beating that she received in a Mississippi jailhouse in 1963. The phrase speaks for itself, and it is often used to express the utter frustration with a given situation. **To be mad as hell**

Identity theft - This term has been around since the 1960s, but its use was limited until the 1990s with the emergence of the Internet and personal computers. It is the process in which **bad actors** steal the identity of a person using information acquired over the Internet or other means. Several measures have been implemented in recent times to curtail such fraud, including the safeguarding of pertinent information such as Social Security numbers and credit information

If God did not exist, it would be necessary to invent Him - This statement is attributed to the French author and revolutionary Voltaire. In many ways, it is indicative of the Enlightenment period when European and American intelligentsia began to ask questions about the nature and existence of God. **The Enlightenment**, also known as the Age of Reason, featured intellectuals, such as the Englishman Francis Bacon, the Frenchman Rene Descartes, the Jewish-Dutchman, Baruch Spinoza, the German Immanuel Kant and the American Benjamin Franklin. Many of which espoused deist and esoteric ideas. The founding of the United States took place during this period. It was also an age of scientific enlightenment the produced both Galileo and Sir Isaac Newton. It was a period when scientific discovery unveiled some of the natural phenomena that was once deemed supernatural and the absoluteness and infallibility of various religious doctrines were **called into question**. The statement begs the question: Did God make Man in His image or did Man make God, replete with various forms of anthropomorphism, in his image?

If the mountain will not come to Muhammad, then Muhammad must go to the mountain - This phrase originates from the story of Muhammad, as retold by the English statesman, scientist and philosopher, Francis Bacon, in Essays, 1625. The phrase is regularly taken to mean: if a person's plan or endeavor falters, he or she should submit to an alternative. Put more succinctly, if a person won't come to you, you will have to go to that person

If we don't hang together, we will hang separately - This saying is ascribed to Ben Franklin and referred to the members of the Continental Congress that signed the Declaration of Independence. The common usage is: when embarking on any endeavor, it is important that the group functions as one entity and not as individuals. **All for one and one for all; in unity there is strength**

If you are not part of the solution, you are part of the problem - This saying is repeatedly attributed to Eldridge Cleaver, the former Black Panther leader and author of Soul on Ice. Later in his life he converted to Mormonism. It literally means what it says: **you can't have it both ways**, you are either on one side or the other

A COLLECTION OF POPULAR ENGLISH PHRASES

If you are not sitting at the table, you are on the menu - The source of this popular saying is somewhat obscure. Many have attributed it to the American politician and Senator from Wyoming, Michael Enzi. It now means: in order to bring about change, or to have a voice, you must be part of the decision-making process or else you are part of a group subjected to those that make critical decisions that impact your life

If you build it, they will come - This quote is credited to the 1989 film Field of Dreams where the chief character hears a voice say: "If you built it he will come," which is interpreted to build a baseball field on his farm. At some point, the he in the phrase was changed to they. The he is Shoeless Joe Jackson. The quote is often interpreted to mean: if you build or develop something, people will come to use and perhaps pay for it. **Say it ain't so Joe**

If you can't stand the heat, get out of the kitchen - This saying is often attributed to the 33rd president of the United States Harry S Truman (no period after the S) who assumed the office after the death of Franklin D. Roosevelt. It means: don't take on a job, if you can't handle the responsibilities and pressure of the position. **The buck stops here; don't bite off more than you can chew**

If you don't stand for something, [you will fall for anything] - The true source of this quote is unclear. Some have attributed it to the British writer Alexander Hamilton (not to be confused with the Founding Father). Others to Malcolm X and still others to Martin Luther King Jr. Several music groups have also used the phrase including the Rolling Stones. Nonetheless, it has come to mean: at some point, you **have to take a stand and be true to yourself** and exhibit some type of **moral compass** by **speaking truth to power**. Those that take no position and **give silent consent** are in effect, **part of the problem and not the solution**

If you give a mouse a cookie, he will ask for a glass of milk - The source of this saying is from the popular children's book, If You Give a Mouse a Cookie. The book reads: If you give a mouse a cookie; he's going to ask for a glass of milk. When you give him the milk, he'll probably ask you for a straw. When he's finished, he'll ask for a napkin, etc., etc... It means people are never satisfied with what they have, they always seem to want more. **Give an inch and they will take a mile**

If you lie down with dogs, you will get up with fleas - This popular saying is often attributed to the American sage Ben Franklin. It simply means: if you associate with people **of dubious character** or **bad behavior**, you are likely to pick up similar habits or conduct. **As thick as thieves; people judge you by the company you keep**

If you want peace, prepare for war (*Si vis pacem para bellum*) - The origin of this phrase is from Thucydides', The History of the Peloponnesian War. Versions of this quote was used by George Washington (1790) and Teddy Roosevelt (1897). It has proven to be a peacetime aphorism. The common usage is: the best way to avoid war is to be prepared for it

If you want to make God laugh, tell him about your plans - This saying is credited to Woody Allen. So often in life, we make the greatest plans. But **the future is promised to no one** and **the best laid plans of mice and men often go astray**. The phrase means that only God knows the future and **what is wisdom to**

man is foolishness to God. We must be forever mindful that **God has a sense of humor** and his favorite tool for rendering justice is irony. Similarly, Aristotle once wrote: **the gods too are fond of a joke** and Shakespeare wrote in <u>A Midsummer Night's Dream</u> (Act III, Scene II): **Lord, what fools these mortals be**

Ignorance is bliss - This expression is from a poem by the <u>English poet Thomas Gray</u> <u>Ode on a Distant Prospect of Eton College</u>. The expression is regularly interpreted to mean: if you don't know about something, you do not worry about it. It is "**not ignorance but the ignorance of ignorance that is the death of knowledge.**" **What you don't know can't hurt you**

Ignorance of the law is no excuse - This is an axiom of the law profession and was bequeathed to us from Roman law: *ignorantia juris non excusat*. Similar sentiments are echoed in the Bible. It means: all citizens should know the law and pleading ignorance of the law does not mean that one is innocent of a crime

Imitatio Dei - This is a Latin term that has migrated to the English language. It literally means "the imitation of God." The term has its roots in Genesis 1:27, wherein "God created man in his own image." It is a religious concept by which man finds virtue or salvation in his actions by attempting to imitate God. The creation of man in the image of God, which acknowledges a resemblance between man and his Creator, is found in several world religions. Some have also stated that there is a dark side to *Imitatio Dei* as in man's desire to be or play God

Imitation is the sincerest form of flattery - The source of this expression, although others have used similar expressions, is from the English writer <u>Charles Caleb Colton</u>, in <u>Lacon: or, Many things in few words</u>, 1820. It is frequently interpreted to mean: copying someone or something is an implicit way of paying them a compliment. **Play the sedulous ape; monkey see monkey do**

Immaculate conception - The foundation of this saying comes from the doctrine that God preserved the <u>Virgin Mary</u> (Madonna)from the taint of original sin from the moment she was conceived. It was defined as a dogma of the Roman Catholic Church in 1854. It is sometimes incorrectly allocated to the birth of Jesus, but it is assigned to his mother Mary. It therefore refers to something that is great, miraculous, or pure. On a similar note, <u>Black Madonnas</u> are also revered in the Catholic Church as sacred although their relationship to Mary remains obscure

In a nutshell - This idiom was supposedly originally a reference to a copy of the "<u>Iliad</u>," mentioned by Pliny, which was so small it could fit into the shell of a nut. Shakespeare also used this phrase in <u>Hamlet</u> (Act II, Scene II) "O God, I could be bounded <u>in a nutshell</u> and count myself a king of infinite space." It has migrated to mean: in the fewest possible words or ways

In like Flynn - The origin of this saying is believed to have come from the macho exploits of actor <u>Errol Flynn</u> who had a reputation for being quite the **Ladies Man**. The phrase is habitually interpreted to mean: to reach or achieve a particular goal or desire. **I'm in like Flynn**

A COLLECTION OF POPULAR ENGLISH PHRASES

In situ - This is a Latin term that has worked its way into the English language. It means: in its original place; in the natural or original position, place or habitat. **Ex situ** means the opposite: outside, off site, or away from the natural location

In spades - The root of this expression appears to be the card game of Bridge in which Spades is the highest-ranking suit of cards making the **Ace of Spades** the highest card. Hence, the expression **Ace of Spades**. The phrase: *in spades* migrated to general usage in the early 20th century. It generally means: in abundance or to the extreme. **Multiply in spades. In droves** is similar and means: in large numbers

In the arms of Morpheus - In Greek mythology, Morpheus was the god of dreams. The term appears in The Metamorphose by Ovid and is the name of a character in the movie The Matrix. The phrase means: a restful state; to be asleep or not aware, to be in a dreamland. Ex: "After a tireless day, he was soon in the arms of Morpheus". The narcotic morphine was named after Morpheus

In the black/red - The origin of this term seems to have been the use of red ink to denote debt and black to denote otherwise. The phrase is regularly interpreted to mean: in the black- you are making money, In the red- you're losing money

In the buff - The source of this expression is believed to be a type of protective coating worn by English soldiers up until the 17th century. In this regard, *to be in the buff* meant to be wearing the leather type protection. Because of its yellowish flesh-like color it was equated with human skin. Over time the expression migrated to mean to be naked. **In your birthday suit** is similar in connotation

In the country of the blind a one-eyed man is king - This phrase originates from a Latin proverb. It has come to mean: the person with the least disability wins or that a person who is not particularly capable can attain a powerful position if the people around him or her are even less capable. **He who has only one eye must guard it well**

In wine there is truth - This saying: *'In Vino Veritas'* is ascribed to the Roman philosopher Pliny the elder as well as the Greek poet Alcaeus. This idea is common in a number of different languages. It has migrated to mean that when people consume alcoholic beverages, they tend to disclose their true feelings

Indian summer - The source of this term is unknown but is believed to have been derived from contact with Native Americans when Europeans arrived on the North American continent. It means: a period of warm weather in Autumn similar to a summer month

Insanity is doing the same thing over and over and expecting a different result – This famous quote is normally attributed to Albert Einstein. However, recently some doubt has been raised as to if he actually said it. Nonetheless, the phrase is often interpreted to mean: it is futile to repeat something that does not work over and over again if the output remains the same

IN A NUTSHELL

Intelligent design - The origin of this term lies in the <u>debate between Creationism and Science</u> **over** the origins of life and the cosmos. In fact, many scientists view Intelligent Design (ID) as a euphemism for Creationism. These scientists evoke the <u>Anthropic Principle</u> which means: what we observe must be restricted by the conditions necessary for our presence as observers. Notwithstanding, intelligent design is defined as: the theory that life, or the universe, cannot have arisen by chance and was designed and created by some intelligent entity. **Science doesn't make eyes but spectacles**

Intelligence quotient (IQ) - This term was coined by psychologist William Stern in 1912. It is a series of test designed to measure a person's intelligence relative to others with the mean set around 100 and high IQ above 125 and low IQ around 70. It is estimated that only 2 percent of the population is above 130. It is often used as an indicator of academic success. In recent times, however, **IQ tests** have come under scrutiny as a barometer of intelligence with other factors such as **emotional Intelligence** considered as part of a person's overall cognitive ability

Iron Curtain - This phrase was coined by Winston Churchill in a post-World War II speech given in the United States. The source of this term, however, is an ideological and geographical line drawn between the Soviet Union (and its satellite states) and the rest of free Europe after World War II; perhaps best exemplified by **the Berlin Wall**. A relic of the **Cold War**, it existed from 1945 until 1990 when the Soviet Union was divided into several independent states. The term has since migrated to mean: any barrier that restricts or prohibits the free exchange of ideas, information or speech. **Behind the Iron Curtain**

Is the Pope Catholic? - The origin of this popular saying is unknown and is analogous to another rhetorical question **does a bear crap in the woods?** It is a question with an obvious answer and is often used to indicate that something should be considered obvious. Something that you **can take to the bank; a sure bet**. On a similar note, **more Catholic than the Pope** is a comparable phrase and means: to be extremely devoted to something

It ain't over until the fat lady sings - This saying appears to have its roots in female opera soprano singers that sung at the end of the opera thus bringing it to a close. It became popular as a commentary to many sporting events where the loss of one team or person appears to be certain. The **Yogism** utter by the baseball player Yogi Berra: **It ain't over till it's over** means the same thing. It has come to mean: the final outcome cannot be determined until the event or situation is completed. Similar phrases include: **anything can happen; Murphy's law; never say never**

It is an affront to treat falsehood with complaisance - This expression is ascribed to Thomas Paine from his <u>Age of Reason.</u> Quite often, we **turn a blind eye** to the truth in favor of what we want to believe or what is expedient. Yet truth is not blind, **nor will the facts cease to exist because we ignore them**. Often, our **silence gives consent** to things that we know to be untrue, and we embrace evil in the face of good and drown the truth in the waters of immorality

It is better to be feared than loved, [if you cannot be both] - This quote is from the **time-honored** classic the <u>Prince</u> by Niccolò Machiavelli. Machiavelli was an observer of his time and the <u>Prince</u> was his **magnum**

opus. It is not only a book about politics, but about human nature. Both fear and love are emotions, and time has proven that it is easier to control people by fear than by love. Love is something that must be inspired from within. **On the other hand**, fear is something that can be induced by the outside and is therefore much less subjective. Fear invokes pain and love evokes happiness. **Love is a many splendored thing** but there is nothing splendored about fear. Thus, you cannot make someone love you, but you can make them fear you. In order to love someone, you must know something about them that is enduring and merits love and is therefore near and **dear to the heart**. But fear can strike at a distance and is easily summoned by power. Consequently, those that have power can always depend on fear to control people and even make them pretend that they love them. Aristotle once said: "no one loves the man whom he fears" **The carrot or the stick**

It is better to wear out than to rust out - This popular expression is frequently attributed to several people. However, there is a difference between someone that popularized a phrase and someone that originated it. The earliest use of this expression was made by the theologian George Whitfield in the early 1700s and most people ascribed it to him. So often in life, particularly in retirement, we look forward to those days when we can **kick back and relax** and **live the life of Riley**. However, remaining active and pursuing a goal or purpose is an important part of life. For example, if we do not use our legs, atrophy will soon set in. The saying has come to mean: it is better to remain active and not succumb to a life of idleness and boredom. Similar phrases include: **give it all you got**; **leave it all on the field**; **if you don't use it, you'll lose it**

It is never too late to be what you might have been - This quote is attributed to the English writer Mary Ann Evans known as George Eliot. She took this male pseudonym because of the gender prejudice of her day. A seminal writer of the Victorian era, she was in many ways an iconoclast particularly when it came to Christianity and associated with free thinkers such as Gerald Massey who may have served as a model for her book Felix Holt, the Radical. It is an old adage that **you are never to old to learn** and this adage is analogous to Elliot's quote. Learning is the conduit that is often used to improve our current condition. So often in life, we give up and say I cannot **do this or that** or defer our hopes and dreams to another day. But if we have the courage and the fortitude to abandon our **comfort zone** and climb the mountain of our potential; we may **reinvent ourselves** and discover our true purpose in life. It is one thing to cherish your dreams when you are asleep, it is quite another to live your dreams while you are awake

It only hurts when I laugh - The origin of this phrase appears to be a book entitled: Memoirs of a Camp-Follower written by Philip Gosse in 1934. He served in the Royal Army Medical Corps during World War I. It is an example of **gallous humor**, because the soldier that responded was in serious condition. It is now used sarcastically in dire situations or when a person wants to indicate the seriousness of a situation. Walt Kelly once said in his comic strip Pogo: **Don't take life so serious, son ... it ain't no how permanent. Laugh to keep from crying**

It takes a village to raise a child - This proverb often attributed to African and sometimes Native American sources is widely used in reference to the raising of our youth. Popularized by the title of one of Hillary Rodham Clinton's books: It Takes a Village, The phrase is regularly interpreted to mean: the community or the nation shares the burden of raising the youth of the next generation and in helping to augment and foster the positive family values that are constantly reinforced in the home

It takes two to tango - This saying was made popular as a result of a 1952 song by Al Hoffman and Dick Manning named Takes Two to Tango. It has migrated to mean: both parties involved in a situation or argument are responsible for it

It was the best of times, it was the worst of times - This expression is from Charles Dickens', A Tale of Two Cities. Other notable works include Oliver Twist (1837–38), A Christmas Carol (1843), David Copperfield (1850), and Great Expectations (1860–61). This phrase is often used to describe life during interesting times or life in general. **May you live in interesting times**

It's not the crime, it's the coverup - This expression comes from the 1972 **Watergate** break-in of the Democratic National Committee Headquarters that took place on June 17, 1972. In itself, the crime was not so bad and Nixon went on to win 49 out of 50 states in November of the same year. Yet, it was the coverup of the crime and the abuse of power that finally forced him to resign. Consequently, this expression is often used, when a small crime is committed and attempts to coverup that crime overwhelm the crime itself. Similar phrases include: **Watergate; follow the money; the cure (remedy) is worse than the disease**

Ivy League - This is the name of a group of schools located in the Northeastern United States. They are, eight colleges: Brown, Columbia, Cornell, Dartmouth, Harvard, Penn, Princeton and Yale. As a group they are among the oldest and most prestigious schools in America, Harvard is the oldest school and was formed in 1636. Because of its record of excellence and prestige, the term, *Ivy League,* is occasionally ascribed to excellence or an elite group

Stands for:

Just when I thought I was out, they pull me back in

IN A NUTSHELL

Jack of all trades [and a master of none] - The origin of this phrase is somewhat obscure, although it has been around for ages. Jack seams to refer to a general person and it appears that Jack of all trades came first and the master of none was added. Greater still, is the belief that this phrase ended with: "but oftentimes better than a master of one." Nonetheless, it has migrated to mean: a person who can do many different types of work but who is not necessarily very good at any of them. However, **A jack of all trades** means: a person who is adept at many kinds of work

Jacob's Ladder - This phrase originates from the Bible (Genesis 28:10-22). It was a ladder to heaven, described in Jacob's dream during his flight from his brother Esau. The phrase is often interpreted to mean: a gateway to heaven

Jacobin - The Jacobins were the most radical and ruthless of the political groups formed in the wake of the French Revolution. In association with Robespierre, they instituted the Terror of 1793–4. The term has migrated to mean: any extreme or radical political person, group or cabal

Jailbait (jail bait) - The origin of this term is uncertain however, the term is derived from the fact that having sexual intercourse with a person below the age of consent is illegal and thus can land a participating adult behind bars. The term often denotes, a person, that is sexually attractive but is below the age of consent often pursued by an adult at risk of being sent to prison for **statutory rape; carnal knowledge**

Jam session - The origin of this term is unclear. Nevertheless, it appears to have its roots in the Jazz culture and has migrated to other forms of music particularly Rock. For example, there was a 1942 short film of the same name, directed by Josef Berne, starring Duke Ellington and his orchestra performing C Jam Blues. It was archived by the U.S. Library of Congress in 2001 because of its historical significance to America's only indigenous artform known as Jazz. Jam session now denotes: a gathering of musician for the purpose of making improvised music, as practice, for fun, or to experiment with new songs, techniques or personnel

Jaundiced eye - This term has its origin in a medical condition in which there is a yellowing of the white part of the eye. The term is defined as: to exhibit envy, prejudice or hostility toward another person. To view someone in a cynical or negative way. **To look with a jaundiced eye; green-eyed monster; green with envy**

Janus-faced - This term is derived from the Roman god Janus who had two faces; one looking forward the other looking backwards. It is defined as: having two sharply contrasting aspects or characteristics; or marked by deliberate deceptiveness especially by pretending one set of feelings and acting under the influence of another. **Two-faced**

Je ne sais quoi - This is a French term "I don't know what" that has worked its way into the English language. Typically viewed as being sort of **bourgeois** in its usage. It means: a quality that cannot be described or named easily; a pleasant quality that is hard to describe. **It has that certain Je ne sais quoi**

A COLLECTION OF POPULAR ENGLISH PHRASES

Jekyll and Hyde - The source of this expression is from a book by <u>Robert Louis Stevenson</u> entitled: <u>The Strange Case of Dr. Jekyll and Mr. Hyde</u> (1886). It is currently used to describe a person or thing that alternately displays two different sides to their character or nature. **Two sides of the same coin**; Janus-faced

Jewish American Princess (JAP) - Sometimes called **Jewish Princess**, it is a stereotypical term alleged to have originated from within the post-World War II Jewish community in the Northeastern United States. It is used to describe a certain female type of Jewish ancestry. <u>Frank Zappa wrote a controversial song</u> using the term in the late 1970s. It is often used disparaging and considered Anti-Semitic or misogynistic by many. It should therefore be used with caution or not at all. It has come to designate a young, upper-middle-class Jewish woman thought of as being materialistic, spoiled, self-indulgent, etc. **Spoiled brat**; daddy's little girl

Jim Crow - This term originated from Thomas Dartmouth Rice, a white man, born in New York City in 1808. He devoted himself to the theater and in the early 1830s, he began performing the act that would make him renowned. He painted his face black and did a song and dance he claimed were inspired by a slave he saw. The act was called <u>"Jump, Jim Crow"</u> (or "Jumping Jim Crow"). It became a pejorative term used to refer to a black person and also racial segregation imposed by whites on blacks known as the <u>Jim Crow era</u>. Similarly, the term **the color line** came into use primarily after American slavery and during the era of <u>Separate but Equal, Jim Crow and Black Codes.</u> W.E.B. DuBois once prophesized that the 20th century would be about the **color line.** These expressions all converge on the discrimination imposed on African Americans from slavery up until the Civil Rights movement. They illustrate the social and legal barriers that separated and limited interactions between people of different races, particularly between blacks and whites in America

Jitterbug - The origin of this term comes from a dance that was popular in America (particularly in the African American community) during the late 1930s and early 1940s. The term now refers to: a young or immature or inexperienced person. **Little jitterbug**

John (Jane) Doe - The name John Doe and Richard Roe were used in English law years ago to describe unknown people (Jane if it is a female). It now describes: an unknown or anonymous person. **Every Tom, Dick and Harry** is similar and means: any and every kind of person, any random person regardless of race, religion, gender or any other distinguishing factors. **John Q. Public** is used similarly

John Hancock - This term was named after a signer of the Declaration of Independence that signed with a bold and distinctive signature. It now refers to a person's signature. **Put your John Hancock here.** Sometimes, **John Henry** {which became popular fifty years after the Declaration of Independence} is also used to designate a signature

John the Baptist figure - <u>John the Baptist</u> is a key figure in the biblical stories of Jesus of Nazareth. According to the Gospels, John's role was to announce the coming of Jesus. Hence, a John the Baptist figure is someone that serves as a mentor (and possibly announce or anoint) someone greater than himself

Jotunheim - One of the nine worlds from Norse mythology and was the homeland of the Frost Giants, Storm Giants, and Mountain Giants. It has migrated to mean: the outer world or land of giants

Judge a person by the content of their character and not the color of their skin - This popular saying is credited to Dr. Martin Luther King Jr.. It was uttered during his seminal I have a dream speech which routinely ranks among the top speeches in history. It states: "I have a dream that my four little children will one day live in a nation where they will not be judged by the color of their skin but by the content of their character." As a result of European domination in the post-Columbian era, **a totem pole** of races emerged in accordance with skin color with whites on the top and blacks on the bottom. Dr. King's statement struck at the core of this racist ideology. It was an appeal to our humanity and the true ideals of which America was founded as stated in its Declaration of Independence that **all men were created equal with certain unalienable rights**. The saying plainly means what it says and strikes at the core of what it means to be human. **The golden rule**

Jump the broom - There are two popular legends associated with this phrase. Some believe that this marriage tradition started in England in the 1700s and migrated to the United States. Yet, others contend that it has its roots in West Africa. In the latter case, it symbolized the sweeping away of past wrongdoing and starting the marriage clean and anew. This phrase was somewhat popularized by the 1977 television miniseries Roots in which black slaves jumped the broom when they were married. Of course, it was difficult for slaves to have official marriages because they were owned by their masters. The term is often used to designate: a marriage or a wedding ceremony, particularly one that is unofficial. **Let's jump the broom** means let's get married. Related terms are: **shack up; common law marriage**

Jungle fever - The source of this term is unknown but was popularized in Spike Lee's movie of the same name. It describes the attraction between a white person and a black person based at first on race; especially a black male and a white female. **Once you go black you never go back**

Just when I thought I was out, they pull me back in - This phrase was made famous by the 1990 film, The Godfather Part III, part of the popular Godfather series about life in the Mafia. It was spoken by the character Michael Corleone played by Al Pacino. Michael did not want to become part of the Mafia, but was **overwhelmed by circumstances** that brought him in. Unfortunately, once in, there was nothing he could do to get away from the sins he committed including killing his brother, Fredo. The phrase is repeatedly interpreted to mean: once you get deeply involved in something or someone, it is very difficult to leave or **put it in your rear-view mirror; in too deep**

Justice [too long] delayed is justice denied - The exact source of this phrase is uncertain. Notwithstanding, it was around as a legal statement in one form or another before it was popularized by Dr. Martin Luther King as part of his Letter from Birmingham Jail. The letter was written on April 16, 1963 just a few months before his seminal I have a Dream speech given in August of that year. It was his response to the procrastination of desegregation in the South. The phrase can be taken literally, however, it is often interpreted to mean that justice should be swift and dispensed **with all deliberate speed**

Justice is blind - The origin of this exact phrase is unknown. However, the concept has been around since antiquity. For example, the Greek goddess of justice, Themis, is mentioned in Homer. She was the representation of order and justice, who summoned the assembly of the gods. She is often depicted as the "Lady of Justice" with a sword in one hand and scales of justice in the other. The scales that she holds represent the impartiality with which justice is served and the sword signifies the power that is held by those making the decision. She is depicted wearing a long graceful robe, and sometimes with a blindfold over her eyes. Justice was a central topic of the Greek philosopher Socrates and it was used in a Socratic dialogue of Plato in which he contemplates "What is justice." In Plato's, The Republic, Socrates wants to define justice, and Plato ends The Republic by defining justice as the greatest good. But justice, although blind at times, is truly **in the eyes of the beholder**. The phrase means what it literally says. In some cases, justice is not rendered, though the truth is apparent and the facts undisputable. The Bible says (Amos 5:24) "let justice roll down like waters and righteousness like an ever-flowing stream." **Let the punishment match the offense(crime)**

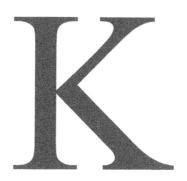

Stands for:

Keep your eyes on the prize

IN A NUTSHELL

Kabuki theater – This term originated from traditional Japanese popular drama performed with highly stylized singing and dancing and known for its elaborate makeup. It has since been used to describe an extremely stylized political show where the roles of the actors (for example Senators) are as predefined as the outcome

Kafkaesque - This term comes from the author Franz Kafka,(1883-1924) and refers to the style with which he wrote his books. Although some of his writings were published prior to his death, Kafka's work became popular during World War II. He is widely regarded as one of the major figures of 20th century literature. Like Virgil and others before him, he had requested that his writings be burned before his death. However, after his death his work gained worldwide acclaim. The Metamorphosis is among his most popular works. Indicative of Kafka's other writings, this book expressed the feeling of anxiety and the mood of despair and alienation that many felt in war plagued Europe which eventually led to the **Theatre of the Absurd** movement in the post war years. **In this regard**, Kafka was a luminary and perhaps a **harbinger of things to come** particularly of the experiences of his fellow Jews in his native land. The term designates: something that is marked by surreal distortion and often a sense of impending danger or doom

Kaleidoscope - This term comes from the optical device containing mirrors and pieces of colored glass or paper, whose reflections create sets of altering patterns that are observable through an eyehole when the tube is rotated. It has since become a metaphor for a continually shifting pattern, scene or a succession of changing phases or actions. **Chameleon**

Kamikaze - The origin of this term comes from a member of the Japanese air attack at the end of World War II that was assigned to launch a suicide bombing attack on American naval vessels by crashing into a ship. It literally means "divine wind." It has migrated to mean: to have or to show little regard for one's safety or personal welfare. A suicidal mission or attack **Kamikaze attack. Suicide bomber** is similar in connotation

Kangaroo court - The exact origin of this term is unknown but appears to be related to Australia the home of the kangaroo or someone with a knowledge of this indigenous animal known for hopping around. It dates back to the mid-1800s and is now used to designate: an informal or itinerant court held by a group to try someone, especially without due process, good evidence and in most cases with a predetermined sense of guilt of a crime. **Star Chamber**

Karma - The origin of this term comes from Hinduism and Buddhism. In these religions, it is the totality of a person's actions in this and previous states of existence, that is viewed as deciding their fate in future existences. Consistent with this view, life is nothing more than a contiguous and cascaded existence in which our current existence is the result of previous states of existence. The westernized version of this term has come to mean: an aura, or spirit that infuses or vitalizes someone or something. An atmosphere, feeling or vibe that one feels or detects. **Good karma; bad karma; guru; nirvana**

A COLLECTION OF POPULAR ENGLISH PHRASES

Keep it simple, stupid (KISS) Principle**)** - This expression has its origin in a principle first espoused by the U.S. Navy in the early 1960s. It states that simplicity should be the key factor in designs. It has since migrated to other fields as a fundamental principle most noted are products and services such as advertising. **Occman's razor**

Keep them barefoot and pregnant (and in the kitchen) - The origin of this saying is unclear. In its current usage, it is derogatory toward women because it means: to restrict them to being dependent and sometimes at the service of men. **Cold feet** is another foot metaphor that means: to hesitate or to lose your nerve, momentum or confidence

Keep your eyes on the prize - This saying has its origin in an old hymn that was adapted and sung during the Civil Rights era. The origin of the hymn is unknown. The hymn has gone by other names including: Hold On, Gospel Plow and Keep Your Hand on the Plow. It was adapted in the 1950s to have lyrics that concurred with the Civil Rights movement. "Keep your eyes on the prize, hold on; Freedom's name is mighty sweet; And soon we're gonna meet; Keep your eyes on the prize, hold on." Forever linked to the Civil Rights era and etched in the minds of those that sung and marched to it, it has since found other applications centering on remaining focus on a goal and **keeping the big picture in mind,** particularly during times of adversity and strife. **We shall overcome**

Keep your friends close and your enemies closer - This saying was made famous by the movie The Godfather Part II but has also been ascribed to Sun Tzu and Machiavelli's The Prince. The saying is repeatedly used to mean: although you keep your friends close, you really need to know what your enemies are doing at all times. **False friends are worse than open enemies.** Sun Tzu said in The Art of War: **Know thy self, know thy enemy. A thousand battles, a thousand victories**

Keep your powder dry - This saying is habitually attributed to Oliver Cromwell, the English military and political leader and later Lord Protector of the Commonwealth. It is a reference to keeping gunpower dry so that it could be fired at any time. It has migrated to mean: to be prepared and ready for a given situation. **Praise the Lord and pass the ammunition; locked and loaded**

Keeping up with the Joneses - This phrase originates from a comic strip by Arthur R. Momand. It means to try and maintain the living standard of your neighbors

Kettle of fish - The origin of this phrase is the English custom of catching fish from the river and cooking them in kettles alongside of the river as part of a group gathering. Often used as part of the phrase: **a pretty or fine kettle of fish** it means: an awkward or difficult situation. But when it is used as: **a different or another kettle of fish**, it has a dissimilar connotation and means: to be completely different from someone or something

Keystone cops (kops) - The source of this term comes from a silent movie made in the 1920s that depicted incompetent policemen. The term has since come to refer to any group that is considered completely incompetent or inept. **The inmates are running the asylum**

Kicked the bucket - The source of this phrase is unclear. Some believe that it comes from standing on a bucket before hanging, then kicking the bucket to hang. The other is from a device called a "bucket" used in the slaughter of animals. In any case, it now means: to die

Kike - The origin of this term is uncertain. Some believe that it originated as an intra-Jewish term that differentiated German Jews from those of Eastern European descent. However, the more popular belief is that it originated from the Yiddish word for circle (kikel). More specifically, from Jewish immigrants entering the United States at the turn of the 20th century that could not sign their names and refused to use the traditionally X because they saw it as a sign of Christianity. Consequently, they signed their names with a circle instead. Nonetheless, it has come to be used as a derogatory term aimed at Jews and hence should not be used when referring to them as a race, religion or people

Kilroy was here - The exact origin of this phrase is unclear. However, in December 1946 the New York Times credited James J. Kilroy, a welding inspector at the Bethlehem Steel shipyard in Quincy, Massachusetts, with starting the craze but he was not the originator of the cartoon that accompanied the phrase. During World War II, it was popularized by American servicemen fighting mainly in Europe but also in the Pacific. It was the graffiti of a baldheaded man looking over a wall and it became symbolic of an American having been there. In many ways, the symbol of Kilroy became **a calling card** for the daring American serviceman. Consequently, during World War II, it was everywhere including on the walls of an exclusive restroom for the Big Three in Potsdam, Germany, in July 1945. It was reported that Stalin emerged from the restroom demanding to know who was Kilroy. Though the phrase is somewhat obsolete or archaic, it is still sometimes used to designate that an anonymous person was at a particular location

Kill two birds with one stone - The origin of this term is unclear. Yet, the concept has been around since antiquity. Some have linked it to the legend of Daedalus' and his son's escape from the Cretan labyrinth. Others to the Latin writer Ovid but these references are unclear. However, it appears to be a hunting metaphor that revolves around a slingshot or the throwing of a stone to kill birds. Nonetheless, this popular idiom now means: to solve two problems or to achieve two goals at once; to accomplish two tasks with only one effort. **Double play**

Kindred (spirit) souls - This is an old English term and probably goes back as far as the word kindred which dates back to the Middle Ages. It has migrated to mean: when the spirits of two humans seem to automatically connect. An individual with the same beliefs, attitudes or feelings as oneself. **Brother from another mother**

Kingmaker - The first time this term appears to have been used, at least in the English language, was Richard Neville the 16th Earl of Warwick. He was a key figure in deposing the English king Henry VI during the War of the Roses. The War of the Roses (1455-1485) was a series of civil wars fought between the House of York (the white rose), and the House of Lancaster (the red rose) and eventually ended by the victory of Henry VII over Richard III which established the Tudor dynasty. Kingmaker is very similar to **Grey**

A COLLECTION OF POPULAR ENGLISH PHRASES

Eminence or *éminence grise*. It means: a person who brings leaders to power through the exercise of political or economic influence. **Power behind the throne; puppet master; king me**

King's ransom - This term seems to have its origin in the feudal system of Europe where nobles were often kidnapped and held for money. One of the largest cases of a king being held for a ransom was Richard I also known as Richard the Lionheart. He was the King of England and the leader of the Third Crusade that started in 1190. Like most of the crusades, it was unsuccessful. One of the most famous of all the Knights of Templar, Richard left **the Holy Land** in October 1192 after securing a truce with the Muslim leader Saladin. On his way back, bad weather forced him ashore and he was imprisoned by Duke Leopold of Austria. He was later handed over to German emperor Henry VI, who ransomed him for the huge sum of 150,000 marks. He spent a year and a half in captivity. During his absence, his younger brother Prince John schemed against him and did not want to pay the ransom. After the ransom was paid in 1194, Richard was crowned for the second time. He died five years later of a battle wound and Prince John became king. Because of the fame attached to Richard, it is highly probable that his ransom is the event that popularized this term. The phrase is regularly interpreted to mean: a very large sum of money. So popular was his fame that a person who is brave and forthright is often called **a Richard the Lionheart. Robin Hood; crusade; Magna Carta; to cost an arm and a leg**

Kitchen cabinet - The source of this presidential term was the presidency of Andrew Jackson. Skeptical of the Washington establishment, Jackson appointed men to his cabinet from outside the Washington circle and his cabinet became known as the "Kitchen cabinet." Over the decades, the term evolved to mean close associates of the president that are not part of his official cabinet. An unofficial group of influential advisers

Klu Klux Klan (KKK) - This is the name of a white supremacist hate organization founded in 1866 with the paramount purpose of suppressing the rights and terrorizing's the lives of newly freed black slaves. It consisted of confederate veterans and other Southerners that elected the famed Civil War general Nathan Bedford Forest as its first grand wizard. It derived its name from the Greek word "kyklos," meaning circle. Within five years, it had extended into all Southern states and became an effective means of resisting Reconstruction and Republican Party initiatives. Even though this organization denounced immigrants, Catholics and Jews; its animus, vitriol and terrorism was primarily aimed at black people. Sometimes referred to as "the Invisible Empire", this organization **under the banners** of **the Lost Cause** and the Southern ethos, conducted cross burning events, staged rallies, parades and marches throughout the United States including several in the nation's capital. However, their main tool of intimidation was lynching. In fact, from 1882-1968, 3,446 blacks were lynched mainly in the South. While this organization had a tendency **to wax and wane**, at its peak in the 1920s its membership exceeded 4 million people nationwide. Although it is known as an organization, the terms: Klan, Klansman or Klan territory also refer: to any person, group or territory that espouses the beliefs, attitudes or actions associated with the behavior of the KKK. **Grandfather clause; The Lost Cause; redneck**

Knights-errant - The origin of this term is from a knight, often portrayed in medieval romances, who wanders in search of adventures to prove his chivalry. It The term now means: a person given to adventurous or quixotic conduct. **Don Quixote**

Knock on wood - The origin of this expression is unknown or unclear. However, it is a superstition that appears around the globe. For example, the British use the term "touch wood" instead of knock on wood. Some believe that people knocked on wood to chase away evil spirits. Some Christians have often linked the practice to the wood of the cross from Christ's crucifixion. Nonetheless, it has come to be used as a way of hoping for good luck or **to ward off** bad luck. <u>Knock on wood was a popular song by Eddie Floyd</u>

Know the ropes - Many may think that the origin of this phrase comes from boxing and every good boxer knows how to use the ropes to his advantage. But the true source of this expression comes from sailing. Ropes, are important in sailing because the sails required for navigation are often controlled by ropes. It can be interpreted to mean: to have experience or knowledge of the proper procedures; to know your way around or to be knowledgeable about the details or routines of a situation or task

Know them by their fruits - This phrase is from the Bible (Matt. 7:16) "<u>Ye shall know them by their fruits. Do men gather grapes of thorns, or figs of thistles?</u>" This saying is from the New Testament and the Sermon on the Mount. The Sermon on the Mount is a collection of many popular sayings of Jesus and imparts much wisdom. This particular saying has been expressed several ways. For example: **actions speak louder than words; when someone shows you who they are, believe them the first time; people are who they are; a man is known by the company he keeps**

Knowledge is power - This is a translation of the Latin phrase *scientia potential est* and Sir Francis Bacon is often credited with popularizing it. The original source of this axiom, however, is probably the Bible (Proverbs 24:5). Similar phrases or connotations were used by Shakespeare (a contemporary of Bacon) and by Thomas Jefferson. Although the literal interpretation is apparent, most people in history that are admired are also knowledgeable. Perhaps because knowledge also serves as a gateway to wisdom and understanding. Therefore, a leader or a person in a position of power who refuses to learn is one that is **doomed to fail**

Known unknowns - This phrase is attributed to Donald Rumsfeld, US Secretary of Defense under George W. Bush. Although he may have been the one that popularized it, the phrase was in existence before Rumsfeld. The phrase is frequently taken to mean: There are known knowns. These are things we know that we know. There are known unknowns. **That is to say**, there are things that we know we don't know. But there are also unknown unknowns. There are things we don't know we don't know"

Knucklehead - This term appears to have its origin in a mechanical device that was used in the mid-1800s. In the mid-1900s, it was popularized by R.F. Knucklehead the fictional poster character of World War II. It later migrated into its current usage which means: a stupid or ignorant person. Similar terms are **wise guy; dunce; jerk; egghead**

A COLLECTION OF POPULAR ENGLISH PHRASES

Kosher - This is a term that has its origin in the Jewish faith. In Hebrew it means: fit; proper; according to Jewish law and often applies to food and other dietary traditions such as not eating pork or shellfish. It therefore has a legal and a moral connotation. This term now denotes: something that is legitimate, genuine or proper; **the real deal**. Something that has gone through some type of validation process or certification. **It is not (ain't) kosher. It doesn't pass the smoke (smell) test**

Kryptonite - This term originated from the 1939 Superman comic strip. It was a radioactive fragment from the planet Krypton and was created by fusion during the explosion that destroyed the planet. This radioactive element interfered with the internal electromagnetic waves that gave **Superman** his powers. It means: something that is a weakness or threat to a person or group. Similar terms are: **an Achilles' heel; a chink in the armor.** In addition, superman has also been used as a metaphor for a man that has greater strength, intellect, stamina, etc. than the average man. Nietzsche used the term superman as a philosophical construct and the term was also popularized by a play written by George Bernard Shaw entitled: Man and Superman (1903)

Stands for:

Like two ships passing in the night

IN A NUTSHELL

Labor of love - The source of this saying is from the Bible (Hebrews 6:10 and Thessalonians 1:3). It means: something demanding or difficult done for pleasure rather than money

Lafayette, we are here - This saying *"Lafayette, nous ici!"* (Lafayette, we are here!) is a saying uttered by Americans in France during World War I to show the French their gratitude, for them in general and Lafayette in particular, for their help in the American Revolutionary War. From that day to this, a ceremony is held at Lafayette's tomb and a new American flag is placed there every Fourth of July. It has been used by others in incidents when one person offers their help to someone who helped them in the past or to a friend in need

Laissez-faire - This is a French term for "allow to do" that has become part of the English lexicon. The origin of its use is uncertain, but folklore suggests that it is derived from the answer Jean-Baptiste Colbert, controller general of finance under King Louis XIV of France gave in regard to financial affairs. It means: a policy or attitude of letting things take their own course, without interfering; the less the government is involved in the economy, the better off it is. **Hands off**

Lame duck - This term originally comes from the London Stock Market and referred to investors who were unable to pay their debts. It now means several things: first, an elected official or group continuing in office. Second, in the period between an election defeat and a successor's assumption of office. Third and perhaps the most used: a president who is completing a term of office and chooses not to run or is ineligible to run for reelection. Anyone or anything soon to be supplanted by another. And lastly, a person or thing that is disabled, ineffective, or inefficient

Lamourette's kiss - This eponym is named after Abbe Lamourette who temporarily united different factions of the French government in 1792. It now means: a temporary reconciliation or resolution to a problem

Land of Goshen - This expression comes from the Bible (Genesis 45:10) and was the fertile land promised to the Israelites in Egypt. It was a district in Egypt where Jacob and his family settled, and in which they remained until the Exodus. After Moses led the Jews out of Egypt (Goshen) and Joshua finally led them into Canaan, they named a portion of the Promised Land, Goshen. Thus, it has a duel and **bittersweet** meaning. "And thou shalt dwell in the land of Goshen, and thou shalt be near unto me, thou, and thy children, and thy children's children, and thy flocks, and thy herds, and all that thou hast." It now denotes: any land of plenty or a place of peace and freedom from fear and evil: (the Canaanite Goshen}. And in another sense, it is used as an exclamation of astonishment and sometimes frustration. Similar phrases include: **The Promised Land; a utopia; land of milk and honey**

Land of nod - This expression originated from the Bible (Genesis 4:16) and was a region to the east of Eden to which Cain went after he had killed Abel. "And Cain went out from the presence of the Lord, and dwelt in the land of Nod, on the east of Eden." It now refers to an imaginary land of sleep, hence the term nodding. **In the arms of Morpheus**

142

A COLLECTION OF POPULAR ENGLISH PHRASES

Last full measure of devotion - The origin of this phrase comes from the *Gettysburg Address* given by Abraham Lincoln on November 19, 1863. The address was a funeral oration given to consecrate the Confederate and Union soldiers that died at that site in the most devastating battle ever fought in the Western Hemisphere. The phrase is frequently used to honor Americans that have given their lives for their country, their community or some noble cause often **above and beyond the call of duty**. Similar expressions include: **gave the ultimate sacrifice**; **now he belongs to the ages**

Last infirmity of noble minds - This expression is from a quote by the English writer John Milton. The expression commonly denotes: the quest for fame, being the last vice of a noble person as he grows old

Last Supper - The origin of this expression is the last meal that Jesus shared with his disciples before his arrest and subsequent crucifixion. As an idiom, it is frequently used as a last meal or gathering before a significant event such as someone leaving. **Last cigarette**

Laugh, and the world laughs with you; Weep, and you weep alone - The origin of this saying comes from a poem by Ella Wheeler Wilcox entitled: Solitude published in 1883. It was inspired by a young weeping woman dressed in black that Wilcox met on a train as she was on her way to the governor's inaugural ball. The ending of this saying is somewhat similar but opposite to an old Latin phrase: weep and the world weeps with you. The phrase has come to generally mean: we all wish that life is always **a bed of roses** but unfortunately it is not. Therefore, when you are happy, people will want to be around you and share your joy, but when you are sad or depressed, people will try to avoid you. People generally gravitate to a smile and run away from a frown. Yet, we tend to forget that **a frown is nothing more than a smile turned upside down**. In life, there are some roads that we walk with friends and others that we walk with family. However, there is always that lonely road of despair that we must find the courage and sometimes the dignity to walk alone in the presence, and under the guidance, of **a merciful and benevolent God**

Lead, follow, or get out of the way - This quote has been attributed to several people such as Thomas Paine and the Canadian educator Lawrence J. Peters. The expression can be interpreted to mean: If you cannot lead, then you should follow or not participate

Left-handed compliment - This expression has its origins in morganatic marriages (marriage between two people of unequal social standings, e.g., a royal person to a commoner) of the Middle Ages. It is a compliment with two meanings, one of which is unflattering to the receiver the other a criticism or insult disguised as a compliment. **Left hand marriage, sinister**

Lèse-majesté' - This term is of Latin origin and migrated to French, and it has also become part of the English language. It literally means "an affront to the majesty or royal authority." Although it is still used in this sense, it has taken on the context of an affront or offence to a person or an institution

Let the chips fall where they may - This expression has its origin in the chopping of wood. In this case, the woodcutter should pay attention to the cutting of wood and not the small chips that result from such activity. The phrase means: to continue regardless of the consequences. To let things, develop naturally and to accept the outcome without regret. **Roll the dice; come what come may.** Similarly, **a chip off the old block** also refers to a chip off a piece of wood and means: someone who is very similar in character to their father or mother; i.e., made from the same stuff

Let the punishment match the offense(crime) - This saying is ascribed to the Roman orator and statesman Cicero. He established a model for Latin prose and rules for rhetoric. A supporter of Pompey against Julius Caesar, he condemned Mark Antony in favor of Octavian. For this offense, Mark Antony had him put to death and his hands and tongue were attached to the podium. At least in this case, **the punishment did not fit the crime.** The phrase can be interpreted to mean that justice must be just and equal to the crime committed. **Justice is blind**

Let them eat cake - This phrase is widely attributed to Marie-Antoinette (but this may not be true). However, it does date back to the French Revolution. It has migrated to mean: a rich person or group that has no regard for the plight of the poor

Let there be light - The origin of this phrase is from the Bible, (Genesis 1: 3). "And God said, Let there be light: and there was light." This phrase is often used to denote the beginning of something new. It is also worthy to note that light is habitually used as a metaphor for knowledge

Lick your wounds - It has long been known and widely observed that some animals (and dogs in particular) lick their wounds and the wounds of others once they have been injured. This seems to be innate in them and some scientists are beginning to believe that performing such activities have therapeutic benefits as the saliva of animals contain antibodies that can help to keep the wound clean and **ward off** infections. The metaphor has been extended beyond the animal realm to apply to humans. It therefore means: to recover from a defeat, scolding or an embarrassing incident. To go away physically or emotionally wounded or harmed. To take some time to regain your strength or joy after a disheartening experience. **Go away and lick your wounds**

Life can only be understood backwards; but it must be lived forwards - This quote is credited to the Danish philosopher Soren Kierkegaard. Known along with Nietzsche, Dostoevsky and others as one of the founders of Existentialism, Kierkegaard spent his life trying to understand the purpose and nature of the human existence. He wrote: "Life can only be understood backwards; but it must be lived forwards. Life is not a problem to be solved, but a reality to be experienced." The phrase can be interpreted to mean: when you are young, **your future seems bright** and you have your whole life before you. You are in the process of learning what life is all about through your experiences. However, you cannot really determine if any of those experiences were good or bad without the benefit of retrospect. Introspection of past events helps you to understand your future experiences. Yet, you cannot afford **to live in the past** because **what is done is done. Life moves on** and you must learn to move on with it. Ben Franklin once wrote: "Life's tragedy is that we get old too soon and wise too late"

144

A COLLECTION OF POPULAR ENGLISH PHRASES

Life flashes before your eyes - This term has been around for centuries. It is a phenomenon where in some life-threatening situations, critical chronological events are recalled in a matter of seconds. Research by scientists and psychologists into this phenomenon suggests that under such circumstances, critical areas of the brain that host autobiographical memories are activated; perhaps as a defensive mechanism. Whereas such psychic phenomena may be viewed as part of our imagination, we are just beginning to **scratch the surface of** cognitive actions that may **lay at the bedrock** of our self-awareness. The phrase is often used to denote **a close call** or a very threatening or near-death situation. **My life just flashed in front of my eyes**

Life is a marathon, not a sprint - The origin of this often-quoted phrase is unclear or unknown. It is sometimes quoted in the reverse, **life is not a sprint, it's a marathon** and is interpreted differently by different people. Some have interpreted it as **anything worth having is worth waiting for**. Others that there are many difficulties in life that one must endure, and we should not look for quick and easy solutions to difficult problems. In this **microwave world** where so many people expect instant everything, it is all the more important that we **keep the big picture in mind**

Life of Riley - One possible origin of this expression is from a character in a 19th century song with a similar title. The expression was made popular before World War I and more so by the 1940s radio show by the same name casting William Bendix in its lead role. The subsequent film and TV series (1953) also contributed to the popularity of this phrase. The expression can be interpreted to mean: a life of luxury; a carefree, comfortable, and thoroughly enjoyable way of living. **Living the life of Riley**

Light bulb moment - The source of this term is the invention of the light bulb by Thomas Edison in 1879. Among the first of his numerous inventions, it was more than a source of light, it was the beacon to a new electrical era and an unprecedented new infrastructure not seen since the advent of plumbing. In 1883, Roselle, NJ was the first city in the world to have an electrical infrastructure. Perhaps more important is that the light bulb was the antecedent of the vacuum tube and ushered in a new wave of electronics, most noted was the radio as we know it today. Resembling the Eureka moment, it means: an epiphany or the sudden realization of a good idea. So much so that the light bulb has become a symbol of a great idea particularly when displayed above the head of a person. **The light bulb came on**

Light-year - This is a term that has been borrowed from the science realm more specifically Astronomy. It is the distance that light travels in one solar year (5.88 trillion miles). Hence, it is a distance and not a time. It is sometimes used colloquially to designate something that is very far away. **Light-years away, warp speed**

Light at the end of the tunnel - The origin of this phrase dates back to the Great Depression that resulted from the stock market crash of 1929. A time that gave birth to other expressions such as "brother can you spare a dime" and **breadlines**. The common usage is: a long-awaited indication that a period of hardship or adversity is nearing an end. Happy days are here again

IN A NUTSHELL

Lightning never strikes the same place twice - This saying is an old myth that has proven time and time again to be wrong. Lightning has hit the same place more than once and tall building such as the Empire State Building have been hit multiple times. Nonetheless, it has come to mean: something that's very improbable and unlikely to happen or will never happen to the same person or group twice. **Once in a blue moon**

Like a lamb to the slaughter - The origin of this expression is the Bible. It appears twice in the Old Testament: Isaiah (53:7) "He was oppressed, and he was afflicted, yet he opened not his mouth: he is brought as a lamb to the slaughter, and as a sheep before her shearers is dumb, so he openeth not his mouth" and Jeremiah (11:19) "But I was like a lamb or an ox that is brought to the slaughter; and I knew not that they had devised devices against me, saying, Let us destroy the tree with the fruit thereof, and let us cut him off from the land of the living, that his name may be no more remembered." It is often interpreted in the New Testament as: an omen of Jesus being the lamb and his crucifixion or unjust killing -- the slaughter. The common usage is: to be unaware of pending doom or danger. **Judas goat**

Like a moth to a flame - This popular phrase has been around for centuries and was used by Shakespeare in The Merchant of Venice (Act II, Scene IX). "Thus hath the candle singed the moth."It is an allusion to a well-known fact that moths are attracted to bright lights. The phrase means: an irresistible and dangerous attraction or allure to someone or something. **A fatal attraction**

Like two ships passing in the night - This expression is from a poem by the American poet Henry Wadsworth Longfellow. It is commonly used to express: people who meet for a brief but intense moment (sometimes involving sex) and then part, never to see each other again. **Ships that pass in the night**. **One-night stand** is a sexual relationship lasting only one night; **a hook up; booty call; Netflix and chill**

Lingua franca - The earliest recording of the use of this term is the Frankish language. But it may have been used earlier as a mixture of Italian with French, Spanish, Arabic, Greek, and Turkish, formerly spoken on the eastern Mediterranean coast. It now means: a language that is adopted as a common language between speakers whose native languages are different

Little green men - This term was first used as part of the alien awareness/phobia that emerged in the early 1900s perhaps best exemplified by the 1938 radio broadcast of War of the Worlds by the American filmmaker and actor Orson Wells. This Halloween broadcast caused mass hysteria, convincing thousands of terrified listeners across the United States that earth was being invaded by **Martians.** The term really came of age in the post-World War II era when the United States and the Soviet Union started **the race for space.** The common usage is: imaginary beings from outer space, e.g., aliens, Martians and extraterrestrials (ETs), **ET phone home**

Lock, stock and barrel - This phrase can be traced back to the early days of firearms. When muskets consisted of three major parts. A lock, a stock of wood and a metal barrel. A musket was made up of a flintlock that produced the power to fire the ball, a wooden stock that held the lock and the barrel, and the barrel through which the musket ball was shot. Put all three together and you have **the whole shooting match**. Yet, it wasn't until the 1800s that the phrase became popular in its current form. It has come to mean, including everything; completely. The **whole nine yards, the whole shooting match** are also used in the same way. **Locked and loaded** means you are ready for whatever comes next

Locus poenitentiae - This phrase originated from the Bible, (Hebrews 12:17). It is in reference to Esau: "For you know that afterward, when he wanted to inherit the blessing, he was rejected, for he found no place for repentance." It means: the interval when it is possible to withdraw from a bargain or course before being committed

Long day's journey into the night - This is a title of a play by the American playwright Eugene O'Neil. Considered by many to be his **magnum opus,** it was released posthumously at his request. It is viewed by many to be a metaphor for the **ebbs and flows** of life as the day represents life and the night death. Also used to indicate a long arduous journey or task

Look what God has wrought - The source of this expression is from the Bible (Numbers 23:23). This was the statement that American inventor Samuel F.B. Morse sent via a telegraph message from the U.S. Capitol to a railroad station in Baltimore, Maryland on May 24, 1844. This invention changed the infrastructure of the nation and the world allowing people to communicate in near real-time. The expression can be interpreted to mean: Man is the instrument of God therefore anything that he manifests can only be through the glory and grace of God. **All praises to the Lord**

Looking glass - The origin of this phrase is from the English writer Lewis Carroll's novel Through the Looking Glass. It has evolved to mean: what is spoken or written is to be accepted in the reverse sense or turned upside down. **The mirror image; Alice in Wonderland**

Loose cannon - This is one of those maritime expressions that has become a popular idiom. It the days of wooden ships, cannons were mounted on one side of the ship to engage in battle with other ships. Teddy Roosevelt, an avid reader, used it as a metaphor around the turn of the 20th century, but its origins probably dates back earlier. References to use of the expression has also been mentioned. The expression is now used to describe: an unpredictable or unstable person capable of inflicting damage. **Nitroglycerine** is used similarly

Loose lips sink ships - This saying originated during World War II as part of the United States' campaign to limit the amount of useful information given to the Japanese and Germans. This was during an era when German submarines were sinking American convoys to Europe with badly needed supplies. This saying was also popularized during the 1960s by the comedian Flip Wilson. It now denotes: to be careful what you say or write because information could be used against you or others. In the era of emails and text messages, this is **all the more important. Careless talk costs lives. The walls have ears** is another phrase that was popularized during World War II, although its roots date back to the Elizabethan era. It was rumored that during this time in England, there were hidden holes in the palace walls that allowed other people to listen to conversations. The common usage is: be careful what you say because people may be eavesdropping

IN A NUTSHELL

Lord of the flies - The source of this expression is the title of a 1954 novel by the Nobel Prize-winner William Golding's. While the expression has been used to designate **the devil incarnate**, it is also used to describe a dystopian existence in which humans succumb to their darkest instincts. A world without rules or morals, where evil can flourish unabated

Love means never having to say you're sorry - This expression comes from a line in a novel entitled: Love Story, written by Erich Segal and the subsequent 1970 film. A common interpretation is: true love masks many words and has a silent language of its own. Therefore, there is no need to say them because they are already understood

Loving v. Virginia - This is the name of a landmark Supreme Court case in which an interracial couple sued the state of Virginia over its interracial laws. It is one of those seminal cases, e.g., *Dred Scott v. Sandford, Roe v. Wade, Brown v. Board of Education* that changed the landscape of a nation. In 1958, during the nascent days of the **Civil Rights movement**, the Lovings were married in defiance of Virginia law which stipulated that no person with one drop of nonwhite blood could marry a white person. At that time, 16 states prohibited interracial marriages because of their anti-miscegenation laws. At 2am in the morning, the Lovings were arrested and later convicted of violating Virginia laws. However, on June 12, 1967, the Supreme Court reversed the decision and deemed anti-miscegenation laws illegal. In that same year, *Guess Who's Coming to Dinner* starring Spencer Tracy, Sidney Poitier, and Katharine Hepburn depicting interracial dating was a **box-office hit**. At that time, only 3 percent of the marriages in the United States were interracial, however, 50 years later, the number approached 20 percent. The Loving case is often used as an example of post-Reconstruction **Jim Crow laws** that changed as a result of the Civil Rights movement and allowed "loving" couples to marry regardless of their race. This milestone case also helped **to pave the way** for same sex marriages. In addition, **Guess Who's Coming to Dinner** has become a catchphrase for interracial dating or when a black person or couple are invited to something that is traditionally white

Low man on the totem pole - The origin of this expression comes from the tradition of some Native American tribes of erecting a pole or pillar carved and painted with a series of symbols. It has since migrated to the English vernacular as a **pecking order** with the most important person at the top and the least important person at the bottom

Lucifer - The source of this term is the Latin name for the planet Venus. This planet, known as **the Morning Star**, was associated with several mythologies as it is one of the brightest objects in the sky appearing in the morning before sunrise or in the evening just after sunset. This is because it is an internal planet and thus lies closer to the sun. Over time, it became associated with God's chief angel that rebelled against God (Isaiah 14:12). "How you have fallen from heaven, morning star, son of the dawn! You have been cast down to the earth, you who once laid low the nations!" Both Dante's Divine Comedy (1321) and John Milton's Paradise Lost (1667) did much to proclaim this name as a moniker for the devil within the Judeo- Christian structure. **Prince of Darkness; fallen angel**

148

Stands for:

May you live in interesting times

IN A NUTSHELL

Machiavellian - Niccolo Machiavelli was an Italian Renaissance political philosopher, statesman and secretary of the Florentine republic. However, he was expelled from public life when the Medici family returned to power. His **magnum opus** was a book entitled: The Prince. It is now defined as: a person who follows Machiavelli's ideas of deceitfulness as outlined in his book The Prince. One that uses cunning, double-dealing, and opportunist methods to achieve a goal. It has been even said that "Old Nick", the popular name of the Devil among Anglo-Saxon races, derives its origin from that of Niccolo Machiavelli. **Old Nick Machiavellian**

Madame Bovary - This expression is from the French writer Gustave Faubert's novel Madame Bovary. It has migrated to mean: a woman that has an inflated or glamorous image of herself

Magic carpet (ride) - It is commonly believed that the origins of the legend of a magic carpet comes from 1001 Nights. However, it appears that the earliest mention of a magic carpet comes from the days of King Solomon. Legend has it that the Queen of Sheba had such a carpet made as a gift to King Solomon. Nonetheless, the term now refers to: something that is amazing particularly as it pertains to methods of transportation. A joyful and blissful ride or trip. **Flying on a magic carpet; take you on a magic carpet ride**

Magna Carta - This is a charter of liberty and political rights obtained from King John of England, brother of Richard the Lionheart in 1215. It is seen as the pivotal document of English constitutional practice. It is a document that recognizes or guarantees rights, privileges, or liberties. It is sometimes referred to as a seminal **piece of work**, rules or laws

Magnum Opus - This is a Latin phrase meaning 'great work' that has become part of the English vernacular. It means: a magnificent work, especially the chief work of a writer, artist or composer. It is sometimes applied to any splendid work or achievement. Chef d'oeuvre is a similar French term and means a masterpiece, a great creation in any field

Maiden voyage - This term, originally meaning the first voyage of a ship, was first recorded in 1901. Yet, the use of maiden to signify "the first time" dates from the mid-1500s. It now means: the first journey of a ship or aircraft; in general terms, it means the first experience. It is also the title of a popular jazz song by Herbie Hancock

Make a mountain out of a molehill - The origin of this saying is from the second century Greek writer Lucian in which he compared an elephant to a fly. The mountain and the molehill were later substituted for the elephant and the fly. It means: to make something big out of something that is small

Make bricks without straw - This phrase comes from the Bible (Exodus 5:7). It refers to the Jews in Egypt prior to the Exodus. "You are no longer to supply the people with straw for making bricks; let them go and gather their own straw. But require them to make the same number of bricks as before." It means: to try to do something without the proper tools, materials or means

A COLLECTION OF POPULAR ENGLISH PHRASES

Make haste slowly - This popular adage was originally a Greek expression that comes to us through the Roman translation of *Festina Lente*. At first, it appears as an oxymoron. However, it means: to do something with speed but carefully. **Haste makes waste; more haste, less speed**

Make him an offer that he can't refuse - This saying has been around for some time. It was popularized in the 1972 movie The Godfather Part I. It was first uttered by Vito Corleone (played by Marlon Brando) the head of the Corleone Mafia family. It means: to convince someone of your position or to do something that you want them to do. The incentive could be positive or negative depending on the situation. **The carrot or the stick**

Make my day (Go ahead, make my day!) - This term is from the movie Sudden Impact and was uttered by the character, Dirty Harry, played by Clint Eastwood in a number of films during the 1980s. It was so popular that President Reagan used it. The popular interpretation is: to go ahead and do something that will make me happy

Man does not live by bread alone - This expression is from the Bible and could be found in (Matthew 4:4, Deuteronomy 8:3). "But he answered and said; It is written, Man shall not live by bread alone, but by every word that proceedeth out of the mouth of God." It appears two places because Jesus is quoting the Old Testament when he replies to the devil in the desert in Matthew. It means that physical nourishment is not sufficient for a healthy life; man, also has spiritual needs

Man is a wolf to man - The origin of this phrase is the Latin phrase *Homo homini lupus* and it is often credited to the Roman playwright Titus Maccius Platus (254–184 BCE). The countless wars and acts of genocide throughout history has proven this phrase to be an axiom. The phrase has been used by writers and philosophers throughout the ages. Arthur Schopenhauer used the phrase in his book The World as Will and Representation, and Sigmund Freud also made references to it. It has served as the backbone of Thomas Hobbes' Leviathan. In this seminal book Hobbes asserts that man is driven by three perpetual forces: competition, difference and glory which he concludes is the catalyst for conflict. The phrase simply means: the natural state is for men to prey on each other. **Man's inhumanity towards (to) man**

Man is the measure of all things - This saying is from Plato's Theaetetus a dialogue written on the nature of knowledge written in 369 BCE. It along with Sophist form the basis of Plato's epistemology. In it, Socrates discusses the subject of knowledge with Theaetetus. The common interpretation is: man is the center of all things. However, throughout the centuries, many have pondered if the statement is an aphorism or a testimony to the hubris and ignorance of man

Man's inhumanity towards (to) man - This quote is ascribed to the Scottish poet Robert Burns from his play Man was made to mourn. "Man's inhumanity to man. Makes countless thousands mourn!" It can be interpreted as a testament to the morbid winds of slavery, genocide and war that swept across **killing fields** and barren lands now only fit for graves. It is a memorial to the human cost of countless **holocausts** paid in blood and engraved on cold tombstones in the graveyards of our inhumanity. What a fool is Man, who bathes in the tub of his ignorance and showers in the waters of his immorality, barbarism and greed.

IN A NUTSHELL

The Chinese philosopher Lao Tzu allegedly said: "Man's enemies are not demons, but human beings like himself". Maybe this world is another planet's hell; Man is a wolf to man

Manchurian candidate - The origins of this expression is from the title of a 1959 novel by the American novelist Richard Condon. It is about a former prisoner of war who becomes brainwashed as an unwitting assassin for an international Communist conspiracy. Even though the expression may have been known previously, it was this book and the subsequent 1962 movie that popularized and defined it. It was further popularized, at least in some circles, by conspiracy theories surrounding the assassination of President Kennedy in 1963. Such theories were enhanced by the fact that in late 1963, the film was removed, some say because it had simply played out. Yet, when the time came to renew it in 1972, it was not renewed. Some say because Frank Sinatra (a friend of President Kennedy) opted to take the movie back and bury it. Furthermore, the association of the Manchurian candidate was also assigned to Sirhan Sirhan the killer of Robert Kennedy in 1968. Hence, at least in the minds of some, the term is linked to the assassination of the Kennedy brothers. The expression can be interpreted to mean: a person who unbeknownst to himself has been convinced to act toward some interest; a person, especially a politician, being used as a puppet by an enemy power. **Useful idiot**

Mandate from heaven - The source of this expression is from the Chinese doctrine initiated during the Zhou dynasty (1046-256 BCE). It was used as a reason for the overthrow of the Shang dynasty and was based on the moral right to rule. Many, however, will argue that this doctrine was in place well before this time as the Pharaohs of Egypt (dating back to its first dynasty around 3200 BCE) also ruled with *a mandate from heaven*. Today, it generally applies to: the God-ordained right to rule. **Divine right of kings; Eye of Providence**

Manifest destiny - This term has its origin in the 19th century doctrine that first appeared in print in 1845, in the July-August issue of the United States Magazine and Democratic Review. It is based on a belief that the expansion of the U.S. throughout the American continent was justified, inevitable and God-ordained. The Mexican American War and the completion of the transcontinental railroad made this proclamation real. The general interpretation is: a future event that is believed to be sure to happen. **A forgone conclusion**

Manna from heaven - This expression is from the Bible (Exod. 16). Manna is food that God miraculously gave to the Jews during the Exodus, after the food they had brought with them out of Egypt had run out. It is interpreted to mean: an unexpected aid, advantage, or assistance that comes at the right time. **A friend in need is a friend indeed**

Mantle of Elijah - This expression is from the Bible and the story of the transfer of power from Elijah to Eisha. (I Kings 19:19) It now means: when someone succeeds to the established authority of a predecessor. **Pick up the mantle**

A COLLECTION OF POPULAR ENGLISH PHRASES

Many a true word is spoken in jest - The source of this popular aphorism is unclear. However, similar connotations were echoed by Chaucer and Shakespeare. Nevertheless, it means: a humorous remark or comment that contains an underlying truth. Something that is said as a joke but was meant to be said as a truthful observation or a fact. We must be forever mindful that a joke is often made **at someone's expense. Just kidding**

March comes in like a lion and goes out like a lamb - This popular proverb goes back at least to the 18th century. Although it is not always true, it could be used **as a rule of thumb** to describe the coming of spring and the end of the cold winter months. March is a transition month and traditionally has cold and moderate days. It has come to mean: at the beginning of March, you can expect some wintry days. But at the end of March, the weather should be much milder, leaves begin to return, and **spring is in the air. March winds and April's showers bring forth May flowers; Harbinger of Spring**

Martial law - The origins of this term is unclear. However, it is defined as: military government that involves the suspension of ordinary law. A law temporarily imposed upon an area by state or national military forces when civil authority has broken down or during wartime military operations

Mary Jane - Even though this term is sometimes associated with a type of woman's shoe, it is also used as a euphemism for marijuana. In this context, it has is origins in the corruption of the Spanish name Maria Juana. Also designated as weed, pot, herb or reefer, it was used by jazz musicians in the early 20th century and by the 1960s, it had become a staple of the Hippie and college culture. Since that time, it has become an integral part of the **Rap and Hip-hop** culture and so prevalent that it was legalized in some states in the early 21st century. First for medicinal purposes and later for recreational use; a sharp contrast from the reefer madness propaganda of the 1930s. In the 1970s, Rick James wrote a song entitled: Mary Jane as an ode not to his love of women, but to his love of this seductive drug. **420 or 4-20 (four twenty)** is also a euphemism for marijuana or smoking it, and likewise, April 20th is designated as the day to annually honor the love of this drug. The origin of this designation is attributed to a group of California high school students that got high after school at 4:20 and dates back to the 1970s. To **smoke 420, 24/7** is to smoke weed all the time, **aka a pothead. Hotboxing** is another term that is related to smoking marijuana, more specifically, to a group smoking a lot of weed in a confined area such as a car. **Exotic cheroot. On a similar note, China White** is often used as a euphemism for a type of heroin

Mason Dixon line - This line takes its name from the two men that surveyed it in the 1760s as part of a land dispute between Maryland (The Calvert family) and Pennsylvania (the Penn family). As time progressed and slavery was abolished in the northern United States, it became the line of demarcation between the North and the South or slave states and non-slave states (above the line were free states below the line slave states). **As fate would have it,** Pennsylvania was occupied by Quakers who over time became the most vocal and active group against slavery and a cornerstone of the Underground Railroad and the abolitionist movement. Thus, during slavery, it represented **a beacon of hope** for slaves escaping the south. In another ironic twist, the two streets that converge on the west side of the U.S. Capitol (the side with the Mall and White House) are Maryland Ave and Pennsylvania Ave perhaps a sign of union between the North and the South. Sometimes, this term is used to denote a line of demarcation particularly as it relates to the social and political landscape of the United States

Masquerade - Although the wearing of masks has been around for centuries in various customs around the globe, the origin of the word and the wearing of masks in public and in private at social events seems to have originated in Venice, Italy in the 15th century and spread across Europe in the following centuries. Similar masked tradition existed in West Africa and the Caribbean. It was the French explorer Pierre: Le Moyne who brought the custom to America and established it a Point de Mardi Gras located just outside of current day New Orleans (although some claim that an earlier tradition was established by French soldiers in current day Mobile Alabama). Henceforth, in America, the celebration of Mardi Gras became an integral part of the New Orleans "Big Easy "culture. The tradition has long been associated with **Fat Tuesday** a prelude to **Ash Wednesday** and the Catholic tradition of **Lent**. By wearing masks, there was no class distinction and people could engage regardless of class while at the same time adding a chic mystique and sexual allure. In New Orleans, the tradition has gone beyond wearing masks to **masquerading around** drunken and nearly nude in your **birthday suit** with beads. The term now means: to pretend, to hide behind a façade. **Hiding in plain sight**

Maxwell's demon **-** Is an imaginary creature that the mathematician and physicist James Clerk Maxwell created to contradict the second law of thermodynamics. The demon is trying to create more useful energy from the system than there was originally. Hence, it is often used to refer to something that is impossible to achieve, e.g., **a perpetual machine**

May the force be with you - The source of this expression is from the Star Wars series of movies. It was said by numerous characters throughout the series and in many ways, has become symbolic of the series. It was first said by the character General Dodonna in the original movie that was released in 1977. It is regularly used today as a parting wish of good luck. In a humorous way, engineers and geeks sometimes say: may the product of your mass and the second derivative of your distance, be with you, F = ma

May you live in interesting times - This phrase probably originates from an ancient Chinese saying that has worked its way into the English vernacular. Some have interpreted it to be a curse; others a challenge to life or both. It is frequently used as a parting wish. On a similar note, President Kennedy once said: "when written in Chinese, the word 'crisis' is composed of two characters. One represents danger and the other represents opportunity." **The best of times and the worst of times**

Maybe this world is another planet's hell - This quote is ascribed to the English writer Aldous Huxley. It can be interpreted as a statement regarding the nature of our reality. A state in which we all must kill something to survive. It is the only reality that we know. When looking upon our blue planet from space, it looks so majestic, peaceful and sublime. Yet on this planet, many of its denizens go hungry every day. Often it is beleaguered by war, genocide, slavery and other forms of **Man's inhumanity towards man**. A state that could only be described as **hell on earth**. Perhaps on some unknown planet revolving around **a**

twinkling star; there exist a **utopian state** in which there are no words to describe hell and its inhabitants **walk around heaven all day**

Mea Culpa - This is a Latin term which means "through my fault" that has become part of the English lexicon. It is used as: an acknowledgment of one's fault or error

Mecca - The origin of this term comes from the holiest city within the Islamic faith located in Saudi Arabia. It is the birthplace of the prophet Muhammad, and the place of his early teachings before his emigration to Medina (the second holiest city) in 622 (the Hegira). He later returned to Mecca in 630 and henceforth it became the center of the Muslim faith. All Muslims pray toward Mecca five times a day. Additionally, all Muslims are required to make a pilgrimage to Mecca (the Hajj) at least once in a lifetime if able. It is important to note that during the European Dark Ages, it was from this city that the torch of knowledge was carried to the European continent using Moorish Spain as its conduit. Today the term designates: a place that is regarded as a center for a specific group, activity, or interest or a place that attracts people, e.g., **a Mecca of learning**

Melting pot - This term has its origin in a crucible used to blend or fuse different types of metals into a single unit. It has since migrated to describe a place where people of different races, religions, and ethnic backgrounds come together and function as a single group. While in existence as a metaphor since the 1700s, it was later popularized by a 1908 play of the same name. No better example can be cited than the United States of America, a nation comprised of immigrants from around the globe. Still, in this great nation, exceptions have been noted. For instance, Thurgood Marshall once said: "The United States has been called the melting pot of the world. But it seems to me that the colored man either missed getting into the pot or he got melted down"

Men are rarely fit to command, who have not been accustomed to obey - The source of this proverb is from Erasmus' Book on Proverbs and Adages, although many others such as Niccolo Machiavelli have echoed similar sentiments. The phrase is often interpreted to mean: good leaders have the experience of being in the position of those they are leading thus bringing that perspective to their leadership. Furthermore, it implies that no one is fit to govern others, who has not obtained a command over his own passions and affections

Ménage à trois - This is a term of French origin that has worked its way into the English language and literally means: "household of three." It has come to denote a sexual agreement between three people often involving a married couple and another person that share an everyday living space

Merci beaucoup - This is a term of French origin that has migrated to the English language. It literally means "thank you" and has come to be used as a chic way of expressing gratitude. Likewise, **Merci beaucoup mon bon ami** means: thank you very much my good friend

Messiah complex - This term takes its origin from Jesus who according to Christian theology was the messiah. It denotes: a state in which the individual believes themselves to be, or destined to become, the savior of the particular field, a group, an event, a time period, or in an extreme scenario, the world. **God complex** is a similar term and means: a person that has an unshakeable belief that he or she is infallible and thus incapable of being incorrect or failing at any task no matter how difficult or daunting it might be

Met his Waterloo - This phrase originates from the battle at Waterloo, Belgium where Napoleon was soundly defeated by the allied forces led by the British military leader Wellington. It now means: to meet one's final and insurmountable challenge. To encounter one's ultimate obstacle and to be defeated by it

Metamorphosis - This is a term that has its origin in the scientific realm more specifically Biology. In Biology, it is used to describe a profound or a series of changes, e.g., from a caterpillar to a butterfly. This term has migrated from the science realm to general use and is used to designate: a significant transformation of any kind or a major change in appearance, character or habits. **Cocoon** is a term that is related to a metamorphosis. It is the protected coating that houses the insect under transformation. It is generally used to describe a protective place or environment often isolated from others. A place or situation that someone feels comfortable in. **Comfort zone; security blanket**

Mickey Mouse - The source of this term is the famed Walt Disney cartoon character that entertained generations of Americans and has become **as American as apple pie**. The term is often used to describe something that is not **on the up and up,** such as an organization, person or group that is **subpar** or not as good or serious as it should be. Something or someone that should not be taken seriously. **Mickey Mouse organization**

Midas touch - It is named from a legendary king of Phrygia who was believe by the Greeks to turn anything that he touched into gold. The expression is interpreted to mean: the gift of profiting from whatever one undertakes. **Green thumb** is a similar term and means a natural talent for growing plants

Might as well be hanged for a sheep as a lamb - This is an old English proverb that goes back to the 17th century. The common interpretation is: might just as well be punished for a big misdeed as for a small one

Milk of human kindness - This idiom is from Shakespeare's play Macbeth (Act I, Scene V). "Glamis thou art, and Cawdor; and shalt be; What thou art promised. Yet do I fear thy nature; It is too full o' th' milk of human kindness." The phrase is habitually interpreted to mean: the kindness, sympathy or empathy shown to others. Similarly, **to kill someone with kindness** means: to pamper with kindness to the point of being absurd or to cause anxiety to someone by treating them in a way that is extremely kind or helpful

Millennial generation - A millennial is a period of one thousand years. The origin of this term is the new millennial of the 2000s. It designates a generation of kids born between 1980 and the start of the new millennial 2001 sometimes referred to as Generation Y and was preceded by Generation X, people born between 1965 and 1980. Similarly, **Baby Boomer** is a term assigned to a group of people born in the aftermath of World War II. They were preceded by the Silent Generation, people born between 1925 and

A COLLECTION OF POPULAR ENGLISH PHRASES

1945. The baby boom was a period of a major increase in the birth rate. It traditionally designates people born between 1946 and 1964

Mills of the gods grind slowly, (but they grind exceeding fine) - The earliest known use of this expression is by the 3rd century Greek philosopher Sextus Empiricus, who wrote: "The mills of the gods grind slowly, but they grind small." The common interpretation is: good things take time to develop; e.g., justice or truth maybe slow but it will come eventually. Similarly, Martin Luther King is quoted as saying "**the arc of the moral universe is long, but it bends toward justice**"

Millstone around your neck - This saying comes from the Bible (Matt. 18:5). It has migrated to mean: a problem or responsibility that you have all the time which prevents you from doing what you want. **Albatross around your neck**

Miranda rights - The origin of this term is a 1966 Supreme Court decision in Miranda v. Arizona. As a result of this landmark decision, everyone is entitled to be informed of their rights before being interrogated when in custody. These rights include: the right to remain silent, the right to an attorney, and that anything you say can and will be used against you. **Take the fifth**

Misanthrope - The origin of this term comes from combining two Greek words *misein* 'to hate' and *anthrōpos* 'man'. The term is defined as: a person who dislikes humankind and avoids human society. The African American abolitionist Charlotte Forten Grimké wrote regarding the treatment of black people in antebellum America. "I wonder that every colored person is not a misanthrope. Surely we have everything to make us hate mankind"

Miscegenation - The origin of this term comes from an 1863 pamphlet entitled Miscegenation: The Theory of the Blending of the Races, Applied to the American White Man and Negro. The was derived by combining two Latin words: *miscere* (to mix) and *genus* (race). It was, in many ways, a response to Northern fears of race mixing as a result of the Emancipation Proclamation issued by Lincoln on January 1 of that year. It appeared before the 1864 election and was a feeble attempt by Democrats to paint Republicans as promoters of race mixing. Even though such actions were pervasive in the South between the white slave-master and the black female slave (with the progeny of such unions deemed slaves by law). The term is defined as: the interbreeding of people believed to be of different racial groups. **Jungle fever**

Misery loves company - The sentiments expressed in this phrase dates to antiquity and could be found in the Bible (Psalms 7:15, Matt. 15:14). The current form of the phrase is often attributed to Christopher Marlow from his Doctor Faustus however, similar phrases appear in writings of John Ray and the 14th century Italian historian Dominick de Gravina. The phrase is often interpreted to mean: People who are suffering find comfort in knowing that they are not alone and that others are suffering as well. **Cry in each other's beer**

Misogyny - The origin of this term dates back to Joseph Swetnam's 1615 attack on women, vividly entitled: The Arraignment of Lewde, idle, froward, and unconstant women. Swetnam and his followers were labeled "Misogynos." The term is a combination of two Greek words Greek *misos* 'hatred' and *gunē* 'woman. The term designates: a dislike, hatred or contempt for, or deep-rooted prejudice against women

Modus operandi - This is a Latin term that literally means "way of operating". Abbreviated as, M.O., it has retained its meaning in the English language. The term is frequently associated with criminal behavior but is also generically applied **to all walks of life**, e.g., the way in which something works or operates

Monday morning quarterback - The source of this expression is from American football. Football games were traditionally played on Sundays. Therefore, quarterbacks and others could look back, often with regret, on the mistakes that they made during Sunday's games on Monday morning. The expression means: someone with the benefit of retrospect that criticizes the acts of another. **Hindsight is 20/20** is a similar expression and means: to look back at past events with perfect (20/20) vision. **To second guess** is also similar and means: to criticize or correct something or someone's judgement after an outcome is known or determined

Monday's child is fair of face - The source of this expression is a children's poem first recorded in England in 1838. Monday's child is fair of face; Tuesday's child is full of grace, etc. It stems from the belief that a child's personality is dictated by the day of the week and was intended to be used to help children remember the days of the week. In accordance with this belief, those born on a Monday were attractive and as an idiom it is used to designate someone that is attractive

Mono e mono - This is a Spanish term that has incorrectly worked its way into the English language. The correct Spanish term is mono a mono which literally means "hand to hand." It has been used incorrectly for so long that it has become a **mumpsimus**. It is currently used to mean one on one

Montezuma's revenge - This expression originated from a sickness attributed to the Spanish that conquered Mexico during the reign of Montezuma and became ill from the water and food. It is defined as: diarrhea or other sickness suffered by travelers, especially visitors to Mexico

Moonwalk - This was the title of a walk (dance) that was made famous by Michael Jackson at the Motown 25 Awards in 1983. A seminal entertainer and former child star, he helped to revolutionize the use of video and cable to reach millions of fans. It was a dance that glided backwards while appearing to make forward walking motions. Since that time, the term has been used to describe: leaving in a fashion as to be elusive or to move backwards while appearing to move forward. To sneak out of something. **Do the moonwalk; you can't moonwalk out of this**

Moral compass - The root of this phrase is unclear. However, it means: a natural feeling that makes people know what is right and what is wrong and how they should behave; a person's ability to judge what is right and wrong and act accordingly

A COLLECTION OF POPULAR ENGLISH PHRASES

More fun than a barrel of monkeys - The source of this phrase dates to the mid-1800s when it was first used as more fun than a cage of monkeys or a wagon load of monkeys which makes more sense. In its current form, however, it is much more sarcastic and funnier because it doesn't make sense. Popularized by the late 1800s, it inspired the children's game Barrel of Monkeys which further increased its popularity. The current usage is: something that is fun or enjoyable. **Barrel of fun**

More in sorrow than in anger - The origin of this expression is from Shakespeare's Hamlet (Act I, Scene II). There are times in life when we feel sorrow or sympathy for someone instead of being angry at them for what they did. There are other times when both emotions are combined. Yet, others when we first feel angry and then sorrow or vice versa. This expression is repeatedly interpreted to mean: to have sympathy for someone or some action which often involves a deeper understanding of the circumstances in which the action took place

More sinned against than sinning - This saying is from Shakespeare's King Lear (Act III, Scene II) "Close pent-up guilts; Rive your concealing continents, and cry; These dreadful summoners grace. I am a man; More sinn'd against than sinning." The common interpretation is that admits to his or her mistakes or sins but also thinks that they were a victim of more serious sins or wrongdoings. **Righteous indignation**

Moron - This term is rumored to have come from a character in a play by Moliere. But its origin may have come from a Greek term for foolish. In one of Moliere's plays, *Le Bourgeois Gentilhomme (The Bourgeois Gentlemen),* the character Mr. Jourdain is a moron. American psychologist Henry H. Goddard is also credited with making the term popular and taking it directly from the Greek source. Regardless of its origins, the term means: a very stupid or foolish person

Mother lode - This expression originated from an old mining term for a principal vein or lode of a region of gold or silver. It now refers to a principal source of supply

Motley crew - This is an old expression that dates to the 1700s (although the word motley is much earlier). Originally, the term motley referred to a mixture of colors and was associated with **court jesters**. Motley was later applied to a mixture of something. Eventually, the expression *motley crew* was associated with a group of sailors before migrating to its current usage which means: a group of undisciplined and sometimes disruptive people. It was also the name of a popular heavy metal group of the 1980s

Move the goalposts - This term has its origin in football and other sports that employ the use of goals to score points. The metaphor has come to mean: to unfairly alter the conditions or rules of a procedure during its course in order to give one side an advantage over the other. Or, to abruptly change the rules of the game, situation or negotiation. **Change horses in the middle of a race**. **Bait-and-switch** is somewhat similar and means to offer one thing; and exchange it for something inferior. **Move the ball down the field (move the chains)** along with **homefield advantage**, **spike the football**, **block and tackle** and **out of bounds** are additional football metaphors that are repeatedly used

159

IN A NUTSHELL

Mozart effect - So named after the famous classical composer Wolfgang Amadeus Mozart. It is the belief that listening to, playing or studying music improves cognitive skills. It is also the belief that the cognitive skills required for mathematics and music are similar. Although making your child listen to Mozart may or may not turn him or her into **an Einstein**, it is clear that Einstein loved playing the sonatas of Mozart on his violin

Much ado about nothing - This expression originated from the title of a comedic play by William Shakespeare. The common interpretation of this phrase is: a lot of trouble and excitement about something which is not important. **A big nothing burger; there is no there there**

Multitasking - Although this term was around before the computer age, it is safe to say that it was popularized during the personal computer (PC) age. These computers were able to do more than one task simultaneously. The term now generically means: to perform more than one task at a time. **Walk and chew gum**

Mumpsimus - This term dates to at least Henry VIII of England. It originally referred to a forgery so fixed in long established error that that it could not except correction. It is defined as: a traditional custom or notion adhered to although shown to be unreasonable or incorrect

Murphy's law - It is believed to be named after Edward A. Murphy, who was working at Edwards Air Force Base on a project and found a technical error and uttered: "If anything can go wrong, it will go wrong." Others believe its origin was named after a fictitious Murphy, allegedly the name of a bungling mechanic in U.S. Navy educational cartoons of the 1950s. Nonetheless, it means: the facetious proposition that if something can go wrong, it will

Music is not in the notes, but in the silence between - This saying is attributed to the Austrian composer Wolfgang Amadeus Mozart and also to the French composer Achille-Claude Debussy. Some may argue that the ability to appreciate music is one of the greatest gifts that a benevolent Creator bestowed upon humanity. However, without the silence between the notes, it would be a mesh of audible frequencies and its pleasure removed. When we think of music, we think of those pleasant notes spaced in time and we take the silence for granted. Yet, it is the balance between the silence and the notes that gives music rhythm which is the essence of its being. While music varies from culture to culture, it is one of the things that helps to define what it means to be human. Often in life, we see what is there without realizing that what is not there may be equally as important. Likewise, sometimes what is not said or done, is just as important as what is said or done. The English poet John Keats wrote: "Heard melodies are sweet, but those unheard are sweeter " **The absence of evidence is not evidence of absence**

Music of the spheres - This phrase and idea is one of the many in antiquity credited to Pythagoras. Trained in Egypt and the Middle East for nearly a quarter century, he started a school in Greece and is most famous for the Pythagorean Theorem named after him. He also contributed to the understanding of music and was the first to generate the diatonic musical scale used in music today. However, some of the things ascribed to him were known in the ancient world and later consolidated at his school. Perhaps Pythagoras' most significant contribution was the establishment of a learning paradigm that was later emulated by other Greeks. The expression "music of the spheres" has come to mean: there is a certain amount of harmony to the workings of the universe which is analogous to harmony in music. Clockwork universe is similar and was developed by Sir Isaac Newton centuries later. It was supported by observation and science. It compares the universe to a mechanical clock wound up by God and ticking along, as a **fine tuned** and **well-oiled machine**, with its gears governed by the laws of science

Music soothes the savage beast - The source of this often-quoted phrase is from the British playwright William Congreve, in The Mourning Bride, written in 1697. "Music hath charms to soothe a savage breast, to soften rocks, or bend a knotted oak." The quote we are familiar with substitutes beast for breast which, over the ages, has become more palatable. The popular interpretation of this phrase is: music has a soothing effect on people and beast alike. It tends to reduce anxiety and to calm the nerves during periods of stress and, in some cases, the power to arouse holiness by releasing the bounded spirit in all of us. **Mozart effect; Van Gogh's ear for music**

Mutt and Jeff - The source of this expression is from a very popular American comic strip by cartoonist Bud Fisher that ran for decades in American newspapers. They were two contrasting characters that somehow got along. The expression generally means: a pair of mismatched people or contrasting figures such as a **good cop or bad cop**, tall and short, skinny and fat, etc. who are habitually paired as companions, teammates, or associates

Mutton dressed as lamb - This phrase was first found in print in the journal of social gossip that Mrs. Frances Calvert compiled in 1811. It now refers to an aging woman who is dressed or made up as if much younger but could also be applied to similar situations

My fellow Americans - This was a phrase that was popularized by Franklin Delano Roosevelt in his first Inaugural Address given on March 3, 1933. As president during the years of the Great Depression and World War II, it was important to send a message to the American people that we were all in it together. It was also used by subsequent presidents, most noted was President Lyndon Johnson in his **State of the Union** address. It is regularly used as a salutation when one American is addressing his or her fellow countrymen

My mind's eye - This phrase has been around for centuries and was used by Geoffrey Chaucer as early as the 14th century. It was also used by Shakespeare in Hamlet (Act I, Scene II). The term means: the mental ability to reconstruct things or form images in the mind, it is an important part of human imagination, creativity and dreams. **In my mind's eye**

Myrmidon - Originally from a member of a warlike Thessalian people led by the Greek hero Achilles at the siege of Troy. It now means: a faithful follower who unquestioningly obeys orders

IN A NUTSHELL

Mystic chords of memory - This phrase is attributed to Abraham Lincoln from his first inaugural address. It is a prelude to a much more moving quote and another example of America's 16th president's poetic acumen. "<u>The mystic chords of memory</u>, stretching from every battle-field, and **patriot grave**, to **every living heart and hearth-stone,** all over this broad land, will yet **swell the chorus** of the Union, when again touched, as surely they will be, by the **better angels of our nature**." Lincoln was a man that knew the power of words and he had the **uncanny ability** to be succinct and direct, yet masterfully vague in his use of metaphor, e.g., linking mystic chords to the chorus of the Union. This allows the listener to form his or her unique interpretation of its meaning. Mystic chords of memory could be interpreted to denote: the precious nature of the past and how such memories could be used to project hope for the future. **The past is prologue**

Stands for:

No good deed goes unpunished

IN A NUTSHELL

Naboth's vineyard - The source of this term comes from the Bible (1Kings 21) Naboth, owned a vineyard next to the palace of King Ahab at Jezreel. The king offered to purchase Naboth's vineyard or trade it for a better one. Naboth completely refused. Instead of using his royal authority to confiscate Naboth's vineyard, Ahab returned home to sulk and Queen Jezebel had Naboth convicted on false charges and stoned to death. Ahab seized the vineyard, but the prophet Elijah stepped in to foretell the downfall of Ahab's dynasty. It is interpreted to mean: any object converted by another or a possession to be secured at any cost. **Ill-gotten gains**

Nature or (versus) Nurture - This is an old debate that dates back at least to Victorian England. Many accredit the popularization of this phrase to the British polymath Sir Francis Galton. At its heart, is the dichotomy of heredity versus environment as the dominant and controlling factor of human behavior and development. In modern times, it has extended to races with some claiming that a particular race is superior/inferior to others based solely on genetics. **Is it nature or nurture?**

Napoleonic complex - This expression originated from the French emperor Napoleon who was notoriously short. It is a personality complex that consists of power trips and false machismo to make up for short height and feelings of inferiority. **Vertically challenged.** For those math enthusiasts, there is also a **Napoleon's theorem** which states: if equilateral triangles are constructed on the sides of any triangle (all outward or all inward), the centers of those equilateral triangles themselves form an equilateral triangle

Necessity is the mother of invention - The true source of this saying is unknown. However, history has proven it to be an aphorism particularly **during hard times** or war. War has always been a **catalyst** for invention. It means: when the need for something becomes imperative, you are forced to find ways of getting or achieving it

Needle in a haystack - The source of this phrase is unclear. However, Thomas More used a similar phrase with the same connotation in the 16th century. Instead of haystack he used meadow. There is also some evidence to suggest that the phrase is much older, and it may have originated outside of Europe. The common interpretation is: something that is very difficult, if not impossible, to find or uncover. Something that has a high probability of failure. **Like looking for a needle in a haystack**

Neither a borrower nor a lender be - This saying is from William Shakespeare's play Hamlet, (Act I, Scene III). The phrase is often interpreted to mean: it is difficult to be friends with someone who owes you money or with someone to whom you owe something, so it is better not to borrow or lend in the first place

Netherworld - This is a term that comes to us from antiquity. The concept of a netherworld, underworld, Hades or hell was first articulated in Ancient Egypt in the legend of Osiris who became the god of the underworld after he was murdered by his brother Seth (Set). Greek mythology is full of stories of heroes and others dissenting into or dwelling in the underworld(Hades) or the land of the dead. The term means: the land of the dead or a land of unknown secrets or consequences. **Caught in a netherworld. Purgatory**

A COLLECTION OF POPULAR ENGLISH PHRASES

Never give a sucker an even break - This saying has been attributed to several people including <u>P.T. Barnum</u> and W.C. Fields. The prevalent interpretation of this saying is: don't allow a person who's easily fooled a fair chance. **There is a sucker born every minute** is another saying that is often credited to Barnum. Whether he or Fields uttered such phrases is uncertain nonetheless, they continue to be attributed to them

Never hold discussions with the monkey while the organ grinder is in the room - This is a quotation from <u>Winston Churchill</u>. The monkey is trained to perform with the organ grinder and therefore his focus is on performing for him while he is in the room. In a similar manner, if a person's boss or a person's parent is in the room, the person is not able to speak freely about something because he must take the opinion of the boss or the parent into consideration. There are somethings that can only be discussed on a **one on one** basis. **Looking over your shoulder**

Never interrupt your enemy when he is making a mistake - This saying is accredited to Napoleon Bonaparte. The phrase is habitually interpreted to mean: if you know that your opponent is making a mistake, let him finish before you act

Never mistake motion for action - This quote is accredited to the American author Ernest Hemmingway. Often, motion is mistaken for action, yet they are **two different beasts**. It is very easy to have useless motion without action but difficult to have action without motion. Action is motion with a purpose of producing a desired outcome, result or achievement. In this regard, motion is **much ado about nothing; going through the motions.**

New Age - This is a term that became popular in the second half of the 20th century and has at its core the philosophical works of <u>Sir Godfrey Higgins</u>, Helen Blavatsky and other spiritualists that were popular at the dawn of the 20th century. Many believe that it was also inspired by the coming of **the Age of Aquarius.** Such ages are associated with <u>the precession of equinoxes</u>, which causes the sun to appear in a different constellation every 2,150 years. The term is now associated with a spiritual movement that takes a holistic view of life by incorporating the mind, body and soul. **New Age movement; the coming of the New Age**

News - It is a common belief that the origin of this term comes from the acronym: North, East, West and South (NEWS). However, recent research seems to have traced it back to the word new with the "s" being added to it. Nonetheless, it means: newly received or noteworthy information, especially about recent or notable events or facts. Most recently, the term **Fake News** has entered the English vernacular as the result of untrue, undocumented or salacious information available over the Internet

Nice guys finish last - This is a saying made famous by New York Giant baseball player Leo Durocher. The common usage is: nice guys who play by all the rules lose to those who are willing to break the rules to win. Similar phrases include: **sportsmanship is fine but winning is better. Second place is the first loser**

IN A NUTSHELL

Night owl - This term has been used fugitively since the 1500s. Owls are nocturnal birds and **as wise as an owl** means to be aware. The term night owl has migrated to mean: a person that works or stays up all night. **Graveyard shift**

Nip it in the bud - This is a phrase that was carried over from gardening. When a bud was nipped off, it could no longer bear fruit. It has migrated to mean: to put a stop to something before it starts or gets moving or gets worse. To put an end to a potential problem. To stop doing what you are doing. **Pouring good money after bad** has the same connotation

Nirvana - This term has its roots in Buddhism. It is a transcendent state in which there is neither suffering, desire, nor sense of self. In such a state, the person is released from the effects of **karma** and the cycle of death and rebirth. It represents the final goal of Buddhism. The westernized version of this term is: a place or state of oblivion to pain, or external reality. To be in a state of internal bliss. **Seventh heaven; guru**

Nitroglycerine - The source of this idiomatic term originates from a very explosive liquid first developed in the mid- 1800s. It was highly unstable and as a result caused many accidental deaths. It was Alfred Nobel who was able to stabilize it and it is the main ingredient in dynamite. Nobel used his wealth to create the Nobel Prize. Because of its unpredictability and explosive nature, it became a metaphor for a person, a thing or a situation that is also unpredictable and explosive, thus, difficult to deal with. **It's like working with nitroglycerine**

No dice - The source of this term comes from gambling in which dice were used to gamble. Early in the 20th century, gambling was outlawed in many American states, and being caught with dice was enough evidence to convict someone of gambling. As a result, gamblers took extreme measures to hide their dice. The term is now used to denote: to refuse a request or to indicate no chance of success

No good deed goes unpunished - The origin of this saying is unclear and may go back centuries. It has been used by several writers and it is often ascribed to playwright Clare Boothe Luce. Also, credited are: playwright Noel Coward, writer Oscar Wilde, journalist Walter Winchell and the late Washington Post writer Bill Gold. The common usage is: life is often unfair or that rewards are often not commensurate with the acts performed

No man is an island - The source of this saying is from John Donne's poem Devotions upon emergent occasions and several steps in my sickness - Meditation XVII. The phrase is regularly interpreted to mean: people do not prosper when isolated from others. **We are all in this together**

No man's land - This term became popular during World War I but its origins is much earlier and predates at least to the American Civil War. It was the area between the trenches of opposing sides so named because of the devastation that each side took once leaving their trenches to attack the other side.

A COLLECTION OF POPULAR ENGLISH PHRASES

Soldiers inside no man's land had a **one in a million** chance of getting out of there alive. It is frequently used to describe a dreadful and isolated place

No one can make you feel inferior without your consent - This quote is credited to Eleanor Roosevelt, although it is not clear if she uttered such words but rather conveyed the sediment. The wife and distant cousin of President Franklin Roosevelt, she was an advocate for women's rights and a powerful voice in the White House. It is a powerful statement about one's self esteem. The common interpretation of this quote is: although others may try to pull you down for various reasons, you are **the captain of your own ship. In the final analysis,** you must have faith and confidence in your abilities; and not yield to the wants, desires or criticisms of those that do not want to see you succeed. Martin Luther King Jr. once said: **a man can't ride your back unless it's bent**

No soup for you! - This expression was made famous by an episode from the sitcom Seinfeld. It was a phrase uttered by the Soup Nazi (played by Larry Thomas). He was a soup chef who frequently denied his customers soup if they misbehaved. It is often used when someone changes his or her mind about giving something to someone else based on their actions

No strings attached - The roots of this idiomatic expression lie in the practice of attaching strings to places in fabric to denote imperfections. It later migrated to mean: unattached or to do something without requesting something in return. In recent times however, *no strings attached (NSA)* means a relationship that is solely based on physical attraction and sex

No such thing as a free lunch - The origin of this saying is unclear but has been attributed to a response of a post-World War II war proposal by former Vice President Henry Wallace. The term "free lunch" has been associated with free lunches given to people to buy drinks. The common interpretation is: nothing is really free, that there is a cost to making the lunch and those costs are often hidden elsewhere. **After the feast comes the reckoning**

Nom de plume - The origin of this term is French for "pen name." It is defined as: an assumed name used by a writer instead of their real name, e.g., Mark Twain is the ***nom de plume*** of Samuel Clemens who took the name from a steamboat term for shallow water (less than twelve feet). **Moniker** is similar and means a nickname

Non sequitur -The origin of this term is a Latin phrase that literally means "it does not follow." It is now defined as: something that is illogical or does not follow a logical sequence. **Non sequitur argument, statement or conclusion**

Not everything that is faced can be changed, but nothing can be changed until it is faced - This saying is ascribed to the African American author and activist James Baldwin. A seminal figure of the 1960s, Baldwin was disappointed with the progress made during the Civil Rights era and articulated the African American experience in his writings. The saying can be interpreted as: We all must **be the change that we**

want to see in the world. However, **change is not easy,** and we must be willing to make the associated sacrifice if we want to change the world

Not just whistling Dixie/whistling Dixie - "Dixie" was the battle song of the Confederacy. It was popularized by the 1859 minstrel song performed by D.D. Emmett, who made fun of black people in his blackface minstrel act. Ironically, the song was originally sung by black slaves that were moved from the South to other regions such as Ohio. It is highly possible that Emmett heard the song there. "I Wish I was in de land ob cotton; Old times dar am not forgotten; Look away! look away! look away! Dixie Land." It was so popular in the South that it was played at Confederate President Jefferson Davis's inauguration in February 1861 and it later became synonymous with the South itself. (Dixieland). Lincoln had it satirically played after Robert E. Lee surrendered at Appomattox Courthouse. It is so engrained in American culture that it could be considered the national anthem of the South. So much so that the owner of the Washington Redskins, the last team in the NFL to have a black player, Bobby Mitchell, made him sing it and played it for 23 years. Thus, the term is forever linked to the Civil War, Reconstruction and **the Lost Cause.** The phrase **whistling Dixie** is much more intricate. For instance, if you **whistle Dixie:** you are singing the battle cry of the side that lost. Ergo, a useless act. If you are **not whistling Dixie,** then it means that there is validity to what you have said or what you are doing relating to the side that won. Hence, **to not whistle Dixie** means: to be saying something important or useful. Conversely, **to whistle Dixie** means: to engage in unrealistic fantasies; waste one's time, **a pipe dream**

Not my cup of tea - This saying has its roots in the fact that a cup of tea in England was considered to be something pleasurable. **Not my cup of tea** became popular during World War II as an easy way of saying that you did not like or care for something. The phrase is habitually interpreted to mean: not one's choice or preference. Of course, **my cup of tea** means the opposite

Nothing comes from nothing - This expression comes from Epicurus', Letter to Herodotus. It has recently been expressed as nothing from (times) nothing leaves nothing. It is antithetical to the phrase **creatio ex nihilo** (creation out of nothing). It means: if you want to have something (greater), you need something to start with

Nothing is certain but death and taxes - This saying is attributed to Ben Franklin and sometimes to Daniel Defoe in The Political History of the Devil, 1726. It means that we cannot escape death and in most cases the price for living. Cervantes wrote: **There is a remedy for all things except death**

Nothing ventured, nothing gained - This is a very old quote. Some say that it goes back to Geoffrey Chaucer in the 1300s, others attribute it to Shakespeare's Merchant of Venice and still others to Ben Franklin. Quite often, when a phrase is both old and popular, it is used by famous people at various times and thus credited to them. Not so much because they originated it, but because they helped to popularize it. Nonetheless, it has come to mean: if you do not take risks in life, you will never accomplish anything. Therefore, it is worth trying to do something because one might succeed even though success is not guaranteed. Similar phrases include: **risk versus reward; risk averse; to save all we must risk all; no chance take, no money make**

A COLLECTION OF POPULAR ENGLISH PHRASES

Now he belongs to the ages - These are the words that Secretary of War Edwin M. Stanton spoken to a small gathering of people that were mourning at Lincoln's bedside on the morning, of April 16, 1865. Though his exact words have been somewhat disputed, the sentiment remains the same. Lincoln was the first president of the United States to be assassinated at a time when the nation was trying to **heal the wounds of war**. Contrary to public opinion, Lincoln was a president that was mostly misunderstood during his presidency and just months earlier his reelection in November 1864 (at least in his own mind) was unsure. Although this phrase is forever linked to America's 16th president, it has applied to other people that helped define and shape an age. When Muhammad Ali died, I thought of this phrase because there will always be other boxers, some of them great, but none, except for him, will ever be the greatest. Not so much because of the things he did inside the ring, but because of those things he did outside of the ring

Now is the winter of our discontent - This expression originated from Shakespeare's Richard III, 1594 (Act I, Scene I). "Now is the winter of our discontent; Made glorious summer by this son of York; And all the clouds that low'r'd upon our house; In the deep bosom of the ocean buried." The phrase is repeatedly interpreted to mean: the time of unhappiness is past. Similar phrases include: **light at the end of the tunnel; the beginning of the end**

Nuclear proliferation - This is a term that emerged during the **Cold War** between the United States and the Soviet Union. It was the result of the potential escalation of nuclear arms which has since expanded to other nations. This escalation not only included the increase in quantity of nuclear weapons but also the various ways of which they could be deployed. Moreover, the overall increase in the power of such weapons, e.g., the migration from the Atom Bomb to the Hydrogen Bomb caused an additional threat. The proliferation of these weapons not only poses a threat to world peace, but to life on this planet. Consequently, the risk of a **nuclear holocaust** is much greater today than it was during the **Cold War** because of the number of nations with nuclear arsenals. The term now means: the massive spread of nuclear weapons throughout the world and the danger of **Armageddon** that they impose

Number of the beast - This phrase originated from the Bible (Revelations 13:18) and is associated with the number 666. Throughout history, there have been many that have tried to associate this number with a particular world leader including Ronald Wilson Reagan because the number in his name (six in each name) are 666

Nuremberg defense – The source of this phrase is the Nuremberg Trials of 1945-46 in which some Germans were accused of hideous war crimes. The defendants claimed that their actions were the results of carrying out orders given by their superiors and therefore they were innocent of such atrocities. The use of such techniques has been used in other legal cases. **Ignorance of the law is no excuse**

Nuts and bolts - The origin of this popular idiom seems to be unknown or unclear. It relates to something physical as many things consists of nuts and bolts used to hold things together at the lower level. The widespread interpretation is: the basic practical details as opposed to theoretical or conceptual ideas, e.g., the building of something or detailed practical information about how something works or how something can be achieved in the real world. **What's the nuts and bolts?** Nitty-gritty is similar and means: the most important aspects or the practical details of a subject or situation. **Let's get down to the nitty-gritty**

Stands for:

Open sesame

IN A NUTSHELL

O captain! My captain! - The origin of this expression comes from a poem written by the American author Walt Whitman. It was written in 1865 as a tribute to Abraham Lincoln and the eminent death of slavery. "O Captain my Captain! our fearful trip is done. The ship has weathered every rack, the prize we sought is won." It is sometimes used in the same context and spirit as Whitman's poem; to bestow respect or to pay tribute to a great leader

Occam's (Ockham's) razor - Also called the **law of economy** or the law of parsimony, is a principle stated by the philosopher, William of Ockham. It is a line of reasoning that says: the simplest answer is often correct or the most suited. It also states that in explaining or deducing something; no more assumptions should be made than are necessary. **The simplest solution is always the best; keep it simple, stupid (KISS); entities must not be multiplied beyond necessity**

Odor of sanctity - This saying originated in the Middle Ages with the belief that dead saintly people gave off a sweet smell. The common interpretation of this sayings is: inflated or hypocritical piety, an assumption of moral superiority; feeling that you are better than others and that the rules do not apply to you. **Holier than thou; on your high horse; to act high and mighty**

Oedipus complex - The name of this expression originally comes from the story Oedipus the King by the Greek playwright Sophocles. It is about a man who married his mother and killed his father. The complex was identified by Sigmund Freud. In Freud's theory, it is the complex of emotions aroused in a young child, typically around the age of four, by an unconscious sexual desire for the parent of the opposite sex and a wish to exclude the parent of the same sex. The term was originally applied to boys, the equivalent in girls is called the **Electra complex. Penis envy**

Of biblical proportions - The source of this expression is the Bible, specifically the Old Testament replete with its Great Flood and stories of creation. The expression is now used to denote: something that is huge or catastrophic in size, scope or magnitude. **Seismic proportions**

Old Glory - The origin of this term, a nickname for the American flag, dates to the American Civil War. It is a story of fidelity and patriotism of one loyal countryman during that bloody fratricidal war. Like the flag that flew over Fort Sumter at the beginning of the Civil War, and the one that flew over Fort McHenry during The War of 1812, it is revered not as a relic of its times, but rather as a national emblem of loyalty and patriotism. The original Old Glory, now part of the Smithsonian museum, was flown by William Driver on his ship before the war. Originally from the North, he defiantly flew the flag he called Old Glory at his home in Nashville Tennessee during the early part of the war. When Union soldiers captured Nashville in 1862, he gave the flag to them to fly over the state capital. It was at this time that it was given the moniker *Old Glory,* an endearing term that was used in subsequent wars and generically to mean: the flag of the United States of America. **Stars and stripes** is another nickname for the American flag. The original flag had 13 stars and 13 stripes, and an additional star and stripe was added to the flag for each state, e.g., the flag that flew over Fort McHenry and inspired the Star-Spangled Banner written by Francis Scott Key had 15 stars and 15 stripes). As the number of states continued to grow and with the possibility of many states entering the Union as a result of the Louisiana Purchase, the adding of stripes for each state became impractical. In 1818 Congress passed a law stating that each additional state would be represented by a star, and that the 13 stripes would forever represent the 13 original colonies or states. **Flag Day** is celebrated in the United States on June 14 the anniversary of the first recognition of the American flag on June 14, 1777. **Rally around the flag**

Old soldiers never die [they simply fade away] - This saying originally comes from a song but was made famous by <u>General Douglas MacArthur</u> in his farewell speech after he had been fired by President <u>Harry S Truman</u> (no period after the S). The friction between MacArthur and Truman existed long before his firing with MacArthur referring to him, at least once, as **the temporary occupant of the White House**. While the expression "<u>Old soldiers never die,</u> they simply fade away." was in use before MacArthur, it Is normally associated with him and the Korean War. It means that being a soldier at heart lives on long after your fighting days are over. **Once a soldier, always a soldier**. Yet, it could apply to any person in a profession whose working days are nearly over

Old wives' tale - The source of this phrase comes from the Greek philosopher Plato. The "old wives" refers to people in their older days that give advice based on superstition. The phrase is habitually interpreted to mean: a common belief about something that is not based on facts and that is usually false. It is sometimes mistaken as: old "wise" tale

On steroids - This expression emerged during the late 20th century as the use of steroids became popular in sports. <u>Steroids</u> are considered to be performance enhancing drugs and as such, they were banned from many sports. The expression now means: to enhance a situation or condition; to change or alter the state of something in a powerful way

On the down low (DL) - This term originated in the African American community to describe black men that lived double lives appearing straight on the outside but also have sex with men. Until recent times, homosexuality, particularly among men, was a serious **taboo** in the African American community. The term has come to mean: a person who is heterosexual in public, but homosexual or bisexual in private. Similarly, a **bean queen** is a term used to describe a white man that is attracted to Latino men. Other terms that are often used to describe heterosexual activities are **AC/DC** a term borrowed from the electrical industry and **switch hitter** a term that has its origin in baseball. **The love that dare not speak its name; come out of the closet**

On the wrong side of history - The exact source of this phrase is unclear; however, many have attributed it to Karl Marx. There is no doubt that phrases that echo this sentiment have been used throughout history. In recent time the phrase has resurfaced as a **prologue of the past**. It is often used to describe a political decision that in retrospect proves to be incorrect

On your soapbox - The expression originates from a wooden crate that was used to ship soap. Because of its size and availability, it was used as a makeshift stand by a public speaker. It has migrated to mean: to emphatically express your opinion about something. particularly about something that people are tired of hearing or is boring. **Standing on your soapbox; get up on your soapbox**

IN A NUTSHELL

Once in a blue moon - This expression dates back to medieval times. A blue moon is the second full moon that appears in one month and is rare because the moon requires about 29 days to complete all phases. The expression means: something that rarely happens. **Gibbous moon** is a moon having the lit part greater than a semicircle and less than a circle. **Wax and wane; harvest moon**

Once you go black, you never go back - This saying has its origin in the African American community but has since migrated to the general public. It is based on the long-standing stereotype that black men are "well endowed" and have long sexual stamina and a strong sexual appetite (note the scene in <u>Blazing Saddles</u>). It has come to mean: once a(white) woman sleeps with a black man, no white man will be able to satisfy her again, so she sleeps only with black men from then on. A similar saying applies to black women: **the blacker the berry, the sweeter the juice.** However, it is not as prominent. **Redbone** is also a term used in the African American community to designate a light skinned black person (typically a female); **Jungle fever**

One bad apple spoils the whole bunch – This is an old proverb that dates to the 14th century. It was used by Geoffrey Chaucer in <u>The Cook's Tale</u> and by Ben Franklin which attest to its longevity. It generally means: it only takes one person or one action to ruin the entire group, situation, etc.. **Rotten egg**

One hit wonder - This term as it is applied today emerged in the late 1970s. It means: a musical performer, group, or composer who produces a one hit song and then has no further success. A product or a thing that cannot duplicate its previous success. **Flash in the pan**

One small step for man, one giant leap for mankind - The source of this saying is the <u>1969 moon landing</u> and was uttered by Astronaut Neil Armstrong. His actual words, however, have been a point of discussion and ambiguity for decades. Armstrong maintained until his death that he said "for *a* man" and not man, which makes sense because man and mankind are interchangeable making the statement "for man" erroneous. To the extent that there have been some that have argued that the "a" was **lost in space**. Notwithstanding, the phrase is often used to describe a significant or unprecedented achievement. **Space::the final frontier**

Only a man who has felt ultimate despair is capable of feeling ultimate bliss - This expression is attributed to the seminal French author Alexander Dumas. There is something to be said about being humbled that makes one appreciate the basic things in life. It has been said that there is no greater joy than the relief of pain. **From rags to riches; you never miss your water till your well runs dry**

[Open] confession is good for the soul - The source of this phrase appears to be an old Scottish proverb that over time has become an axiom. Although not directly mention in the Bible, Psalms 119: 26-28 seems to echo this theme. "26) I have declared my ways, and thou heardest me: teach me thy statutes.27) Make me to understand the way of thy precepts: so shall I talk of thy wondrous works.28) My soul melteth for heaviness: strengthen thou me according unto thy word." Confession is an integral part of Catholicism and has proven to be therapeutic and cleansing of past sins. Sincere confession and contriteness are germane to redemption as illustrated by the aforementioned biblical verses. The phrase can be interpreted to mean: the act of confessing helps to alleviate the stress and strain of a guilty conscience. **Come clean**

Open sesame - The source of this expression is from the magical formula in the tale of Ali Baba and the Forty Thieves in One Thousand and One Nights. Casted in an Arabian setting, One Thousand and One Nights is a collection of enduring and sometimes erotic stories told by the young Shahrazad under sentence of death ordered by King Shahrayar. Ali Baba is the person in one of the tales who discovered this magic formula that opened a cave where forty robbers kept their treasure. Open sesame was also the title of a hit song by Kool and the Gang in the mid-1970s. It is currently used as: a phrase uttered that allows a free or unrestricted means of entry or access; or something that allows a person or a thing to enter or to do something successfully or easily. **Shibboleth**

Open up a can of whoop ass - The origin of this expression is alleged to be a prank caller who habitually called into radio stations and said he was going to open up a can of whoop butt. Often mistaken for whip ass, it is one of the phrases that contain the word whoop: as in **whoop dee do.** The phrases generally means: to threaten physical harm or to assault someone them verbally

Opposites attract - The origin of this exact phrase is uncertain, but it has been around for quite some time. It is a fact of nature that things, such as magnets are attracted to **polar opposites.** Perhaps opposites attract because there is a need to feel complete, to do things that are out of the norm and in some cases antithetical to our natural instincts. There is an overall balance to any healthy relationship and often this balance is maintained by differing opinions, perspectives and prospective. We often admire in others those essential qualities that complement our strengths or our weaknesses. The phrase is often used to describe a **mutual attraction**

Oracle - In classical antiquity, an oracle was a priest or priestess acting as a medium through whom advice or prophecy was sought from the gods. Two of the famous oracles in antiquity were the oracle at Delphi and Dodona. Herodotus claimed that these oracles were founded by the arrival of two black doves from Thebes in Egypt. Delphi was the most famous. However, Dodona is mentioned in both the Iliad and the Odyssey. Alexander the Great consulted the Oracle of Ammon. Ammon(Amen) was the chief Egyptian god and the source of the word Amen used in the Bible to end prayers. This oracle was located in the Siwa Oasis which was a 50-mile stretch of trees and vegetation found deep in the northern Sahara Desert. This particular oracle was known for its accuracy and it was widely believed that the Greek mythological hero **Heracles (Hercules** to the Romans) and perhaps Perseus made pilgrimages there to consult Ammon. It had no strategic value to Alexander but apparently had strong personal value. This trip was a perilous journey so much so that the Persian army had previously lost thousands of men in this desert. A series of supernatural legends and stories, some reported by his generals present at the time, came out of Alexander's excursion that continue to mystify historians today. None more important than the reappearance of black birds (in this case, ravens or crows) that led them to the oracle along with Alexander's unwavering desire to ask the oracle who his father was. Alexander's mother, Olympias, had repeatedly told him that he was the son of a god and apparently, he needed to confirm this before he embarked on a quest to conquer the known world. Alexander was told by the oracle that Ammon, not

Philip, was his true father and **the rest is history**. He never lost a battle after receiving this conformation. The term oracle is frequently used to designate: a person or thing regarded as an infallible authority or guide on something. On a similar note, the sibyls were female oracles in ancient times believed to utter prophecies of a god. In fact, on the ceiling of the Sistine Chapel, Michelangelo alternated sibyls and prophets. Sibylline Oracles (Books) were a collection of closely guarded oracle sayings that the Roman leaders kept in secret and used as a **palladium**. They were kept in a room beneath the Temple of Jupiter on the Capitol. In times of great threats or peril, these books were consulted by the *decemviri sacris faciundis* (ten-men). These men were like the Supreme Court Justices and held office for life. They were responsible for keeping the books in safety and secrecy. At the command of the Senate, these officials consulted the Sibylline Books in order to discover the religious observances necessary to prevent extraordinary misfortunes or natural disasters such as comets, earthquakes, plague, etc. **Extrasensory perception (ESP)**

Order(s) of magnitude - This is a term that has its roots in the science and mathematics realm. It is based on the logarithmic scale and means to increase or decrease something by a factor of ten. Hence, 10 has a magnitude of one, 100 two and so forth. For example, to increase something by an order of magnitude of three means to multiply it by 1000. It is generally used to state that something is increased or decreased by a considerable number. For instance, to say that something is **orders of magnitude** greater than something else means that it is much larger

Originality is undetected plagiarism - This saying is ascribed to the English author William Ralph Inge. It is perhaps best exemplified by numerous scientific discoveries such as Newton's Laws of Physics and the works of William Shakespeare. Although Shakespeare was a genius **in his own right**, he drew from numerous sources some of which were not available in his native language and many were of Italian origins. For example, when we read Othello or Romeo and Juliet. **Beneath the veil** of this Englishmen's genius, lies Italian stories that form the foundation of these plays. They lay undetected amid the **Elizabethan and Jacobean** milieu and the polymathic intellect of a literary genius. We must be forever mindful that **no man is an island;** and advancements are made because (as Newton once said) he is **standing on the shoulders** of others that came before him

Oriole - This is a term that has its roots in the African American community. It is closely related to the term Uncle Tom and takes its name from the famous cookie that is black on the outside and white on the inside. It has come to mean: a black person that totally identifies, not with the black race, but with the white race. Sambo, which is an archaic pejorative term for a black person, is sometimes used with the same connotation within the African American community, e.g., **Smiling Sambo**. As in other cases involving race, i.e., nigger; people outside of the African American community should use this term with caution or better yet not at all when referring to black people because some blacks may find it offensive

Osmosis - This is a term that was borrowed from the science realm; more specifically, biology. In biology, it is the diffusion of a solvent (such as water) across a membrane (normally flowing from a lower concentration to a higher) until a state of equilibrium is reach. It has migrated to mean: the subtle or gradual absorption or assimilation of information or knowledge. **To learn through** osmosis

A COLLECTION OF POPULAR ENGLISH PHRASES

Out of God's blessing into the warn sun - The source of this phrase is unknown, but Shakespeare used a similar phrase in <u>Hamlet</u> (Act I, Scene II). The phrase is frequently interpreted to mean: from good to less good

Out of sight, out of mind - This term goes back to the days of the Greek poet Homer and appears in the <u>Odyssey</u>. It is often interpreted to mean: you soon forget people or things that are no longer visible, present or of use to you. **What you see is what you get**

Out-Herod Herod - This phrase is inspired by the Bible (Matt. 2:13), and from Shakespeare's <u>Hamlet</u> (Act III, Scene III). According to the Bible, <u>King Herod the Great</u> was a wicked king who saw the baby Jesus as a threat and wanted to murder him. It is interpreted to mean: to outdo in extravagance, violence, or excess. To surpass in evil, excesses, or cruelty. For example, his cruelty out-Herods Herod. **Draconian measures**

Over the barrel - The source of this is said to be placing someone that was saved from drowning over a barrel to get water to come out of the lungs. Some think it was also used as a form of punishment. It has migrated to mean: in a helpless position; at someone's mercy. **You got me over the barrel**

Stands for:

Praise the Lord, and pass the ammunition

IN A NUTSHELL

Paint the town red - The origin of this expression is uncertain. However, some believe it to have originated with the riotous acts by the Marquis of Waterford and a group of friends who once painted parts of the town red. There are others that say it originated from the type of riotous behavior that alluded to blood being spilled in the streets. For the movie lover, there is a 1973 Spaghetti Western called High Plains Drifter starring Clint Eastwood where he has a **vertically challenged** sheriff paint the town red and renames the town "Hell." Nonetheless it has come to mean: to go out and outrageously enjoy oneself; have as much fun as you can. To celebrate something such as a graduation or a birthday. **Let it rip; let it all hang out; let's go out and paint the town red!**

Palace intrigue - The source of this term appears to be the events surrounding the Kings and Queens of Europe as part of palace life and the power of the throne. The term goes back centuries and appears to have been used first in France as: *intrigues de palais* and migrated to other languages. The common usage is: all of the maneuvers that go on **behind the scenes** such as **jockeying for position,** and **power plays** in a court or place of authority such as the White House

Palladium - The palladium was a statue of Pallas in great antiquity on which the safety of Troy and later Rome was said to depend. It is defined as: something believed to ensure protection; safeguard. The Constitution of the United States is a palladium. **Sibylline Books**

Panacea - This expression originated from the name of the daughter of Asclepius the Greek god of healing. It is defined as: a cure for all; a solution or remedy for all difficulties or diseases; something that will make everything about a situation better

Pandora's box - In Greek mythology, Pandora opened up her box which contained all of the evils of humankind. Thus, it is a source of many unforeseen troubles. Interesting enough, the last thing left in the box was hope. Which has led some to question why hope is in a box that contained all the evils. The expression can be interpreted to mean: something that will lead to many problems **Let the genie out of the bottle; open up a can of worms**

Pantheon - The source of this term comes from a circular dome temple with a hole in its center located in Rome. It was completed around 125 CE and was built during the reign of Hadrian and dedicated to all the gods. It is the best-preserved building from ancient Rome. The term now refers to: a group of selected individuals that are honored together sometimes in a place such as the hall of fame. **Pantheon of heroes.** Many confuse the Pantheon with the Greek Parthenon which is the temple of Athena Parthenos, built on the Acropolis in 447–432 BCE by Pericles. It was built to honor Athena and to memorialize the recent Greek victory over the Persians. The Lincoln Memorial in Washington DC, is modeled after the Parthenon

Paper lion - This expression originated from the Chinese revolutionary and leader Mao Tse-tung in reference to the United States. It now refers to: a person or a thing that appears to be more formidable than it is. **An idle threat**

A COLLECTION OF POPULAR ENGLISH PHRASES

Par for the course - This expression has its roots in golf where every player is expected to achieve a par or better. Par is the number of strokes a player should normally require for a particular hole or course. It means: what is normal or expected in any given circumstance; an amount or level considered to be average; a standard. **Above par; below par; up to par**

Paradigm shift - This term was first coined by Thomas Kuhn in his 1962 book entitled: The Structure of Scientific Revolution. It is often used to describe a sudden or fundamental change so profound that the previous approach or method becomes obsolete. Similarly, **paradigm paralysis**, a term attributed to Joel Barker, is the inability to recognize, accept or act beyond the current **status quo** and is the greatest obstacle to a paradigm shift

Pareto principle - So named after economist Vilfredo Pareto that specifies an unequal relationship between inputs and outputs. The Pareto principle, also known as **the 80/20 rule**, is a theory maintaining that 80 percent of the output from a given situation or system is determined by 20 percent of the input

Part and parcel - This is an old phrase that dates to the Middle Ages and was used as a legal term before it migrated to its current usage. Like **hale and hearty,** it is a phrase comprised of two redundant words, the second word is used for emphasis. The current usage is: an essential or integral component of something

Parting is such sweet sorrow - This phrase is from Shakespeare's Romeo and Juliet (Act II, Scene II). Their sorrowful parting is also "sweet" because it makes them think about the next time they will see each other. The expression can be interpreted to mean: it is difficult and painful to part with someone you love, however, the thought of meeting again is sweet. **Until we meet again**

Pascal's Wager - So named after the French philosopher and mathematician Blaise Pascal. It is an argument according to which the belief in God is rational whether or not God exists. Falsely believing that God exists leads to no harm, whereas falsely believing that God does not exist may lead to eternal damnation. It has migrated to mean that it is better to prepare for something that does not happen then to ignore it and **suffer the consequences**. The **Atheist's Wager** is a response to Pascal Wager. Similar phrases include: **If you want peace, prepare for war, chance favors the prepared mind**

Pass away (on) - This is an old term that has been around at least since the Middle Ages. It reflects the belief that the physical body pass on to a spiritual realm. Today, however, it is mostly used as a euphemism for dying, because during a time of grief some people have a difficult time saying that a loved on has die

Paul Pry - The origin of Paul Pry comes from the name of the title character of Paul Pry (1853) by the English playwright John Poole (1786-1872). The common usage is: an inquisitive, meddlesome person

Pay no attention to the man behind the curtain - The origin of this phrase is from the Wizard of Oz. When Dorthey goes to see the wizard, he is a large frightening figure that is being manipulated by a man behind a curtain. Her dog pulls back the curtain and the man is revealed. Thus, **"letting the cat out of the bag."**

The jig is up, etc. It is now used as a phrase when the truth is finally revealed or when someone is pretending to be something that they are not. **To hide behind the curtain; and your little dog too**

Pay the (pied) piper - This is an old saying of origins unknown that has been around since the late Middle Ages. It appears in several languages and was memorialized in English in a Robert Browning poem. According to legend, the pied piper charmed away all the rats in town? When one person refused to pay him what was promised, he obtained his revenge by leading all the town's children away as well. It means: To face, accept, or suffer impacts for one's actions or words or to pay a price for something that is too high or outrageous rather than suffer the consequences of not paying. **He who pays the piper calls the tune; Hobson's choice**

Pearly gates - This term comes from the Bible (Rev.21:21) "And the twelve gates were twelve pearls; every gate was of one pearl: and the street of the city was pure gold." The term now means: the gates of heaven or heaven itself. **Streets are paved with gold**

Pecksniffian - This expression originated from the character, Seth Pecksniffian, in the Novel Martin Chuzzlewit by Charles Dickens. It now denotes: hypocritical benevolence or insincere moral principles. An example of Pecksniffian is a political campaign that seems to appeal to ethics and values but really appeals to peoples' wants and desires. **Hypocrisy is the compliment vice pays to virtue**

Peeping Tom - This saying originated from the legendary Peeping Tom of Coventry, England, who was the only person to see the naked Lady Godiva. According to folktale, he was struck blind in punishment. Her husband promised that he would decrease unpopular taxes only if she rode naked on horseback through the marketplace. It has migrated to mean: a pruriently prying person: a voyeur. Similar phrases include: **mind your own business; nosey people don't live long**. On a similar note, **a Lady Godiva** is sometimes used to denote a naked lady

Penelope's loom (weavings)(labor) - This term is derived from Homer's Odyssey. According to this legend, Penelope is the wife of Odysseus who resists the advances of many suitors by telling them that she will choose one to marry as soon as she finishes weaving a burial shroud for her ailing father-in-law, Laertes. She spends each day at her loom weaving and at night, she returns to undo what she has done during the day so that she never finishes her project. She does this for twenty years in hope that Odysseus will eventually return from the Trojan War which he does. The term has migrated to mean: an endless task. **Sisyphus' rock**

Penis envy - Is a theory postulated by Sigmund Freud to account for some aspects of female behavior (notably the castration complex) but controversial among modern theorists. The common usage is: envy of the male's possession of a penis. Similarly, a **phallic symbol** is any object such as an obelisk, a cigar or skyscraper, that may broadly resemble or represent the penis, especially in an object that symbolizes power, e.g., an automobile

182

A COLLECTION OF POPULAR ENGLISH PHRASES

Penultimate - This word has its roots in a Latin root from *paene* ("almost") and *ultima* ("last"). It is repeatedly misused to mean something that is above the ultimate or the highest, when in fact it means next to the last

People generally see what they look for and hear what they listen for- This quotation is from: To Kill a Mockingbird by Harper Lee. It can be interpreted to mean: we all have our prejudices and biases that are developed as part of our life experiences. We tend to gravitate toward those things that benefit us and stray away from things that do not. Such actions could be a function of our rectitude or perhaps our innate instinct to survive

People who live in glass houses shouldn't throw stones - The expression has been traced back to Geoffrey Chaucer's Troilus and Criseyde. It generally means: you should not criticize other people for having the same faults or qualities that you yourself have. **Take a look at the man in the mirror**

Perception is reality - Like so many popular expressions, the source of this expression is unclear or unknown. However, one of the first documented examples of this phenomena is from the cave analogy put forth in Plato's Republic known as **Plato's cave**. The nature of our reality continues to be a subject of debate. For example, Albert Einstein is quoted as saying "Reality is merely an illusion, albeit a very persistent one." The expression means: the perception of something being true, based on limited knowledge; prejudice or overexposure to a particular belief, view or situation

Perpetual (motion) machine-This is a scientific term that has worked its way into common usage. It is a machine that does not require any energy to maintain its motion; thus, a perfect machine. Yet, such a machine is impossible because it would violate the first and second laws of thermodynamics. Like the alchemist of old that went in search of a method of making gold, many scientists and philosophers have proposed and sought out such machines. The term is habitually used to denote something that moves on its own (without dissipating energy) or something that is impossible to achieve

Persona non grata - This is a Latin term that has entered the English language. It means: an unacceptable or unwelcome person: It is regularly compared with **persona grata** which means the opposite. **Blackballed; blacklisted**

People may hear your words, but they feel your attitude - This quote is credited to the American author John C. Maxwell. So often we forget, that verbal communication is just one form of communication. Most times, our true feelings are encoded in our voice and gestures and thus are more enduring. Often, people remember not only what you say, but how you make them feel which is the essence of charisma. **Actions speak louder than words** and your body language and tone are the true indicators of your message

Pet peeves - This is an expression that came into existence around the turn of the 20th century with the term peeve or peevish meaning: easily irritated, especially by unimportant things and dates much further back. The term generally means: something that a particular person finds especially annoying. **One of my pet peeves; we all have our pet peeves**

IN A NUTSHELL

Peter Pan (syndrome) - Is a character created by the Scottish novelist and playwright J. M. Barrie. He is a boy with magical powers who never grew up. The term is now associated with a person that never seems to grow up

Peter Principle - Is a theory that originated with the Canadian educator Laurence J. Peter and bears his name. The theory, that all members in a hierarchy rise to their own level of incompetence is habitually applied to a person that has reached the apex of his or her abilities. "**Every employee tends to rise to his level of incompetence**"

Philadelphia lawyer - During colonial times, this was a colloquial term that was initially a compliment to the legal expertise and competence of an attorney due to the outstanding reputation of the Philadelphia Bar. It now means: a very shrewd lawyer who is an expert in the exploitation of legal technicalities. **White shoe lawyer**

Philippic - The origin of this term is a speech given by the Greek statesman, Demosthenes against Philip, king of Macedon and the father of Alexander the Great. A contemporary of Plato and Aristotle, Demosthenes was recognized as the greatest of ancient Greek orators. He had a **speech impediment**, that he overcame by speaking with pebbles in his mouth and by reciting verses when running or out of breath. He also practiced speaking before a large mirror. His **work ethic** proves the adage that **practice makes perfect**. The term now means: any bitter verbal attack; a long angry speech or scolding

Phishing - Pronounced fishing is another term that emerged with the popularity of the Internet. Like **Trojan horses, clickbait** and scams, it uses the Internet to grab access to the user. It is a fraudulent attempt to gain financial or other confidential information from Internet users often without their knowledge. In this regard, the perpetrator is fishing for pertinent information that could be later used for gain. Frequently, the attacker **masquerades** as a friend or reputable entity in an email or text message. It is a common form of **Identity theft** using the Internet as its conduit

Physician heal thyself - This phrase originates from the Bible (Luke 4:23). The common usage is:to attend to your own faults, instead of pointing out the faults of others. Similar phrases include: **take a look at the man in the mirror; take the mote out of your eye (Matt. 7 3-5)**

Pick up the mantle - In the Bible, when Elijah was taken up into heaven, Elisha "took up also the mantle of Elijah that fell from him" (2 Kings 2:13) thus taking Elijah's place. The phrase is habitually interpreted to mean: to take the place of someone; to continue someone's work or mission. **Hand over the baton is** similar in connotation. **Pick up where you left off; pick up the gauntlet**

Pickwickian - This expression originated from Mr. Pickwick, central character of The Pickwick Papers, the first novel by Charles Dickens. It now means: something marked by simplicity and generosity; intended or taken in a sense other than the obvious or literal one: someone who is jovial, plump or generous; of, relating to, or characteristic of Mr. Pickwick

A COLLECTION OF POPULAR ENGLISH PHRASES

Pièce de résistance - This is a French phrase that has become part of the English vernacular. It means: the most outstanding, remarkable accomplishment. The best or most important thing. Regarding food, the principal or featured dish of the meal

Pig in a poke - The origin of this expression goes back to the Middle Ages and was recorded in the 1500s. A poke, in this case, is a sack or a bag and thus the pig is unseen. The phrase is regularly interpreted to mean: something that is bought or accepted without knowing its value or seeing it first. To buy a pig in a poke; sight unseen. Let the cat out of the bag is similar because in some cases a worthless cat was substituted for a valuable pig which was only discovered once the buyer opened the bag (or hears a suspicious meow). Thus, this term means: to give away a secret or to hide something. I've been had; bamboozled

Piggy bank - The origin of this term dates back several hundred years and has nothing to do with a pig. In the Middle Ages jars were made of pygg a type of clay. It was customary for people to use such jars to save money. Over the years these pygg banks containers were called piggy banks. Serendipitously, the shape of these pygg banks was perfect for a small bank and manufactures began to make small banks in the shape of a pig and the rest is history. The term has migrated to mean: a container for holding money especially coins. Money that has been save especially for a rainy day

Pile Pelion on Ossa - The source of this phrase is the Greek myth of two large mountains that were pile atop each other in an attempt to reach heaven. The phrase now means: to add difficulty to something that is already difficult, tedious or challenging; a futile attempt

Pinocchio's nose grows - The source of this expression is from the Italian children's writer Carlo Collodi's The Adventures of Pinocchio (serialized in 1881-1883). Pinocchio is born a natural liar. Every time he told a lie his nose grew larger. Today, the growing nose of Pinocchio is associated with a person that lies. Liar, liar pants on fire is similar and is believed to have been derived from an 1810 poem entitled: The Liar by William Blake

Pipe dream - The source of this saying comes from the dream or the vision that people got after smoking opium. The common usage is: an unattainable or fanciful hope or scheme. What have you been smoking?

Piqued my curiosity (interest) - The origin of this term is unclear or uncertain. However, it is one of those terms such as "whet your appetite" and "bated breath" that are sometimes misused. It is frequently written as: peeked or peaked my curiosity. Piqued means to stimulate as opposed to peeked (to look) or peaked (to maximize) one's interest. Although such sayings sound correct, and for the most part make sense, they are incorrect. The phrase means: to stimulate one's curiosity or interest

Placebo effect - Even though the phenomenon has been around for some time, the term placebo and its effect were first identified in a paper by Dr. Austin Flint Sr., in 1863. A prolific writer, he wrote several books and published over 240 articles on almost every possible aspect of internal medicine. The placebo effect is one in which a patient's condition is improved by a dummy drug or fake treatment that cannot

185

be attributed to the properties of the drug or treatment. It must therefore be the result of the patient's belief in the benefit of the drug or treatment. **Mind over matter**

Plato's cave - This term comes from Plato's Republic. Plato's allegory of the cave is one of the best-known, most insightful attempts to explain the nature of reality. It describes prisoners in a cave who were only exposed to shadows of puppets and took that to be reality. Plato was one of the foremost philosophers of ancient Greece. Often viewed as the mouthpiece of his mentor Socrates; it is very difficult to discern where the philosophy of Socrates ends, and Plato's begins. **In turn,** Plato was the mentor of Aristotle who in turn was the mentor of Alexander the Great. The term has evolved to mean: to believe in a false reality based on your limited experience or ignorance

Platonic love (friendship) - The term is named after Plato, who was the first to describe this kind of love. It means: a type of love that is chaste and non-sexual. **A platonic relationship**

Plausible deniability - This term has its roots in the post-World War II Intelligence community. Although it was widespread during the Cold War, it was popularized in 1975 when the Church Committee, a U.S. Senate committee, investigated U.S. intelligence agencies. A perfect example of plausible deniability is the **Watergate** investigation: What did he know and when did he know it. Plausible deniability has since migrated to other aspects of industry, government and politics. In most cases, it relates to legal matters or jeopardy. The common usage is: a situation in which a denial of responsibility or knowledge of misconduct cannot be demonstrated as true or false because of a lack of evidence

Play it again, Sam - This expression was made famous by the 1942 movie Casablanca starring Humphrey Bogart and Ingrid Bergman. In the movie, the song, As Time Goes By is symbolic of the old relationship between Rick, played by Humphrey Bogart and Ilsa, played by Ingrid Bergman. So, the song is a bitter-sweet reminder of lost love, a love now forbidden because she is now married. Although often quoted, these words were not spoken in the movie instead she said the following: "Play it once, Sam, for old time's sake...Play it, Sam. Play "As Time Goes By." Nonetheless, it has come to mean to repeat something, in some cases over and over. **We'll always have Paris** is another line from the same movie and means: memories, particularly between former lovers, are everlasting. Another famous line is: I am shocked, shocked, to find gambling is going on here which was stated by the corrupt officer (Captain Renault) just before he collects his winnings. It is repeatedly used as the ultimate statement of corruption and hypocrisy. Additionally, the phrase the usual suspects appears to have its origins from a line spoken by Captain Renault in this movie. This phrase now refers to: a usual group of criminals suspected of a crime and has recently been normalized to include any group that regularly meets. Other lines from this **time honored** movie include: here's looking at you kid: and of all the gin joints, in all the towns, in all the world, she walks into mine

Play possum - The origin of this term is from the behavior of the opossum that pretends to be dead when defending itself against predators. It has migrated to mean: to pretend to be asleep or unconscious; or to be deceitful about something. **Playing dead**

A COLLECTION OF POPULAR ENGLISH PHRASES

Play second fiddle - In an orchestra, there are two roles played by violins which are called first fiddle and second fiddle. The player or performer who played the first fiddle was considered the main and important musician in orchestra. It means: to be subservient or inferior to someone, to follow someone or something. **Can't hold a candle; second banana; always the bridesmaid, never the bride**, virtually mean the same thing

Play the sedulous ape - This expression originated from an essay by the Scottish writer Robert Louis Stevenson. The common usage is: anyone who slavishly imitates someone; one who is conscientiously attentive and tries to learn by intentionally imitating others. Similar phrases include: **imitation is the sincerest form of flattery; monkey see monkey do**

Play the trump card - This saying takes its origin from a card game. The trump card is the winning card. It has come to mean: to use your most powerful or effective means to solve a problem or to get out of a bad situation. **Get out of jail free card** is another card metaphor and comes from the board game Monopoly. It denotes: a means or method used to work your way out of a bad or difficult situation

Playing musical chairs - The source of this idiom is from the name of a popular party game in which players compete for a decreasing number of chairs by going around in a circle until the music stops. At that time, they must have a seat to sit or be expelled from the game. The phrase now refers to: moving from one place to another before finally staying; any situation involving several people in a series of interrelated changes. Similarly, **Pop goes the weasel** comes from a nursery rhyme and singing game and is sometimes used to indicate excitement

Playing the race card - The term "race card" was first used in horseracing. Its current usage may have derived from a cartoon of Lincoln playing cards against a Confederate soldier in which he plays the Ace of Spades, which in this case, symbolized the Emancipation Proclamation. In the 19th century, politicians and others looking for a euphemism for racial politics coined the phrase "playing the race card." After the Civil Rights movement and during the election and presidency of Barack Obama, the term was sometimes used to direct criticism toward black people and President Obama by accusing people of color of playing on white guilt. The common interpretation of this phrase is: an attempt to gain an advantage, especially in politics, using race as a factor. **White guilt; white privilege**

Pocket dial - This term emerged with the advent of cell phones. Because of their **pocket size** and portability, cell phones could inadvertently make a phone call while in someone's pocket. The term now means: to unintentionally call someone

Poetic justice - This phrase was coined in the late 17th century by the English literary critic and historian Thomas Rymer in his essay entitled: The Tragedies of the Last Age Considere'd. It means: a fitting or deserved reckoning for one's actions in which vice is punished and virtue is rewarded. **You reap what you sow**

IN A NUTSHELL

Poets(geniuses) are born not made - This term originated from a Latin proverb and has means: poets, like all true artists, possess talent that cannot be taught, somethings require a certain amount of natural ability, e.g., **a natural born leader.** The English writer Edward George Bulwer-Lytton once said: "talent does what it can; genius does what it must"

Point-blank - The origin of this phrase appears to be medieval archery in which targets were painted white (typically in the middle of a circle). The blank comes from the French word for white which is *blanc*. The term migrated to mean: a shot fired very close to its target or in some cases; to be direct

Poker face - The source of this term is the card game poker. In this game, it is essential that players do not show any indication of the cards in their hands and bluffing is an essential part of the game. It means: to wear a face that does not reveal your inner thoughts. Other poker/card metaphors are: **know when to hold them; play the hand that is dealt to you; it's (ain't) in the cards; several cards short of a full deck; lay your cards on the table; keep your cards close to your chest; play your cards right; show your cards; wild card; cards/odds are stacked against you; play the trump card; hole all the aces; have a card up your sleeve; buy the pot**

Politically correct - This term has been around since the late 1970s and early 1980s. As the Civil Rights of individuals was expanded, so was the usage of this term. It now means: conforming to a belief that language and practices which could offend political sensibilities such as matters of sex, race, religion, sexual orientation and handicapped people, should be abolished. Similarly, **political football** means: a debated issue, usually between political parties that is difficult to resolve. It is often used to gain leverage over the other party

Pollyanna - So named after the heroine of the novel Pollyanna, by the American children's writer Eleanor Hodgman. It means: an excessively or blindly optimistic person. Adjective: also, Pollyannaish. Unreasonably or illogically optimistic

Pomp and circumstance - The origin of this expression comes from Shakespeare's Othello (Act III, Scene III) "Farewell...the royal banner, and all quality, pride, pomp, and circumstance of glorious war." In recent times, it has been associated with a series of ceremonial marches made famous by Sir Edward Elgar. It now has the following meaning: impressive activities or ceremonies

Portmanteau **word** - This is a word of French origin that eventually worked its way into the English vernacular. It is a word that is a linguistic merger of two words into one sharing the meaning of combined words such as Medicare which equals medical care or the moniker given to Trump's daughter and her husband (javanka) a combination of Jared and Ivanka

Possession is nine-tenths of the law - This is an old expression that dates back centuries. One of the earliest recorded usage is in a play by the English writer Colley Cibber, Woman's Wit or the Lady in Fashion, from the late 1600s, early 1700s The popular interpretation of this phrase is: ownership is easier to maintain if one has possession of something, unless there is sufficient evidence that it was stolen or fraudulently obtained

A COLLECTION OF POPULAR ENGLISH PHRASES

Potemkin village - So named after Potemkin, the Russian army officer and politician, who was said to have built fake villages to impress Catherine the Great on her tour of the Crimea: a story now generally considered untrue. It has migrated to mean: a façade or something that appears impressive but is ineffective and insubstantial

Pour oil over troubled waters - The ancient Greeks believed that pouring oil over stormy waters calmed the waves. The common interpretation of this phrase is: to smooth or calm a situation by tact or diplomacy

Power corrupts, and absolute power corrupts absolutely - The English historian and writer Lord Acton, expressed this opinion in a letter to Bishop Mandell Creighton in 1887. History **bears testimony** to this powerful axiom. It means: if someone is given absolute power, they will eventually be corrupted by it. Likewise, **if you want to test a man's character, give him power.** This quote is often erroneously attributed to Abraham Lincoln. The true source is Bob Ingersoll and is about Lincoln. The full quote is as follows: "Nearly all men can stand adversity, but if you want to test a man's character, give him power." **The strong do what they can, and the weak suffer what they must**

Practice makes perfect - This popular phrase has been around in its current form for centuries (at least the 1500s) and may have evolved from the phrase 'use makes mastery.' It has become an axiom and true for every endeavor as the human brain, and moreover the subconscious mind, is trained toward efficiency resulting from repetition which is the essence of skill. A person can never achieve perfection; but without practice he/she will never reach their full potential. Quite often in sports, we see the execution and not the long hours of practice that tuned such skills. The phrase means: regular practice of an activity or skill is the only way to become proficient at it. It is also important to have the right coach or mentor to encourage a person and to set an example that it could be done

Practice what you preach - This expression was inspired by the Bible (Matthew 23:3) although it does not appear in the Bible. The widespread interpretation of this phrase is: to set an example and to do what you advise others to do. Similar phrases include: **The golden rule; actions speak louder than words**

Prejudice, not being founded on reason, cannot be removed by argument - This quote is ascribed to the British author and polymath Samuel Johnson. No one comes into this world with a prejudice for or against anything. Prejudice is something that is a product of our environment and **sense of moral compass.** Over time, attitudes and perceptions are **baked in** and thus form the foundation of our reality. Once established, it is very difficult, and in some cases impossible, to change. When life is viewed through the prism of prejudice, the light of truth is distorted and sometimes obscured by what we believe or want to be true. Emerson wrote: "People only see what they are prepared to see." **Perception is reality**

Praise the Lord, and pass the ammunition - This phrase comes from an American patriotic song by Frank Loesser, and published as sheet music in 1942. The general interpretation of this phrase is: although a person may place his faith in God; earthy actions are still required to achieve a goal(s)

189

IN A NUTSHELL

Preaching to the choir - This exact phrase originated in the 1970s but is a variant of a much older English phrase: **"preaching to the converted."** It means: to pointlessly try to convince a person or a group of something that they already agree upon. **A foregone conclusion**

Presto chango - The origin of this expression is unclear. However, it appeared in a 1929, Business Week, advertisement, "Just one touch lets you go from black to a second color. Presto. Chango. Or back to black. Presto. Chango. Color copies have never been easier." A subsequent cartoon by the same name in 1939 helped to popularize it. It was also used in magical acts. It now means: to change quickly or a change occurring suddenly and as if by magic. **Abracadabra!; hocus pocus**

Pride goes (comes) before a fall - This expression has its origin in the Bible (Proverbs 16:18). "Pride [goeth] before destruction, and a haughty spirit before a fall." The common interpretation of this expression is: overconfidence leads to mistakes which in turn leads to destructions or defeat

Prima donna - This term comes from Italian opera and is the principal female singer in an opera or concert. The term has migrated over to general use and means: a vain or disobedient person who finds it difficult to work under direction or as part of a team; someone that thinks that they are special and that the normal rules do not apply to them. **Jewish American Princess (JAP)**

Prima facie - This is a Latin term that has entered the English vernacular. It literally means "first face or first appearance." It generally means: something based on the first impression; accepted as correct until proven otherwise; something that is sufficient to establish a fact or raise a presumption unless disproved or rebutted. In law it means: a motion for a directed verdict which should be granted unless the defendant provides proof to the contrary sufficient to deny the motion. **Guilty until proven innocent**

Primrose path - The origin of this expression comes from Shakespeare's Hamlet (Act I, Scene III) "the primrose path of dalliance treads; And recks not his own rede." The expression can be interpreted to mean: the pursuit of pleasure, especially when it is seen to bring disastrous consequences: **a course of action** that is easy or tempting but also hazardous; **the easy way out of** a difficult situation. **Lead you down the primrose path**

Procrastination is the thief of time - This phrase was first articulated by the English poet Edward Young. It is frequently interpreted to mean: time is a precious thing and we should not hesitate to do the things that we want to do or are required to do. Furthermore, delay or indecisiveness may have unfortunate or devastating consequences. Similar phrases include: **he who hesitates is lost; time and tide wait for no man; strike while the iron is hot; opportunity knocks but once**

Procrustean - This expression originated from, Procrustes, the villainous son of Poseidon in Greek mythology. He was renowned for forcing travelers to fit into his bed by stretching their bodies or cutting off their legs. It is used to describe a person or institution that forces people to conform. **Draconian**

A COLLECTION OF POPULAR ENGLISH PHRASES

Prodigal son - The source of this term is from the Bible (Luke 15: 17-24). One of the parables of Jesus, it is about a misbehaving son who wastes his inheritance but returns home to find that his father forgives him. It is therefore defined as: a wayward person (particularly a child) that after the experiences of life repents and returns home or to his roots. **Return to the fold.** Similarly, a **Native son** means: someone born in a particular place and still lives there or is associated with it, as opposed to an **expatriate** who is a person who lives outside their native country typically in exile

Profile(s) in courage - This was the title of a book written by John F. Kennedy that won a Pulitzer Prize although the phrase may have been in use before him. It commonly denotes a demonstration of courage amid adversity and strife. An exemplary example of bravery, strength and fortitude. **Speak truth to power; moral compass**

Prometheus's fire - Prometheus is known for stealing fire from the gods thus bringing knowledge to mankind. He was severely punished by the gods for his crime. As punishment, Zeus chained him to a rock where an eagle fed each day on his liver, which grew again each night. According to the Greeks, humankind is forever indebted to him. But after Prometheus's theft of the secret of fire, Zeus ordered Hephaestus to create the woman **Pandora** as part of the punishment for mankind. The term habitually refers to something that is enlightening or innovative. **Promethean** means something that is exceptionally creative and original. **Sisyphus' rock; Pandora's box**

Prove it! I'm from Missouri - Missouri's unofficial nickname is the Show-Me State. The most popular origin of this nickname comes from a speech given by Representative Willard Duncan Vandiver who was a member of the United States Congress and served during the late 1800s. While he may not have coined the phrase, he popularized it. Henceforth, it became something that the inhabitants enthusiastically embraced, and **the rest is history.** This phrase is regularly used as a response by someone who is skeptical about something that is being said or done and needs additional confirmation or proof. **Put up or shut up**

Public enemy number one - This term has its origin in law enforcement. More specifically, the Federal Bureau of Investigations (FBI) during the Roaring Twenties and the Great Depression when prohibition and a depressed economy spun a host of organized crime figures and gangsters. Chief among them were Al Capone, John Dillinger, Bonnie & Clyde and Baby Face Nelson. It designated a criminal at the top of the FBI's list of the ten most wanted criminals. It was during the early days of the FBI, that men such as Elliot Ness, J. Edgar Hoover and other **G-men** (Government Men) became national figures in their battle against organized crime and bank robbers. The term has since been used to designate a chief enemy, nemesis or adversary. Another term that emerged from this era of crime is **hitman,** a person who is paid to murder someone, especially for a criminal or political organization or more generically a person designated to destroy an adversary

Pull the wool over your eyes - This expression appears to have its roots in the practice of judges and lawyers wearing wool wigs in court. Pull the wool or wig over their eyes inhibited them from seeing the truth. It means: to deceive someone by telling untruths. **Fool me once shame on you, fool me twice,**

shame on me. This also seems to be the origin of the term **bigwig** as only people of importance wore wigs during colonial times

Pull up by your bootstraps - The source of this phrase is unknown. However, it was used by the Irish novelist and short story writer James Joyce in Ulysses, 1922.This expression has given rise to the computer term bootstrap program or simply to boot up. It currently means: to improve yourself by your own efforts without any help from others. In a humorous note, Al Franken once wrote: "To pull yourself up by your bootstraps, you've got to have the boots." **Do it on your own; tighten up your bootstraps. A self-made man(woman)** is someone that has pulled himself or herself up by their bootstraps

Purgatory - The basis of this term is the Roman Catholic doctrine of a place or a state of suffering inhabited by the souls of sinners that are in the process of expunging their sins before they can go to heaven. It is habitually used to describe: a place between heaven and hell, good or evil, having the potential to be purified. An in between state or a place of waiting. A perpetual state of torture or unhappiness. **Netherworld**

Push the envelope - The origin of this expression is from aviation jargon in which envelope refers to the known limits. At the end of World War II, the **sound barrier** was one of the obstacles that was challenged before the **race for space** began. On October 14, 1947, Chuck Yeager broke the sound barrier in his Bell X-1 jet. At the time, it was uncertain if a person could survive the **sonic boom** that occurs at the speed of sound. He did, and **the rest is history.** It was the most historic flight since the Wright Brothers. After the sound barrier was conquered, space became the new envelope. The phrase generally means: to challenge the limits of something or go right to the top. **Push the limits; stretch the envelope**

Put the cart before the horse - The earliest reference to this saying is in a work by the Roman orator and statesman Cicero (106 BCE - 43 BCE) entitled: On Friendship. It has migrated to mean: to reverse the proper order or procedure of something, **Through the looking glass; ass backwards**

Put your finger in the dyke - The origin of this story is from The Little Dutch Boy Who Saved Holland. In which a little boy saves Holland by putting his fingers in a hole in the dyke. The story is part of a novel entitled Hans Brinker. It is interpreted to mean: to stop the flow of something before it becomes too large to stop. **An Ounce of prevention is worth a pound of cure**

Putting lipstick on a pig - This phrase was first recorded in 1946, in the aftermath of World War II but did not become popular until later. Although both terms had been around for some time, with pig used in various saying to denote something ugly, e.g. **fat pig**, Miss Piggy, **pig out**, and lipstick to designate the practice of trying to make oneself more attractive. The two were never combined into a phrase until this time. Like many phrases, this one stuck. The common interpretation of this phrase is: an attempt to make something that is ugly appear better than what it is, without improving it. To make something or someone look appealing or attractive when it quite clearly will not work or will only fool the most naive or dumbest of people. **Mutton dressed as lamb.** On the other hand, **to take the gift off the gingerbread** means: to ruin something that would otherwise be good

Pygmalion effect - There is a story from ancient Greece of how a person turned a statue from ivory to life and married her. The movie My Fair Lady is based somewhat on this premise. The story of Pygmalion is the story of the **self-fulfilling prophecy.** The Pygmalion effect is based on the work of Rosenthal and Jacobsen (1968) and illustrates that teacher expectations influence student performance. This is particularly true when it comes to the expectations of certain minority groups and women in areas such as **Science Technologies Engineering and Mathematics (STEM).** It means: if you think negative thoughts they will eventually happen and vice versa. If you believe something is true it will become true. Similar phrases include: **Mozart effect; the power of positive thinking**

Pyrrhic **victory -** King Pyrrhus of Epirus (c. 318 BCE – 272 BCE) landed on the southern Italian shore with 20 elephants and 25,000-30,000 men to defend his fellow Greek speakers against Roman domination. Although Pyrrhus won the first two battles, he lost a large number of his men and as a result, lost the war. It means: a victory won at such great cost to the victor that it is equal to a defeat or a draw in the long run. **Risk versus reward**

Stands for:

Quantum leap

IN A NUTSHELL

Qualitative versus quantitative - The origin of the use of these two terms used together is unclear. However, they are often contrasted against each other. Qualitative analysis of data seems to be inductive whereas quantitative analysis or data is more deductive. **As a rule of thumb**, analysis or data is deemed quantitative if it is expressed in numerical form and qualitative if it is in written form. For example, qualitative data characteristically consists of words while quantitative data normally consists of numbers, e.g., spreadsheets, probabilities, statistics, etc. Typically, quantitative analysis or information is grounded in a quantitative assumption or premise. In this regard, qualitative data could be used to support quantitative data and vice versa

Quality of mercy is not strained - This is yet another saying by William Shakespeare and it appears in The Merchant of Venice (Act IV, Scene I). "The quality of mercy is not strain'd; It droppeth as the gentle rain from heaven; Upon the place beneath; It is twice blest; It blesseth him that gives and him that takes." The phrase is regularly interpreted to mean: mercy is something that has to be freely given; no one can force someone else to be merciful, kindhearted or to forgive someone. These things, in their truest and sincerest forms, emanate not so much from the mind or the body; but from the **inner sanctums** of the human soul

Quantum leap(jump) - This term is borrowed from the Physics field of Quantum Mechanics. A field which deals with particles on the subatomic level. The term generally means: a sudden and dramatic change or increase. **A gigantic step**

Que sera sera - This phrase, used in several languages, was popularized by the 1956 Alfred Hitchcock's film: The Man Who Knew Too Much and sung by Doris Day. It was also the theme song of her TV show. It means "whatever will be will be" and is often used to express a situation in which you cannot control

Queen Anne is dead - When Queen Anne died, her death was not announced until it was clear that George of Hanover would become George I of Great Britain and that there would be no war. By the time of the official announcement of the Queen's death to the public, everybody who mattered already knew that she had died. The common interpretation of this phrase is: your news is stale; everyone knows what you are talking about already. **Old news; tell me something new**

Queer as a three-dollar bill - This was an American colloquialism which was originally meant to denote counterfeit money, as in American currency there is no three-dollar bill. The term was later used to denote a homosexual and later shorten to just **Queer. The love that dare not speak its name**

Quid pro quo - This is a Latin term which means "this for that" that has worked its way into the English language. It means: something for something; an equal exchange or a favor or advantage granted or expected in return for something. **You scratch my back, I'll scratch yours; pay to play; you have to give in order to receive**

Stands for:

Revenge is a dish that is best served cold

Railroaded - This term originated from the early railroad days when railroad lines were placed in geographical areas without much regard for the effects on the population. They were intentionally placed to get from point A to B and to connect to other railways thus making a contiguous chain between larger destinations. The general interpretation is: to press or force someone into doing something in great haste or against someone's will. To act unjustly or without regard for the welfare of others. **I got railroaded**

Rain check - This term originated from the early days of American baseball when a rain check or ticket was given if a game was rained out. It generally means: a ticket given for later use when a sports event or other outdoor event is interrupted or postponed by rain or when a product that is on sale has run out of stock. It is also used generically to postpone any event or invitation, e.g., **I'll take a rain check** on our lunch. Similar phrases include: **catch you later; catch you on the rebound**

Raining cats and dogs - In 17th century England, after heavy rains, many of the streets were filled with filth including dead cats and dogs. It appears in Richard Brome's: The City Witt (1652). The phrase has evolved to mean: heavy rains. **It's pouring down; when it rains it pours**

Raise Cain - This term is a biblical reference to Cain the eldest son of **Adam and Eve** and murderer of his brother Abel (Genesis 4). It means: to behave in a wild, noisy manner; to cause a loud disturbance; to protest angrily against something or someone; to create trouble or a commotion. **Cain and Abel**

Rally around the flag - The source of this expression is attributed to General Andrew Jackson at the Battle of New Orleans during the War of 1812. He later became the 7th president of the United States and he has an entire era named after him called "The Age of Jackson." The expression generally means: to come together or show support especially during tough times. To **circle the wagons** is a similar metaphor with its origin in the wagon trains in the United States that went west and formed a circle to ward off attackers. This phrase has migrated to mean: to unite in defense of a common interest. **Raise a red flag; wave a white flag**

Rapprochement - This is a French term that has migrated to the English language. It literally means "to bring together." It has evolved to mean: diplomatic terms established between two states or bodies moving towards each other or an agreement

Rat race - This term originated from the 1920s-30s Jazz culture in America. It was the name of a dance that was difficult to keep up with. It now means: keeping up with the everyday world. The comedian Lily Tomlin once said: the trouble with the rat race is that even if you win, you're still a rat. David Lee Roth one said: just when you think you've got the rat race licked – Boom! Faster rats. **Don't get caught up in the rat race; keeping up with the Joneses**

Ré·pon·dez s'il vous plait (RSVP) - This is a French term that has become part of the English language. It simply means respond please. The acronym, RSVP, in its current usage, means: the invited guest(s) must tell the host **whether or not** they plan to attend the event and is usually used by the host to determine how many people will attend. The expression, *ré·pon·dez s'il vous plait,* is sometimes used sarcastically in conversation when you want to get someone to respond to what you said or did. **Get back to me**

Read between the lines - This phrase is believed to have come from the fact that sometimes secret messages were written between the lines in invisible ink or other forms of cryptography used in letters and in documents. It means: to look for or discover a meaning that is hidden or implied rather than explicitly stated. **Read the small(fine) print** means: to be aware of the specific terms, conditions, restrictions, limitations, details, etc., of an agreement, contract, or other binding document

Read the Riot Act - The Riot Act was a law that was passed in England in 1714 to prevent riots. When riotous groups assembled, they would simply read them the act before taking action, if needed. It generally means: to reprimand rowdy characters or to warn them to stop behaving badly; to give someone a severe scolding. **Rake (Haul) over the coals** is a similar expression and has its origin in the medieval treatment and punishment of heretics in Europe. It means: to criticize or reprimand someone severely. **Procrustean**

Read the tea leaves - The origin of this phrase comes from the practice of forecasting future events by reading smeared or spotted substances known as tasseography. Although in practice during the Middle Ages, as tea became prominent, the practice moved from molted metals and other substances to tea. It is conducted by interpreting symbols formed by-tea leaves on the sides or the bottom of a cup of tea or coffee. It has migrated to mean: to interpret signs leading to an event or action to predict the future. **Know which way the wind is blowing**

Real men don't eat quiche - The origin of this phrase is from the title of a book by the American author Bruce Feirstein published in 1982. Analogous **to real men don't wear pink** it is a phrase that speaks to the traditional **red line** between masculine and feminine acts and is also similar in connotation to **men are from Mars, women are from Venus**. In recent times, however, such traditional **lines of demarcation** have been challenged and the definition of masculine and feminine blurred. Notwithstanding, the phrase means: the stereotypical male does not wear or behave in a manner that could be considered effeminate

Reap what you sow - This expression originated from the Bible, (Galatians 6:). There are many that believe that a sense of fairness or **karma** pervades life on earth. In this regard, **what goes around comes around**. Reap what you sow has come to mean: **you get what you deserve**, or you eventually have to face up to the consequences of your actions. Similar phrases include: **face the music; get what's coming to you; old sins cast long shadows; as a man sows, so shall he reap**

Rebellion to tyrants is obedience to God - This saying is attributed to the American Founding Father Ben Franklin. He wanted to make it part of the Great Seal because it echoes the sentiments of the American Revolution and the Declaration of Independence. Many believed that it was inspired by the Bible (Acts 5:29). "Then Peter and the other apostles answered and said; We ought to obey God rather than men." It is currently used as a statement of freedom and that we put our trust in God rather than in man. **Render unto Caesar what is Caesar's**

IN A NUTSHELL

Recherché - This is a French term that has migrated to the English Language. It literally means "carefully sought out." It means: something that is rare, exotic or obscure. Something that is known to a chosen few; or something that is marked by rare and exquisite quality, known only to connoisseurs or aficionados. **Recherche' collection or selection**

Reckless abandon - The origin of this term is unclear. However, it could have been derived from the legal term reckless abandonment, which has a different connotation. It means to engage in reckless or careless behavior without regard for the consequences, unintended or otherwise. **Bull in a china shop; with reckless abandon**

Red badge of courage - This is a phrase that was popularized by the title of a book written by the American author Stephen Crane about the American Civil War. Like so many popular novels, it was made into a 1951 film which further helped to popularize the phrase. During the Civil War, there was a group of soldiers that did wear a red badge. Metaphorically speaking, the red badge could symbolize a red blood stain on a uniform resulting from a wound inflicted in battle (although this was not the case in Crane's novel). The term has migrated to mean: a sign of courage, bravery or honor. **Blood and guts** is a similar term that is ascribed to General George Patton so much so that it became his moniker. **On a side note**, the Medal of Honor was created in 1861 and first given to soldiers during the Civil War. It is the highest U.S. military decoration, awarded by Congress to a member of the armed forces for gallantry and bravery in combat at the risk of life **above and beyond the call of duty.** It is therefore the ultimate badge of courage

Red flag - The origin of this term dates back to antiquity. It was common to raise a flag as a symbol and the red flag became a symbol of revolt. For example, the slaves in ancient Rome **raised a red flag** in their revolt and the use of raising a red flag during revolutions is well documented. Gradually, it became a symbol of warning throughout the world. Red is a symbol of warning perhaps because it is the color of blood and we psychologically identify with it as impending danger (such as in **crossing a red line, stopping at a red light**, etc.). Today, the term denotes: a warning of danger or a potential problem. Something that demands immediate attention or provokes action or a response. Similar expressions are: **draw a line in the sand; knock the chip off your shoulder; to sound the alarm. Raise a red flag in front of a bull. Raise a white flag** is similar but is used as a sign of a truce, surrender or a request for mutual dialogue

Red herring - The source of this term appears to be the belief that in the 17th century, escaping criminals would drag a dried smoked herring, which turned red by the smoke, along their escape route to get the dogs to lose their scent. It is currently used as: something, especially a clue, that is, or is intended to be, misleading or distracting. **Smoke and mirrors**

Red hot - The origin of this term comes from heating a substance such as a metal to the point when it glows red. Though this is hot in comparative terms such as room temperature, it is not very hot when compared to the thermodynamic heat spectrum which is the source of the glow. The heat color sequence is as follows: red, orange, yellow, white, and bluish white as an object is heated to successively higher temperatures. **As you can see**, in comparison, red hot is the lowest and we can tell how hot a star is by looking at its color spectrum. Nonetheless, the term "red hot" has come to designate something that is very hot. Similarly, **ice cold** designates something that is very cold or cold enough to freeze. Both terms use room temperature as a reference. It is important to note that hot and cold are used as metaphors for many things. Hot often as something good, cold as something bad. For example, colloquially speaking, a basketball player could be **red hot** meaning he can't miss or **ice cold** meaning he can't find the basket. Similarly, **Red hot momma** or **to be hot** means someone that is very attractive

Red meat - Traditionally, red meat is meat such as lamb or beef that is red when it is raw. Most recently, the term has been applied to politics. In this context it means: to give or say things appealing to one's political base or something that they feel strongly about even if it is not in line with the general population. **Dog whistle**

Red tape - In the early 1900s, lawyers and government officials often tied their papers together with a red ribbon. It now means: excessive bureaucracy or adherence to rules and formalities, especially in public business. **Cut the red tape; cut to the chase**

Red wedding - This phrase became popular from the Game of Thrones series in which a happy wedding between Edmure Tully and Roslin Frey turns into a bloodbath. The phrase has become synonymous with an event that turns into a disaster

Redneck - The source of this term is the sunburned necks of white field workers of the American South. Such red necks became a symbol of their meager status. Consequently, the term was used, sometimes derogatorily, to denote a poor white person. It is used mostly today to denote a working-class white person, especially a politically reactionary one from a rural area. **Poor white trash (PWT)**

Remember the Alamo - The Alamo was a battle fought in Texas between Mexican soldiers and American settlers. In that region, the settlers were soundly defeated. It featured such notables as: Jim Bowie, William Travis and Davy Crocket along with the Mexican general Santa Anna. One of the catalysts of this war, was that the settlers brought slaves into the region which was a violation of the original agreement with Mexico after they gained their independence from Spain. "Remember the Alamo" has been used since as an American rallying cry. It has entered American folklore in a similar manner to **Custer's last stand**

Renaissance man - So named after a prototypical polymath of the Renaissance period. A period in the revival of art and literature under the influence of classical models in the 14th - 16th centuries that produced Leonardo da Vinci and others. It is defined as: a cultured person who is knowledgeable, educated, or proficient in a wide range of fields, someone who is **well read** on several subjects, **a polymath**

Render unto Caesar - This expression is a saying of Jesus from the Bible (Matthew 22: 20-22). Jesus was asked the question about paying taxes in hope that he would answer "yes" or "no" and he gave this response; meaning that his followers should be law abiding citizens of their country while also following

IN A NUTSHELL

God's laws. This saying gives rise to multiple possible interpretations concerning under what circumstances it is desirable for Christians to submit to earthly authority. It is also used by everyday people to yield or not yield to the government or even on the job when workers may refer to management as the ruling authority. **The powers that be** is similar and also comes from the Bible (Romans 13:1)

Resistance is futile - The original source of the phrase appears to be the British Dr. Who series in which the Vogon guard says: resistance is useless. The Borg in the American Star Trek series uttered the current phrase which of course is very similar in meaning. Though the origin is sometimes disputed, between the earlier Dr. Who (1963) and Star Trek (1966), there is no doubt that the current phrase was popularized by the Star Trek series along with: **beam me up Scotty, live long and prosper, to boldly go where no man has gone before** and of course my favorite: **revenge is a dish that is best served cold**. The phrase means exactly what it says; that it is useless to resist, and in other circles, such as gaming, as a prelude to an **all-out attack** that cannot be defended. **An exercise in futility** is similar and means: any activity that is unsuccessful, pointless or does not yield positive or constructive results. **Carrying coals to Newcastle** is another phrase that is an exercise in futility. It has its origin in Great Britain. Newcastle was a town that was known for its coal production. Hence, carrying coal to this town was a fruitless endeavor. The phrase therefore means: to do something that is pointless or totally unnecessary. **Does not bear fruit**

Rest in Peace (RIP) - This phrase goes back centuries, perhaps as early as the 1st century CE. Other variants such as "may he sleep in peace" have also been used. However, around the late Middle Ages, it became quite popular among Christians to say, often after someone dies and later written on tombstones (most frequently in its abbreviated form RIP). Today that tradition continues at gravesites and memorials. It is used to express the hope that the beloved person's soul has found peace and happiness in the hereafter. **May God have mercy on your soul** is a phrase regularly used by judges after they pronounced a sentence of death or by a person that believes that God is the ultimate judge of a person's fate

Rest on your laurels - The origin of this saying comes from Ancient Greece where wreaths of laurel were worn across the head as an emblem of victory. These wreathes were associated with the god Apollo and given to victors at the Pythian games in his honor. The phrase now means: to be satisfied with past achievements and to become complacent or comfortable with **the status quo**

Return on investment - This is a term that comes out of the financial realm that has worked its way into the public sphere. Often referred to as (ROI), it can be calculated in many ways. It is the first question that investors want answered to determine their **risk versus reward**. In the public sphere, it is habitually used: to weigh one's options, such as going to college, type of degree, buying a particular home, etc. **What's the return on investment; is it worth it**

Revenge is a dish that is best served cold - The origin of this saying is unclear, and many think it is of French origin. However, it was made famous in a Star Trek episode: The Wrath of Khan. It means that revenge is best served not fresh or hot after the insulting or offensive incident, but at a time of your choosing so that the person or group is unaware of your actions and their response is nullified or impeded. **Vengeance is mine, saith the Lord**

Reverse engineer - This is a term that has its origin in the engineering realm. In engineering, it means to start out with a developed product and work backwards to determine how it works or how it was conceived. The term has worked its way into the English vernacular to mean: to start out with a conclusion or a solution to a problem or a dilemma and to justify it **by any means necessary.** To take something apart and **to see what makes it tick. The end justifies the means**

Ride shotgun - The origin of this term comes from the old stagecoach days in the Western United States. As the territory of the United States expanded as a result of the Louisiana Purchase, people took stagecoaches west. These stagecoaches were vulnerable to attack. The person next to the driver carried a shotgun **to ward off attack.** As the railroad emerged, stagecoaches became obsolete. Still, this term was not popularized until the beginning of the 20th century and made even more popular by the numerous Westerns that depicted stagecoaches as movies and television developed. Though currently used to designate an armed guard in the seat next to the driver of a vehicle, it is sometimes used to designate the person in the passenger seat or even someone that plays a secondary role or a person that protects someone while on travel. **Second banana**; sidekick

Ride the gravy train - The term is believed to come from 19th century railroad slang, although the earliest recorded use dates from the early 1900s and the musician W.C. Handy also known as the *Father of the Blues*. It has migrated to mean: to experience excessive ease, success, or profit, especially undeservedly. Similar phrases include: **on Easy Street; parked on the corner of Easy Street and Gravy Lane; sitting pretty**

Ride the pine (bench) - This is a sports term that probably originated in baseball and was later extended to other sports, e.g., football, basketball. In the old days, benches were made of pine and a reserve player who sat on the bench more than he played rode the pine. It means: to be used as a substitute player or to be on the team and not play at all. Similar expression **are: left guard of the water bucket, right end of the bench; benchwarmer; second string**

Right as rain - The origin of this saying is unclear. But it is a common belief that it originated in Great Britain; a country known for its rain. The earliest usage dates to the late 1800s. The expression means: feeling well and healthy, particularly after an accident or illness or **being under the weather**; correct. **As right as rain; it's raining cats and dogs; when it rains it pours; hale and hearty**

Right the ship - This phrase has its origin in the maritime experience of a ship being turned on its side or capsized. The common interpretation is; to return something to its original state, form or position. To make a correction in a positive manner

Righteous indignation - The origin of this term is unclear. However, it is closely related to the biblical verse (Ephesians 4:26-27) "Be angry, and yet do not sin; do not let the sun go down on your anger, and do not give the devil an opportunity." It means: an emotional response of anger and contempt based on a belief that malice or an injustice has been enacted against a person or group

Ring finger - The fourth finger on the left hand was believed by the Ancient Egyptians to be connected directly to the heart. This is why it is called the ring finger today and the finger that one wears their wedding band. It is one of the many customs the we inherited from this great ancient civilization

Rip van Winkle - This expression originated from Rip Van Winkle a children's story written by American author Washington Irving and published in 1819. It is about a man who wandered into the mountains and slept for twenty years. It has evolved to mean: someone who has outdated views and is completely out of touch with contemporary ideas. **Lost in a time warp; old school; as old as Methuselah**

Rise from the ashes of a Phoenix - In Egyptian mythology, a phoenix is an immortal bird that when it dies bursts into flames and is reborn from its own ashes. Hence, bringing something back to life. It generally means: to make a miraculous comeback, to be resurrected. The Egyptian obelisk is also a symbol of resurrection

Rivers of Babylon - The origin of this saying is from the Bible (Psalm 137). It is one of the best-known psalms and is about the captivity of the Jews in Babylon. "**By the rivers of Babylon,** we sat and wept when we remembered **Zion**." Zion was the hill of Jerusalem on which the city of David was built and thus the historic land of Israel and a symbol of the Jewish people. It is important to note that the Babylonians did not exile all of the Jews. The king of Babylon, Nebuchadnezzar, only exiled the most prominent citizens of Judah, i.e., professionals, priests, craftsmen, and the wealthy, **the best and the brightest**. Many of the Jews in Babylon formed the foundation of some of today's Jewish traditions, literature and religious infrastructure as well as the development of a paradigm for later life in the diaspora. Seventy years later, when the Babylonians fell to the Persians under Cyrus the Great, the Jews could return home. Rivers of Babylon is often interpreted to mean: a remorseful time or place, sometimes alluded to by those that are mourning the dead or the destruction of something that they valued dearly. **A bad situation.** On a side note, **Next Year in Jerusalem** is a phrase that is unique to the Jewish culture and is related to this event and other episodes of expulsion. Most Jews are familiar with it as: *le-shanah ha-ba'ah bi-Yerushalayim*, and is said at two times during the Jewish calendar: at the conclusion of the Passover Seder and at the conclusion of the Ne'ilah service of Yom Kippur. This phrase is significant because Jews pray for Jerusalem's reconstruction and the reestablishment of the Davidic monarchy. Because of its historical and sacred nature, it is not recommended that non-Jewish people use this phrase. It is only mentioned here to make the reader aware of its significance to the Jewish people

Road to Damascus (moment) - This expression originated from the Bible (Book of Acts Chapter 9) and is in reference to Saint Paul's epiphany and his conversion to Christianity. It is a common belief within Christianity that after this experience, Paul changed his name from Saul to Paul (Acts:9:13-16) a common motif echoed in the Old Testament. His epiphany and conversion **set in motion** a series of actions that help to form the foundation of one of the world's largest and most pervasive religions. It means: an important moment of insight, typically one that leads to a dramatic transformation of attitude or belief. **On the road to Damascus**; **Eureka moment**

Rob Peter to pay Paul - Many believe that the origin of this expression goes back to Saint Peter and Saint Paul that one would crucify Paul in order to redeem Peter. It generally means: to take money or something from one thing and use it for another

Robinson Crusoe - This term originated from the novel of the same name by the English novelist and journalist Daniel Defoe. A long-standing classic first published in 1719, the first edition assigned the book to Robinson Crusoe as its author, leading many readers to believe he was a real person and the book a record of true events. The exploration of the globe and the tales of faraway places and exotic islands **piqued the curiosity** of people and **fed into this narrative** and gave rise to men like Captain Cook. It has migrated to mean: anyone who lives alone like a hermit for a long time. **Girl Friday**

Robot - The source of this term comes from a play written by the Czech writer Karl Capek entitled: R.U.R which stood for Rossum's Universal Robots. The name came from the Czech word "robota" meaning 'forced labor.' Written in the 1920s, it was one of the first dystopian works in which "robots" or anthropomorphic machines were used to do all of the work for humans. It now means: a machine capable of carrying out a complex series of actions automatically, especially one programmable by a computer or a person that acts like one. **Acting like a robot**

Rock of Gibraltar - This ancient landmark lies where the Mediterranean joins the Atlantic Ocean. It derives its name from the Moorish General Jabal Tariq who conquered it and most of the Iberian Peninsula in 711 CE. The Moors occupied Spain until they were conquered by Ferdinand and Isabella in 1492. It has evolved to mean: any person or thing that has strength and endurance that can be relied on. Similar phrases include: **pillar of strength**; **steady as a rock**; **to be a rock of Gibraltar**

Roe v. Wade - This was a landmark Supreme Court (7-2) decision rendered on January 22, 1973 which made abortions legal within the United States. A **political football** for decades, with **Pro-choice** advocates on one side and **Pro-life** advocates on the other. The term is now frequently used to refer to the ongoing debate between the two groups and **women's reproductive rights. Pro-choice and Pro-life** are terms that emerged after this decision and respectively denote: the right of the mother to choose and the right to protect the life of the unborn baby

Roger that - The source of this term is early radio communication, especially in the military. Often, a phonetic alphabet was used to avoid confusion especially in critical situations. Roger indicated received and "Roger that" was used to denote received and understood and the term migrated to general usage with the same connotation. Sometimes phonetic alphabets were used to spell out words to avoid confusion, e.g., A as in apple. G as in George, etc..

Roland for an Oliver - Roland was the greatest of the warriors in the Charlemagne cycle of the *chansons de geste*. He was renowned for his prowess and the manner of his death in the Battle of Roncesvalles.

IN A NUTSHELL

Most memorable was his five days of combat with Oliver in which neither was the victor. It is said that Roland and Oliver became friends. It means: an effective retaliation or **tit for tat**. **To give as good as one gets. Die like Roland** is another related phrase and recounts the way Roland died. He allegedly died of hunger and thirst while crossing the Pyrenees in 778. It therefore means to die of hunger or thirst

Roll (give) the golden apple - The source of this saying comes from Greek mythology. **The Golden apple (apple of discord)** was thrown on the table by Eris the god of discord at a wedding to which all the Greeks gods were invited except her. She uttered: "**for the fairest**" which meant someone or something that causes trouble. A practical joke meant to cause chaos. According to the Greeks, this was the start of the Trojan War. The common interpretation is: the cause of a dispute. **To sow discord**

Roll out the red carpet - The origin of this expression appears to be unknown. Some have suggested that it dates back at least to ancient Greece based on the classical play Agamemnon which is the first of three linked tragedies that make up The Oresteia; a trilogy written by the ancient Greek playwright Aeschylus. In this play, a reference is made to a red (crimson) carpet that was used to welcome Agamemnon upon returning a hero from the Trojan War "floor of crimson broideries to spread; For the King's path." In an ironic twist, because he walked on this "crimson" carpet, the gods abandoned him and he was soon murdered. Nonetheless, the expression has evolved to mean: to formally welcome an important guess that has just arrived. In most cases, it is a long, narrow red carpet laid on the ground for a distinguished visitor to walk on when arriving. It is used in Hollywood to welcome the stars during awards. **Red carpet treatment** is very special or **royal treatment**

Roman a clef - This expression comes from the French *livre aclef* and means "a novel with a key." Common examples of roman à clef are Aldous Huxley's Point Counter Point and Simone de Beauvoir's Mandarins. In both cases, the disguised characters are immediately recognizable only to a small circle of insiders. It is used to tell a real event anonymously or to describe a real life behind a façade of fiction

Roman holiday - The Romans obtained their enjoyment at the expense of doomed gladiators who fought in the arena as part of their "**bread and circus**" culture. It now means: an occasion on which enjoyment or profit is derived from suffering or discomfort of others; a holiday obtained at the expense of others **Not on my nickel**

Rome wasn't built in a day - This phrase was adapted into English in the 16th century from a medieval French proverb. The common interpretation of this phrase is: if you want to do something great you must be willing to invest the time to do it right. **Patience is a virtue**

Romeo and Juliet - These two lovers were made famous by Shakespeare's play of the same name. Like so many of Shakespeare's tragedies, the true source is Italian. The Russian writer Fyodor Dostoevsky once wrote when comparing Shakespeare to Pushkin: who is Shakespeare but an Italian dressed in an English suit? Not much is known about them except that they were real lovers who lived in Verona, Italy and died for each other in the year 1303. It has migrated to mean: two lovers who are willing to die for each other or a pair of youthful often helpless lovers. Pyramus and Thisbe is similar and is an ancient story about two young Babylonian lovers who were forbidden to marry and committed suicide under tragic circumstances. **Courtly love; the lover is destined to share the fate of the beloved**

Romulus and Remus - According to Roman legend, these two twin brothers were nursed by a she-wolf and became the founders of Rome. The common usage is: founders or exemplars of something great, in once sense and a **Cain and Abel** in another because Romulus killed his brother Remus. Hence, according to legend, the name Rome comes from Romulus its first king. However, a more comprehensive history of Rome is delineated in the Aeneid by Virgil and traces its roots back to the Trojan War. On a similar note, **raised by wolves** has become an idiom and applies to a person or a group that appears ill-mannered, unrefined or socially inept; **no class**

Room 101 - This term is taken from the novel Nineteen Eighty-Four (1984) written by George Orwell in 1949. It is a **dystopian** type novel, like Orwell's earlier Animal Farm written in1945 that emerged in the aftermath of World War II and Stalinism as a **harbinger** of future totalitarian states. Room 101 (so named after a conference room at BBC where Orwell sat through meetings) was an interrogation room where the subjects were confronted with their **worst nightmare,** fears and phobias in an effort to break them down. It was a futuristic version of the **Inquisition,** replete with its gang of inquisitors using techniques that would make **Machiavelli** look like a saint. The interrogators knew everything about a person including their dreams and nightmares. In many cases today, Room 101 serves as a metaphor of our worst fears and phobias and what would happen if someone or a group had control over them and fearfully over us. **Orwellian** is a term that describes the dystopian state outlined in some of Orwell's novels. **Big Brother**

Root and branch - The origin of this term is uncertain. It has come to express the thorough or radical nature of a process or operation; something that must be completely changed, removed or destroyed. **Chapter and verse**

Rope-a-dope - This phrase was made famous by Muhammad Ali after the George Foreman fight (Rumble in the Jungle) in Zaire in 1974. It is a boxing tactic of pretending to be trapped against the ropes, provoking an opponent to throw ineffective punches until he tires himself out or **runs out of steam**. It has since been used in situations when you want to fool someone or get them to adopt a strategy that in the long run works against them often using a professed strength as a weakness

Roscian **[performance]** - This expression originated from the Roman actor Roscian who became the greatest performer of his time. Roscian was a friend and contemporary of Cicero and it was Cicero who first coined the term. Shakespeare acknowledges the superiority and versatility of Roscius's work in Henry VI, part 3: "What scene of death hath Roscius now to act." It now means: a performance of outstanding skill

Rose colored glasses - This expression was first recorded in Tom Brown at Oxford a novel by the English lawyer Thomas Hughes in 1861. In the story, Oxford is a sort of utopia. The popular interpretation of this phrase is: an attitude of cheerfulness or seeing things in an optimistic light. **To see the world through rose colored glasses**

Rosetta Stone - The origin of this idiom is the discovery, in 1799, of a decree issued in 196 BCE on the behalf of Ptolemy V. It was written in three different languages: **hieroglyphic,** demotic, and Greek. This decree became known as the Rosetta Stone and was the key to deciphering the Egyptian hieroglyphics by Jean-François Champollion in 1822. It was discovered by the French and given to the British as part of the **spoils of war** and it now resides in the British museum. The term has migrated to mean: something that is a key to deciphering or unfolding a hidden meaning

Round robin - The source of this expression is from the practice of arranging the signatures of a petition in a circular form to disguise the order of signing. It has migrated to mean: a tournament in which each competitor plays in turn against every other. **A battle royal** is a fight involving two or more people and the last one to survive is declared the winner

Round table - The source of this term comes from the legend of King Arthur and the 150 knights that sat around a round table that was made by **Merlin.** When sitting at a round table, all participants are equal. In fact, the North Vietnamese demanded a round table during the Paris peace negotiations in 1969. The term generally means: an assembly for discussion, particularly at a conference in which ideas and opinions are shared. **Let's have a round table meeting. Siege Perilous** is another term that comes from this legend and was the seat at the Round Table that was fatal to all except Sir Galahad, the son of Sir Lancelot and the knight who was to find the Holy Grail (the cup that Jesus drank from at **The Last Supper**). It is interesting to note that Lancelot, the most famed of all the knights of the Round Table, was denied the Grail because of his adulterous behavior which. ironically conceived Galahad the knight that conquers the Grail. **Camelot** is another term that emanated from the King Arthur legend. It was the place where King Arthur held his court. It means: a time, place, or atmosphere of tranquil and blissful happiness. For example, the early days of the Kennedy presidency is often referred to as Camelot. **The search for the Holy Grail**

Rug rat - This is a term that emerged during the 1970s and was popularized by the American television series of the same name. It generally means: a child, toddler or someone that is not old enough for school. **Preschooler**

Rule by fiat - This is an old English expression that originally applied to the king or members of the clergy. Fiat is a Latin term that means let it be done. Most recently, it has become associated with a tyrannical or autocratic form of government. It generally means: to rule by decree. Similar expressions include: **so let it be written, so let it be done; to rule by fiat; rule with an iron fist**

Rule of thumb - The origin of this phrase appears to come from an old English law that allowed a man to beat his wife with a stick if it was no thicker than his thumb. In 1782, Judge Sir Francis Buller is reported as having made this legal ruling. It now means: a broadly accurate guide or principle, based on experience or practice rather than theory or scientific calculations. **As a rule of thumb**

A COLLECTION OF POPULAR ENGLISH PHRASES

Run around like a chicken with its head cut off - The source of this expression comes from the fact that chickens and other poultry can run around for several minutes after their heads have been decapitated. It therefore means: to run around in a frenzy or in a state of confusion or chaos

Run with the hare and hunt with the hounds - The origin of this saying is unclear or unknown. Nevertheless, it evolved to mean: to remain on both sides of an argument or to be on good terms with both sides. **To be on both sides of the fence; to play both sides (ends) against the middle**

Running out of steam - The origin of this phrase dates back to the days when steam engines were used to power locomotives and other pieces of machinery. The steam engine is the product of the diligence and genius of Thomas Newcomen and James Watt and was an integral part of the Industrial Revolution. The phrase now means: to suddenly lose the energy or interest to continue doing something. **To gather (gain) steam** means the opposite. **Blow off some steam** comes from the relief valve that prevents explosions by relieving the pressure in a boiler by venting excess steam and pressure. It means: to release emotional tension by talking or getting angry, getting drunk or even having sex. Other steam related terms are: **full steam ahead; under your own steam; pick up some steam; head of steam**

Rush of adrenaline (an adrenaline rush) - This term has been in use since the 1970s. Adrenaline is a hormone secreted by the adrenal gland. It is normally activated by stress or excitement and prepares the body in cases of **fight or flight**. This term is often used to describe a sudden burst of energy under such conditions

Russian roulette - This expression originated from drunken Russian soldiers of the Czar's court who popularized this game. It is the practice of loading a bullet into one chamber of a revolver, spinning the cylinder, and then pulling the trigger while pointing the gun at one's own head. It is repeatedly used to describe a dangerous situation in which the outcome is decided by chance. **Playing Russian roulette**

Stands for:

See no evil, hear no evil, speak no evil

IN A NUTSHELL

Sackcloth and ashes - The basis of this expression is from the Bible (Matt. 11:21, Luke 10:13). Sackcloth is a coarse, black cloth made from goat's hair that was worn together with the burnt ashes of wood as a sign of mourning for personal and national disasters. It was also worn as a sign of repentance and at times of prayer for deliverance. The term is often interpreted as: a sign that you are very sorry for something you said or did wrong or something that you should have done but didn't do. A sign of morning or remorse. **Wear sackcloth and ashes. Wear the willow** is similar in connotation and means to grieve

Sail under false colors - This expression originated from pirate ships that at the moment of attack, lowered their friendly flag and raised the pirate flag. The common interpretation of this phrase is: to pretend to be something you are not, a hypocrite. **Under false colors; two faced**

Salad days - This expression originated from Shakespeare's <u>Anthony and Cleopatra</u> (Act I, Scene V) and refers to the difference between how <u>Cleopatra</u> loved Caesar and how she loved <u>Marc Anthony</u>. "My <u>salad days</u>, When I was **green in judgment: cold in blood.**" It refers to an earlier or youthful time, accompanied by inexperience, enthusiasm and idealism. **You are only young once; vale of years**

Saint Nick - The source of this moniker, as it is applied to Santa Claus, is the Greek Saint Nicholas known for his gifts and is celebrated as the patron of children on December 6. Although the term first appeared in Europe, we owe its current popularity to America. Nicholas was neither fat nor jolly but rather he assumed these **Falstaffian** characteristics through the evolution of legend. It was Washington Irving's 1809 book entitled: <u>Knickerbocker's History of New York</u> that first portrayed Saint Nick as a pipe-smoking gift-giver replete with stealth rooftop visits in the middle of the night. This motif was further enhanced by an 1821 anonymous poem entitled: <u>A Children's Friend.</u> The image of Saint Nick as **Santa Claus**, who lived in the North Pole, continued to evolve along with the celebration and exploitation of merchants that enhanced the gift-giving theme. Additional themes were added including the biblical narrative of the <u>three wisemen and baby Jesus.</u> It was the convergence and amalgamation of such themes that led to the formation of the traditions of Christmas that most Christians celebrate today. **Good old Saint Nick; Easter bunny and eggs**

Salt of the earth - The source of this saying is from the Bible (Matthew 5 :13). In the Sermon on the Mount, Jesus tells his followers, "Ye are the <u>salt of the Earth.</u>" It has evolved to mean: a person or group of people of great kindness, reliability, or honesty: an individual or group considered as representative of the best or noblest elements of society. **Better angels of our nature**

Savior faire - This is a French expression that has worked its way into the English language. It literally means "know how to do." It was also part of a phrase: "**Savior faire is everywhere**" uttered by the Warner Bros, cartoon character Pepe LePew and made popular by the mouse named <u>Savior Faire from the Klondike Kat cartoon</u> produced by Total Television. The term means: the ability to act or speak appropriately in social situations; the ability to behave in a correct and confident way in different situations

A COLLECTION OF POPULAR ENGLISH PHRASES

Say hello to my little friend - This line was made famous by the 1983 movie Scarface. The little friend refers to a weapon, in this case a gun. It is regularly used when someone wishes to do harm to another person or to show a person that they are armed

Say it ain't so Joe - This phrase relates to Shoeless Joe Jackson, the baseball player with a 356-lifetime batting average that was convicted in the 1919 World Series gambling conspiracy. The phrase is used in reference to any hero that has betrayed his trust. Be careful how you pick your heroes because they may disappoint you. **I don't believe my eyes; can't trust anybody; I am not a role model**

Scapegoat - The origin of this term comes from the ancient Hebrew practice of using a goat to cleanse the sins of their people by laying their sins on the head of the goat and then setting it free in the wilderness. (Lev. 16) It means: a person that takes the punishment or blame for someone else or a group. **Fall guy; walk the plank**

Scarlet letter - Was the letter "A" that a woman convicted of adultery was formerly made to wear, especially among the Puritans of 17th century New England. It was also the title of a popular book written by the American novelist and short-story writer Nathaniel Hawthorne. It means: a mark or a sign of some type of condemnation or denunciation. **Mark of Cain; damaged goods**

School of hard knocks - The origin of this phrase is attributed to the American, writer, artist and philosopher, Elbert Hubbard. It now means: difficult or challenging experiences that are considered to be instructive; to learn something the hard way; practical experiences as opposed to book knowledge. **No matter how many books you read on swimming, eventually you must get in the water; pull yourself up by your bootstraps**

Schrödinger's cat - So named after the Austrian physicist, Erwin Schrödinger. The paradox lies in the clever coupling of quantum and classical physics. It is a thought experiment about the unknown fate of a cat in a box and whether the cat is dead or alive under certain conditions. It has come to refer, mostly in the field of science, as an unsolvable mystery, a paradox. Something that cannot be easily or definitely determined. **Schrödinger's cat is it dead or alive? Maxwell's demon**

Scorched-earth - This is a military term that has worked its way into general usage. The technique has been around for centuries and is perhaps best exemplified by General Sherman during the American Civil War in which he destroyed the civilian infrastructure to prevent Southerners from using it. Sometimes, it is used to prevent an invading army from using valuable resources. In this instance, the objective is to destroy, crops, infrastructure or anything that could be used by the enemy against them. The term is defined as: deliberate widespread destruction of something normally as a means of defense

Sea legs - This expression has its origins in the ability of passengers on ships to adjust to the movements of the boat. It now means: the ability to adjust to a new situation. **Get your sea legs. To sail the seven seas** is another term of maritime origins that means: to travel around the world

IN A NUTSHELL

Search engine - This is a term that has emerged with the Internet and the advent of Google in the late 1980s and early 1990s. It is defined as: a program that searches for and identifies items in a database that correspond to keywords or characters specified by the user. It is used especially for finding particular sites on the World Wide Web. **Google it**

Second Amendment rights - This term refers to the Second Amendment of the Constitution which is the right to bear arms. In recent times, however, this amendment has come under scrutiny as many believe that the intent of the amendment was for self-defense and therefore should prohibit the acquisition and use of certain automatic weapons or those deemed weapons of war. On the other hand, there are those that contend that such weapons are within the purview of the Constitution. This term is often used to denote the ongoing debate

Security blanket - This term emerged in the 1920s and was first used domestically. It was later used during World War II in reference to the security of military operations and information. However, it was popularized by Charles Schulz in his Peanuts cartoon strip in the mid-1950s and became a staple of the character Linus. As a result, it has several meanings. The first, is a familiar blanket or other object, e.g., favorite toy or teddy bear, held by young children as a source of comfort. The second: a set of security measures, typically imposed in order to maintain complete secrecy about something or to protect a person from harm; and finally, generically as something; or perhaps even someone, that gives psychological aid and comfort to someone. **Throw a security blanket around; good luck charm**

See no evil, hear no evil, speak no evil - The source of this proverb is unclear, and some believe that it has its origin in China and ascribed to Confucius. The order is sometimes reversed but the connotation remains the same. Nonetheless, the concept is universal and could be found at the bedrock of many religions. It was popularized using three monkeys with their hands over their eyes, ears and mouth. The general interpretation of this phrase is: not to participate in any evil that you come in contact with, do not perpetuate any evil and to be virtuous in the midst of evil. Similar phrases include: **monkey see monkey do; there are none so blind as to those that will not see; there are none so deaf as those who will not hear**

See sharp or be flat - This was a saying that was made famous by Muhammad Ali when he said: "Musically speaking, if Larry Holmes don't C sharp, he'll B flat." In addition to his exemplary boxing skills in the ring, Ali was truly **one of a kind,** and he dubbed himself "the greatest of all time (GOAT)." He was known for his witty saying and rhymes and his predictions of the outcome of the fight in kind. However, his greatest battle did not take place inside the ring, but rather outside of it. He took a courageous and financially damaging stand against the Vietnam War which caused him his championship and stripped several years off his boxing career. Furthermore, he was a strong voice for the Civil Rights struggles of his day. Scorned in his **salad days** by many, praised in his **vale of years** by most; he was a charismatic and iconic figure, who **now belongs to the ages.** The phrase can be interpreted to mean: if you don't focus on what you are doing then you will not achieve your goal

A COLLECTION OF POPULAR ENGLISH PHRASES

Seek and ye shall find - This saying comes from the Bible (Matt. 7:7). "**Ask and it will be given** to you; seek and you will find; **knock and the door will be opened to you**." The common interpretation is: if you search hard enough for something, you will find it

Selective amnesia - This is a psychological term that has worked its way into general usage. In psychology, it is also referred to as *dissociative amnesia* which is the loss of memory regarding certain events normally induced by stressful or emotional situations. In recent times however, it often refers to the intentional or disingenuous loss of memory used to avoid remembering an event, situation or action that could be self-incriminating or convenient, e.g., **I don't recall**; **to the best of my memory**; **take the fifth**

Self-inflicted wound - The origin of this term is uncertain or unclear. Some soldiers would shoot themselves in the foot to avoid going back into combat and this is one example of such a wound. **Generally speaking**, it now means: a mistake or **faux pas** that was caused by oneself that may have dire or harmful consequences. **Shoot yourself in the foot** is very similar and means to carelessly make a situation worse for yourself or to demonstrate incompetence or inaptitude in a given situation

Self-preservation is the first law of nature - The source of this expression is unclear, but it has been attributed to the English poet Samuel Butler (1835-1902). It has come to reflect the Darwinist belief of **survival of the fittest** or that the number one goal in life is to survive

Senators are good, but the Senate is evil - This is a Latin proverb which means although individuals may be good, when they form a group, they can become bad

Seneca Falls - The origin of this term is a town located in central New York. It was the site of the first women's rights convention in the United States held between July 19-20, 1848. It was attended by Elizabeth Cady Stanton, Lucretia Mott, Frederick Douglass, and other prominent people to address women's suffrage. This movement ultimately resulted in the ratification of the 19th amendment to the Constitution established on August 18, 1920. Seneca Falls was **ground zero** of the women's suffrage movement and has therefore become its symbol. **Stonewall Inn**

Separate the sheep from the goats - This expression originated from the Bible (Matthew 25: 33) and generally means: to divide the good from the bad, the worthy from the unworthy. Similar to: **Separate the wheat from the chaff**

Serpent in one's bosom - This expression originated from the Greek myth of the shepherd that found a frozen snake and put it under his shirt only to have the snake revived to bite him. It can be interpreted to mean: someone whom one has befriended, taken care of, or treated well but proves to be traitorous, untrustworthy, deceitful, or ungrateful

Seven-year itch - The origin of this phrase appears to be in a skin irritation that lasted for about seven years. It appeared to be more prevalent in the United States. The current usage of the phrase was popularized by the 1955 film of the same name starring Marylyn Monroe as the stereotypical "**dumb blonde**" and featured the iconic picture with her dress blowing up on the street. The phrase now means:

a supposed tendency toward infidelity after seven years of marriage perhaps because **"familiarity breeds contempt"** and the initial happiness declines. **The Honeymoon is over** is similar and means that the early pleasant beginning, i.e., at the start of a marriage, has ended but can also be applied to other initial endeavors such as the presidency

Seventh heaven - The source of this term comes from the Jewish belief that heaven was divided into seven levels. This was somewhat supported by the Ptolemaic view of the ancient world where Ptolemy divided the space above earth into concentric circles. It generally means: the highest place or a state of extreme happiness or bliss. **I'm in seventh heaven**

Shake it like a Polaroid picture - The origin of this phrase is from a song by Outkast entitled: Hay Ya! released in 2003. In the days before digital photography, Polaroid instant film was the only way that a person could get near real-time photographs. The photos developed **right before your eyes** and many believed by shaking it helped the picture develop faster (which is untrue). A casualty of the digital age, Polaroid closed its last plant in 2008. The phrase means: to **shake your booty** while dancing or walking. Shake your booty, by KC and the Sunshine band, was a popular song in the 1970s Disco era. **Shake that booty**

Shell-shock - The source of this term is the trauma experienced by soldiers during World War I. Although artillery was used in previous wars, the advancements in this type of warfare and the pervasive exposure to artillery fire gave rise to a new wartime symptom that inflicted mental as well as physical damage to those constantly exposed to it. It was among the first post-traumatic stress symptoms diagnosed and treated. The term now means: a state of astonishment or bewilderment normally induced by stress, fatigue or surprise; to be stunned, distressed, or exhausted from a prolonged trauma or an unexpected difficulty: to be overwhelmed by something. **Basket case**

Shibboleth - This expression originated from the Bible (Judges 12:4-6). It was a word used by the Gileadites as a test to detect the fleeing Ephraimites, who could not pronounce the sound. In its current usage, it means: a word or way of speaking or behaving which shows that a person belongs to a particular group or an old idea or opinion. Sometimes used as a secret code that gives one inclusion or entry to a group

Ship of fools- This is a popular expression that has been the title of several books, songs, and movies and may have its origin in Plato's Republic. Even though, it is not specifically used in this ancient Greek classic. In the Republic, there is an allegory that depicts a ship populated by people who are deranged and playful aboard a ship without a pilot. Consequently, they are seemingly ignorant of the ship's direction or course. However, centuries later, this phrase became well known after the publication of a book with the same title by Sebastian Brant, a German theologian in the 15th century. Around that time, a famous painting of the same name by Hieronymus Bosch appeared and is now a masterpiece on display in the Louvre Museum in Paris. The phrase has evolved to mean: any group of people that act like fools when they get together while heading toward an unknown direction or course of action. Shakespeare wrote in As You Like It (Act V, Scene IV) "Here comes a pair of very strange beasts, which in all tongues are called fools." In other words, we all know fools when we see them and there is nothing more dangerous than a group of them acting together on a ship or otherwise

Ship of state - This popular saying is frequently ascribed to the Greek philosopher Plato (429-247) in his Book VI of The Republic. However, the true origins of the metaphor can be traced back to the lyric poet Alcaeus (620 -580 BCE) who preceded Plato by more than a century. This term is also found in Aeschylus who also preceded Plato. The Republic of Plato is a **time honored** classic and its philosophy has enriched readers for millenniums. Germane to Plato's ship of state paradigm is the concept of a **philosopher king** who is the captain of the ship. A monarch not only **well-versed** in the nuances of administration; but a statesperson trained to think philosophically as well. A leader whose overall knowledge of the world and historical events enables him or her to rule impartially and in accordance with the circumstances of their times. The term ship of state is regularly interpreted to mean: a nation or its affairs are like a ship under sail; and thus, must have a wise captain (philosopher king) to guide it through the turbulent waters of time. Men and women such as Alexander the Great, Queen Elizabeth I, and Abraham Lincoln are examples of leaders that have met this criterion

Shirt of Nessus - The source of this saying comes from Greek mythology and was the blood-soaked shirt of the centaur that Hercules killed with a poison arrow. The dying centaur naïvely convinced Hercules' wife that his blood had the power to keep Hercules from having adulterous love affairs. She made Hercules a shirt that was soaked in the centaur's blood. Instead of keeping Hercules away from other women, it tortured him so bad that he had himself burnt on a funeral pyre. The saying has migrated to mean: a source of misfortune from which there is no escape; a fatal present; anything that unknowingly wounds or serves as a destructive force or influence, it is also referred to as: **Tunic of Nessus, Nessus-robe**, or **Nessus' shirt**

Shot across the bows - This saying derives from the naval practice of firing a cannon shot across the bows of an enemy's ship to show them that you are prepared to do battle. It now means: a statement or gesture intended to frighten someone into changing their course of action; **a warning shot.** Similarly, an **opening salvo** is the first of a series of simultaneous discharges of weaponry (normally artillery) that typically comes at the beginning of battle. It is sometimes used as a metaphor for the beginning of a series of things or events to follow

Shotgun wedding - The origin of this term is uncertain, however, according to historians, in America between the 18th and 19th centuries, the use of violence or physical harm was used to force weddings, and possibly the gun was used as a threat. Because the honor and dignity of the family was **called into question** if the female became pregnant before marriage, quick arrangements were made to assure that the family's dignity was upheld and with the prospects that the unborn child would be raised in a family consisting of a father and a mother. Being a **spinster** was one thing, but being an unwed mother was a serious **taboo**. The term now pertains to a quick wedding arranged to avoid embarrassment due to an unintended pregnancy

IN A NUTSHELL

Show me a hero and I will write you a tragedy - This is a quote from the American writer F. Scott Fitzgerald and means: the fate of a hero often ends in tragedy; or in order to have a hero there must first have been a tragedy. **Cut from the cloth** of a Shakespearean tragic play, the phrase can be interpreted to mean: heroes, tragedy and valor are often inextricably linked

Show me the money - The primary source of this expression comes from the movie Jerry Maguire starring Tom Cruise and Cuba Gooding Jr.. Although it was in use earlier, it was popularized in this 1996 film. The common interpretation is: **put up or shut up; put your money where your mouth is**

Shrinking violet - The origin of this term appears to be the flower, violet, and it probably originated in England. As an idiom it means: a shy person. **Wallflower** is another flower term that is similar in connotation, however, another popular phrase used to describe personal behavior; **a clinging vine** is: a person who is submissively dependent on another

Shylock - The origin of this term is from a Jewish moneylender Shylock in Shakespeare's Merchant of Venice, who lends money to Antonio but demands in return a pound of Antonio's own flesh should the debt not be repaid on time. It generally means: a ruthless and unscrupulous moneylender. Likewise, **a pound of flesh** refers to: a payment or punishment that involves suffering and sacrifice on the part of the person being punished

Sideburns - This term is derived from the Civil War General Ambrose Burnside who was known for his side whiskers. Appointed head of the Army of the Potomac by Abraham Lincoln, he was just as ineffective as his predecessor. His name was inverted, and this is the source of the term sideburns. It has migrated to mean: a strip of hair grown by a man down each side of the face in front of his ears

Silence gives consent - This expression is attributed to the Greek philosopher Plato, and it has been used by many authors. Its literal interpretation is perhaps the most concise. It means that keeping quiet, especially in situations which a definitive yes or no is required, is the same as giving permission. Martin Luther King Jr. once said: **In the end, we will not remember the words of our enemies but the silence of our friends.** Similar phrases include: **speak truth to power; conspiracy of silence; deafening silence**

Silent majority - This term became popular during the Nixon administration in the late 1960s as a result of Vietnam War protests. The common interpretation is: a significant proportion of a population who choose not to express their views, often because of apathy or because they do not believe their views matter

Silhouette - The origin of this term comes from Étienne de Silhouette who was a French author and politician. Why it is named after him **remains a mystery** because he was not the originator of this technique that was popular during his day. Nonetheless, it means: the dark shape and outline of someone or something visible against a lighter background, especially in dim light

A COLLECTION OF POPULAR ENGLISH PHRASES

Silicon Valley - This term gets its name from an article written in 1971 by journalist Don Hoefler entitled: Silicon Valley USA. The area was so named because the transistors manufactured there were made of silicon instead of germanium. Long before the article, however, this area of Northern California was known for its innovation in electronics. William Shockley the coinventor of the transistor moved from New Jersey (which was previously the **Mecca** of electronics) to return, like a **prodigal son**, to his native roots where he formed an electronics company. He employed **the best and brightest** from neighboring Stanford University many of them would later leave to join Fairchild Semiconductor (the inventor of the first Integrated Circuit (IC)). This group of iconoclasts eventually formed their own company, Intel, and **the rest is history**. Today Silicon Valley is the **high-tech** Mecca of the world with revenue that exceeds the revenue of many nations. **The cutting edge**

Simon-pure - The origin of this term is from the phrase "the real Simon Pure," which was the name of a character in the play A Bold Stroke for a Wife (1717) by Susannah Centlivre. She was one of the most successful female playwrights of the 18th century. In the play, Simon Pure is impersonated by another character. It now means: completely genuine, authentic, or honest; of untainted purity or integrity. **The real McCoy**

Since time immemorial - This is a popular phrase whose meaning has been changed **by the hands of time**. In England, it was first used to designate the time before Richard I came to power. The phrase now means: ancient, beyond the memory of man

Sing from the same hymnbook - The source of this phrase is the practice in some churches of singing selective hymns from a hymnbook during services. **Like playing from the same sheet of music** and **being on the same page**, this phrase has migrated into general usage. It means: to have the same understanding, goals, or motives; **to be on the same team**

Sine quo non - This is a Latin phrase that means "without which not" that has worked its way into the English lexicon. It means: an essential condition; a thing that is absolutely necessary

Sinister - The origin of this term is the Latin word for left side. The Romans believed that anything left was a sign of evil. This also gave rise to the phrase: **getting up on the wrong side of the bed**, which meant to get up on the left side. Lefthanded people were also victims of this "sinister" belief. It generally means: something harmful or evil; the specter of evil

Sisyphus' rock - Sisyphus was the son of Aeolus, punished in Hades for his misdeeds in life. The gods had condemned Sisyphus to ceaselessly rolling a rock to the top of a mountain, whence the stone would fall back of its own weight. They had thought with some reason that there is no more dreadful punishment than futile and hopeless labor. Hence, it evolved to mean: a dreadful punishment or an arduous task. **Sisyphean task**. Prometheus

IN A NUTSHELL

Skeleton at the feast - According to the historians Herodotus and Plutarch, the Egyptians like to place a skeleton at the feast to remind guests of their mortality. The common interpretation of this phrase is: **a party pooper, a wet blanket** or someone that won't be invited the next time

Skeleton in your closet - This is an old English saying going back to the 1800s. Some say that the source was doctors that kept skeletons in a closet out of sight to be examined later. It now means: a secret source of shame, potentially ruinous if exposed, which a person or family makes efforts to conceal. **Keep it in the closet**

Skid row - The source of this phrase appears to be *skid roads* that were laid by loggers at the turn of the 20th century. During this time there was an increase in the demand for lumber and the building of roads consisting of logs placed diagonally and adjacent to each other was essential to transportation. Exactly how *skid road*, migrated to *skid row* remains **a matter of conjecture**. Some argue that these loggers stayed in a cheap area of town, others that destitute people lived or slept near such roads during the **Great Depression**. Regardless of origin, the term was popular in the United States during the 1930s. The term now means: a poor local section of town frequented by vagrants, those suffering from **substance abuse,** mental illness or those that are homeless. **On skid row means** to be destitute or **down on your luck.** To hit rock bottom. **Ghetto**

Skin flick - This term seems to have emerged with the popularity of **X rated** movies in the early 1970s, when movies such as <u>Deep Throat</u>, <u>Behind the Green Door</u> and <u>The Devil in Miss Jones</u> debuted. Although pornography has been around since antiquity, with some even inscribed as graffiti in Egyptian tombs, it was the advent of motion pictures at the dawn of the 20th century that launched it into a new phase. **Stag film** was a term that preceded skin flicks and during the early 1970s, movie houses, known as adult theaters, catered to such movies. This gave rise to other pornographic terms such as **triple (XXX) rated** which in itself has become associated with adult or mature content. The presence of home video recorders and players in the 1980s allowed viewing to take place within the home and also increased the amount of available adult content dramatically. The advent of the Internet provided a ubiquitous conduit for such content, including acts that would be considered **taboo**. The term *skin flick* has become synonymous with pornography and is sometimes used euphemistically. These movies are designed to stimulate erotic or sexual rather than aesthetic or emotional feelings, often depicting sexual organs and **erogenous zones** of both male and female. **Show some skin**

Skin in the game - The origin of this expression is unclear; however, it was popularized by the billionaire Warren Buffet. The skin is the person and the game is the endeavor. In the general sense it means: to incur some risk or to have a personal stake or investment in something. **To have some skin in the game; to have a horse in the race**

Skunk Works - This term originated at <u>Lockheed Martin</u> in the late 1940s early 1950s in the nascent days of the Cold War. Takings its name from the comic strip Li'l Abner, it was the brainchild of Kelly Johnson and under his leadership produced innovative aircraft such as **the** <u>U-2 and SR71</u> (Blackbird) spy planes.

A COLLECTION OF POPULAR ENGLISH PHRASES

Quite often, they worked on developmental projects known as **black projects** which were generally unknown to the general public. The term has migrated to mean: an experimental laboratory or department of a company or institution, typically smaller than and separate from its main research division. **Think tank** is similar and means: a group of experts providing advice and ideas on specific scientific, political or economic problems

Smoke and mirrors - It is believed that the origin of this expression lies in the use of optical illusions by magicians while performing tricks on stage. It has migrated to mean: the concealing or exaggerating of the truth of a situation with misleading, irrelevant or false information. **Pulling the wool over someone's eyes; bread and circuses**

Smoke em (them) if you got em (them) - This term emerged during World War II, specifically in the United States military. A somewhat archaic phrase and a relic of its times, it was frequently used before cigarette smoking became **taboo**. It means: to take a break; to relax. **Do your thing; whatever turns you on**

Smoke test - This is a term that originated from electrical engineering. It was a test that turned on the device and looked to see if there was any smoke. It has since migrated to other areas such as software. It generally means: a quick and dirty test designed to see if the unit under test has any major flaws associated with it. **Give it the smoke test; beta test. A trial balloon** is similar and means: a tentative measure taken, or a statement made to see how a new policy or idea will be received

Smoking gun - The origin of this expression is the 1893 Sherlock Holmes short story by Sir Arthur Conan entitled: The Gloria Scott. In the short story, it is referred to as a smoking pistol. It now means: a piece of undeniable incriminating evidence. **No smoking gun**

SNAFU- This is an acronym for Situation Normal All Fouled Up - Even though this acronym was popularized during World War II, it may have its roots in the telegraph era and migrated to the US military, although the evidence for this claim is not well documented. Within military use, however, the fouled was often replaced with the curse word F**ded. The term now means: a chaotic or confused situation

Snail mail - Although this term has been in existence since 1942, it did not become popular until the advent of Email and the Internet. Often associated with the US Postal Service established by Ben Franklin in 1775, it means: the slowness (snail-like) and sometimes inefficiency of the postal service, which takes days instead of seconds to deliver information or products that could be easily downloaded

Snake oil salesman - This term is believed to have its origin in the Chinese immigrants that came to America during the mid-19th century. Among the items that these Chinese immigrants brought with them was a type of **snake oil** used in their native land to cure several ailments. It was not long before peddlers in the American west began to sell fake snake oil and other products as a panacea or elixir. These products were far less effective and as a result gave the term snake oil a bad name. Consequently, snake oil became synonymous with: a bogus substance with no medical value. Subsequently, the term *snake oil* *salesman* was associated with anyone that sold or promoted an idea or product that fraudulently deceives the public or a person. **A con man**

Snowball effect (snowballing) - The origin of this term comes from the rolling of a snowball down a hill in which it gets bigger and rolls faster as the momentum changes due to the increase in its size and velocity as it gathers more snow. The term now refers to: something that starts out in a small or initial state and grows bigger or stronger as time goes on. **Domino effect**

Social media - This is a term that has its origins in the emergence of the Internet. In addition to being a marketing conduit, the Internet has been used to link people socially together with the advent of popular websites such as Facebook, Twitter, Instagram, etc. The long-term **pros and cons** of such websites have been the source of recent debates, some of them centered around Civil and **First Amendment** rights and security. In such a social milieu, one may have a hundred social media friends but not one true friend that they interact with **face to face in the real world. Social currency** is another related term that has emerged and means: the potential resources which arise from the presence of social media platforms

Sock it to me [Sock it to me] - This saying is from the Laugh-In TV show of the late 1960s and early 1970s. Hosted by Dan Rowan and Dick Martin and featuring Goldie Hawn and others, it was a popular variety show, along with Sonny and Cher and Flip Wilson. It made fun of social and political issues during the early days of the Nixon presidency. It remains an iconic show of that turbulent era. It means: **to let me have it; do your worst! Hit me with your best shot; rock my world; give it to me baby**

Socratic **irony(method)** - So named after the classical Greek philosopher Socrates. It is a means by which the pretended ignorance of a skillful questioner leads the person answering to expose his own ignorance. It often means: when a person pretends to be ignorant to expose the ignorance or inconsistency of someone else. A series of questions intended to place a person on the defensive and lead them to a desired result

Sodom and Gomorrah - The source of this term is from the Bible (Genesis 13:13) Sodom and Gomorrah were two cites in the Bible that were notorious for their wickedness and decadence. So much so that before God ordered it to be destroyed, he graciously agreed to spare Sodom if only ten righteous people could be found there. Upon destroying the cities, God warned Lot and his wife not to look back as they left the towns. But Lot's wife disobeyed God and looked back. Consequently, she was turned into **a pillar of salt.** (Genesis 19:26). The term Sodom and Gomorrah has come to be associated with wickedness and depravity of any kind, particularly among groups of people or conducted in specific places (**dens of iniquity**). The word **sodomy** comes from Sodom. **Fire and brimstone**

Sola scriptura - This is a Latin term that means by scripture alone. It originated out of the observation that certain Christian teachings and practices (especially some of those formulated during the medieval period) had little or no biblical foundation. It became the theological doctrine adopted by some Christian (Protestants) that scripture alone is the primary and absolute source for the dogma and practices of their religion. At its core, is the belief that the Bible is the direct and inerrant revelation from God, and this belief is the cornerstone of Lutheran and Reformed theologies. **Sola scriptura** differs slightly from **Solo scriptura,** the latter being the interpretation (exegesis) of scripture

Sold down the river - This saying has its origin in American slavery in which black slaves were sold from the Chesapeake tobacco region to the Southern cotton regions as cotton replaced tobacco as a major crop requiring manual labor after the invention of the cotton gin by Eli Whitney. His invention "made cotton king" and revolutionized the Textile Industry which led to the Industrial Revolution. The original meaning of this phrase, now obscured by the annals of history, has migrated to signify a profound betrayal. **Judas kiss**

Some rise, by sin, and some by virtue fall - The source of this phrase comes from Shakespeare's play, Measure for Measure (Act II, Scene I). It is regularly interpreted to mean: some people achieve high positions by dubious or dishonest means and some honorable people fall or do not advance because of their virtue or honesty. **Virtue is its own reward**

Something is rotten in Denmark - This expression originated from a line from Shakespeare's play Hamlet (Act I, Scene IV). At the time Denmark, is festering with moral and political corruption. It is repeatedly used to describe corruption or a situation in which something is drastically wrong. **A fish rots from the head down**

Sop to Cerberus - In Greek mythology, Cerberus was a three-headed giant dog that guarded the entrance to Hades, (Hell). A 'sop' in this context seems to be a sort of bribe. The common interpretation is: a gift or bribe given to appease a potential source of trouble or danger

Sophomore jinx - The origin of this tern is unclear. However, the word sophomore seems to have come from the Greek words *sophos* meaning wise and *moros* meaning fool. The English usage of the word dates back to the 16th century. In the 1700s, it was used to designate a second-year student at Harvard and Yale. While the first year is difficult, the second year is not without its challenges. It was noted that some students perhaps overachieved in their first year, only to have a slump in the second year for various reasons. This phenomenon was also true in other endeavors such as sports to the point of some athletes being superstitious about it. The term now means: an instance in which a second, or sophomore effort falls short of the standards established by the first

SOS - The folk etymology of this term is an abbreviation for Save Our Souls. It has its origin in Morse Code used on the telegraph. The telegraph system was invented by Samuel Morse in 1837 and revolutionized communications. For the first time in human history, messages could be sent long distances in near real time. SOS was a series of three dashes which stood for the letter S, followed by three dots which stood for the letter O, followed by three more dashes indicating the letter S. Thus, it had a particular cadence and was easy to send and receive. It could even be sent using a flashlight. It was adopted as an international signal of distress. It therefore means: a signal of extreme distress, used especially by ships at sea or people in desperate situations. **Send out a SOS.** Mayday is used similarly

IN A NUTSHELL

Soul brother (sisters) - In the fifties, the term "soul" began to be associated with African Americans as in soul food, soul music, etc. Such terms arose as part of a black awareness or nationalist movement in the 1960s. For example, James Brown wrote a song entitled: Say it Loud - I'm Black and I'm Proud and he was often designated as "Soul Brother Number One." Though such terms are still popular, in the case of soul brothers and sisters, it has been abbreviated to just brothers and sisters

Sowing wild oats - This is an old English saying that has a duel meaning. Wild oats were a type of grass that was very hard to cultivate to the extent that it was a useless endeavor. Which is one-way that it is used today. Another way is more prevalent and has a sexual or exploratory connotation as in a young man sowing his wild oats or spreading his seed. As part of the maturation process, this stage often involves doing something, stupid, rebellious or foolish at a young age

Space: the final frontier - The source of this expression is the opening lines from the Star Trek television series aired from 1966-1969. "Space, the final frontier. These are the voyages of the Starship Enterprise. Its continuing mission to explore strange new worlds, to seek out new life and new civilization, **to boldly go where no one has gone before.**" This seminal series viewed in the nascent days of space exploration and the quest to land a man on the moon, initiated a new generation of earthlings raised in a milieu of exploration that transcended terrestrial boundaries. It means to go beyond the limits of the earth and into an area once reserved for the gods

Space-time continuum - This is a term that was borrowed from the science realm. Specifically, Albert Einstein's Theory of Special Relativity. Our reality is divided into segments of space and time and we define events by when and where they happened. In this regard, it is a **barometer** of our reality. Consequently, it has been used colloquially to explain or describe the nature and bounds of our reality and everyday existence. **Within the space-time continuum**

Spare the rod and spoil the child - This expression appears to have originated from the Bible (Proverbs 13:24). "He that spareth his rod hateth his son: but he that loveth him chasteneth him betimes." It now has the following meaning: discipline is necessary for good upbringing

Speak softly and carry a big stick - A phrase first used by Teddy Roosevelt which he attributes to an African proverb. One of four faces on Mount Rushmore, he was president of the United States during a time when it was expanding from an isolated nation to an international empire. He started the Panama Canal and was against big corporations. This phrase embodies his personal and national persona at the turn of the 20th century. It advises the tactic of caution and non-aggression, backed up by the ability to use military force if required. Although this concept was made famous by Teddy Roosevelt and the saying used by other presidents, it is embodied on the back of the dollar bill in which the eagle, the symbol of America, has arrows in one hand and an **olive branch** in the other

Speak truth to power - This phrase is alleged to be coined by the Quakers during the mid-1950s. But it appears to have been coined earlier by Civil Rights leader Bayard Rustin in the 1940s. The phrase is repeatedly interpreted to mean: to speak what you believe to be true, regardless of the negative consequences particularly against authority or those that have the power to retaliate against you

Speedy Gonzales - The origin of this term comes from a Warner Brothers cartoon character which was part of the Looney Tunes and Merrie Melodies series. He was known for his speed and claimed to be the fastest mouse in all of Mexico or **south of the border**. Introduced in 1953, he is an iconic figure of the Warner Brother cartoon empire along with: Bugs Bunny, Daffy Duck, Porky Pig, Elmer Fudd, Silvester, Foghorn Leghorn, Road Runner, Wile E. Coyote, Tasmanian Devil, Tweety bird and Yosemite Sam, that entertained a generation of **baby boomers**. As his name implies, Speedy was always in a rush to do things fast and efficient. As a result, his name became associated with such actions. It has come to mean: someone that does something quick and fast. **Who do you think I am, Speedy Gonzales?**

Sphinx - The source of this ancient term is the legendary sphinx of Egypt that has graced the Giza plateau alongside the Pyramids for millenniums. With the head of a pharaoh (believed to be Khafre) and the body of a lion, the Sphinx dates back to the Old Kingdom and its true name is Hor-em-akhet "Horus on the Horizon." The enigmatic nature and lore of the sphinx is a legacy of the Greeks that once proposed a riddle to it. The term has migrated to mean: an enigmatic or mysterious person or thing

Spic - This derogatory term seems to have its origin in the building of the Panama Canal. More specifically referring to the phrase 'No spik d' English' used by Panamanians to denote that they didn't speak English. As in many terms, it migrated to its current form and was applied to people of Hispanic or Latino descent. It is now used as a derogatory term that applies to people of Latin or Central America whose native language is Spanish or their descendants. **Wetback** is similar in usage. As in most cases involving terms that are derogatory to a specific group, the aforementioned terms should not be used when addressing the group

Spill the beans - In ancient Greek secret societies, votes were counted using beans: dark beans for no votes, which were kept in a container. Only certain officials were to know how many negative votes were casted. Occasionally, by accident or otherwise, the container would be knocked over thus spilling the beans and revealing the secret votes. It therefore means: to reveal secret information unintentionally or indiscreetly

Spin doctor - This term originated in the United States during the 1980s. It means: a spokesperson employed to give a favorable interpretation of events to the media, especially on behalf of a political party or person

Spring forward, fall backwards - This phrase has its origins in adjusting the clock to compensate for the difference in available sunlight and is aligned with the equinoxes'. At the time of both equinoxes, sunlight and darkness are equal (twelve hours each day) and the sun rises directly in the east and sets directly in the west. After the **Spring Equinox**, in the Northern Hemisphere, the days get longer reaching peak sunlight at the **Summer Solstice** and continue to decline until the **Winter Solstice** (when the available sunlight is at its minimum point). This saying is used to remind people to spring their clocks forward in the Spring and fall their clocks backwards in the Autumn or fall

IN A NUTSHELL

Squeaky wheel gets the grease (oil) - This saying is credited to Josh Billing the pen name of the American humorist Henry Wheeler in a poem entitled: <u>The Kicker</u>. The phrase is habitually interpreted to mean: the loudest complaints get the most attention. **Silent majority**

Strait-laced - This term goes back to the Middle Ages. It was popularized by a woman's undergarment (bodice) during the **Victorian era**. A woman with a strait-laced bodice has the bodice laced tightly. Like the term **dire straits**, it is repeatedly confused with its homonym 'straight' to the extent that the latter has become acceptable in some circles. It now means: having or showing very stern moral or social attitudes or convictions. **Straight and narrow** is similar and comes from the Bible (Matt. 7:14), "strait is the gate, and narrow is the way, which leadeth unto life." It means the proper way or conduct. **Goody two shoes**

Straitjacket - The source of this term is a device invented in France in 1790 by Guilleret at Bicêtre, to restrain mentally ill people that may cause harm to themselves or to others. It is often used to describe a situation that restricts or confines a person; something that limits the development in a way that could be damaging. **Being put in a straitjacket**

Standing on the shoulders of giants - This is a phrase first used by <u>Isaac Newton</u> to describe his accomplishments. Newton was paying homage to scientists such as <u>Copernicus</u> and <u>Galileo</u> who came before him. In fact, Newton was born on Christmas day the same year that Galileo died. The phrase is often interpreted to mean: to use the understanding gained by major thinkers who have gone before in order to make intellectual and continuous progress. Similar phrases include: **a dwarf on a giant's shoulders sees the farther of the two; it is difficult to begin without borrowing; originality is undetected plagiarism**

Star Chamber - The source of this expression was an English court system that tried cases affecting the interests of the Crown. Called the *Star Chamber* because of the star on its ceiling, it now means: an unfair, secret judicial act; any tribunal, committee, or the like, which proceeds by arbitrary or unfair methods. **Kangaroo court**

State of the art - The first recorded use of this term appears in 1910, in a book on the gas turbine and was used as a technical term. It is defined as: the most recent stage in the development of a product, incorporating the newest ideas and the most up-to-date features. **High-tech** is similar and means: employing, requiring, or involved in high technology

State of the Union - The source of this expression is a yearly address delivered each January by the president of the United States to Congress, in accordance with Article II, section 3 of the U.S. Constitution. It gives the administration's view of the state of the nation and plans for legislation. It was first given by George Washington on January 8, 1790, and from that date until 1946 it was referred to as the Annual Message. It has also been applied generically to other situations such as when someone wants to know how things are going. **What's the State of the Union?**

A COLLECTION OF POPULAR ENGLISH PHRASES

Statue of Liberty - The origin of this iconic American symbol is a gift given to the United States by France in 1886. This lady of freedom resides in the New York harbor reminiscent of the famed Statue of Rhodes with a crown on its head. At the turn of the 20th century, it served as a **welcome mat** for people around the world **yearning to be free**. Inspired by the Union victory during the Civil War and the abolition of slavery in the United States, in the initial design it held the torch of freedom in one hand and the broken chains of slavery in the other. Such symbolism, however, was viewed as to provocative for its times and the broken chains were replaced by a tablet with July 1776 inscribed on it. In its final design. the broken chains were placed at the statue's feet which can be seen today. It now serves as a symbol of American freedom and democracy
.

Status quo - This is one of many Latin terms that has worked its way into the English language. It literally means in Latin "state in which." It means: the existing state or condition of affairs. **To maintain the status quo; go along with the program**

Status symbol - This term dates to the mid-1900s but the source of the saying is unclear. It denotes: a possession that is taken to indicate a person's wealth or high social or professional status such as a big house, fancy car(s), jewelry, etc. **Trophy wife**

Still waters run deep - This phrase is just one of many Latin proverbs that has worked its way into the English language. First used in English in the 15th century, its roots go back to antiquity in one form or the other. For example, Shakespeare wrote in <u>Henry VI Part II</u> (Act III, Scene I): **smooth runs the water where the brook is deep**. During the 1960s, it was the title of a hit song by the popular R&B group, <u>The Four Tops.</u> It, in effect, means: a quiet or mild manner may obscure a more passionate or even wise nature. Some people who are quiet or shy are often very intelligent and interesting; in the same manner that the deepness of a river could be concealed by its calmness. **You can't judge a book by its cover; the more one knows, the more silent he becomes**

Stinks to high heaven - The origin of this saying appears to be from Shakespeare's Hamlet (Act III, Scene III) It was spoken by King Claudius. "O, my offense is rank, it smells to heaven. The common interpretation is: to have a very strong and unpleasant scent; something that is extremely corrupt or suspicious. **It stinks (smells) to high heaven**

Stockholm syndrome - So named after an incident in Stockholm in 1973, during which a bank employee became romantically attached to a robber who held her hostage. It is a phenomenon in which victims of trauma or kidnapping sympathize with their captors. **Florence Nightingale effect**

Stonewall (Inn) - The source of this expression (not to be confused with stonewalling or to stonewall) is a gay bar located in Greenwich Village, New York. It was <u>the place where violent riots took place starting on June 28, 1969</u> in protest of unjust treatment of homosexuals. Historically, it is considered ground zero of the Lesbian, Gay, Bisexual, Transgender and Queer/Questioning (LGBTQ) movement. Later, it was designated as a historical site and considered, by many within the movement, as a shrine and gathering place to express their commitment to equal rights for the LGBTQ community. **Seneca Falls**

227

IN A NUTSHELL

Straight, no chaser - The origin of this expression comes from drinking a straight shot of liquor without mixing it or taking another non-alcoholic drink afterwards to drown out the alcohol. It has come to mean in some circles: to give the information straight, regardless of how bad or offensive it could be. **Straight talk; give it to me straight (no chaser)**

Straighten up and fly right - The source of this saying seems to have emanated from the African American community around World War II. It was the title of a hit song by Nat King Cole in 1943 and may have been used by the Tuskegee Airmen. The phrase is regularly interpreted to mean: to get serious and start behaving properly

Strain at the gnat and swallow the camel - This saying comes from the Bible (Matt. 23:24). "Blind guides! You strain your water so you won't accidentally swallow a gnat, but you swallow a camel!" The common usage is: to quibble about something small but ignore something that is really big or important; to criticize someone for minor faults while ignoring major ones. **Make a mountain out of a molehill**

Strange bedfellows - The source of this expression is from Shakespeare's The Tempest (Act II, Scene II). It has migrated to mean: unlikely companions or allies. Similar phrases include: **politics (war) makes strange bedfellows; the enemy of my enemy is my friend; a common danger causes common action**

Stream of consciousness - This saying is ascribed to the American psychologist and philosopher William James. It is from his Principles of Psychology (1890). The common usage is: a person's thoughts and conscious reactions to events, perceived as a continuous flow

Stubborn as a mule - This is an old proverbial saying that has been around for centuries. Historically, mules have been used as draft animals. A mule is one of those rare animals that is a product of two different animals, a female horse and a male donkey. As a result, the mule has an odd chromosome count and is therefore sterile. It is believed that **"the quote, unquote"** stubbornness of the mule is a trait associated with the donkey. However, researchers have shown that mules are not necessarily stubborn but instead are very intelligent. In fact, they are more intelligent than a horse, a donkey or even dogs. Nonetheless, the phrase generally means: to be extremely obstinate or a person who will not listen to the advice of others and won't change their way of doing things

Sub rosa - This term comes from the legendary Greek god of silence and secrets, Harpocrates, who stumbled upon Venus while she was making love to Cupid and given the first rose as a bribe to keep quiet about it. Thus, the rose became the symbol of silence. Harpocrates was the Greek interpretation of the Egyptian god *Harpa-Khruti* (Horus the Child) who was usually depicted as a small boy with a finger held to his lips; an Egyptian gesture symbolizing childhood which the Greeks mistook for a hush for silence. *Sub rosa* means "under the rose" or something happening or done in secret

Substance abuse - Since antiquity, alcohol and other drugs have been abused and known to be addictive. However, it wasn't until recently that it has been recognized that some people are genetically more prone to addiction than others. It was the **Founding Father** Dr. Benjamin Rush who was one of the first to propose the idea that alcoholism was more than a moral weakness and was therefore linked to the alcohol itself. With the rise of other addictive drugs, the term substance abuse came into use to describe the overarching phenomena of addiction and to propose methods to alleviate or eliminate the condition. The term means: the abusive and addictive use of alcohol and drugs such as heroin, cocaine, or prescription drugs. **Under the influence of**: is a similar term that describes the impact or impairment of a person's ability to function

Suffer fools gladly - The source of this saying is from the Bible New Testament. (2 Corinthians 11:19). The common usage is: to have patience with someone even if you think they are ignorant or have senseless ideas. **Not to suffer fools gladly** is probably used more often and means the opposite

Sugar Daddy - The origin of this term is uncertain. It is a wealthy, middle-aged man who spends freely on a young woman in return for her companionship or intimacy. If married, she is sometimes referred to as a **Trophy wife** which has come to mean: a young, attractive wife regarded as **a status symbol** for an older man

Sulk in his (your) tent - The source of this expression comes from the Iliad and the episode in which Achilles sulks in is tent and refuses to fight because Agamemnon took his girl away from him. He only returns to battle after his dear friend and lover, Patroclus, is killed by Hector. The phrase generally means: to withdraw from the action or quit because you think you've been insulted or treated dishonorably or unjustly. **Take your ball and go home; everyone hates a quitter**

Survival of the fittest - This expression originated from Charles Darwin's theory of evolution. Although Darwin was the first to popularize the theory of evolution, he was not the first to espouse it. Such distinction belongs to the Muslim polymath Al Jahiz who first proposed it over 1000 years before Darwin. The notion that humans evolved from simian ancestors gave rise to the Scopes Monkey Trial and other idioms such as **I'll be a monkey's uncle. Darwinism**, at least in its early days, was laden with racist ideology and dogma which led to the fabrication of data perhaps best exemplified by Piltdown Man. This dogma ultimately converged on whites having a separate and more advanced evolutionary track than other races placing them at the top of the racial **totem pole** and other races behind them in accordance with their hue. To this end, blacks were placed on the bottom next to apes. Anthropological discoveries were **reengineered** by white scientists to justify the social milieu and supremacy of the white race. Such theories have now been proven false using mitochondrial DNA and Y chromosome testing techniques. The general interpretation is: those that are strong survive while those that are weak will perish. Similar phrases include: **only the strong survive; the strong do what they can, and the weak suffer what they must**

Sweet Fanny Adams - This expression originated from a story about a very young child by the name of Fanny Adams, who was gruesomely murdered in England in 1867. For some reason, the phrase developed the informal meaning of "absolutely nothing at all," perhaps as an unfortunate and grotesque indication of how little of poor Fanny remained intact after the murder. The expression can be interpreted to mean: nothing at all or nothing. **Much ado about nothing**

Sword of Damocles - The expression comes to us from the writings of the Roman politician, orator, and philosopher Cicero (106-43 BCE). The phrase generally means: something that threatens to bring imminent disaster or something that is always present as a danger or a threat to a person, place, or situation; a precarious situation. Example: the nuclear sword of Damocles hangs over the region by a thread

Symbiotic relationship - This is a term that has its origin in the scientific realm; more specifically biology and ecology. It is a relationship where two different species work together in a mutual association helping each other to the benefit of both species. For example, humans take in oxygen and exhale carbon dioxide and plants take in carbon dioxide and exhale oxygen. It is defined as: a cooperative relationship of mutual benefit or dependence between two groups or two people. **Cross pollination** is another biological term that has migrated to the general public. In biology it means: to pollinate a flower or plant with pollen from another flower or plant. Generally, it means: to influence something or someone by association or proximity

Stands for:

The higher the monkey climbs,

the more he shows his tail

IN A NUTSHELL

Table d'hote - This is a term of French origin that has become part of the English vernacular. It literally means: "table of the host." It now means: a full meal with all courses, offered at a set price. **A la carte**

Taboo - The origin of this word comes from the Polynesian word for "forbidden" and was introduced to the English language after the voyage of Captain James Cook to this area. It has therefore migrated to mean: something that is prohibited or restricted by social custom. **Off limits; out of bounds**

Taj Mahal - The origin of this term comes from a magnificent edifice in India, erected by the Mogul emperor Shah Jahan in 1649. It is a white marble mausoleum with a large reflecting pool built in honor of his deceased wife and known worldwide for its splendor, elegance and excellence. Consequently, in modern times, the term has been associated with splendor, elegance and excellence particularly in reference to an architectural achievement

Take a chill pill - The source of this expression appears to be the introduction of a pill to alleviate Attention-Deficit/Hyperactivity Disorder (ADHD) in the 1980s. The term easily migrated to mean: **to chill out** or calm down

Take a licking and keep on ticking - This expression comes from a TV ad produced by the Timex Corporation to promote the longevity and reliability of their watches. It means: to endure, to persevere through difficult and challenging situations. On a similar note, the **Energizer Bunny** is another advertisement that echoes the same sentiments. It was produced to demonstrate the longevity of the Energizer battery; like the bunny, it kept going and going and going

Take a page (leaf) out of someone's book - The origin of this popular saying is unclear. However, it has come to mean: to behave or to do something in a way that someone else would; to follow someone's example. **Imitation is the sincerest form of flattery; follow the leader; to play the sedulous ape**

Take (plead) the fifth - This phrase originated from the right to invoke the Fifth Amendment in the Bill of Rights, part of the American Constitution, which says that a person can't "be compelled in any criminal case to be a witness against himself." It has become a response to a question that you do not intend to answer. **I'll take the fifth**

Take with a grain of salt - The origin of this saying is often attributed to the Roman author Pliny the Elder's, Naturalis Historia (77CE) and the belief that putting salt on your food protected it from poison. The common interpretation is: to accept something with reservations

Tall, dark and handsome - This expression goes back to at least the early 19th century, although its origin is obscure. The term *dark* may refer to a tan or even to the person's hair color. But in some cultures, e.g., India, dark skin is not considered to be something positive and the preference is for light skin. Nonetheless, at least in the West, it is used to denote a handsome man, **an Adonis.** one that most women would fine extremely attractive

A COLLECTION OF POPULAR ENGLISH PHRASES

Tar and feathers - This term comes from the colonial period practice of covering a person in tar and then attaching feathers to the tar as a form of public punishment and humiliation. While sometimes hilarious to the spectators, it was painful to the person subjected to it. Quite often, this practice is linked to the American Revolutionary War, perhaps because it appears to have been more prevalent in the American colonies. Yet, it is more of a product of its time and not the war. The common interpretation is: to harshly criticize, condemn or reprimand someone; especially in a public setting or before a group. **Rake them over the coals**

Tar baby - The source of this expression comes from a fictional character in the African-American folktales Uncle Remus by Joel Chandler Harris published in 1881. It was a doll made of tar that would stick to you. The use of the term 'tar baby" can have derogatory connotations depending on the context in which it is used. Members of the African American community are extremely sensitive to its usage because of its past negative connotation when it referred to them. Whereas malice may not be the original intent, it may in fact be the final result. It should therefore be used with caution or perhaps not at all. It denotes: a difficult problem that is only aggravated by attempts to solve it. **To make matters worse**

Teflon - The source of this term comes from a tough synthetic resin that is used to coat cooking utensils in order to give them a nonstick coating. It was first used as a metaphor in 1983, in reference to Ronald Reagan in a speech by Pat Schroeder as he referred to Reagan as the *Teflon President* because nothing stuck to him. Since that time, the term Teflon and **Teflon Man** denotes: something or a person that nothing sticks to permanently. Someone who is immune to criticism and perhaps **above the law** or the criteria used to judge others

Tell it not in Gath - The origin of this phrase is the Bible (2 Samuel 1:20) "Tell it not in Gath, publish it not in the streets of Askelon; lest the daughters of the Philistines rejoice, lest the daughters of the uncircumcised triumph." The common interpretation is: don't mention this, especially to someone who might take pleasure in it or celebrate the news at our expense

Tempest in a teapot - The source of this saying is unknown, but many have attributed a similar saying to the Roman statesman Cicero. It now means: a great commotion over an unimportant matter. Another way of saying: **much ado about nothing; small potatoes**

Term of endearment - The origin of this term is unclear. The use of endearing terms probably goes back as far as language itself. Ironically, many of these terms use the sense of taste as a metaphor such as sweetie, sugar, honey, cupcake, etc. particularly when referring to a spouse. Babe or baby is also used as a term of endearment for the female spouse and sometimes daddy is used to designate the male spouse although it may have Freudian implications. Terms of endearment are also used to express affection for someone that has died. The phrase is frequently used as: a word or expression often intended to address affection

Thank God (the Lord) for small favors(mercies) - The origin of this popular saying is unclear, but it was probably inspired by the Bible. It simply means: to be grateful for what you have; regardless of how large or how small; to appreciate the blessings of the Lord particularly in times of strife. Shakespeare wrote in King Lear (Act IV, Scene I) **"The worst is not so long as we can say; This is the worst." The patience of Job**

Thanksgiving - The story of Thanksgiving originating with the Pilgrims sharing a Thanksgiving meal with Native Americans remains a **matter of conjecture**. Although etched in the collective memory of Americans, it may have more to do with folklore than fact. The Thanksgiving that Americans celebrate today, however, was established by Abraham Lincoln in 1863. In fact, during that year there were two Thanksgivings, one after the battle of Gettysburg on August 6, 1863 (although the battle ended on July 4th which Lincoln interpreted to be an omen from God) and another after Lincoln's seminal speech at the battlefield in November which would be honored henceforth on the last Thursday of November. Lincoln saw the resurrection of the Pilgrim based holiday as a means of unifying the nation. His speech at Gettysburg consecrated the dead of both Union and Confederate soldiers that died in that epic battle. But much credit should be given to Sarah Hale who wrote Lincoln and strongly suggested that he make Thanksgiving a national holiday. Controversy loomed for decades over the last Thursday in November because many Americans did not start their Christmas shopping until after Thanksgiving and sometimes the last Thursday shorten preparations for the Christmas celebration. In December 1941, however, Congress passed a law making the fourth Thursday in November the national day of observance. This allowed enough time for people to do their Christmas shopping something that brought **season greetings** and joy to most merchants. Hence, Thanksgiving as we know it today in America, may have more in common with Lincoln's **mystic chords** and the battle of Gettysburg than it does with the Pilgrims. **Black Friday; Cyber Monday**

That government is best which governs least - This expression is regularly ascribed to Thomas Jefferson but has also been attributed to the American author Henry David Thoreau from his book Civil Disobedience. Assigning this saying to a Founding Father rather than Thoreau gives more credence to its current usage. In modern times, this expression is repeatedly used by those that want the government to interfere with their lives as little as possible. **Laissez-faire**

That takes the cake - This saying has its origins in American slavery in which black slaves would have a cakewalk contest and the winner was awarded a cake. It was intended to satirize the stiff ballroom events of white plantation owners and in some ways to make fun of Ol' Master. It has since evolved to mean: someone or something that is so unusual as to be unbelievable. Similarly, a **Cakewalk** is an absurdly or surprisingly easy task, **a piece of cake**, and **a walk in the park** essentially mean the same thing

The American dream - This term was first used by the French politician and historian, Alexis de Tocqueville, in his book Democracy in America (1835). The book is a foreigner's perspective of the fundamental characteristics and rules of governance that have made America great. Being a foreigner, he could be candid and concise in his observations. For example, he wrote: "The surface of American society is covered with a layer of democratic paint, but from time to time one can see the old aristocratic colours breaking through." It is a large book that is frequently quoted but few have read it in its entirety. The phrase means: the idea of prosperity in America: owning a home, having a good paying job, living a happier life, e.g., **a chicken in every pot and a car in every garage. Living the American dream**

The apple doesn't fall far from the tree - This saying goes back, in one form or another, to the 1800s and was used by such notables as Ralph Waldo Emerson who apparently was one of the first to use it in the English language. It appears in several different languages and is a popular proverb with various connotations. In its current usage, it is frequently used to describe familial similarities particularly when one precedes the other such as the son's resemblance to the father; in looks, habits, aptitude, etc. **Like father like son; chip off the old block**

The beginning of the end - This phrase in the 16th century, was used only to describe an approaching death. It gained a new meaning after the French lost the Battle of Leipzig (Battle of Nations) in 1813. This battle was one of the most devastating battles of the Napoleonic Wars (1800 - 15). It marked the end of the French Empire east of the Rhine and was a **harbinger** of future defeats. The phrase now means: the event to which ending or failure can be traced; the point in which something starts to get gradually worse, until it fails or ends completely. Winston Churchill once said referring to World War II "it's not the beginning of the end... but perhaps the end of the beginning." **Point of no return**

The best laid plans of mice and men often go astray (The best laid schemes of mice and men often go awry) - This phrase is an adaptation from a line in: To a Mouse by the Scottish poet Robert Burns 1786. It now refers to the belief that things often, and can go, wrong even though you have planned them well. **Murphy's law**

The best surprise is no surprise - The origin of this expression is unclear. Nevertheless, it became the slogan of the Holiday Inn hotel franchise. It simply means that it is best to get exactly what you expected rather than to get something bad or wrong that you did not expect. **No news is good news**

The best things in life are free - The source of this saying appears to be from a song in the musical "Good News" which opened in 1927. A movie version was produced in 1930 and remade in 1947. This song was sung by several music groups in various decades most noted were the 1940s and 1950s group the Ink Spots. "The moon belongs to everyone; the best things in life are free; the stars belong to everyone; they gleam there for you and me." It generally means: **money doesn't buy you happiness** or **peace of mind**. The things that we truly value, such as love, true friendship, good family, etc., do not **come with price tags**, but from the heart and the spirit that a **benevolent Creator** has bestowed upon us

The best way to predict the future is to create it - This quote is often attributed to the 16th president of the United States, Abraham Lincoln. But he may not have been the source or even used it. Some have also credited to Peter Drucker. Notwithstanding, Lincoln was known for his witty sayings and wisdom and perhaps he said something similar and it was therefore attributed to him. Like many famous people, his life was **riddled with** failure and strife. Yet, in many ways, he was a luminary and now rests as a seminal figure, not only in American history but in world history. Thanks to people like him, that dared to pursue their dreams and potential, America, through **Yankee ingenuity** helped to shape the modern world. This

235

quote can be interpreted to mean: **No one can predict the future**, but in the words of <u>Thomas Edison</u>; through **"one percent inspiration and ninety-nine percent perspiration"**, they can help to create it

The Bible Belt - The term was first used by the American writer and satirist H.L. Mencken when he was reporting on the <u>Scopes Monkey Trial</u> which took place in Dayton, Tennessee in 1925. It is defined as those areas of the South where Protestant fundamentalism is widely practiced. Despite the professed religious observance, educational and college graduation rates in this region are among the lowest in the United States. Whereas, cardiovascular and heart disease, obesity, homicide, teenage pregnancy, and sexually transmitted infections are among the highest rates in the nation. Furthermore, these southern states are traditionally conservative and many of them voted Democratic before the Civil Rights act of 1964. In more recent times, since 1980 and the election of Ronald Reagan, they have trended Republican and historically the white population has been on the opposite side of equal rights for people of African descent leading many to wonder if they **practice what they preach**

The Big Apple - The origin of this term is believed to have come from the African American community. It originated in the American south (New Orleans) in connection with horseracing and as part of the migration of the jazz movement of the early 20th century and became the signature of <u>New York City</u> because it was the place to be. It now refers to <u>New York City</u>. -Similarly, **the Big Easy** is another name for New Orleans

The blind leading the blind - The source of this saying is the Bible, (Matt.15:14). The general interpretation is: the uninformed attempting to inform the others; someone who is not capable of dealing with a situation is guiding someone else who is not capable of dealing with it

The blood of the martyrs is the seed of the Church - The origins of this expression comes from a paraphrase of a statement made by the renowned early church leader <u>Tertullian</u> in 197 CE. It is from his book entitled: <u>The Apology</u>. It generally means: nothing great is achieved without great sacrifice

The bogyman (boogyman) - The origin of this popular term is uncertain. However, a version of such a mythological creature appears in many cultures around the world. It is most often used to scare children into doing something that you want them to do. It is also used to designate a fear or phobia of something or someone; something to fear or something that haunts you. **The bogyman is coming to get you; beware of the bogyman; there is nothing to fear, but fear itself**

The buck stops here - This expression originated from a statement made by President Harry S Truman. It has migrated to mean that responsibility is not passed any further; the responsibility for something cannot or should not be passed to someone else

The business of America is business - This saying is attributed to President <u>Calvin Coolidge.</u> It means: business and big business in particular is an integral part of the American fabric and essential to its economy. **Big business**

236

A COLLECTION OF POPULAR ENGLISH PHRASES

The Byronic hero - This term comes from an idealized but flawed character exemplified in the life and writings of the English writer and politician Lord Byron. The common interpretation is: a melancholy and rebellious young man, distressed by a terrible wrong he committed in the past

The carrot or the stick - This phrase is an old proverb regarding rewards of the carrot and punishment of the stick. Perhaps the best example of this phenomena is exemplified in Ancient Egypt in which the pharaoh is depicted with his arms equally crossed bearing a shepherd's crook in one hand and a whip (flail) in the other. Balance or equilibrium is achieved by the correct application of these two dynamic influences symbolized within that portrayal and to some extent control human behavior. The phrase has migrated to mean: rewards and punishments that influence someone's behavior or actions

The cave you fear to enter holds the treasure you seek - This quote is credited to, Joseph Campbell, the renowned American scholar of myth and religion. But Campbell was more than a professor, orator and prolific writer. He was **a guru** that desperately tried to discern the nature and purpose of the human existence. Fear is an emotion that can only be conquered by courage, faith and fortitude. We must be forever mindful that **there is nothing to fear but fear itself**. In life, great things are normally achieved through great sacrifice. Yet many of us refuse to enter the cave because we fear the unknown or failure thereby forsaking the treasures not only of our minds but of our existence. Fear is that **fire breathing dragon** often wounded but seldom slain. Those that refuse to battle it will never know how great they can truly be. **The Dutch philosopher** Baruch Spinoza wrote: "all things excellent are as difficult as they are rare." Follow your bliss

The church of what's happening now - This was a phrase that was made famous by the comedian Flip Wilson. On his television show, there was a skit that aired periodically in which he played a minister of a church. It means the current thing, what is in vogue. **What's going on; what's happening**

The coast is clear - This saying originated from the days of pirates and smugglers that sailed up and down the coast. If the coast was clear of warships that were on the lookout for pirates, then they could sail. The common interpretation is: no observers or authorities are present and it's safe to proceed or come out of hiding. **When the cat is away, the mice will play**

The course of true love never did run smooth - This expression originated from Shakespeare's A Midsummer Night's Dream, 1598(Act I, Scene I). "Could ever hear by tale or history; The course of true love never did run smooth." The play contains all of the aspects that love consists of; and this is represented in the constantly twisting plot line. Its meaning is simple: true love always encounters problems or difficulties in which the lovers must endure. **Nothing comes easy**

The crown jewels - The origin of this phrase comes from the crown, other ornaments and jewelry worn or carried by the sovereign on certain state occasions. It now means: a particularly valuable or prized possession or asset

IN A NUTSHELL

The cure for boredom is curiosity. There is no cure for curiosity - This quote is sometimes attributed to Dorothy Parker. However, further investigation ascribes it to Ellen Parr. The popular interpretation is: people that are innately curious are seldom bored because they occupy their time investigating things, people or events that they find interesting. The renowned physicist Richard Feynman known for his curiosity and **out of the box thinking** once said: **I would rather have questions that can't be answered than answers that can't be questioned. Curiosity may have killed the cat,** but at least that cat was not bored

The cure (remedy) is worse than the disease - This expression is accredited to the English statesman, scientist and philosopher, Francis Bacon. The expression can be interpreted to mean: the solution to a problem can have **unintended consequences** that are worse than the original problem

The devil can cite scripture for his own purpose - The original source is the Bible (Matthew 4:1-11) and the devil's temptation of Christ, in which the devil indirectly quotes scripture. This phrase originated from William Shakespeare's play: The Merchant of Venice. (Act I, Scene III). "The devil can quote Scripture for his own use. An evil soul using a holy story is like a criminal who smiles at you. He looks like a good apple but he's **rotten at the core. Oh, liars can look so honest.**" This expression is meant to communicate that displaying knowledge of religious scripture, or even being able to cite scripture to support one's plans and intentions is insufficient evidence that one is actually morally upright. **Hood or cowl does not make the monk**

The devil is in the details - This phrase seems to have been derived from an older phrase "God is in the details." It simply means: the details of a matter are its most problematic aspect. **Look inside the box; read the fine print**

The dickens - The earliest used of this term is found in Shakespeare's The Merry Wives of Winsor. (Act III, Scene II) It is generally used for emphasis or euphemistically invoking the devil, e.g., **they work like the dickens**

The dozens - The source of this saying appears to be unknown and is a term popular in the African American community. It is a game of friendly insults exchanged between two people. For example: your momma is so fat that her ass needs two zip codes. To which a person may respond: Your daddy is so poor, he can't pay attention. Also, known as: "playing the dozens" or **"to do the dozens"**

The eagle flies tomorrow (on Friday) - The origin of this saying is unknown or unclear. But it has been popular in the African American community for some time. The eagle is in reference to the eagle on the back of the American dollar bill. The phrase now means: to get paid

The easiest person to deceive is one's self - This quote is ascribed to the English novelist Edward Bulwer-Lytton. The common interpretation is: deception is a part of human nature and we all are guilty of it at one time or another. However, most of us are oblivious to how we deceive ourselves. Sometimes out of self-preservation, other times out of envy and greed, it is **a double-edged sword** that can yield positive or negatives results. Sometimes we fool ourselves into thinking that something that is right is wrong or that something that is wrong is right. Our hopes and our dreams can be the biggest enablers of our inner deception which is nothing more than a distortion of our current reality in search of **better days**. It can be like waiting for Godot, he cannot come today, but he will surely come tomorrow but **deep down inside** we know he will never come. The renowned American physicist Richard Feynman once wrote: "The first principle is that you must not fool yourself and you are the easiest person to fool." **True deception goes unnoticed.** Jane Wagner, the American writer, director and producer once said: "**the ability to delude yourself may be an important survival tool; to live in a fool's paradise**

The eleventh hour - The source of this idiom is from the Bible (Matthew 20: 6-10). It has migrated to mean: the latest possible moment. It is worthy to note that World War I ended on the eleventh hour. of the eleventh day, of the eleventh month of 1918 perhaps a slight reference to this saying

The emperor has no clothes - This saying originated from the Danish writer Hans Christian Andersen in his "The Emperor's New Clothes." The story is about an emperor who loved wearing fine clothes and spent all of his people's money on them. He had a different set for each hour and was, without doubt, the finest dressed man in the land. But he was fooled by dressmakers into wearing nothing and thinking it was clothing until a child told him that he was naked. It generally means: any obvious truth denied by the majority of people despite the evidence to the contrary, particularly when proclaimed by the government. In many cases, the failure to admit the obvious is because of **fear of the consequences.** It is also used sometimes to express something in general that is untrue. Similar phrases include: **the elephant in the room; deep meaning often lie in childish play**

The end justifies the means - This saying is regularly attributed to the Italian statesman **Machiavelli** but, it actually comes from the Roman poet Ovid. One of the foremost writers of the **Augustan era,** Ovid is known for his mournful love poems such as the Amores and the Ars Amatoria and his **magnum opus** the Metamorphose. The phrase generally means: the methods of achievement are not as important as the final result. Similar phrases include: **it doesn't matter how you get there; the end crowns the work**

The enemy of my enemy is my friend - This is an ancient proverb. It means that it is easy to unite with someone if you have a shared or common purpose or foe. **Strange bedfellows**

The eyes are the mirror (window) of the soul - This quote is attributed to the Brazilian author of the Paulo Coelho. "The eyes are the mirror of the soul and reflect everything that seems to be hidden; and like a mirror, they also reflect the person looking into them." It means that by looking into the eyes of someone you can, on occasion, gaze into the abyss of their soul

The face that launched a thousand ships - The source of this phrase is Greek mythology, specifically the Trojan War. Helen of Troy was believed to be the most beautiful woman in the world and her adduction by Paris was the cause of the Trojan War. The phrase now means: a person or a thing that causes disaster, particularly war. **A Judgement of Paris** is another idiom that stems from the choices given to Paris by the gods. It now means: any difficult decision

IN A NUTSHELL

The fog of war – This phrase is attributed to <u>Carl von Clausewitz</u> from his **magnum opus** entitled <u>On War</u>. He was a Prussian officer that wrote extensively on the moral, psychological and political aspects of war. It has also been used by armies around the world as a handbook of various aspects of war. It generally means: the confusion, chaos, and disorder caused by war or conditions on the battlefield. It frequently addresses the uncertainty and **unintended consequences** of war. It has recently been applied to other unpredictable, chaotic and stressful situations in which the outcome is determine in real-time. <u>The Art of War</u> by Sun Tzu is another seminal book about the tactics and strategies of war that have **stood the test of time**

The fool thinks himself to be wise, but the wise man knows himself to be a fool - This saying is from Shakespeare's play: <u>As you like It</u> (Act V, Scene I). Similar quotes are credited to others such as the Latin writer Lucius Anaeus Seneca who wrote: "He is a fool who cannot be angry; but he is a wise man who will not." The expression can be interpreted to mean: there is a difference between a fool and a wise man because wisdom teaches a person how to behave and how to think within a logical framework; something that a fool finds difficult to do. The wise man knows that he is capable of being fooled simply because he knows he can never know everything. Similar phrases include: **fools rush in where angels dare to tread; a fool and his money are soon parted**

The ghost sitting on the grave - The source of this expression is credited to the English philosopher <u>Thomas Hobbes</u> who wrote: The Church, the papacy became nothing other than the ghost of the deceased Roman Empire, sitting on its grave. This phrase is sometimes used to describe: a situation where one thing ceases to exist but is quickly replace by something that resembles it

The glass is half empty(full) - The source of this expression is unclear. It is used as a saying to indicate if someone tends to look at things in a positive or a negative way. If it is half full, the person is optimistic; if it is half empty, the person is pessimistic

The good Samaritan - The source of this adage is from a parable in the Bible (Luke 10:33). The parable of the Good Samaritan tells the story of a man traveling from Jerusalem to Jericho, and while on the way, he is robbed of everything he had, including his clothing, and **is beaten to within an inch of his life.** He is passed by several people including a priest that refuse to help him. Finally, a Samaritan comes to his aid. It generally means: a kindhearted, charitable or helpful person

The gospel truth - The source of this saying is from the Bible and refers to the inerrancy of the four gospels: <u>Matthew, Mark, Luke and John.</u> Since the 1780s, Matthew, Mark and Luke have been referred to as the **synoptic gospels** because they comprise many of the same stories of Jesus, often in a similar arrangement and language. **On the other hand,** the Gospel of John was written later and gives a different perspective on <u>the life of Jesus.</u> Even though Matthew is the first gospel book of the New Testament, <u>most biblical scholars</u> believe that Mark was the first gospel written and that Matthew and Luke used Mark and another document called Q as the foundation of their gospels. They believe that the <u>Q document</u> contained the themes and parables that are common to Matthew and Luke such as the virgin birth that are not contained in Mark. Accordingly, the stories that are unique to Matthew are designated

240

A COLLECTION OF POPULAR ENGLISH PHRASES

as M and those unique to Luke are designated as L. This is repeatedly referred to as the <u>Synoptic Problem.</u> Regarding John, the biggest discrepancy between John and the synoptic gospels centers around when was Jesus arrested: before or after the **Passover meal**. The saying, the gospel truth, has been used since the 1600s. It largely means: something that is absolutely true and unquestionable

The greatest remedy for anger is delay - Although sometimes ascribed to the American political activist Thomas Paine, the true source of this saying appears to be the Roman stoic philosopher and tutor of Nero, Lucius Annaeus Seneca. It means what it literally says; when people are angry, they tend to do things that they would not normally do or come to regret later. Anger tends to **bring out the worst and not the best** in people. **Go and cool off; chill out**

The Greeks had a word for it (them) - This phrase has its origins from the title of a play by the American Pulitzer Prize winner Zoe Akins in 1929. The common interpretation is: something unmentionable. On a similar note, Shakespeare, in Julius Caesar (Act I, Scene II), coined the phrase: **it was Greek to me** "But those that understood him smiled at one another and shook their heads. But for mine own part, <u>it was Greek to me."</u> The common usage is: a way of saying that you do not understand something that is said or written. **It's all Greek to me**

The hand that rocks the cradle rules the world - The source of this expression comes from a poem written by the American poet <u>William Rose Wallace</u> in 1865. The poem emphasizes the role of the mother in shaping the children of the next generation. "Blessings on the hand of women! Angels guard its strength and grace; In the palace, cottage, hovel; Oh, no matter where the place." Such is the sacred gift given to all mothers; to see in their children not what they are, but what they can be. The phrase now means: the person who raises a child determines the character of that child and so influences the type of society that the next generation will create. **It takes a village to raise a child**

The higher the monkey climbs, the more he shows his tail - This saying is sometimes credited to the American singer-songwriter, Thomas Waits. However, it has been in existence since the 14th century and was written by the English philosopher and theologian <u>John Wycliffe</u>. "<u>The higher the Ape goes, the more he shews his tail</u>." Nonetheless, it generally means: the further an unsuitable person is promoted, the more apparent his inadequacies become. **Peter Principle: person rises to his level of incompetence**

The inmates (lunatics) are running the asylum - The source of this expression is unclear. Nevertheless, it is believed to have been derived from the motion picture industry in the 1920s and used in various forms throughout the 20th century to refer to total incompetence. Some have credited Charlie Chaplin with the phrase. The popular interpretation is: the people that are the least capable of running an organization, institution or group are now in charge. A total chaotic and irrational situation. **Keystone cops**

The iron fist in the velvet glove - Napoleon seems to have originated this phrase. It means: a person who has a gentle, sweet, or unassuming appearance or disposition, but who in reality is particularly severe, forceful, and uncompromising. **Janus-faced.** On a similar note, **to rule with an iron fist** means to rule in a very strict or disciplined manner; to rule with absolute authority. **Rule by fiat**

IN A NUTSHELL

The judgments of the Lord are true and righteous altogether - This phrase is ascribed to Abraham Lincoln's <u>Second Inaugural Address</u> delivered on a rainy March 4, 1865. **For all intents and purposes,** the American Civil War was **all over but the shouting.** Lincoln had turned his face away from the dark shadows of war and toward the bright horizon of a peaceful new day. So often in his speech and in his thoughts, Lincoln evoked God as the sole judge of human fate. This speech was an attempt to **heal the wounds of** a much-divided nation so that **the government of the people, by the people and for the people would not perish from this earth.** "Within 701 words, Lincoln references God fourteen times, quotes the Bible four times and invokes prayer three times. He once called his beloved nation **"the last best hope on earth."** On this day he spoke from his heart, as if he intuitively knew that his soul would soon be called to **the house of the Lord.** Almost four years to the day, the war that killed more Americans than all of the previous wars combined was indeed over and its leader assassinated. Buried in the same suit that he gave this seminal and heartfelt speech, his tall body along with the dead body of his young beloved son, Willie, made its solemn train ride across a grieved and bereaved nation toward his final resting place. And as the train traveled along its morbid path, the nation finally felt, the end of God's long wrath. This phrase can be interpreted to mean: literally what it says that God's wisdom is unknown and unbounded, and **His judgments are true and righteous altogether. He now belongs to the ages**

The L word - This term was popularized in the late 20th century. It is sometimes used as a euphemism for Lesbianism. The origins of the term "Lesbian" comes from the name of the Greek island, Lesbos. According to the Greek female poet <u>Sappho</u>**,** it was believed to be inhabited by women or a place where friendly or sexual relations between women frequently occurred. Sappho was one of the few female poets of antiquity, and she is regularly associated with lesbianism because it was the theme of some of her poetry. Similarly, **Butch, dyke** or **bulldyke** have been use in the past to describe a lesbian of masculine appearance or manner

The last trump - The source of this term is the New Testament 1 Corinthians 15:52 and 1 Thessalonians 4:16. "In a moment, in the twinkling of an eye, at the <u>last trump</u>: for the trumpet shall sound, and the dead shall be raised incorruptible, and we shall be changed." It is a reference to the last trumpet call on earth before the righteous are called to heaven. It means the final call. **Clarion call**

The law of unintended consequences - The term is regularly attributed to the American sociologist Robert K. Merton but has been witnessed and articulated in other ways long before this phrase was coined. Ancient myths and the Bible are full of stories that confirm this law. It is a cross between **Murphy's law** and the phrase: **the best laid plans of mice and men often go awry**. It is also referred to as the **precautionary principle.** The common usage is: actions of people, government and corporations always have effects that are unanticipated or unintended. Such effects can be positive or negative but cannot be foreseen. Similar phrases include: **cause and effect; sometimes we look for one thing and find another**

The lion shall lay down with the lamb - This quote is often ascribed to the Bible, (Isaiah 65:25), but is not directly found in the Bible although (Isaiah 65:25) is similar in content and probably served as the inspiration of the expression. The common interpretation is: a promise of a peaceful utopia

242

A COLLECTION OF POPULAR ENGLISH PHRASES

The Lost Cause - Immediately after the Civil War, the South began to develop a construct of the Civil War that depicted them not as losers of the war, but rather as defenders of their rights. Perhaps best exemplified by the movies <u>Gone with the Wind</u> and <u>The Birth of a Nation.</u> From this construct emerged heroes, some depicted on <u>Stone Mountain</u> and statues throughout the South, and a new Southern heritage was borne from the simmering ashes of slavery. This construct became central during the years of Reconstruction although the monuments were built later. Today, "<u>The Lost Cause</u>" continues to be a means in which some Southerners continue to cope with losing the Civil War, perhaps best illustrated by the use and display of the Confederate flag and the slogan: **the South shall rise again. I wish I was in Dixie.** On a similar note, **Southern hospitality** is a stereotype attributed to some Southerners as being welcoming and friendly, gracious hosts, in contrast to the South being the cesspool of racism, discrimination and segregation

The love that dare not speak its name - The origin of this expression comes from the British author and poet Lord Alfred Douglas who used it in his poem <u>Two Loves</u>. He was a friend and lover of <u>Oscar Wilde.</u> Homosexuality was a criminal offense and serious taboo at this time in Britain and Wilde was later imprisoned. "The love that dare not speak its name" was a constant theme of the trial and the phrase has been attached to it historically. The phrase is now used as a euphemism for homosexuality. Related phrases include: **in the closet; on the down low;** Stonewall Inn

The luck of the Irish - This is a phrase that goes back at least to the migration of the Irish to America as a result of the <u>Potato Famine in the mid-1800s</u>. Contrary to popular opinion, it was a negative term that meant that the Irish have bad luck. Yet today, it is a sign of good luck and is often associated with a **Leprechaun and a pot of gold**

The mark of Cain - This expression is from the Bible (Genesis 4:15 and relates to a stain placed on Cain for the murder of his brother Abel. It is most unfortunate that in some religious circles, (most noted was the Mormons) this mark or curse was extended to black people and because of such beliefs, <u>the Mormons</u> refused to give black men priesthood until 1978. "They were a mixture of all the seed of Adam save it was the seed of Cain, for the seed of Cain were black, and had not place among them (Moses 7:22)." It has migrated to mean: a stain on one's reputation

The meek shall inherit the earth - The source of this saying is from the Bible (Matthew 5:5) (Psalm 37:11). Meek as in this expression means people see themselves as servants of God and those that serve God will inherit the earth. Jesus described himself as "meek and lowly" (Matthew 11:29). God's promise of the kingdom is a new heaven and a new earth. This phrase generally means: to be humble in your actions, live a life of humility and being willing to sacrifice your privileges for the benefit of others without seeking a reward other than the pleasure of giving

The N word - This term was popularized in the late 20th century. It is a euphemism for the pejorative term "nigger." The origins of the term "nigger" has its roots in <u>the Transatlantic slave trade</u> and was first used by Spanish and Portuguese slave traders. This term has become one of the most pejorative terms in the English language when used by a non-black person to designate a black person. Before the Civil Rights movement, it was used freely as depicted in the novels of the American author and humorist Mark Twain. Among some black people and in rap music, the term is still widely used in various connotations without any offense taken by many blacks within the African American community to designate themselves. Other pejorative terms used to designate black people include: **coon, tar baby, boy, jungle bunny, sambo, Jim Crow, monkey, ape, gorilla, spear chucker, spade, etc.**, all of which should be avoided when addressing blacks as individuals or as a group. On a similar note, **sand nigger** is a derogatory term that is sometimes used to denote a person of Middle Eastern descent

The nature of the beast - This saying goes back to the 17th century and is of unclear origin. The phrase is frequently interpreted to mean: the inherent or essential quality or character of something, which cannot be changed

The only thing necessary for the triumph of evil is that good men do nothing - This popular quotation is regularly attributed to Edmund Burke. Though Burke wrote something quite similar, the exact words cannot be found in any of his writings. It was also used by President Kennedy and attributed to Burke. The common interpretation is: **turning a blind eye** to evil will only allow it to flourish at a faster rate. It is very similar in connotation to the quote by Leonardo Da Vinci. Similar expressions include: **"He that does not punish evil commands it to be done"**; silence gives consent

The only thing we have to fear is fear itself - This expression is credited to President Franklin D. Roosevelt's first inaugural address given on March 4, 1933. Roosevelt was the last president sworn in in the month of March and he inherited a nation amid an economic depression. Perhaps this is why this saying resonated so much. Fear is a human emotion that can manifest itself in many ways. The fear of dying, the fear of failing, the fear of losing a love one or your job are just some of the fears that we must confront. Faith and courage are the two vehicles that are often used to combat fear. The expression is frequently interpreted to mean: that we must confront our fears and accept them as part of the human experience because the only way to eliminate a fear is not to fear it at all. **Fear has many eyes**

The opposite of love is not hate, it is indifference -This quote is attributed to the Jewish Holocaust survivor and writer Elie Wiesel. So often in life, we associate something with its **polar opposite**, e.g., up, down; left, right; love, hate. Most people experience love before they experience hate. However, it is the voyage between these two states that is often overlooked and is just, if not more important. In this case, hate is the destination, but indifference is the journey. Nelson Mandela said: "No person is born hating another person," it is something that a person learns and the only way that we can begin to understand hate, is to understand the individual steps of the journey

The original sin - This is a Christian doctrine that asserts that after the **Fall of Adam**, in the **Garden of Eden**, his descendants (all humans) are born with an innate urge to sin as a consequence of his fall. This was a concept that was developed in the writing of the Christian theologian St. Augustine: "the deliberate sin of the first man is the cause of original sin." It is habitually used as a metaphor for the initial cause of many problems that emerge from a single immoral act, e.g., slavery in America

244

A COLLECTION OF POPULAR ENGLISH PHRASES

The passion [hatred] of a thousand burning suns - The origin of this exact term is unclear but, a similar phrase appears in the, _Bhagavad Gita,_ the holy book of the Hindu religion. Many have attributed it to J. Robert Oppenheimer, who was familiar with the Hindu concept, and his quotation after the explosion of the first Atomic bomb. The phrase is habitually interpreted to mean: extreme passion or hatred for someone or something

The patience of Job - This expression originated from parables in the Bible, the Book of Job. Job was a prosperous man whose patience and piety were tried by undeserved misfortunes, and who, in spite of his bitter lamentations, remained confident in the goodness and justice of God. It has migrated to mean that patience and fortitude can conquer all things. **Patience of Griselda** is similar in connotation. **Patience is a virtue**

The pen is mightier than the sword - This adage was coined by the English novelist and poet Edward Bulwer-Lytton in his play: Richelieu; Or the Conspiracy, 1839. It means: writing is more effective than military power or violence. To choose **diplomacy over war; words cut more than swords.** A similar saying is attributed to Muhammad: **the ink of the scholar is more sacred than the blood of the martyr**

The plot thickens - The origin of the phrase appears to be a play or a book in which a mystery unfolds. It generally means: a situation that becomes more and more complicated and puzzling **as time goes on**

The pot calling the kettle black - This saying dates back to the 1600s. It has migrated to mean: the criticisms a person is aiming at someone else could equally well apply to themselves. **Take a look at the man in the mirror**

The price of wisdom is above rubies - The origin of this saying is from the Bible (Job 28:18) "No mention shall be made of coral or of pearls, for the price of wisdom is above rubies." The phrase has migrated to mean that wisdom is something that **can't be bought or sold,** it is something that must be earned through experience and is priceless

The prince and the pauper - This term is regularly attributed to the American author and humorist Mark Twain and was the title of one of his novels although the term was probably in use before. It means: a contrast in people; one rich and the other poor

The proletarians have nothing to lose but their chains - This saying is ascribed to Karl Marx. This quote is regularly interpreted to mean: the working class and poor people are already enslaved by the rich and the powerful. They therefore have nothing to lose if they revolt or rebel against them

The Promise Land - This expression originated from a story in the Bible and the land of Canaan, which was promised to Abraham and his descendants (Genesis 12:7). The promise of land was assured to Abraham, and later confirmed to Isaac, Jacob, and Jacob's sons; the Jewish people and the nation of Israel. It is now used to define something and especially a place or condition believed to promised or a final satisfaction

245

or realization of hopes. During American slavery, the North was called the Promised Land by the slaves. **Land of milk and honey**

The prospect of hanging concentrates the mind wonderfully - This quote is credited to Dr. Samuel Johnson. He was an English essayist, literary historian, lexicographer and poet who was a prominent figure in 18th century England. An expert on Shakespeare and memorialized in Boswell's The Life of Samuel Johnson, perhaps his greatest contribution was A Dictionary of the English Language. The quote is regularly interpreted to mean: there is something about impending danger or a crisis that focuses the mind on things that are relevant or on a particular goal. In difficult situations; without any apparent escape or recourse; things that were once significant **shrink to insignificance in comparison**. Take for example in times of war, when some of the greatest inventions have been made amid life threatening circumstances and the most perilous of times. Similar phrases include: **when your back is against the wall; necessity is the mother of invention; existential threat**

The rabbit died - The origin of this expression comes from an early pregnancy test in which the urine of a human female was injected into a female rabbit. The rabbit was killed, and its hormones examined. The common belief was that the rabbit only died when the test was positive, however, the rabbit died in either case. The phrase is sometimes used to denote that the female, in question, is pregnant. On a similar note, **the red river flowed** is another female expression and is sometimes used as a euphemism for a woman's menstrual period. **To knock someone up** means to get them pregnant

The race is not to the swift (nor the battle to the strong) - This phrase was inspired by the Bible (Ecclesiastes 9:11) It has come to mean: nothing is for certain. This phrase has been used by several writers in some cases, the phrase "but that's the way to bet" was appended to i **Tortoise and the hare** t.

The real McCoy - The source of this saying has been debated. Some say that it goes back to a boxer named McCoy, others attribute it to the African American inventor Elijah McCoy. Nonetheless, it means: **the real thing,** not an imitation or a substitute. Something that is genuine and not an imitation or fake, the genuine article. **The real deal**

The remembrance of things past - The source of this saying is Shakespeare's Sonnet 30. The phrase is regularly interpreted to mean: something remembered; a reminiscence of things that have happen both good and bad, a remembrance of a time or era. In some cases, it could be nostalgia and in others, plain retrospect. **It was the best of times, it was the worst of times**

The report of my death has been [greatly] exaggerated (Rumors of my (demise)death have been greatly exaggerated) - This expression originated from Mark Twain's response after hearing that his obituary had been published. The popular interpretation is: something that is taken to be true that is false or something that is assumed to be over but is not. Or that **it ain't over until it's over; It ain't over till the fat lady sings**

A COLLECTION OF POPULAR ENGLISH PHRASES

The revolution will not be televised - The source of this saying appears to be a song/poem by the late Gil Scott-Heron. Released in 1970, it echoed the revolutionary sentiment of the sixties. Since that time, it has been used as a rallying cry for revolt or change

The road less traveled - This phrase comes from a popular poem written by the American author <u>Robert Frost</u> in 1920 entitled: <u>The Road Not Taken</u>. At its core, this poem is about choice: and how one choice can change a person's life and thus make all of the difference: "I shall be telling this with a sigh; Somewhere ages and ages hence: Two roads diverged in a wood, and I; I took the one less traveled by, And that has made all the difference" The phrase is generally interpreted to mean: we all come to critical junctures in our lives, **the fork in the road**, where one decision can alter the path of our lives. Often the road less traveled is the most difficult one. **When you see the fork in the road take it; Buridan's donkey**

The road to hell is paved with good intentions - The expression is regularly attributed to Saint <u>Bernard of Clairvaux</u> (1090 – 1153). It may have been influenced by the Bible (Ecclesiasticus 21:10). It is interpreted to mean: people often mean well but do bad things; or that promises and plans must be put into action, or else they are useless. **Going to hell in a handbasket** is similar and means: to be rapidly deteriorating or to be on a course that is heading for disaster. To be on the inevitable path toward utter failure or ruin. **Primrose path**

The Seal of Solomon - The Seal of Solomon or **the Shield or Star of David**. Under both symbols the same thing was denoted. According to legend, Solomon had a ring or seal from God in which he could control demons. The seal is a hexagonal figure consisting of two interlaced triangles, thus forming the outlines of a six-pointed star as denoted on the Israeli flag. It has been traditionally used as a symbol of the Jewish heritage, and during the Jewish holocaust it was used as a way of designating Jews. It has since been used as a seal of approval or a sacred symbol within Judaism. **Solomon's Judgement; the wisdom of Solomon**

The secret is in the sauce - The origin of this expression is obscure but, it was first popularized during the fast food burger wars between McDonald's and Jack in the Box in the 1970s. The phrase is frequently interpreted to mean: an essential ingredient to doing something well or to success. Something that gives it that certain *je ne sais quoi*. This expression can be applied more generically as the term **secret sauce** is also widely used, which means: a special feature or technique kept secret by an organization or a person and is regarded as being the chief reason for its success. **What's the secret sauce?**

The slings and arrows (of outrageous fortune) - This phrase comes from Shakespeare's play; <u>Hamlet</u> (Act III, Scene I). Slings and arrows are weapons used to attack people, and fortune means things that happen to you. It has come into usage as: unpleasant things that happen to you that you cannot prevent

The spirit is willing but the flesh is weak - This saying is from the Bible, the New Testament (Matthew 26:41), in which Jesus tells his disciples: "Watch and pray, that ye enter not into temptation: <u>the spirit indeed is willing, but the flesh is weak</u>." The quote is often interpreted to mean: someone that has good intentions but fails to live up to them or someone that would like to undertake something but hasn't the energy or strength to do so. **The road to hell is paved with good intentions**

The stone that the builder rejected - The source of this saying is from the Bible (Psalm 118:22) (Acts 4:11) "The stone which the builders rejected has become the head stone of the corner." In the New Testament, it is clear that Jesus is the stone that was rejected. This saying is frequently used to denote: a situation in which a person is rejected or falls short of expectations but later finds himself or herself achieving or exceeding expectations. **Cornerstone**

The straight and the narrow - The source of this saying is from the Bible (Matt. 7:14). It has migrated to mean: the honest and upright way to live; a straight and law-abiding path through life

The straw that broke the camel's back - There was a story in England about a horse that could only carry so much on his back. This story was later changed to the straw that broke the camel's back by Charles Dickens in Dombey and Son. However, it may have been adapted by Dickens from an Arab proverb. The common interpretation is: the limits have been exceeded. **Everything has its limits; you got on my last nerve**

The strong do what they can, and the weak suffer what they must - The source of this expression is from the Melian Dialogue as recorded by the Greek historian Thucydides in his History of the Peloponnesian War. This was a twenty-seven-year long war between Athens and Sparta in which Sparta defeated Athens. This expression has been repeated for over two thousand years and history has proven it to be an axiom. It means literally what it says and verifies the adage: **Power tends to corrupt and absolute power corrupts absolutely**

The struggle is real - This is a phrase that entered the lexicon of millennials in the early 2000s along with **First World problems** and **white whine**, which are sometimes used synonymously. While popularized in Rap Music, its origins are unknown. The phrase generally means: to experience a hardship or a problem; something that a person is going through as a result of living in a well-developed society (First World) such as America, which on the outside appears to be good but not without its share of hardships (real or imaginary). **First World problems** such as having to many choices of what to eat, or not going on the right vacation, etc., **pale in comparison to** those experienced in Third World countries. Perhaps these are symptoms of an ever-increasing world of materialism and a vague sense of **the best things in life are free**

The tail wagging the dog – The origin of this phrase is unclear but has been in use since the 19th century. It is related to the observation of dogs wagging their tails. The common interpretation is: to distract attention from something that is bad or to change the subject from something that is more important to something that is less important. To place emphasis on something that is less important or significant in front of something that has more merit **To wag the dog**

The thrill of victory and the agony of defeat - This catchphrase was made famous by Jim Mckay, the announcer of the popular ABC's Wide World of Sports TV series. It was one of the longest run sports TV series in history depicting the challenges, achievements and perils of sports. This quote goes beyond sports and speaks to the spectrum of life. The highs and the lows, the peaks and the valleys that are so prevalent in all aspects of life and to the human capacity to overcome or to succumb to such endeavors

A COLLECTION OF POPULAR ENGLISH PHRASES

The truth is stranger than fiction - This phrase is regularly ascribed to the American author and humorist Mark Twain. However, it appears to have earlier origins. It was used in <u>Lord Byron's</u> satirical poem <u>Don Juan</u> in 1833. So often, when a well-read person such as Twain repeats a phrase that is not well known, its popularity is attributed to him and not the original author. The common interpretation is: that sometimes it is easier to understand fiction than it is the truth. Fiction can be made up, whereas truth cannot

The truth shall make you free - The source of this quote is from the Bible (John 8:32) "Then said Jesus to those Jews which believed in him; If ye continue in my word, then are ye my disciples indeed; And ye shall know the truth, and <u>the truth shall make you free</u>." This expression has been interpreted several ways. One interpretation is that there is something that is liberating about the truth and when it is finally revealed, everyone seems to recognize it for what it is. Another interpretation is that all lies eventually converge on the truth. **Liars can look so honest**

The wages of sin is death - This expression originated from the Bible. (Romans: 6:23). "For <u>the wages of sin is death</u>; but the gift of God is eternal life through Jesus Christ our Lord." It simply means that if you continue to do bad things, they will eventually catch up with you. **You reap what you sow**

The war to end all wars - This phrase will be forever linked to <u>World War I.</u> Known as **The Great War** in its day, it was so devastating that it was foolishly believed that it would end all future wars. Few saw it as a **harbinger** of future destruction. Yet a score years later, the world found itself engulfed by yet another world war more devastating than the first. The seeds of the second world war were **sowed in the soil of** the first. So much so that it could be viewed as one continuous war with a twenty-year intermission or germination period. The unparalleled mechanization and weaponry of the first world war was only enhanced during this period of germination. It was this war, fought in the early years of the 20th century, that left its indelible mark on the century and set the trajectory of future technologies including nuclear war. This phrase now stands as a testimony to Man's ignorance in believing that on the eleventh hour of the eleventh day of the eleventh month of 1918; something even as devastating and terrible as war, could eventually find a morbid end; and that Man would finally **lay down his burden and study war no more.** This phrase is sometimes used as a euphemism for a **Nuclear holocaust.** "Only the dead have seen the end of war." "War does not determine who is right—only who is left"

The White House – This familiar term takes its name from the color of the building located at 1600 Pennsylvania Ave. It is the home of the president of the United States and the symbol of the presidency and the executive branch of government. To foreign governments, however, it is the mouthpiece of the nation. It is in the center of the city and aligned with the Washington Monument and the Jefferson Memorial and like the nation's capital it was built by black slaves. John Adams was the first president to live in the White House and during the War of 1812 it was partially burned by the British. During the inauguration party of Andrew Jackson, it was open to the public and nearly trashed. So much so that people took home items. Although the term is well known today, it was originally called the Executive Mansion and it was also referred to as "the people's house." The White House didn't get is current name until 1902 when Teddy Roosevelt officially endorsed it

249

IN A NUTSHELL

The whole is greater than the sum of its parts - This expression is credited to Aristotle. The expression can be interpreted to mean: it is not enough to have the pieces, they must fit or work together as a cohesive unit, e.g., the United States and not individual states. **All for one and one for all; in unity there is strength**

The wisdom of Solomon - The source of this saying is from a story in the Bible (I Kings 3) regarding Solomon. There are several stories in the Bible that illustrate his wisdom. For example: there is the story about the two women that claimed to be the mother of a baby and Solomon ordered that the baby be cut in half to discern which was the true mother, because she would rather give her child to the other than to have it cut in half. (1 Kings 3:16–28). The **Queen of Sheba** also found that Solomon was wise (I Kings 10, 11, II Chronicles 9) "When the queen of Sheba saw all **the wisdom of Solomon** and the palace he had built, the food on his table, the seating of his officials, the attending servants in their robes, his cupbearers, and the burnt offerings he made at[a] the temple of the Lord, she was overwhelmed." But we must keep in mind, that **"before God we are equally wise and equally foolish."** The phrase now refers to being wise beyond one's years; or to exercise good judgement

The wish is the father of the thought - The proverb can be traced back to Latin and appears in a slightly different form in Shakespeare's <u>Henry IV, Part II</u>. The common interpretation is: people sometimes come to believe something that they wish were true

The world is your oyster - This expression originated from Shakespeare's: <u>The Merry Wives of Windsor</u> (Act II, Scene II). The original inference of the phrase is interpreted by some as a lack of character and integrity. Pistol is going to use violent means (sword) to steal his fortune (the pearl one finds in an oyster). We inherited the phrase, absent of its original negative connotation, to mean that the world is ours to enjoy and we are in a position to take advantage of the opportunities and challenges that life has to offer

The writing(handwriting) is on the wall - This expression originated from the Bible (Daniel 5) and the story of Daniel in the narrative of Belshazzar's drunken feast. Belshazzar was the son of the Babylonian King Nebuchadnezzar and ruled alongside his father. He used sacred goblets to drink wine thus, debasing these Jewish sacred temple glasses. Suddenly, a mysterious writing (*mene mene tekel upharsin*) appeared on the palace wall which could only be read by Daniel. These words were the **harbingers** of doom and destruction. Soon, the Babylonians were conquered by the Medes and Persians. Belshazzar was slain and his power was passed to Darius the Mede and the Persians. Hence, the general interpretation is: imminent danger has become apparent or the end is near. **Coming events cast their shadow before**

Theatre of the absurd - This is a phrase that was coined by Martin Essin. It was derived from an essay by Albert Camus entitled <u>Myth of Sisyphus'</u>, written in 1942. The birth of <u>the theater of the absurd</u> as an art form has its roots in post-World War II Europe specifically as an **avant-garde** movement in France. This theme of absurdity was first popularized by a play written by <u>Samuel Beckett</u> entitled: <u>Waiting for Godot.</u> At first it only applied to theater, but now the phrase generally means: events or actions that seek to represent the absurdity and ludicrous nature of the human existence. Something that is illogical, ridiculous or bizarre in its scope or content. **By virtue of the absurd; Kafkaesque**

A COLLECTION OF POPULAR ENGLISH PHRASES

There are lies, damned lies and statistics - This saying is attributed to Benjamin Disraeli, the British Prime Minister under Queen Victoria. Yet, it was made famous by the American author and humorist Mark Twain who credited it to Disraeli. The expression can be interpreted to mean: numbers and statistics can be misleading because they could be manipulated or misquoted. **The numbers don't lie**, but this expression implies that they do

There but for the grace of God go I - This expression originated from the English martyr John Bradford on seeing several criminals being led to hang. In an ironic twist, he was later executed as a heretic. It has migrated to mean: to compare one's blessing to the lesser fate of another

There came a pharaoh that knew not Joseph - This famous expression originated from the Bible (Exodus 1:8) of the Old Testament and relates to a new pharaoh from another dynasty that came to power in Egypt and did not know Joseph. Many biblical scholars relate this to the expulsion of the Hyksos, a Semitic group that conquered Egypt during the Second Intermediate period; and the rise of Ahmose I the founder of the New Kingdom which is recorded in Egyptian history. It has evolved to mean: a change of power with the new leader bringing in his own staff that has no allegiance to the policies of the previous regime. **Out with the old, in with the new**

There goes the neighborhood - This is an old expression, but its roots seem to be unclear. It appears to have been used any time "the other" moved into the neighborhood. However, once African Americans began to migrate to northern areas, this phrase became synonymous with black people moving into white neighborhoods and housing discrimination against black people. In fact, there were sundown towns or towns that did not allow black people in their town after dark thereby openly discriminating against black people. The warning to African Americans was to not "let the sun go down on you." **"There goes the neighborhood"** has since migrated to other areas; and has been used on occasions in which blacks have ventured into areas once deemed **for whites only**, e.g., when Barrack Obama became president. Although sometimes used today without racial connotations, because of its history, "there goes the neighborhood" could be viewed as impolite or offensive by some African Americans. Therefore, non-blacks, should be cautious in its usage. **The N word**

There is a tide in the affairs of men - This phrase is from Shakespeare's play Julius Caesar, (Act IV, Scene III) "There is a tide in the affairs of men. Which, taken at the flood, leads on to fortune." It simply means: there is a time and place for everything and we must take advantage of opportunities that are placed before us. **Opportunity knocks but once; no time like the present**

There is no there there - This saying is ascribed to the American writer Gertrude Stein. The expression can be interpreted to mean: there is nothing to see here. It is repeatedly used to convey a lack of substance or evidence as it pertains to the subject under discussion or accusations being made. Similar phrases include: **nothing up my sleeves; I've got nothing to hide; much ado about nothing**
There is nothing more dangerous than security - This quote is ascribed to Sir Francis Walsingham, spymaster under Queen Elizabeth I. A seminal figure in Britain's espionage history, Walsingham protected Queen Elizabeth I against many Catholic threats at **home and abroad.** These threats eventually led to the

defeat of **the Spanish Armada** in 1588. The saying is commonly interpreted to mean: during secure times, people become complaisant and take their security for granted. **As a consequence**, they become unaware of the dangers around them. But during times of peril and chaos, there is a **heightened sensitivity** to danger

These are the times that try men's souls - The origin of this saying is from Thomas Paine written in The American Crisis during the Revolutionary War. Paine was a professional revolutionary having participated in both the American and French Revolutions. This phrase is regularly quoted during critical or difficult situations when strong but perhaps controversial measures must be taken, e.g., **When your back is up against the wall** or **desperate times call for desperate measures**

Theseus's cord - In Greek mythology, Theseus was the legendary hero of Athens who slew the Cretan Minotaur (half man and have bull) with the help of Ariadne the daughter of King Minos of Crete. He was given a ball of golden cord by her to navigate his way through the labyrinth after he killed the Minotaur. Thus, following Theseus's cord is a way to work yourself out of a difficult situation. **Trail of Breadcrumbs** is similar and originated from the popular Grimm's fairytale, Hansel and Gretel. In this fairytale, the two were taken deep into the forest in the hope that they would not find their way out. However, clever Hansel left a trail of breadcrumbs to show their return path

Think outside the box - This expression comes from a puzzle in which the dots in a square grid must be connected without the pen leaving the paper. It can only be accomplished if some of the lines extend beyond the square or the box. It regularly denotes: to think in an original or creative way to arrive at a different or unique solution. **Keep an open mind. Color within the lines or stay in your lane** are metaphors that essentially means the opposite

Think tank - This term first appeared around the turn of the 20th century but did not become popular until the 1950s. It is a research institution or organization formed to solve difficult and complex problems

Third world - The genesis of this term appears to be a derivative of the **Cold War** and emerged during the 1950s. It represented countries that were not part of the West or within the sphere of the Soviet Union or their form of government. Those under the designation of the West, were referred to as the **First World** and the Communist block as the **Second World**. In effect, the Third World consisted of nations that were previously or currently colonized by Europeans. Many of these developing countries, particularly in Africa, gained their independence from Europe, yet remain within the realm of the Third World. It means: the developing countries of Asia, Africa, and Latin America. An underdeveloped country that lacks the economic, social and physical infrastructure of a modern nation. **Banana Republic**

Thirty pieces of silver - The source of this expression is from the Bible (Matt. 26:15), It is a reference to the money that Judas took to betray Jesus. "And said unto them, What will ye give me, and I will deliver him unto you? And they covenanted with him for thirty pieces of silver." According to the New Testament, after taking the funds, Judas repented and later hung himself. The term has come to be used as a symbol of ultimate betrayal. Similar phrases include: **sold for thirty pieces of silver**; **Benedict Arnold**; **turncoat; sold down the river**

Those that dance are considered insane by those who can't hear the music - This saying is frequently ascribed to Nietzsche. However, additional research reveals that it was used in various forms before Nietzsche and is of unknown origin. Nonetheless, it is often interpreted to mean: it is very difficult to evaluate or understand something without knowing the facts or circumstances in which it occurs. For example, most people familiar with dancing would assume that others moving to an unheard rhythm are dancing. Similarly, it you have never **walked in someone's shoes**, it can be difficult for you to understand their perspective

Those that do not learn from history are doomed to repeat it - This quote is attributed to the Spanish philosopher George Santayana, although these are not his exact words. It is interpreted to mean: history repeats itself and, in many ways, is our greatest teacher. A similar saying is by Karl Marx: **History repeats itself, first as tragedy, second as farce; to be on the right side of history**

Those who give up liberty(freedom) for security (safety) deserve neither - This quote is attributed to the American Founding Father Ben Franklin. In recent times, it has **come under attack** with many believing that it has become **a relic of the past.** Technological advances and terrorist threats have left many to ponder if this 200-year-old adage is applicable to the 21st century. Nonetheless, it means what it says that if you trade your freedom for your safety in the end you will have neither

Thou protest too much - The source of this phrase is Shakespeare's Hamlet (Act III, Scene II). "The lady doth protest too much, methinks. " It is frequently used to describe a situation in which a person is complaining about something that isn't as bad as he or she thinks or would like others to think

Three can keep a secret if two of them are dead - This expression is accredited to the American author, inventor and Founding Father Ben Franklin. It generally means: people should be careful who they confide in, as the more people they tell their secret to, the more unlikely it is to remain a secret. **Sub rosa**

Through the grapevine - This saying appears to have its origin in the telegraph, although It was the title of a hit record Heard it through the grapevine during the sixties by Gladys Knight and the Pips. It has migrated to mean: an indication that a piece of information was obtained via an informal contact or gossip. Often said when someone does not want to give up their source of information. **A little bird told me**

Throw someone a curve (ball) - This expression has its roots in American Baseball, where the pitcher throws a batter a curve ball. The term was transferred to other kinds of surprise, not necessarily unpleasant, in the mid-1900s. It has migrated to mean: to surprise someone with something that is difficult or unpleasant to deal with or unexpected. **The best surprise is no surprise. To call balls and strikes** is another baseball metaphor that means to officiate or to call things in accordance with the law or a predetermined set of rules. Yet another baseball idiom is **to hit one out of the park** or **to hit a home run**

which means to be successful at something or to accomplish a task with extreme grace or ability. **To hit a grand slam** is similar but a more powerful metaphor. **To get to first base** means to just get started and **to touch all the bases (round the bases)** means to have everything covered; **right off the bat** means immediately; without delay and **to bat a thousand** means to be extremely successful at something. **A whole new ballgame** means something different or to start all over

Throw someone under the bus - The exact origin of this term is uncertain however there are two competing theories. The first is that it originated in America among Minor League baseball players specifically Cyndi Lauper. The second is that it originated in England and migrated to America. The current usage in America is more akin to its usage in England as a political metaphor. Notwithstanding it means: to cause someone else to suffer in order to save yourself; to betray someone. Similar expressions are: **save your skin; scapegoat; rat someone out; backstab; drop a dime on someone; sing like a canary**

Throw the baby out with the bath water - The source of this expression comes from the German phrase *Das Kind mit dem Bade ausschütten* (to throw the baby out with the bath water)." The saying first appeared in print in Thomas Murner's satirical work *Narrenbeschwörung* (Appeal to Fools) in 1512. In medieval Europe, taking a bath was a luxury and, in some cases, hierarchal in nature, with the father, mother and children all in that order using the same water. By the time the infants were bathed, the water was completely dirty. Hence the phrase. It now means: to discard something valuable or significant while disposing of something insignificant. **Don't throw the baby out with the bath water**

Throw your hat into the ring - The origin of this phrase appears to be a circular ring formed by bystanders and onlookers which was a prelude to a fight or a boxing match. The challengers would throw their hats into the ring. It generally means: to do something that makes it clear that you want to compete or to initiate a challenge. **Knock the chip off your shoulder**

Time and tide wait for no man - The source of this saying is from Chaucer's Prologue to the Clerk's Tale written in 1395. The phrase is regularly interpreted to mean: if you don't make use of a favorable opportunity, you may never get the same chance again; delay or indecisiveness may have unfortunate or tragic consequences. Similar phrases include: **he who hesitates is lost; procrastination is the thief of time; dip your bread in the gravy while the gravy is still warm**

Time heals all wounds - The exact origin of this aphorism is unclear. In the context of the phrase, it is normally taken to mean emotional and not physical wounds. Often said during times of emotional pain, and sometimes used as **a rule of thumb**, notwithstanding it has its detractors. For example, Rose Kennedy the mother of John and Bobby Kennedy once said: "It has been said, 'time heals all wounds.' I do not agree. The wounds remain. In time, the mind, protecting its sanity, covers them with scar tissue and the pain lessens. But it is never gone." It has also been noted that time is the cause of all wounds

Time is of the essence - The origin of this popular phrase is obscure, perhaps because it is applicable to so many situations. One source believes that it was a legal term, another source links it to the construction of the American Transcontinental Railroad. Nonetheless, the term is used to express: a need to complete

A COLLECTION OF POPULAR ENGLISH PHRASES

a task in a timely manner; to meet a **deadline** or to place time above other matters such as cost. Similar phrases are: **the clock is ticking; get to hopping; let's get the show on the road; keep moving; jump to (on) it; step on it; time and tide wait for no man**

Tip of the iceberg - An iceberg is a massive floating body of ice broken away from a glacier with about 10 percent of its mass (the tip) above the surface of the water and the rest unseen. This maritime phrase became popular after the colossal Titanic, once deemed unsinkable, hit an iceberg in1912 on its **maiden voyage**. It was sunk, losing at least 1,500 lives. This tragedy was one of the deadliest in maritime history. It now has the following meaning: the first hint or revelation of something bigger or more complex lies ahead. The earliest indication, or most apparent appearance, of some forthcoming larger phenomenon or event. **The beginning of the end; it's only the tip of the iceberg**. Additionally, a person who is very cold is sometimes referred to as an **iceberg. Tip of the spear** is a similar metaphor that is regularly used in military operations and is normally used to designate the first or the best of a particular group or action

Titanic - Like so many terms, the origin of this term comes from Greek mythology. The Titans were a primeval race of giants, the progeny of the earth (Gaia) and the heavens(Uranus) and were led by Cronus. They ruled the universe before the Olympian gods. They were eventually overthrown by Zeus (the son of Cronus). Zeus became the leader of the gods on Mount Olympus, the guardian and ruler of humankind and the arbitrator of good and evil. The term has migrated to mean: of exceptional strength, size, or power, something that is very large, colossal. **Herculean; clash of the titans**

Tis better to have loved and lost than never to have loved at all - The source of this expression is from a poem entitled: In Memoriam by the Victorian poet Alfred Lord Tennyson. The phrase is often interpreted to mean: that love is a very special thing, something that every human being needs to experience in one form or another. There are somethings in life worth losing because of the experience gained and the only way to know love is to love and/or to be loved. Similar phrases include: **the course of true love never did run smooth. No matter how many books you read on swimming, you can only learn by getting in the water**

To add insult to injury - The source of this phrase is from Phaedrus' The Bald Man and the Fly. Phaedrus, translated a collection of Aesop's fables into Latin and was known as the Roman Aesop. The phrase generally means: to make a bad situation worse. **Pile Pelion on Ossa**

To be or not to be (that is the question) - This expression originated from Shakespeare's Hamlet (Act III, Scene I). The verse reads: To be, or not to be that is the question; whether 'tis nobler in the mind to suffer **the slings and arrows of outrageous fortune; Or to take arms against a sea of troubles;** and by opposing end them. The phrase is often interpreted to mean: to question whether it is better to live or to die? Life is bad, but death might be worse. A question of being true or false or to hold true to one's convictions or morals. It is **a test of one's mettle**. Similar phrases include: **a coward dies a thousand deaths a hero dies but one; to thine own self be true; speak truth to power**

To bite the dust - This saying is attributed to Homer and comes to us from the Iliad Book 2. "Fall headlong in the dust and bite the earth." Its current form comes from an 1870 translation of the Iliad. A similar phrase can be found in the King James Bible. "They that dwell in the wilderness shall bow before Him; and His enemies shall lick the dust" (Psalms 72.9). Often quoted as **another one bites the dust**, it was the title of a popular song in the 1980s by the British Rock group Queen. It is regularly used as a figure of speech or euphemism for death or to go down in defeat. **Kicked the bucket**

To blow hot and cold - The source of this phrase is from an Aesop's fable entitled: The Man and the Satyr. "I cannot be friends with a man that blows hot and cold with the same breath." It generally means: to change one's mind quickly sometimes **without rhyme or reason**

To call a spade a spade - The origin of this phrase goes as far back as ancient Greece where it was used by the Greek playwright Menander: "I call a fig a fig and a spade a spade." The phrase is frequently interpreted to mean: to speak plainly without avoiding unpleasant or embarrassing issues; to call something as it is or by its right name. **Beating around the bush** means the opposite, to discuss a matter without coming to the point

To cry sour grapes - The source of this idiom is an Aesop's fable, in which a fox tries again and again to jump high enough to reach grapes hanging high on a vine, and finally gives up, asserting that the grapes were probably sour anyway. The expression generally means: a situation in which someone adopts a negative attitude to something because they cannot have it themselves. **A sore loser. Low hanging fruit** is the opposite and means something or someone that is easily won or convinced; something that is achieved with little or no effort

To cry wolf - The source of this expression is from Aesop's fable: The Boy Who Cried Wolf. The phrase is regularly interpreted to mean: to call repeatedly for help when it is not needed; with the effect that one is not believed when one really does need help. **False alarm**

To cut the melon - This is an old saying that was first reported in the Chicago Daily News in 1911. The common interpretation is: to distribute profits among participants in a venture; to divide up the spoils

To decimate - The origin of this term comes from the Roman practice of punishment by lining people up and killing every tenth one. It now means: to kill, destroy, or remove a sizable percentage or part of a group or something

To eat crow - According to etymologist James Rogers, eating crow was the subject of a story reported in the Atlanta Constitution in 1888. It tells the tale of an American soldier in the War of 1812, who shot a crow during a ceasefire and was made by a British officer to eat the crow. Unlike turkey, chicken and other fowl, crow has an unusual **foul taste**. The common interpretation is: to be humiliated by having to admit one's defeats or mistakes. To confess that you are wrong, normally to a group after an embarrassment or shameful act. **Humble pie**

To err is human to forgive is divine - This expression is credited to Alexander Pope's poem entitled: An Essay on Criticism, Part II, published in 1711. It has migrated to mean: the idea that forgiveness is a worthy response to human failings. Similar phrases include: **everybody makes mistakes; it is a man who errs, it is a fool who persists**

To everything there is a season - This expression comes from the Bible (Ecclesiastes 3:1). It is one of the most quoted phrases in the Bible. "To everything there is a season, and a time to every purpose under the heaven: **A time to be born, and a time to die**; a time to plant, and a time to pluck up that which is planted." It means that **there is a time and place for everything**. It is often said when someone is acting in a way that you do not think is appropriate for the situation that they are in

To extend the olive branch - The olive branch in ancient Greece, was a sign of prosperity and peace. It also can be traced to the Bible (Genesis 8:1), in allusion to the story of Noah in which a dove returns with an olive branch after the flood. When you extend the olive branch, you're trying to make peace

To fall on your sword - The source for this saying comes from the Bible (Samuel 31:4-5) and the story of Saul's death. The expression has migrated to mean: to take personal responsibility for a group or personal action; to commit suicide or to offer a resignation. **To walk the plank**

To kill the goose that laid the golden egg - The source of this expression is an Aesop's fable. In this tale, a man and his wife had the good luck to own a goose that laid a golden egg every day. They soon began to think they were not getting rich fast enough and, thinking the bird must be full of gold, they killed it to get all the gold at once. But when they cut the goose open, there was no gold inside. If they hadn't been greedy and killed the goose, it would have kept laying a golden egg every day. It generally means: to foolishly destroy something that is of great benefit to you

To kowtow - The source of this expression comes from the Chinese custom to kneel and touch the forehead to the ground in expression of deep respect, worship, or submission. It now designates: to act in an excessively subservient manner. **Kiss the ring** means essentially the same thing and refers to kissing the ring after having an audience with the pope to show submission to his authority. Similar phrases include: **bend over backwards; suck up to; on bended knees**

To lead apes in hell - The origins of this saying remains a mystery. Some say it gained popularity as a Protestant attack on the Catholic Church insistence that the unmarried refrain for sexual activity. William Shakespeare referenced this phrase in: The Taming of the Shrew and Much Ado About Nothing. The expression now means: women who do not win the company of men will be reduced to the company of apes in hell. **Grass widow** is similar and means: an unmarried woman who has lived with one or more men, a discarded mistress, a woman who has an illegitimate child; or one that is away from a husband for long periods of time. It could also refer to a divorced or separated woman

To leave no stone unturned - There are two competing stories for the source of this expression in Greek mythology and legend. The most prevalent is the response given by the oracle of Delphi when asked where to find the treasure buried by the Persian king Xerxes. The alternate source is: After the death of Hercules, Eurystheus the king responsible for the twelve labors of Hercules, wanted all Hercules' sons dead and demanded to look everywhere. This phrase was used by Euripides in his play, The Children of Hercules. The phrase was popular among the Greeks and bequeathed to the rest of Europe through the Romans. In fact, Pliny the Younger used it in a letter to Tacitus. Perhaps the confusion arises from interpretation. Nonetheless, it means: to search everywhere; to do everything possible to find something or to solve a problem. **A stone's throw away** is another stone metaphor that means something that is very close

To lift the veil of Isis - Isis was an Egyptian goddess that was also very popular in Roman times and she was associated with a very popular Mystery Cult. According to the masonic author and mystic Manly P. Hall: "The face and form of Isis were covered with a veil of scarlet cloth, symbolic of ignorance and emotionalism which forever stand between man and Truth. Isis lifts her veil and discovers herself to the true and wise investigator who unselfishly, humbly, and earnestly seeks to understand the mysteries which surround him in the universe. Those to whom she reveals herself are warned to remain silent concerning the mysteries which they have seen." A similar reference is made in the classic the Metamorphoses of Apuleius or The Golden Ass, written by the Latin writer Lucius Apuleius. To lift the veil of Isis is frequently interpreted to mean: to uncover or unlock a great mystery. There was an Occult popular book written by the renowned occultist Madame Blavatsky entitled: Isis Unveiled that claim to unlock great mystery. **Riddle of the Sphinx**

To play chess(checkers) while someone else plays checkers (chess) - The origin of this phrase is uncertain. It relates to the fact that the two games are not on the same level and neither are the people that play them. For example, checkers is tactical while chess is both tactical and strategic. All of the pieces in checkers start out as equals, not so in chess. In fact, a pawn in chess can emulate a checker piece. It is frequently used to illustrate: two people or opponents that are not playing on the same intellectual level. Additionally, **playing three-dimensional chess** implies strong intellect; and understanding beyond normal comprehension. **Not in the same league**

To play the Cupid - In Roman Mythology, Cupid was the god of love; and the son of Venus. He is represented as a naked, winged boy with a bow and arrows, with which he wounds his victims. The Greek equivalent is Eros. This phrase generally means: to play the role of the matchmaker. **Cupid's arrow**

To sit (live) in an ivory tower - This expression originated from the Bible (Song of Solomon 7:4). It has migrated to mean: to be in isolation, in your own imaginary world aside from everyone else; a state of privileged seclusion or separation from the facts of the real world. **People who live in glass houses shouldn't throw stones**

To stonewall - The source of this saying is the nickname of Confederate **General** Thomas (Stonewall) J. Jackson (1824-1863) that was bestowed at the First Battle of Bull Run in 1861. "There is Jackson standing like a stone wall." Afterward, the nickname stuck, and Jackson was promoted to major general for his courage and quick thinking on the battlefield. In one of the strangest twists of the Civil War, Stonewall Jackson was accidently shot and killed by a Confederate soldier a month or so before the seminal battle of Gettysburg. He is consistently ranked among the top American generals. The common usage is: to delay or block (a request, process, or person) by refusing to answer questions or by giving evasive replies, especially in politics

To test someone's mettle - This phrase dates to the 1600s. It is frequently misquoted as to test someone's "metal." In fact, the term *mettle* and *metal* both have the same origin and were used interchangeably prior to the 1800s. The term mettle then diverged to mean courage, fortitude or character. To test someone's mettle therefore means: to test their courage, or character. **Show your mettle** is used similarly

To the victor belong (go) the spoils - This expression is supposedly derived from a speech by Senator William Learned Marcy (1786 - 1857) in which he stated: "to the victor belong the spoils." On a national scale, the spoils system was installed with the development of two political parties, the Federalists and the Democratic Republicans, and was used by the earliest Presidents. This expression means: the winner is entitled to all of the rewards, bonuses, or benefits of success. **Winner take all; the spoils of war**

To thine own self be true - This expression originated from Shakespeare's Hamlet (Act I, Scene III). "This above all- to thine own self be true; And it must follow, as the night the day; Thou canst not then be false to any man." Even though this phrase has become an axiom, it is normally said after a person subjects himself to retrospection and introspection. It simply means: to be true to yourself; Similar phrases include: **your character is much more important than your reputation; don't sell out; know thyself; have a moral compass; keep it real**

Toe the line - The origin of this expression seems to be arguments between politicians in the British House of Commons who carried swords to meetings. Lines were drawn between the opposing parties that were more than a swords length from each other. This was to prevent the outbreak of violence during heated discussions between party factions. Others believe that it has its origins in placing a toe on a line or a mark to begin a race or start an event. Still others have cited *tow* the line which has nautical origins referring to the ropes on a ship. Yet, "toe" the line seems to be the current and most prevalent use of this popular phrase. The common usage is: to conform to a rule, standard or law. To strictly follow the rules in a manner that is deemed acceptable or correct

Tomboy - This is an old English term that dates back to the 1500s. It was first used to describe a boy that was rude before migrating to its current usage. It now means: a young girl that acts like a boy

Tongue-in-cheek - The origin of this phrase is unclear. However, many believe that it evolved from the practice of holding your tongue in your mouth as a sign of silent contempt. Nonetheless, this phrase had become popular by the mid-1800s. It generally means: insincerity, irony, or fanciful embellishment of a situation or an opinion. It is also an indication that a statement or position should not be taken seriously. **Until you are blue in the face**

Top banana - The origin of this term seems to come from a burlesque routine involving three comedians in which the one that gets the punch line also gets a banana. The term now means: the most important person in an organization or activity. Likewise, **second banana** is the second most important person or a person in a subservient position. **Top gun; second fiddle**

Tortoise and the hare - The source of this expression is an Aesop's fable. It is a story about a race between a fast rabbit and a slow turtle in which the turtle unexpectedly wins. So confident was the hare, that it decided to take a nap during the race and when he woke up, the turtle was near the finish line. It has become a testament to endurance and persistence. **Slow and steady wins the race**; Achilles and the Tortoise

Touché - This is a French term that has worked its way into the English vernacular. It literally means touch and is used to acknowledge a hit in fencing. In English, it is used to admit that someone has made a clever or effective point or remark in an argument

Tower of Babel - This saying is from the Bible (Genesis 11). It was a tower built to reach heaven that ended in a state of confusion in which people spoke different languages. It now refers to a state of confusion or a situation that leads to one. It is also an example of the vanity and hubris of humankind. **Pile Pelion on Ossa**

Treasure trove - The origins of this term is uncertain. The common usage is: a valuable discovery, resource, or collection or valuables of unknown ownership that are found hidden, in some cases declared the property of the finder. **Mother lode; Aladdin's cave; diamond in the rough**

Trinity - The origin of this term is the Christian belief that God exists in three persons: The Father, The Son and The Holy Spirit. This doctrine did not become official until 381 CE with a declaration known as *the Nicene-Constantinopolitan Creed.* Several biblical scholars point out that this belief evolved over centuries with the backing of Roman Emperors such as Constantine and Theodosius. It was the Emperor Theodosius that labeled all that did not believe in the Trinity as heretics. Many argue, that it is based on biblical exegesis and not actual scripture (The Trinity is not mentioned in the Bible). The term is sometimes used to describe something holy. **Immaculate conception**

Trouble knocked at the door, but, hearing laughter, hurried away - This quote is attributed to the American Founding Father and polymath Ben Franklin. Laughter, except in times of **gallows humor**, is a sign of happiness. The expression evolved to mean: we should not let anything interfere with our happiness or to break our spirit even during times of adversity.

Trojan horse - This was a huge hollow wooden horse constructed by the Greeks to gain entrance into Troy during the Trojan War. It repeatedly refers to: someone or something intended to defeat or subvert from within, usually by deceptive means. This event is also the source of the expression: **beware of Greeks bearing gifts; A Trojan horse computer virus is** a term that became popular with the advent of personal computers. It hides within a seemingly harmless program only to install itself and harm the operation of other programs

A COLLECTION OF POPULAR ENGLISH PHRASES

Trolling (Troll) - This is an Internet term that has become quite popular. It is sometimes confused with its traditional meaning of a cave dwelling dwarf or giant, but the term has nothing to do with cave dwellers or seclusion. It means: to deliberately harass someone online by using inflammatory or contemptuous language or other means of verbal harassment

Trouble (right here) in River City - This saying is from the 1957 Broadway musical The Music Man. It was subsequently made into a film in 1962 starring Robert Preston. "Ya got trouble, folks, right here in River City. Trouble with a capital "T"; And that rhymes with "P" and that stands for pool!" It is normally used when there is, or one suspects, trouble in a particular location, especially a town or city. **I'm talking about trouble, right here in River City**

Trust but verify - This is an old Russian proverb that was made famous in 1987 by President Ronald Regan and used during arms control negotiations with Russian President Mikhail Gorbachev. It also has its roots in accounting as a means of double checking the work. The common usage is: although you place the utmost trust and confidence in someone or something; **even the best laid plans go astray**. For example, there could be **underlying currents** that could hinder, impede or destroy one's trust and you want to be aware of those things **as soon as possible**. Verifying assures that the initial trust bestowed is maintained. **Murphy's Law**

Truth needs not the ornament of many words, [it is most lovely when least adorned] - This expression appears in Erasmus' book on Proverbs and Adages. The history of the human experience is littered with stories about people that have tried to conceal the truth, only to have it revealed at the most inappropriate time. The expression is often interpreted to mean: **truth speaks for itself** in a clear voice and one does not need to add or alter it. **The truth will set you free; speak truth to power**

Tub of lard - The exact origin of this expression is unclear; however, it is believed by some to have originated in England. Lard is a fatty substance that comes from the abdomen of a pig. Up until the turn of the 20th century, it was heavily used in cooking. A tub of lard, therefore, meant a pile of pig fat. The expression migrated to mean: a very fat and sloppy person hence a derogatory term for someone that is obese. Related expressions include: **fat pig; Humpty Dumpty; Miss Piggy**

Tubula rasa - This is a Latin term that has migrated to the English language. It literally means "clean slate." It is frequently used in epistemology (theory of knowledge) and psychology, to designate an absence of preconceived ideas or predetermined goals. In this regard, it is often used to refer to the human mind at birth or something existing in a pristine or new state. **A clean slate**

Turn a blind eye - Many people think that this phrase comes from the Bible. Specifically, (Matthew 7:5) which is similar in connotation. "Thou hypocrite, first cast out the beam out of thine own eye; and then shalt thou see clearly to cast out the mote out of thy brother's eye." But, the source of this saying comes from the British Admiral (Lord) Nelson at the battle of Copenhagen in 1801. Nelson was blind in one eye, and he turned his telescope to his blind eye as a means of technically disobeying an order because he looked at something but had **plausible deniability** that he did not see anything. Nelson later became a national hero and is famous for his naval victories over the French during the Napoleonic Wars (1800-

1815). The common usage is: to knowingly ignore a wrongdoing or a situation. To knowingly refuse to recognize something which you know to be factual. Related expressions include: **800-pound gorilla; elephant in the room; sweep it under the rug**

Turn the other cheek - The source of this saying is the Bible (Matthew 5:39). In **the Sermon on the Mount,** Jesus asked his followers to turn the other cheek. The expression now means: to refrain from retaliating when one has been attacked or insulted or to react humbly rather than seek revenge for the act or injury. **Vengeance is mine, saith the Lord**

Turn your wounds into wisdom - This saying is credited to Oprah Winfrey and could be interpreted as follows: Many times in life, we look at our troubled past, the wounds that were inflicted upon us or by us in shame and discontent. Yet, **life is a marathon and not a sprint**, and if we look deep into those wounds, we can not only heal them, but teach others how to heal theirs through the wisdom that we have gained through our experiences. Wisdom is one of those things in life, that is gained by experiences and when we try to give our children only good experiences, we rob them of one of wisdom's greatest tools. It is not the man that is beaten to the ground but the man that picks himself up that is on the road toward wisdom. **To err is human** and no person experiences life, without making a mistake or sufferings some pain or some strife. Still, the greater mistake is not being able to learn from such experiences and to drown in the **troubled waters** of discontented pasts. Don't let the demons of the past doom you, before **the better angels** of the future can consume you

Tweedledum and Tweedledee - This expression originated from the English nursery rhyme in Lewis Carroll's Through the Looking-Glass. It has migrated to mean: two individuals of a group or a pair of things that can barely be distinguished

Twenty-four seven (24/7) - The source of this term is believed to come from the African American community during the 1980s. The common usage is: twenty-four hours a day, seven days a week; constantly; all the time. Similar sayings include: **all year around; around the clock**

Two-edged (Double edged) sword - The source of this term is from the Bible (Hebrew 4:12) "For the word of God is quick, and powerful, and sharper than any two-edged sword." The term means: something that has both an advantage and a disadvantage or something that has favorable and unfavorable consequences. **It cuts both ways**

Typhoid Mary - Mary Mallon, now known as Typhoid Mary, seemed to be a healthy woman when a health inspector knocked on her door in 1907. Nevertheless, **looks can be deceiving** and she was the cause of several typhoid outbreaks. The term has been used to denote a person that brings misfortune. Similar to **avoiding the plague**

Stands for:

Uneasy lies the head that wears a crown

Ugly duckling - The source of this term is the title of an 1843 fairytale by Hans Christian Andersen about a bird that was ridiculed for being ugly but later matures into a beautiful swan. It migrated to mean: someone or something once deemed as unattractive or unlikely to flourish but **exceeds expectations** to become something beautiful or highly successful. **Diamond in the rough**

Unalienable right - The source of the term comes from the Declaration of Independence written by the American president and polymath Thomas Jefferson. It was signed by the Second Continental Congress in Philadelphia on July 4, 1776 declaring the independence of the thirteen colonies from Great Britain. Its preamble states: "We hold these Truths to be self-evident, that all Men are created equal, that they are endowed by their Creator with certain unalienable Rights, that among these are Life, Liberty and the Pursuit of Happiness." Many of the ideals in this **time-honored** document such as **the pursuit of happiness** were first espoused by the English philosopher John Locke and adopted by Jefferson. We need not point out that such rights were not granted to people of African or Native American descent and thus are universally antithetical to the document itself. Alexis de Tocqueville wrote: "Americans are so enamored of equality that they would rather be equal in slavery than unequal in freedom." Nonetheless, the term means: rights given to us by our Creator rather than by government such as the right of personal liberty, and the right to acquire and enjoy property

Uncle Sam - This term is a nickname for the United States because of its initials (U.S.). It has its origin in a meatpacking plant during the War of 1812 to denote the United States. Uncle Sam is typically portrayed as a tall, thin, bearded man wearing a red, white, and blue suit. It was first the nickname of the Army and then migrated to the entire nation. "**Uncle Sam wants you**" has long been a recruiting slogan for the U.S. military. Similarly, **Uncle Sugar** is a term that is a combination of Uncle Sam & **Sugar Daddy** and refers to the benevolence of the United States federal government in bestowing money and benefits. Whereas Uncle Sam generally refers to the U.S. military or the nation, Uncle Sugar refers to the generosity of the U.S. government

Uncle Tom - This term is from the character in Harriet Beecher Stowe's novel Uncle Tom's Cabin. Perhaps more than any book of its era, this book (parts published in June, 1851) did more to change the attitudes toward slavery in the United States and Great Britain and was a prelude to the Civil War. Yet, over the years, particularly within the black community, the term "Uncle Tom" developed a negative connotation. The common usage is: a black person who is regarded as being subservient or excessively deferential to white people. A black person who is overeager to win the approval of whites (as by servile behavior or uncritical acceptance of white values and goals). An **Aunt Jemima** is the female equivalent of an Uncle Tom. It was the face of a stereotypical black mammie that graced the boxes of pancake mix and syrup produced by Quaker Oats. Similar phrases include: **an oriole; go along to get along**

Unconditional surrender - This is a saying made famous by General Grant during the American Civil War. In many ways, it became a rallying cry from the North after its victories at Gettysburg and Vicksburg on July 4, 1863. The expression can be interpreted to mean: a surrender in which no guarantees are given to the surrendering party, in effect a **Carthaginian peace; to the victor belong (go) the spoils**

A COLLECTION OF POPULAR ENGLISH PHRASES

Under the radar - This is a term that has its roots in the aviation arena. Invented in the 1940s and used throughout World War II, radar is a means of detecting the presence, speed and location of a moving object. **To fly under the radar** means to go undetected. **Under the radar** has been adopted to mean the same thing; to go undetected or unnoticed

Uneasy lies the head that wears a crown - This expression is from Shakespeare's Henry IV, Part 2 (Act III, Scene I). The common explanation is: although **it is good to be the king** or the president, the job comes with great responsibility and authority. Many times, he is the **arbitrator of life and death** for his people. Thus, he **bears a heavy weight on his shoulders**. Furthermore, he is besieged by internal and external problems and in some cases afraid of losing his position. All of these factors contribute to the angst and the stress that is induced by the job

Until death do us apart - The origin of this popular wedding vow was inspired by the Bible but is not specifically stated in the Bible. It could, however, be traced back to the Book of Common Prayer by Thomas Crammer (1489- 1556) Archbishop of Canterbury during the English Reformation. "For better or for worse, for richer, for poorer, in sickness and in health, to love and to cherish; from this day forward until death do us part." Ironically, he helped to build the case against the Catholic Church in Henry VIII's divorce from Catherine of Aragon. This led to the establishment of the Church of England. Thus, breaking the vow that Henry VII took. **Ring finger**

Until hell freezes over - The origin of this expression seems to be unknown. It is predicated on the fact that hell is an extremely hot place, a perpetual inferno that is too hot to ever freeze over. It is similar in usage to **a cold day in hell**. Until hell freezes over, however, has evolved to mean: for an extremely long time or forever and a cold day in hell means: unlikely or impossible that it will ever occur or never. **As cold as hell** is another idiomatic expression which means that it is very cold. Whereas it is oxymoronic in nature, there are some religions that perceive a portion of hell as being cold and Dante in his Inferno alludes to such a section of hell. In this case, the term **as hell** means extreme and one could easily say it is **hot as hell** or **hard as hell**. Additionally, **a snowball chance** in hell means: something that has little to no chance of being successful, a **fool's errand**

Until the cows come home - The origin of the phrase seems to be linked to when cows are set out to pasture. They don't return until the next morning to be milked. The milking of cows in the morning sort of signified the beginning of the workday on the farm or a time when you had to be somewhere or do something. The expression can be interpreted to mean: out for a very long time; usually all night. Other farm idioms include: **Put out to pasture** which comes from putting draft animals out to pasture after they were too old to perform their duties or to bring animals to pasture to feed on the grass. **Until (before)the cock crows** which was used in the Bible in reference to the betrayal of Jesus by Peter (Matthew 26:34). "Jesus said unto him, Verily I say unto thee; That this night, before the cock crow, thou shalt deny me thrice." **Up at the crack of dawn** is the time when the sun first appears and now means: to wake up very early, this is also the time when the cock(rooster) crows. Similar phrases include: **from sunup to sundown**; **all night long**

IN A NUTSHELL

Until you are blue in the face - The source of this idiom appears to come from the face turning blue as a result of holding one's breath for a long period of time. When there is no or little oxygen in the blood, it turns from red to blue. This is why the bodies of dead people turn blue or have a bluish tint over time. It is also true of "blue babies" a condition that develops when organs, cells and tissues do not receive enough oxygen. While in the mother's womb, these babies receive oxygen from the mother and are not blue. This condition was finally resolved by Vivian Thomas as portrayed in the movie Something the Lord Made. The expression is regularly interpreted to mean: for a long period of time or something that is exhaustive from physical strain or from anger. **Blue bloods**

Up to snuff - The origin of this phrase comes from 'snuff', the powdered tobacco that had become chic to inhale in the late 1600s. There were different grades of snuff and the **aficionados** could tell the difference between good snuff and very good snuff. The common usage is: meeting the required standard

Uriah Heep - This expression comes from a fictional character created by Charles Dickens in his novel David Copperfield. It now denotes: a person who is uninteresting humble but dangerously malicious

Useful idiot - The exact origin of this term is unknown, but it is regularly associated with Vladimir Lenin. Perhaps because it was used to identify Soviet sympathizers in Western countries during the **Cold War**. The earliest recorded usage of this term was in 1948 in an Italian newspaper. The term is used generically to denote: someone who unwittingly or naively supports a bad or malicious cause; someone that is used by someone else or is easily manipulated

Utopia - This word is derived from the Greek which means "no place." Throughout history, various utopias have been described, e.g., Plato's Republic, Thomas More's Utopia (the first to use this term), Francis Bacon's New Atlantis, etc. However, in the 20th century, several books emerged under the heading of utopia such as Capek's, RUR, Huxley's Brave New World and Orwell's 1984 that are not utopias but **dystopias** which is an imagined place or state in which everything is unpleasant or bad; as far as the human race is concerned. It is important to note that these books started out in search of a utopia but ending up being the opposite. The word utopia means the opposite and is an imagined place or state of things in which everything is perfect. For example, James Hilton's novel, Lost Horizon, written in 1933 depicts a utopia in the form of Shagari-La. **There are no utopias**

Stands for:

Virtue is its own reward

IN A NUTSHELL

Vade mecum - This is a Latin phrase meaning "go with me" that has become part of the English language. It has been used since the early 1600s. It is defined as: a handbook or guide that is kept constantly at hand for consultation. It, however, has been extended to other useful items and aids carried by a person. For example, this book, In a Nutshell could be considered a vade mecum

Vale of years - The source of this adage is William Shakespeare's Othello (Act III, Scene III). "Haply for I am black; And have not those soft parts of conversation; That chamberers have; or for I am declined; Into the vale of years—yet that's not much—She's gone." The phrase now refers to: the declining years of life. The opposite of **salad days**

Vampire - The exact origins of this term and the creature is unknown; however, many believe that it is a relic of the Middle Ages and the plagues that engulfed Europe. Notwithstanding, it was popularized by Bram Stoker's epic novel Dracula published in 1897. His novel crystalized many of the characteristics that we attribute to vampires today, e.g., bloodsucking nocturnal beings. So much so that Dracula has become a household word. The term is used frequently to describe: someone that takes advantage of another especially for personal gain. Something that sucks the life out of something else. **Frankenstein; wolfman**

Van Gogh's ear for music - This phrase is believed to have been coined by the film producer Billy Wilder. It refers to Vincent van Gogh a famous painter that cut off his ear because he was in love with a woman that seemed to reject him. The expression is a musical pun intended to refer to someone being tone deaf. The phrase has migrated to mean: when referred to a singer, it suggests that they tend to go off key a lot. More generally, it refers to someone who cannot distinguish the differences between musical tone or does not have **an ear for music**

Vanish into thin air - The source of the saying is from Shakespeare and appears in two of his plays: Othello, "Then put up your pipes in your bag, for I'll away. Go; vanish into air; away!" and The Tempest "These our actors, as I foretold you, were all spirits and are melted into air, into thin air." The phrase vanish into thin air" is an adaptation of Shakespeare's expressions, first recorded in The Edinburgh Advertiser, April 1822. The phrase has evolved to mean: to **disappear without a trace. A disappearing act**

Variety is the spice of life - This expression originated from a poem by the English poet William Cowper entitled: The Task (1785). He was the foremost English poet of the generation between Alexander Pope and William Wordsworth. The common usage is: new and exciting experiences make life more interesting

Vengeance is mine, saith the Lord - The source of this saying is from the Bible (Romans 12:19). "**Dearly beloved**, avenge not yourselves, but rather give place unto wrath: for it is written, Vengeance is mine; I will repay, saith the Lord.**" My mother would always say that God does not punish you for your sins, it is the sin itself that eventually punishes you. The phrase generally means: vengeance and retribution are reserved for God and God alone. Seneca once wrote: **revenge is an inhuman word**

Vestal virgin - This term comes from ancient Rome. For more than a thousand years, vestal virgins held a level of extraordinary respect and authority as priestesses of Vesta the Roman goddess of health. They were the only female priests within the Roman religious system and the only Roman women with true power and the rights of men. The group numbered six at any one time. They were responsible for maintaining the sacred flame which represented the soul of Rome and served for thirty years. Celibacy was a strict and unforgiving requirement. So much so that the punishment for violating the oath of celibacy was to be buried alive because spilling their blood was a violation of Roman law. A vestal virgin could marry after her term of service was over. Though to do so, was considered **bad luck**. The term has come to be used as something or someone, particularly a woman, that is untainted or **as pure as the driven snow. Sibylline books**

Victorian - The term gets its name from England's Queen Victoria that reign from 1837-1901 one of the longest reigns in British history. In fact, the longest reigns belong to women, Queen Victoria, 63 years and Queen Elizabeth II, 65 years and counting. Victorian defines an important era in the history of Great Britain and also can define a person that lived through that era. Other English periods that preceded it include: **Elizabethan and Jacobean**

Victory has a hundred fathers and defeat is an orphan - This quote is quite regularly attributed to John F. Kennedy, but its source could be older. The expression can be interpreted to mean: many people want to take credit for a successful venture or person, but no one wants to take credit for a failure

Vim and vigor - The exact origin of this expression is unknown, but it seems to not have been used before the mid-1800s. The two words are redundant with the second word used to give emphasis to the first, e.g., **hale and hearty**. The term was originally vis and vigor before it migrated to its current usage which means: to be full of energy. It remains uncertain whether the term gave birth to the more vulgar phrase of piss and vinegar which essentially means the same thing. **Full of vim and vigor, Full of piss and vinegar**

Virtual reality - The concept has been around for over a century. Yet, the term was not popularized until 1987 when Jaron Lanier, founder of the Visual Programming Lab (VPL), used the term. The common usage is: an environment or state in which an alternative reality is generated using a computer or other means to create a three-dimensional simulation or environment that can be interacted in a seemingly real or physical way. An imagined reality created outside of our own

Virtual organization - This term emerged with the Internet and the ability to link people together, virtually or without being in the same physical place using the Internet as the principal conduit. It gave rise to virtual teams, managers and employees that emulated the physical workplace in function and in operation. It enabled employees to work from home in their slippers, avoid long commutes, and linked them to fellow employees and customers around the globe. Although many have argued the need for physical interactions, the number of virtual organizations continues to rise as technology improves

Virtue is its own reward - This expression has been ascribed to the great Roman orator Cicero. It generally means: a person should not be virtuous in hopes of getting a reward, but because it makes them feel good to be virtuous. **Patience is its own reward** is a similar expression

Virtuoso - This is a term that was borrowed from the arts, specifically music. It has recently been applied to any skilled person. **Prima donna; guru**

Volte face - This term is based on the Latin term *"volvera facies"* and similar terms appear in French and Italian. The term has also worked its way into the English language. It means: an act of turning around so as to face in the opposite direction. More practical uses are: to change the strategy completely; to change opinion or attitude in the opposite direction; to make a 180 degrees turnabout; to back away or back out of an agreement or policy; any complete reversal, e.g., **from a smile to a frown. Turn one hundred and eighty degrees; about face**

Voice crying in the wilderness - Like so many sayings that have become staples in the English language, this one also emerges from the Bible and is repeated several times in the New Testament. In fact, it is one of the few that is repeated in every Gospel (Luke 3:4), (Mark 1:3) (Matt. 3:3), (John 1:23) and the Old Testament (Isaiah 40:3). "I am a voice crying in the wilderness, 'Make straight the way of the Lord,'" as Isaiah the prophet said." The quotation is used to imply that John the Baptist was preparing the way for Jesus, as foretold by the prophecy of Isaiah. The common interpretation is: a person, particularly a prophet or a luminary, that is not listened to at first. Yet, over time their prediction comes true. It can also be used as a warning of things to come if things continue its current course. **Who is that voice crying in the wilderness? John the Baptist figure; harbinger of doom**

Voodoo - This term comes from the name of an African based religious cult practiced in the Caribbean, mainly in Haiti, and parts of the southern United States. It combines traditional African magical and religious rites, and is characterized by sorcery, spirit possession and ancestor worship. The term is habitually used to describe a type of magic or sorcery. For example, voodoo economics is a term coined by George H.W. Bush in his 1980 campaign which means: an economic policy perceived as being unrealistic and ill-advised. **Voodoo doctor; working Roots on someone. Hoodoo** is regularly linked to Voodoo. Still, Hoodoo is not a religion but rather, a form of folk magic that originated in West Africa and like Voodoo is mainly practiced today in the Southern United States. For example, Frederick Douglass, the African American abolitionist, editor, orator, author and statesman wrote about a Hoodoo experience he had at a crucial moment in his life. On a similar note, **Black magic** is a term that is often used to denote magic that is used for evil purposes or to worship the devil. However, many **people of color** reject this term and see it **in the same vein** as *angel's food cake* and *devil's food cake* -- subliminal terms, in their view, which portray white as being good and black as being evil

Vote with your feet - The origin of this expression is unclear although many believe that the Russian revolutionary and Communist leader Vladimir Lenin used a similar phrase when he referred to the soldiers of the Czar during the Russian Revolution of 1917. It generally means: to attempt to **make your voice heard** by doing something that changes, eliminates or brings attention to your current situation. To walk away from something or a situation. **Vote your conscience; all politics is local**

Vox populi - This term is of Latin origin and literally means the people's voice or voice of the people. It also can be found in the longer adage, *"Vox populi, vox Dei,"* which means "The voice of the people is the voice of God. In recent times, the term has been abbreviated as **vox pop**. It is regularly associated with majority rule or the opinions or beliefs of the majority. **Silent majority**

Stands for:

Whom the gods would destroy,
they first make mad

IN A NUTSHELL

Walk on water - The source of this expression is the Bible, and the Gospel narratives in which Jesus walks on water (Matthew 14:22-36; Mark 6:45-56; John 6:16-24). Luke is the only Gospel that does not include this miracle. The phrase now means: to do something that is deemed impossible or astonishing; to believe that you are above the rest and that the rules do not apply to you

Walk the plank - This saying has its origin in the practice of pirates forcing a person to walk blindfold along a plank over the side of a ship to one's death in the sea. The common usage is: to suffer punishment at the hand of someone or to force someone to take responsibility for an action of a person or a group. Similar phrases include: **fall on your sword; fall guy; scapegoat**

Wall Street - The origin of this term is the name of a street in New York City. It derives its name from a wall built by the Dutch, when the city was call New Amsterdam to protect them from attacks by Native Americans and pirates. It is now the home of the New York Stock Exchange (NYSE). Historically, it has also been the base of some of the largest brokerages, banks and financial institutions. So much so that the term is now a metonym for the stock market and at times the financial health of the nation. Although the term is a major **barometer** of the nation's economic state, it is not all encompassing, but rather refers to the larger investment community, whereas **Main Street** refers to individual investors, small businesses, employees, etc. Because it is a financial **epicenter**, Wall street has also been used as a metaphor for corporate greed. **Wall Street and Main Street; bull and bear market**

Walls of Jericho - The source of this expression comes from the Bible (Joshua 6: 1-20). Jericho was a Canaanite city destroyed by the Israelites after they crossed the Jordan River into the Promised Land. According to the Bible, it collapsed by the sounds of trumpets. "When you hear them sound a long blast on the trumpets, have the whole army give a loud shout; then the wall of the city will collapse and the army will go up, everyone straight in." Therefore, the saying "the walls of Jericho" is inextricably linked to its collapse and the miraculous conquest of the city. Often quoted as: **and the walls came crumbling (tumbling) down**, it infers a long-waited collapse of something or someone often under its own weight or by the actions of the person

War is hell - The source of the saying is William Tecumseh Sherman the famous American Civil War general. It became his mantra and he is famous for his March to the Sea in which he virtually destroyed the infrastructure of the American South. It is often used to describe the nature of warfare or conflict

Warp speed - The origin of this term is the science fiction realm and was popularized by the Star Trek series of the 1960s. In this context it meant to travel faster than the speed of light, something that physicists deem impossible. It has migrated to mean: something that travels very fast or at the maximum speed. **Light speed**

Watershed (moment) - This term has been around for at least a century. Often used figuratively, the literal meaning of watershed is a point or division in a river or a stream where the river is split into two paths that will never intersect again. It has therefore migrated to mean: a turning point or a point in time that marks an important or significant change in events. Similar phrases include: **cross the Rubicon; point of no return; beginning of the end; high water mark**

Wash your hands with something - This saying is from Pilate in the Bible, (Matthew 27:24). "When Pilate saw that he could not prevail, but rather that a tumult was beginning, he took water and washed his hands before the multitude, saying, "I am innocent of the blood of this just person." It has evolved to mean: to refuse to have anything more to do with someone or something. This aforementioned passage is also the source of the phrase **Blood curse.** In all four Gospels, Pilate declares the innocence of Christ before sentencing him to death. It is only in Matthew does the crowd react so strongly. Henceforth, throughout European history and within some Christian circles, this passage was used to place the blame of Christ's execution on the Jewish people, e.g., **Christ killers** also known as **Jewish decide.** For example, Martin Luther, a seminal figure of the Reformation and one of the fathers of the Protestant movement, was an avowed anti-Semite. In his 1543 treatise: On the Jews and Their Lies, he called for the burning of synagogues and Jewish homes. "We are even at fault for not striking them dead," Luther was not alone in his anti-sematic beliefs and rhetoric. Other Christian denominations, including the Catholic Church, endorsed **blood libel** or the belief that Jews kill Christian children for ritual purposes, especially in the preparation of Passover bread, a belief prevalent throughout the Middle Ages and occasionally used until the early 20th century. Some even used it as justification for the Jewish **Holocaust**

Watergate - The source of this term is a political scandal in which an attempt to bug the national headquarters of the Democratic Party (in the Watergate building in Washington, DC) led to the resignation of President Nixon (1974). Since that time, it has become a metaphor for **plausible deniability** as well as a political scandal to the extent the many scandals have the suffix "gate" attached to them. This scandal has produced other phrases such as **it's not the crime, it's the coverup, follow the money** and the term **Deep Throat** which takes its name from the popular pornographic movie of the early 1970s starring Linda Lovelace and now means: a person who anonymously supplies information about covert or illegal action in the organization where they work. **Tricky Dick; a whistleblower**

Wax and wane - The source of this expression seems to be the changing phases of the moon and it goes back to the 1300s. The common usage is: to undergo alternate increases and decreases; to grow stronger and then weaker again. **Ebb and flow** is the same idea and refers to tides which ironically are caused by the waxing and waning of the moon. **Harvest moon; blue moon**

We come to bury Caesar, not to praise him - This expression originated from Shakespeare's Julius Caesar (Act III, Scene II). This phrase should be taken within the context of the entire speech. By itself, it is often used to denounce a person particularly a tyrant. It refers, however, to the evil that men do lives on after them, and that the good is often buried with their bones. The complete quote is: "**Friends, Romans, countrymen, lend me your ears; I come to bury Caesar, not to praise him. The evil that men do lives after them. The good is oft interred with their bones.**" It is regularly interpreted to mean: people often forget the good things that people do; but they remember the bad things. Similarly, Shakespeare penned in Henry VIII (Act IV, Scene II) **Men's evil manners live in brass; their virtues we write in water**

IN A NUTSHELL

We have met the enemy and he is us - This phrase was made famous by a 1970 cartoon by Walt Kelly that depicted Porkypine and Pogointo in a comic strip and attributed the phrase to Pogo. Kelly did not invent the phrase; it was used earlier on a 1970 Earth Day poster. The origin of the phrase is much older and is an adaptation of a War of 1812 comment by Oliver Hazard Perry: "We have met the enemy and he is ours." The aforementioned phrase resonated in America because it seemed metaphorically appropriate for the Vietnam War and America's status as **the standard-bearer** for democracy around the world, which divided the nation. Wars are started by old people, but they are fought by young people. This was the source of the division between older Americans (Silent Majority) and the so-called Hippie movement of the young. It simply means: sometimes we are our worst enemies. **Things rust from the inside out**, and empires crumble from within long before they fall from the outside. **When the axe came into the forest, the trees said the handle is one of us**

We know what we are, but not what we may be - This saying comes from Shakespeare's <u>Hamlet</u> (Act IV, Scene V). The phrase is often interpreted to mean: only God knows the future, all we can do as mortals is to plan for it. Yet, there is no guarantee that any of our plans will come to fruition because of **unforeseen circumstances**. Because we are mortal, it is most unfortunate that the only thing about the future we can predict is that someday it will no longer exist for us

We need never be ashamed of our tears - This saying is ascribed to Charles Dickens from his book <u>Great Expectations</u>. "Heaven knows <u>we need never be ashamed of our tears</u>, for they are rain upon the blinding dust of earth, overlying our hard heart." Humans are the only species on earth that express sorrow or joy in the form of tears. They are perhaps, the sincerest form of expression. For ages, men have been taught not to cry because they appear weak when doing so. This saying **flies in the face** of such beliefs, and it serves as a reminder not only of our sorrows, or our joys; but of our virtues and our humanity. Sappho wrote: **what cannot be said will be wept**

We shall overcome - This phrase is from a popular song of the same name <u>sung during the Civil Rights movement</u> that became one of its rallying cries. So much so that President Lyndon Johnson used it when he signed Civil Rights legislation into law. It has since become **a rallying cry** for other groups that are seeking Civil Rights and justice for all. **Keep your eyes on the prize**

We wuz robbed - This phrase is attributed to Joe Jacobs. He spoke these words after Max Schemeling lost his fight to Jack Sharkey on June 21, 1932. Although grammatically incorrect, it is reminiscent of those famous yogisms that continued to be quoted by sports fans after a game or a play. Yet, it has extended beyond sports and is often used when someone feels that an injustice was levied against them

Wear your heart on your sleeve - The source of this expression is from William Shakespeare's play <u>Othello</u> (Act I, Scene I). "But I will <u>wear my heart upon my sleeve;</u> For daws to peck at. I am not what I am." The expression can be interpreted to mean: to openly display one's emotions

We're not in Kansas anymore - The source of this expression is from <u>The Wizard of Oz</u> where Dorothy says to her dog Toto, "I've got a feeling <u>we're not in Kansas anymore."</u> The common usage is: to be in a place or situation that is outside of your comfort zone or scope of understanding. Strange or different surroundings. **Wicked witch of the west** is another phrase that has its origin in this **time-honored** classic. The character was played by Margaret Hamilton in the 1939 film. In the film, she is <u>Dorothy's chief nemesis</u>. The term refers to: a very callous, hateful or vindictive woman particularly one that is out to do you some harm; an evil arch nemesis. Other popular sayings from <u>The Wizard of Oz</u> include: **follow the yellow brick road;** I'll get you, my pretty [and **your little dog too**]; **there is no place like home;** off to see the wizard; pay no attention to the man behind the curtain; I'm melting, melting; [ohhhhh what a world, what a world]; ruby slippers

Western civilization - This term has its origin in European and Mediterranean civilizations, more specifically, Greece and the Roman Empire. However, most recently it has been used as a euphemism for white or European values, culture, etc. to the exclusion of the contributions made by the Middle East and other civilizations that donated to its greatness

Western style liberalism - This expression is a product of the **Age of Enlightenment** and a pillar of modern Western civilization. It replaced the norms of hereditary privilege, state religion, absolute monarchy, the divine right of kings and served as an inspiration to the Founding Fathers of the United States. It gave birth to the rights of the individual. It is sometimes used to denote Western democratic values

Wet behind the ears - The origin of this phrase comes from the fact that when an animal such as a colt or calf is born on the farm, it is wet all over with birth fluid. Most of the body dries quickly, except for behind the ears. The common usage is: someone who is young, inexperienced or immature. **Green behind the ears** means the same thing. **Dry behind the ears** means knowing how to do something or experienced. **New to the game**

Whack-a-mole - This term takes its name from the popular arcade game often played at fairs, carnivals, etc.. It is a game in which a rubber mallet is used to hit moles that pop up randomly from holes and it is difficult to whack them all in a timely fashion. The term has migrated to mean: a situation in which problems continue to occur making it difficult to solve, cope or to keep track of them

What do they know of England, who only England know - This quote is attributed to Rudyard Kipling in his poem entitled: <u>The English Flag</u> from 1891, The phrase is often interpreted to mean: if you only know one place or one thing, you are limited in your knowledge and understanding of that thing because you have nothing to compare it to. **All the Whos in Whoville** is a similar expression. This reference is from <u>How the Grinch Stole Christmas!</u> A **time-honored** book written by Dr. Seuss. **Walk a mile in someone else's shoes**

What happens in Vegas stays in Vegas - This saying emerged in 2003 as part of a campaign to brand the city of Las Vegas, Nevada for something other than gambling. Long known as a **sin city**, the task to change the image to increase tourism was much longer in the making. The slogan has been quoted by comedian Billy Crystal and others and has since become a catchphrase for keeping certain activities **in the closet** or **just between friends**

IN A NUTSHELL

What is past is prologue - This expression originated from Shakespeare's play: <u>The Tempest</u> (Act II, Scene I). Events in life are seldom as isolated as some would like, and the past is the **harbinger** of the future. History is arranged like **a series of dominos** with related events unfolding as time goes forward. We should therefore always be mindful of history and the ancillary effects of our present actions on future events because the present is nothing more than the past of the future. The common interpretation is: the past prepares us for the present and the future and that **history repeats itself. Read the tea leaves**

What we have [here] is a failure to communicate - This expression originated from the 1967 movie <u>Cool Hand Luke</u> starring Paul Newman as Luke. It is about a laid back cool Southern **redneck** (Luke) who is sentenced to two years in a rural prison but refuses to conform and later escapes prison only to be returned. It is regularly used when two people do not agree on something or when one person does not understand the point that another person is making. **Don't see eye to eye; can't see it my way**

What we obtain too cheap, we esteem too lightly - The origin of this saying is from the American political activist Thomas Paine written in <u>The American Crisis</u> during the American Revolutionary War. The expression can be interpreted to mean: we often take the things that we are given to us for granted and therefore do not appreciate what it took to achieve or acquire them. In other words: **Easy come, easy go**

What would Jesus do (WWJD) - This is a phrase that became popular in the 1990s. For many Christians, it serves as a constant reminder of their guiding principles and **moral compass.** In many cases, it is inscribed on bracelets as an emblem of their faith and their deep commitment to walking daily in the footsteps of their lord and savior, Jesus Christ

Whatever doesn't kill me will make me stronger - This quote is ascribed to the German <u>philosopher Friedrich Nietzsche's,</u> <u>Twilight of the Idols,</u> published in 1888. This is a saying that is regularly said during times of adversity and strife. Shakespeare wrote in <u>King Lear</u> (Act IV, Scene I) "The worst is not so long as we can say, 'This is the worst." Adversity, strife and suffering are integral parts of the human experience. When we are born, we cry and when we die others cry. But in the dash between two dates that define our lives, if we have the courage to **forge ahead** and to **turn our wounds into wisdom,** we can learn from our mistakes and gain strength from our misfortunes. We must, however, be forever mindful, that in life there are no real mistakes or misfortunes; just misunderstanding of the nature and purpose of our earthly existence. **When you are going through hell keep going**

What's your sign? - This phrase became popular in the 1960s during the **Space Age**. As Man began to explore the universe and sent human beings into outer space, people on earth, particularly in the United States, reached for the stars inwardly by embracing some aspects not of Astronomy but <u>Astrology</u>. <u>Astronomy</u> is a science. **On the other hand,** Astrology is the interpretation of the movement of celestial bodies (planets and stars) and their influence on human affairs. The latter has nothing to do with science. Unfortunately, many people interchange the two, yet they are vastly different. What's your sign, falls into the astrology realm and is based on the zodiac. When someone asks you, what's your sign, they are referring to one of the twelve zodiac symbols that roughly correspond to the months of the year. In the sixties and seventies, it was a popular **pick up line** and everyone knew their sign (by the way I am a Gemini). It was an era when the Age of Aquarius /Let the Sun shine in, a song popularized by the 1967 play Hair and the R&B group the 5th Dimension, alluded to a new age while at the same time helped to define the current age. The latter part of the sixty's decade; highlighted peace and love and was against things like the Vietnam War and gave rise to such terms as: **hippie movement**; **Woodstock**; **flower children**

When America sneezes, the world catches a cold - The source of this phrase is European and not American. The first person to use a similar phrase was the aristocratic Prussian diplomat Klemens Wenzel Furst von Metternich. It was used to designate France's influences over Europe during the Age of Napoleon: "when France sneezes, the whole of Europe catches a cold." The destabilization of Europe by France during those years change not only Europe but led to revolutions across Latin America which also destabilized the Western Hemisphere. The phrase is not only an indication of America's military might, but of its **soft power** which has, at least in the post-World War II era, left an indelible footprint on the world

When in Rome, do as the Romans - This is an old English proverb. Though the Greeks were great, it was the Romans that left their indelible imprint on the European continent as best exemplified by the saying **all roads lead to Rome**. The common usage is: when visiting a foreign land, follow the customs of those who live in it. It can also mean that when you are in an unfamiliar situation, you should follow the lead of those who **know the ropes**

When movies were in black and white, and so was everything else - The source of this expression comes from a song by the African American activist and musician Gil Scott-Heron entitled: B Movie. It was a satirical critique of the Regan administration. Scott-Heron was rapping, in the 1970s, before it was called Rap. For example, some lyrics from this song are: "Nostalgia, that's what we want…: the good ol' days, when we gave'em hell. When the buck stopped somewhere, and you could still buy something with it. To a time when movies were in black and white, and so was everything else…. Before the free press went down before full court press and were reluctant to review the menu because they knew the only thing available was…Crow." The expression is frequently interpreted to mean: there are some in America, particularly in the South, that yearn for those pre-Civil Rights days when black people were considered second class citizens **under the aegis shield** known as **Separate but Equal**

When someone shows you who they are, believe them the first time - The source of this expression is the African American poet, Civil and Women's Rights advocate Marguerite Ann Johnson better known as: Maya Angelou. Popularized by Oprah and others, this phrase simply means: people are who they are; and **a tiger doesn't change its stripes**. Often, they are **harbingers** of their own motives and display their **true colors** even when they try to disguise them. People are normally **true to themselves**, the problem is that we are often, for our own selfish reasons, blind to that truth. Sometimes we see them, not as they are -- but as we want them to be; and therein lies the problem. Similar expressions include: **everybody's somebody's fool**; **you never get a second chance to make a first impression**; **coming events cast their shadow before**; **you know the bird by its song**

IN A NUTSHELL

When the axe came into the forest, the trees said the handle is one of us - This saying is often credited to the legendary sage, Aesop. It is part of a collection of fables entitled: <u>The Woodcutter and the Axe</u>. In this particular case, the trees could not be cut without the aid of one of their own. It can, therefore, be interpreted to mean: often in life, we are silent or unknowing contributors to our own misfortunes or demise. **Straight trees are cut first** is a similar expression and means: a person should not be to honest and upright because people can take advantage of their truthfulness and candor

When the cat's away, the mice will play - This is an old English proverb that has been around since the late 1400s. It was popular during Shakespeare's time and it was similarly used in his play Henry V (Act I, Scene II) written in 1599: "playing the mouse in absence of the cat." It now means: when the person who is in charge is away, the subordinates will do as they please. Related expressions include: **a free for all**; **playing cat and mouse**

When the mouse laughs at the cat, there is a hole nearby - This is an African proverb about the **cat and mouse game** played between **predator and prey**. In this one, however, the prey gets the best of the predator. Reminiscent of the popular <u>Tom and Jerry cartoons,</u> the phrase is often interpreted to mean: when someone smiles or laughs at you in a situation that they otherwise would be frightful, it is because they know they have a way out of the situation and your threats or demands are meaningless. Similar phrases include: **idle threats; when the cat is not home, the mice dance on the table**

When the pupil is ready, the master will appear - This phrase is often accredited to Eastern philosophy and Buddhism in particular. Yet, deeper investigation traces its origin to the Theosophical Society founded by the renowned occultist <u>Madame Helena Blavatsky</u> along with Henry Steel Olcott, and William Quan Judge in 1875. At the turn of the 20th century, this society claimed as its members, Mahatma Gandhi, Thomas Edison, T. S. Eliot and Vice President Henry Wallace who along with President Franklin Roosevelt placed Masonic symbols on the American dollar bill. It was also linked to the independence of India from Great Britain in 1947. Blavatsky's books were highly read within the Occult and some have linked the Swastika, used by the Nazis, to her writing specifically: <u>The Secret Doctrine</u>. The phrase generally means: if you truly seek knowledge and wisdom, eventually someone or something will appear that will serve as a mentor or guide to deeper knowledge and understanding. Related expressions include: **John the Baptist figure; at the feet of the master**

When (if) you are going through hell, keep going - This saying is accredited to the British statesman and historian Winston Churchill. This phrase generally means: in life we go through some difficult circumstances that seem impossible to get out of. Sometimes such situations can blind us from the fact that the human spirit is one of the things that separates us from the other beasts on this planet. Hell comes in many forms and sometimes we create our own hell at the expense of a blissful heaven. Only the devil and his demons are happier in hell than they were in heaven. My father would always say: a person should be able to stay in hell for one day, if he knew he was getting out the next. **The only way to get out of hell is to keep moving through it**

A COLLECTION OF POPULAR ENGLISH PHRASES

When you come to the fork in the road, take it - This is one of the many witty sayings known as "Yogisms", e.g., **the future ain't what it use to be,** attributed to the New York Yankee and Met baseball player Yogi Berra. The statement is so ambiguous, as to have many different interpretations. One is of an eating utensil, fork, that you just pick up and take (LOL). Another is an actual fork in the road that divides the road into two roads of which you are forced to choose one. In this case, taking either road could lead you to the same destination point by different routes. Therefore, it doesn't matter which one you take

When (If) you find yourself in a hole, stop digging - The origin of this popular adage is unclear and perhaps unknown. Notwithstanding, some have attributed it to an early article written around the turn of the 20th century. Yet others attributed to Will Rogers, or even Warren Buffett (however, this may be a case of assigning someone popular to a popular saying). The expression generally means: if you are doing or saying something wrong or if something is not working, stop doing it. On the other hand, **to dig yourself out of a hole** means to find a solution to a problem or to work your way out of a difficult situation. **When (if) you are going through hell, keep going;**

When you look long into the abyss, the abyss looks into you - This quote is ascribed to the German philosopher Friedrich Nietzsche and is from: Beyond Good and Evil. "He who fights with monsters should be careful lest he thereby become a monster. And if thou gaze long into an abyss, the abyss will also gaze into thee." The abyss in this case is a dark place and represents the darker side of humanity. In this regard, the abyss has become a mirror and reflects, not what you think you are, or what you once were, but rather what you have become. Sometimes we cannot recognize the embodiment of evil, simply because we have become the epitome of evil. Take for example, the French Revolution. It started out by killing all of the aristocrats under the banner of Liberty, Equality and Fraternity and ended up with them killing each other including their leader Robespierre. Or Orwell's Animal Farm where the animals revolted against the humans only to become more humanlike when they were given power; replete with pigs walking on their hind legs. The common interpretation is: it is hard to be part of something for a long time, without it becoming part of you. We are all shaped by our environment. **If you lie down with dogs, you will get up with fleas**

Where in the world is Carmen Sandiego - This catchphrase comes from a popular game that was first released in 1985. It is often used when someone disappears from the public or when someone goes on a long trip or away without notifying someone

Where's the beef? - The origin of this catchphrase is from a Wendy's hamburger commercial that was popular in the 1980s, in which an old grandma looks at a competitor's small hamburger with a big bun and asked: where's the beef? Since that time, it has become a phrase the questions the validity, substance or idea of something

Where's Waldo - The origin of this popular phrase comes from a series of popular books by the British illustrator, Martin Handford in 1987. To date, the series of books have sold over 50 million copies and is published in nineteen different languages. In the United States, the name Waldo is used. Yet, in other countries and languages the name is different, e.g., in England it is Wally. The illustrations depict, an elusive man in a red and white shirt often hidden in a crowd. In 2009, researchers made some discoveries about how the brain searches for objects using the Where's Wally? books as a reference. It now refers to: a search for something or someone, an enigma or puzzle, something or someone **hiding in plain sight**, or something that is not obvious. **Where in the world is Carmen San Diego?**

Whet your appetite - This is an old English expression that dates back to the days when the word 'whet' was commonly used to mean to sharpen. It is habitually incorrectly used as "wet" your appetite. Although one may say **wet one's whistle**, it is incorrect to say wet your appetite. The common usage is: **to pique one's curiosity** or desire especially when it comes to food. **To whet your appetite**

Which came first, the chicken or the egg - This is an ancient dilemma that dates at least to the days of Aristotle. Modern science, however, has determined that the egg had to be first. The egg from which the first chicken emerged had to be laid by a chicken-like species from which the chicken evolved as a result of genetic mutations that took place first in the egg. **In a nutshell**, or eggshell would be more appropriate for this analogy, all subsequent "chicken" eggs were laid by chickens, but the first chicken came from an egg and not the other way around. The expression as come to mean: a situation in which it is difficult to discern which thing caused the other, i.e., **cause and effect**. An unresolved dilemma or paradox. **A chicken and egg situation**

While you live, tell truth and shame the devil - This expression originated from Shakespeare's Henry IV. Part 1, (Act III, Scene I) 1597. "And I can teach thee, coz, to shame the devil. By telling truth: tell truth and shame the devil." It means: always try to tell the truth even when you are tempted to lie. Similar phrases include: **speak truth to power; honesty is the best policy**

White Anglo-Saxon Protestant (WASPs) - English Protestants were the first immigrant group to settle in America in the late 17th and early 18th centuries, e.g., the Mayflower Voyage, Plymouth Rock, Pilgrims, etc. It is a term that was frequently used through the 1950s. As an identity, all people of color were rejected, and it also rejected demands for inclusion by Jews and Catholics regardless of skin color. "Anglo Saxon" as an initial term inferred that Irish (presumably Celts) and Latin (French, Spanish, Italian, etc.) were also not members of the WASPs community. Today in many circles, it is used to denote a stereotypical white person of European ancestry

White coat syndrome (hypertension) - So named after the fact that doctors and nurses traditionally wore white coats or white outfits. It is a condition in which the blood pressure of the patient rises while they are being examined by the doctor or nurse. This is not indicative of the patient's normal blood pressure, but rather due to the excitement of being examined

White collar crime - This term was coined by Edwin Sutherland in 1939. He defined the term as "crime committed by a person of respectability and high social status in the course of his occupation." Such people traditionally wore white shirts to work. It therefore designates: the theft, fraud, embezzlement, or some other nonviolent crime committed by a politician, salaried employee or a senior member of an organization. **Differential Association** is another popular theory put forth by Sutherland. It states that people learn deviant or criminal behavior through their interactions with other people. It views such behavior not as innate, but something that is learned and emulated

White elephant - The source of this term is a story told about the king of Siam who gave a sacred albino elephant to a member of his court knowing that caring for this sacred animal would drive him bankrupt. It now means a possession that is useless or troublesome to maintain and difficult to dispose of. **A lemon** is similar but means: a highly flawed or defective item frequently used to describe a defective automobile

White knuckle - The origin of this expression seems to come from a hand clenched in fear thus turning the knuckles white (on some people). The term has evolved to mean: an event or an activity that provokes nervous tension or an experience that causes a very strong feeling of fear or anxiety; such as in a white-knuckle ride on a plane or a roller-coaster or exposure to something strange or unusual. **Room 101**

White lie - The origin of this term is unclear and perhaps unknown. Even the most virtuous among us have been guilty of telling at least one especially if you have children. Some common examples are: Santa came down the chimney. The tooth fairy was too tired, so she left your money on the table. No honey, you don't look fat in that dress. It means: a harmless or minor lie, especially one told to avoid hurting someone's feelings or for the overall good. **To tell a white lie**

White man's burden - This saying originates from a poem of the same title by the English writer Rudyard Kipling (1899). It was the supposed or presumed responsibility of white people to govern and impart their culture to nonwhite people. It was repeatedly used as a justification for European colonialism. It was a relic of the Victorian era, which saw the carving up of Africa and the rise of men such as Cecil Rhodes (1853-1902) founder of the Rhodes scholarship (open to all races) and namesake of the country Rhodesia. It is seldom used today because of its racist connotation

White privilege - As a fact of history, "white privilege" is an artifact of the post-Columbian era. In the 1930s, W. E. B. Du Bois wrote about this concept. One that gave poor whites a phycological advantage over non-whites in general and black people in particular. During the Civil Rights era, when the walls of **Jim Crow** and **Black Codes** were under siege, a greater focus and critique of ""white-skin privilege" emerged. The concept really **came into its own** in the late 1980s, when Peggy McIntosh, a women's-studies scholar at Wellesley, started writing about it. The common usage is: a set of advantages and/or protections that white people benefit from (mostly at the expense of people of color) **on a daily basis** that are not granted either subliminally or otherwise to people of color. Similarly, **white backlash** is the hostile reaction of some white Americans to the advances of the Civil Rights movement but can also be used to describe any counterattack by whites resulting from the perceived advancement of people of color, e.g., the rise of the **Ku Klux Klan** during Reconstruction. Similar phrases include: **white man's burden; Jim Crow; grandfather clause**

White shoe (law) firm - The origin of this term dates to the pinnacle of the **WASP** establishment that did not allow Jews or other non-WASPs as part of their organization. It took its name from the white shoes that many of them sported in the summer at their restricted clubs. The term has since migrated to mean: a leading professional service organization, typically with a **blue-chip** clientele. **White shoe lawyer; gentlemen's agreement.** Similarly, **a barrack-room lawyer** has its origin in military slang. The common usage is: someone who freely offers their opinion or advice, particularly legal advice, of which they are unqualified to give

White whale - The origin of this idiom is the novel Moby Dick by Herman Melville written in 1851. In this classic book, Captain Ahab is obsessed with catching an elusive great white whale (Moby Dick). Although considered a failure in its day, its popularity was established early in the 20th century and endures today. Unfortunately, Melville, who died in 1891, never lived to see his book get the proper respect and recognition. So much so that the names: **Captain Ahab** (a deranged obsessed person) and **Moby Dick** (something big) have become part of the American lexicon. The term white whale or great white whale now means: to be obsessed with something almost to the point that it destroys you; to chase after something and to never achieve it. **Chasing a great white whale; chasing windmills**

Who shall guard the guardians (*Quis custodiet ipsos custodes***)** - This saying is attributed to the Roman poet Decimus Iunius Iuvenalis known to us as Juvenal and comes from his Sixth Satire. It is akin to the phrase **the fox guarding the henhouse.** This phrase is often used to refer to politicians and law enforcement officials who break the laws that they enact

Whole kit and caboodle - The origin of this expression is unknown or unclear although it has been around for over a century. Most experts agree that the original term was boodle and later evolve into caboodle. The phrase has evolved to mean: everything that is. **The whole nine yards** and the **whole shebang** are similar expressions

Whom the gods love die young - The source of this saying is from the Greek myth of Trophonius and it is often interpreted to mean: virtuous or gifted people die at an early age, because God wants those people to be with Him in the afterlife. It is commonly used as an explanation of why young people die. **Only the good die young**

Whom the gods would destroy, they first make mad - This is a phrase spoken by **Prometheus** in Henry Wadsworth Longfellow's poem entitled: The Masque of Pandora. Although used by Longfellow, the source can be traced to ancient Greece and has been attributed to Euripides and Sophocles. The expression is generally interpreted to mean: madness is often a prelude to destruction

Will no one rid me of this meddlesome priest - The source of this saying is the English king, Henry II who spoke these words in 1170 in reference to a quarrel with Thomas Becket, the Archbishop of Canterbury, over the rights of the church. These words ultimately ended in the martyrdom of St. Thomas Becket. The current usage means: to get rid of a problem or a person that continues to haunt you. Similar phrases include: **a stone in your shoe; a pain in the neck; a fishbone in the throat**

Win one for the Gipper - The origin of this phrase is the Notre Dame football player George Gipp known as the Gipper. After his early death at 25, the famed Notre Dame coach, Knute Rockne, urged his team to win one for the Gipper. Ronald Regan portrayed Gipper in a 1940 film and used this phrase as a political slogan. Hence, the slogan is also attached to him. It means; to do something in honor of someone else; to place the interest of others above yourself

Witch-hunt - This term has its origin in the persecution of people believed to be witches or warlocks. It has migrated to mean: the searching out and deliberate harassment of those (such as political opponents) with unpopular views; or when a person decides to target another person for reasons which may, or may not, be obvious. Perhaps the most famous political witch-hunt was conducted by Joseph McCarthy after World War II to **ferret out** Communists in America. It led to the term **McCarthyism**. Since that time, American presidents, mainly Richard Nixon and Donald J. Trump, have used this term in defense of investigations launched against them. **Burnt at the stake**

With all deliberate speed - This phrase comes from the landmark U.S. Supreme Court Civil Rights case, Brown v. Board of Education, issued on May, 17, 1954. These words were used in the decision and thus, have memorialized the phrase. This case overturned Plessy v. Ferguson, the 1896 U.S. Supreme Court ruling that instituted **Jim Crow** laws throughout the South. The Supreme Court ruling in the Brown v. Board of Education ordered the desegregation of public schools and was a **harbinger** of the Civil Rights movement and the end of **Separate but Equal** established in Plessy v. Ferguson. Since that time, the phrase has been used in cases where expediency and swiftness are important to the resolution of a problem or situation

With malice toward none, [with charity for all] - This phrase is attributed to Abraham Lincoln. "With malice toward none, with charity for all, with firmness in the right as God gives us to see the right." It is from his second inaugural address given on March 4, 1865 in the same suit that he would be buried in one month later. It was his way of holding out **the olive branch** to the South. John Quincy Adams expressed a similar thought in an 1838 letter: "In charity to all mankind, bearing no malice or ill will to any human being." Although put in poetic form, as Lincoln so often did, it could be interpreted to mean: we should not hate each other, but rather, show compassion and empathy toward each other

Without fear or favor - This expression is credited to the New York Times reporter Adolph S. Ochs. It was a statement about how the news should be conducted but could apply to other endeavors in life. The expression can be interpreted to mean: an impartial and honest assessment of something or someone. Similar phrases include: **speak truth to power; all the news that is fit to print**

Without further ado - This phrase and the word ado dates to at least Tutor England (1485 - 1603), e.g., Shakespeare's Much Ado About Nothing. Often written incorrectly as without further adieu, the latter is an eggcorn or the improper use of two words that sound the same, particularly if the sentence makes sense in its improper form, e.g. baited breath, wet your appetite, etc. The phrase is repeatedly used to mean: without further delay; immediately. The word adieu means goodbye, and therefore, one would say: **I bid you adieu** not ado

Woke - This is a term that has emerged with the millennial generation. In some ways, it is a generational replacement for the term **I'm hip to that,** which emerged in the sixties. It means: to be aware of what is going on or what's happening around you and in the world. **To be on the ball; You woke?**

Worry is interest paid on trouble before it comes due - This saying is credited to the English author, Anglican priest and professor of divinity William Ralph Inge. The common usage is: we only worry about something when we sense impending strife, trouble or danger. Shakespeare wrote in Macbeth (Act III, Scene II) "Things without all remedy should be without regard. **What's done is done; don't worry be happy**

Wreak havoc - The exact origin of this phrase is unknown or unclear. Yet, it was popular in the 1800s and was used by seminal writers such as Percy Shelly and Charles Dickens. Like bated breath and whet your appetite, this phrase is repeatedly misspelled as "wreck" havoc and makes sense in its incorrect form. The phrase means: to disrupt, to cause chaos. Similar phrases include: **roll the golden apple; to sow discord**

XYZ

Stands for:

Xerxes tears

You can run, but you cannot hide

Zeno's paradox

X

Xanadu - The origin of this term is the name of the palaces of Kubla Khan given by Samuel Taylor Coleridge in his 1816 poem: Kubla Khan. They were known for their luxury and beauty. "In Xanadu did Kubla Khan A stately pleasure-dome decree: Where Alph, the sacred river, ran Through caverns measureless to man." It means: an idyllic, exotic, or luxurious place. **Taj Mahal**

Xanthippe - She was the wife of Socrates. Her allegedly bad-tempered behavior toward her husband made her proverbial as a shrew. It means: any nagging scolding person, especially a shrewish wife

Xenophobia - This is one of a long list or phobias (fears) such as claustrophobia, homophobia, etc.. that permeates the English language. It means: the intense or irrational dislike or fear of people from other countries or anything that is strange or foreign to a particular group

Xerox - The source of this term is the name of a copying company that started as a photographic paper company (Haloid Company) in 1906. The company eventually ventured into copying machines based on xerography technology and changed its name to *Xerox*. A pioneer in the copying industry, its name later became synonymous with an electronic copy. **Carbon copy**

Xerxes tears - Xerxes I (ruled 486-465 BCE), also known as Xerxes the Great, was the king of the Persian Empire. It was reported that Xerxes wept when he sent his men into battle against the Greeks. The expression means: a commander's concern for the lives and welfare of his troops

X-ray vision - This term appears to have started with the emergence of science fiction novels and comic books in which characters such as **Superman** had such vision. A form of electromagnetic radiation, X-rays were discovered by accident in 1895 by the German physicist, Willian Roentgen while he was working with a cathode ray tube in his laboratory. The term is based on the ability of X-rays to penetrate flesh and reveal bone structures. The common usage is: the ability to see through any object such as walls to observe what is inside. **You must have X-ray vision; laser vision**

Y

Yabba-dabba do - This phrase has its origin in the Flintstones cartoon series of the 1960s produced by Hanna-Barbera. It was uttered by its chief character Fred Flintstone and the series was set in **the Stone Age**. It depicted the lives of the Rubbles and the Flintstones families featuring Fred and Barney as best friends and neighbors. It means: an expression of happiness and/or excitement; something that you may say after an accomplishment. **You damn skippy** is similar and is a term of approval or excitement or an indication of agreement. **Yippie Ki Yay**

A COLLECTION OF POPULAR ENGLISH PHRASES

Yahoo - The origin of this term is from a member of a race of brutes in Jonathan Swift's Gulliver's Travels who looked like humans and had all the vices of humans. Although it has recently been popularized by the name of a popular Internet company, the term means: a brute in human form; an uncultivated or crude person; or an exclamation frequently used to express joy or excitement. **Yahoo!**

Yankee ingenuity - The origins of this term stems from the term Yankee. Yankee was originally used as a derogatory term by the British to denote an American colonist. After the American Revolutionary War, the citizens of the free and independent colonies embraced the term as a **badge of courage** and a **term of endearment.** During the American Civil War, it was used to denote a person from the North or the Union. In Britain today, the term Yankee or better yet "Yanks" is used to denote an American. As America's technological prowess **began to bloom**, Yankee ingenuity became popular and was assigned to American inventions and innovation. This term sharply distinguished them from European innovations. It now means: the creativity, innovation, problem solving and technical prowess that is uniquely American. The Panama Canal is a perfect example of Yankee ingenuity. **Made in America; good old Yankee ingenuity**

Yellow belly (yellow) - The exact origin of this term is unclear. One **school of thought** is that it is a term that designated people from a particular area in England and was later Americanized. Another is that it takes its name from a bird that has a yellowbelly. Nonetheless it has migrated to mean: a coward. **Afraid of your own shadow**

Yellow journalism - The origin of the term dates back to the 1890s and the newspaper wars between William Randolph Hearst and Joseph Pulitzer. The term gets its name from a comic strip created by Richard Outcault which appeared in Pulitzer's newspaper that became extremely popular. It featured a bucked-toothed, baby faced kid in a yellow dress. The kid became so popular that both Hearst and Pulitzer had their own versions of the Yellow Kid and was a constant reminder of the rivalry between these two newspaper giants. The common usage is: journalism that is not based on facts or the truth but rather on sensationalism and outlandish exaggerations. **Shoe leather journalism** is another journalistic term that is often used. It is basic reporting in which the reporter travels on foot from place to place to uncover and report a story or an event. This often involves, visiting the site, conducting interviews, pulling documents and sorting the facts

Yippie Ki Yay - This expression has its roots in the American West, specifically among the cowboy culture. Although in use for some time, it was popularized recently by the Die Hard series of movies starring Bruce Willis. It is normally used to express joy or excitement. **Yippie; yabba-dabba do**

You can fool some of the people some of the time; but not all the people all of the time - This quote is attributed to Abraham Lincoln (although no one can find the actual speech or event where he gave it). It means: while some people can be fooled, all the people can't be fooled, forever. **Everything has its limits**

You can lead a horse to water, but you can't make it drink - This is an old English proverb that has been around since the 12th century. It now means: you can present someone with an opportunity or an option, but you cannot force him or her to take advantage of it

IN A NUTSHELL

You can never step into the same river twice - This saying is ascribed to the Greek philosopher <u>Heraclitus of Ephesus</u>. Because the river is always in motion, it serves as a time clock. The idea behind never being able to step into the same river twice is a testament to the continual change of life itself, every second is unique. To a larger extent, take the earth, it can never revolve around the sun at the same spot because the sun is moving relative to the galaxy and the galaxy is also moving relative to space. Each moment in time has its own uniqueness. Hence, you can never go back to where you once were. **The only thing constant is change**

You can run, but you cannot hide - This expression is credited to the American boxer <u>Joe Louis</u>. Known as the "Brown Bomber," he was heavyweight champion of the world 1937–49, defending his title 25 times during that period. It has migrated to mean: sooner or later you must face whatever you are running from. **Face the music**

You can't beat somebody with nobody - This saying is attributed to the celebrated philosopher and educator <u>Nicholas Murry Butler</u> when his group opposed nominating Teddy Roosevelt for Vice President in the 1900 election. Roosevelt became president after the **assassination** of William McKinley in 1901. Often repeated as a political mantra, it now means: if you oppose a person, thing or idea, you must have a viable alternative or solution. **You can't beat a horse with no horse** is similarly used. **If you are not part of the solution, you are part of the problem**

You can't make an omelet without breaking some eggs - This is a translation of a French proverb. It means that it is difficult to achieve something important without causing any unpleasant effects or sacrifice. **Upset the applecart** is similar and means to spoil a plan or disturb the status quo. It originated from the 1800s whereby a farmer would bring a loaded applecart of neatly stacked fresh apples for sale

You can't serve God and mammon - The source of this saying appears to be the Bible (Matt. 6:24). Mammon is wealth regarded as an evil influence or false object of worship and devotion. It was taken by medieval writers as the name of the devil of greediness and rejuvenated in this sense by the English poet John Milton. It now means that in life you must choose between the rewards of the spiritual world and those of the material world. **It is easier for a camel (rope) to go through the eye of a needle than for someone who is rich to enter the kingdom of God**

You can't judge a book by its cover - The origin of this phrase is unclear, but it has been around for centuries. The phrase has evolved to mean: we should not make a judgement of a person or a thing based on what appears on the surface. Similar phrases include: **things are not always what they seem; the first appearance deceives many; the intelligence of a few perceives what has been carefully hidden**

You catch more flies with honey than you do with vinegar - This is an old proverb that has **stood the test of time**. The phrase centers around two contrasting approaches that serves as a metaphor for interactions with people. Honey is sweet and sticky while vinegar is bitter and slippery which implies that people are more receptive to politeness or kindness than they are to rudeness or unpleasantness. Therefore, your words and actions should be sweet, just in case you have to eat them

A COLLECTION OF POPULAR ENGLISH PHRASES

You get what you pay for– This is an old English proverb of unknown origin. Sometimes **cheap is too expensive** because cheap things often have flaws that are discovered later. **In the long run**, it may have been better to choose a more expensive item or option that was more reliable. Although high price does not necessarily mean high quality, often the price of an item is directly proportional to its quality. Similar phrases include: **you get what you deserve**; **you reap what you sow**

You must be the change you want to see in the world - This phrase is attributed to the Indian philosopher and activist Mahatma Gandhi. However, according to the New York Times, Gandhi never said the actual words but rather echoed the sentiment. His nonviolent movement was a central component to the independence of India from Great Britain in the 1940s and served as a model for Dr. Martin Luther King Jr.. The common interpretation of the phrase is: if you want change, you can't wait around for someone else to bring about the change that you want. Each of us has a moral responsibility to make the world a better place for our children and the children of tomorrow. Change is not an easy thing, and every change has required some sacrifice and the courage **to speak truth to power. Actions speak louder than words**

You never get a second chance to make a first impression - The source of this saying is unknown, but it has been ascribed to the Irish author Oscar Wilde and others. It was used in an ad for Botany Suits in 1966 and later by Head & Shoulders. The phrase has evolved to mean: when you first meet someone, people make judgments of you based on several factors: your body language, your attitude, how you dress and speak are some of the key factors that you can control. There are, however, other factors, such as race, gender or physical disabilities that cannot be controlled but can be managed better if you are aware of them. It is most unfortunate, but some people do **judge a book by its cover**. Similar phrases include: **put your best foot forward; appearance rules the world; dress for success**

You never miss your water till the well runs dry - The source of this popular proverb is unknown or unclear. It simply means: so often in life, people take (particularly the essentials} for granted because they become so accustomed to having them. It is only when they are removed that people begin to realize how important or indispensable, they are. This could apply to a person or a thing and evolve over time, e.g., cellphones or hot and cold running water, a dear friend or loved one. **What we obtain too cheap, we esteem too lightly**

Young Turks - The origin of this term has its roots in a young group of Turkish reformers that wanted to modernize Turkey (Ottoman Empire). For decades, Turkey was known as "the sick man of Europe" and their refusal to modernized kept them behind other European nations. As the Ottoman Empire began to crumble, it was a group of three young Turkish men that came into prominence using a modernization platform. This group became known as: The Young Turks. In 1908, they carried out a successful revolution and deposed the Sultan Abdul Hamid II. The term now means; a new group or breed of young people, with different ideas that challenges the existing rule or **status quo; The Jacobins**

Youth is wasted on the young - This quote is credited to the Irish playwright George Bernard Shaw. You are never any younger than you are today and with each moment, you get older. When you are young, you are in good physical and mental condition and you don't have the responsibilities and worries of people that are much older. **The world is your oyster**. Yet, with all of this zeal, the wisdom and knowledge gained by experience is lacking. The phrase is often interpreted to mean: if older people had the zeal, enthusiasm and health of the young, they would make much better use out of it. When you are young you cannot see the mistakes, you will make in the future; and when you are old you cannot change the mistakes you have made in the past. The Irish writer Oscar Wilde sarcastically wrote: "I am not young enough to know everything"

Yuppie - This is a term that emerged in the 1980s and stands for Young Upwardly-mobile Professional. **The Yuppie movement** was an ideological contrast to the hippie movement of the late sixties and early seventies that sought peace and love and preferred a communal lifestyle that frowned upon the establishment and commercial success. There were many however, that viewed the migration of **hippie** to yuppie as **a sell-out**. The term means: a young person with a well-paid job often **living the life of Riley** in the suburbs or affluent sections of the city. Likewise, blacks, many of which were beneficiaries of Affirmative Action programs of the late sixties and seventies, were called **Buppies** which stands for Black Upwardly-mobile Professional. **DINKS (Double Income No Kids)** also emerged during this time period

Z

Zeal without knowledge is a runaway horse - This quote is credited to Thomas Henry Huxley. He was an English biologist, a surgeon and leading supporter of Darwinism, who coined the word agnostic to describe his own beliefs. He was the grandfather of Aldous Huxley the author of the popular book: A Brave New World. It is often interpreted to mean: enthusiasm is something that must be directed or focused on a goal. Therefore, the eagerness of an inexperienced person **may do more harm than good** if not properly directed. **Zeal without knowledge is fire without light**

Zeno's paradox (arrow) - Is a paradox put forth by Zeno of Elea that states: if an object moves with constant speed along a straight line from point 0 to point 1, the object must first cover half the distance (1/2), then half the remaining distance (1/4), then half the remaining distance (1/8), and so on without end. The conclusion is that the object never reaches its point. The frequent interpretation is: something could be plausible theoretically, but totally impractical in the real world. **Achilles and the Tortoise; Everything has its limits**

Zero-sum game - This term originated from economic and game theory and has migrated to other areas such as politics. Sometimes mistaken for *zero sum gain*, it is frequently used to describe a situation when a loss offsets a gain or vice versa. **Nothing from nothing leaves nothing**

List of Popular Internet/Texting Slang Terms

1. 2F4U - Too Fast For You
2. 2Moro - Tomorrow
3. 2nite - Tonight
4. ADL - All Day Long
5. AKA - Also Known As
6. ASAP - As Soon As Possible
7. ASE - Age Sex Ethnicity
8. ASLP - Age Sex Location Picture
9. ATM - At The Moment
10. ATO - Against The Odds
11. AUDY - Are You Done Yet
12. AYPI - And Your Point Is
13. AYW - As You Wish
14. B2U - Back To You
15. B2W - Back To Work
16. B4 - Before
17. B4N - Bye for Now
18. BCNU - Be Seeing(CN) You
19. BF - Boyfriend
20. BFF - Best Friend Forever
21. BLNT - Better Luck Next Time
22. BRB - Be Right Back
23. BRIAB - Be Back In A Bit
24. BTW - By The Way
25. C2C - Cam to Cam
26. CCL - Couldn't Care Less
27. CHOHW - Come Hell or High Water
28. CMCP - Call My Cellphone
29. COL - Crying Out Loud
30. CYA - Cover Your Ass
31. DBA - Don't Bother Asking
32. DGMW - Don't Get Me Wrong
33. DIY - Do It Yourself
34. Dunno - I don't know
35. DWI - Deal With It
36. DYMM - Do You Miss Me
37. EOD - End Of Discussion
38. F2F - Face To Face
39. FAQ - Frequenty Asked Questions
40. FCFS - First Come First Served
41. FKA - Foramlly Known As
42. FYE - For Your Entertainment
43. G2CU - Glad To See You(U)
44. G2G - Got to Go
45. G2K - Good To Know
46. GBNF - Gone But Not Forgotten
47. GBU - God Bless You(U)
48. GLHF - Good Luck Have Fun
49. GMAB - Give Me A Break
50. GOK - God Only Knows
51. GOYHH - Get Off Your High Horse
52. GR8 - Great
53. GTHA - Go The Hell Away
54. GTO - Got To Go
55. GTTP - Get To The Point
56. GWIJD - Guess What I Just Did
57. H911 - Husband In Room
58. HMP - Help Me Please
59. HWMNBN - He Who Must Not Be Named
60. HYK - How You Know
61. IAG - It's All Good
62. IASB - I Am So Bored
63. ICYDK - In Case You Didn't Know
64. IDK - I Don't Know
65. IDTS - I Don't Think So
66. IFTHTB - I Find That Hard To Believe
67. ILY - I Love You
68. ILYSM - I Love You So Much
69. IMO - In My Opinion
70. IOU - I Owe You
71. IRL – In Real Life
72. J/K - Just Kidding
73. J2KYK - Just To Let You Know
74. JFTR - Just For The Record
75. JG2H - Just Go To Hell
76. JIC - Just In Case
77. JTC - Jion The Club
78. JW2K - Just Wanted To Know
79. KIB – OK I Back
80. KMA - Kiss My Ass
81. KYMS - Keep Your Mouth Shut
82. LAM - Leave A Message
83. LMA - Leave Me Alone
84. LOL - Laughing Out Loud
85. LTM - Listen To Me
86. MIQ - Make It Quick
87. MPTY - More Power To You

88. MSH - Me So Horny
89. MWF - Married White Female
90. MWM - Married White Male
91. MYOB - Mind Your Own Business
92. N2B - Not To Bad
93. NHATM - Not Here At The Momment
94. NMJC - Nothing Much Just Chilling
95. NRN - No Reply Necessary
96. OIC - Oh I See(C)
97. OK - Okay
98. OMG - Oh My God
99. OT - Off Topic
100. OTL - Out To Lunch
101. OTT - Over The Top
102. P4P - Pic for Pic
103. PCM - Please Call Me
104. POV - Point of View
105. RBTL - Read Between The Lines
106. ROTFL - Rolling On The Floor (FL)
107. RP - Roleplay
108. S.O.S. - Save Our Souls (Help)
109. STSP - Same Time Same Place
110. Sup - What's Up
111. SWF - Single White Female
112. SWM - Single White Male
113. SWP - Sorry Wrong Person
114. T2UL8R - Talk To You(U) Later (L8R)
115. TBC - To Be Continued
116. TBNT - Thanks But No Thanks

117. TC - Take Care
118. TDTM -Talk Dirty To Me
119. TFS - Thanks For Sharing
120. TGTBT - To Good To Be True
121. TISC - That Is So Cool
122. TLC - Tender Loving Care
123. TMI - To Much Information
124. TMK - To My Knowledge
125. TSM - Thaanks So Much
126. TTYL - Talk To You Later
127. TYT - Take Your Time
128. UDY - You(U) Done Yet
129. W911 - Wife In Room
130. WAU - What About You(U)
131. WAYN - Where Are You Now
132. WBU - What About(B) You
133. WCW - Woman Crush Wednesday
134. WDYA - Why Do You Ask
135. WHS - Wanna Have Sex
136. WIP - Work In Progress
137. WTHAYW4 - What The Hell Are You Waiting For
138. WUWH - Wish You Were Here
139. XOXO - Hugs and Kisses
140. YAM - Yet Another Meeting
141. YGM - You Got Mail
142. YMMD - You Made My Day

References

1. Ammer, Christine, The American Heritage Dictionary of Idioms, Second Edition, Houghton Miffin Harcourt, New York, 2013

2. Archer. Peter and Archer, Linda, 500 Foreign Words & Phrases, Adamsmedia, Avon, MA, 2012

3. Ayers, Donald, M., English Words from Latin and Greek Elements, The University of Arizona Press, Tucson, AZ, 1986

4. Ayto, John, Brewer's Dictionary of Phrase and Fable, Collins, New York, 2005

5. Berlitz, Charles, Dictionary of Foreign Terms, Thomas Crowell Company, New York, 1975

6. Blaisdell, Bob, The Wit and Wisdom of Abraham Lincoln, Dover Publications, Mineola, New York, 2005

7. Bloom, Harold, Shakespeare, Riverhead Books, New York, 1998

8. Chapman, Robert, L., The Dictionary of American Slang, Pan Books, 1987

9. Ciardi, John, A Third Browser's Dictionary, The Akadine Press, New York, 1987

10. Dahlskoo, Helen, A Dictionary of Contemporary and Colloquial Usage, Avenel Books, New York, 1972

11. Dickson, Paul and Clancy, Paul, The Congress Dictionary, John Wiley and Sons, New York, 1993

12. Dickson, Paul, Slang, Pocket Books, New York, 1998

13. Erasmus, Desiderius, Collected Works of Eranmus, University of Toronto Press, Toronto Canada, 1982

14. Evans, Ivor H. Brewer's Dictionary of Phrases and Fable, Harpers and Row, New York, 1981

15. Farlex, Idioms & Slang Dictionary, Farlex International, USA, 2017

16. Funk, Wilfred, Word Origins, Bell Publishing Company, New York, 1950

17. Garrison, Webb, Why You Say It, MJF Books, New York, 1992

18. Geary, James, Geary's Guide to the World's Great Aphorists, Bloomsbury, New York, 2007

19. Gross, John, The Oxford Book of Aphorisms, Oxford University Press, Oxford, 1983

20. Gordon, Karen, Elizabeth, The Disheveled Dictionary, Houghton Mifflin Company, New York, 1997

21. Hendrickson, Robert, QPB, Encyclopedia of Word and Phrase Origins, Dorset Press, New York, 1972

22. Hendrickson, Robert, The Dictionary of Eponyms, Facts on File, New York, 1997

23. Makkai, Adam, Boatner, and Gates, J.T., A Dictionary of American Idioms, Barrons, Hauppauge, New York 1995

24. , Dictionary of Eponyms, Sphere Books Limited London England, 1991

25. McCraw -Hill, McCraw-Hill Dictionary of American Idioms and Phrases, New York, 2002

26. Merriam- Webster, 12,000 Words, Merriam-Webster, Springfield MA, 1986

27. O'Toole, Garson, Hemingway Didn't Say That, Little A, New York, 2017

28. Servi, Katerina, Greek Mythology, Ekdotike Athenon S.A. Athens, 2009

29. Sheidlower, Jesse, Jesse's Word of the Day, Random House, New York, 1998

30. Sholl, Andrew, Bloomers, Biros, &Wellington Boots, Past Time Oxford, England, 1996

31. Sociometer, Shakespeare's English Plays, Oxford University Press, London, 1977

32. Tannen, Deborah, Communication Matters, Modern Scholars, 2004

33. Terban, Martin, Dictionary of Idioms, Scholastic Reference, New York, 1996

34. Wilson, Kenneth, G., The Columbia Guide to Standard American English, Columbia University Press, New York,1993

Internet references:

1. Britannica.com
2. Dictionary.com
3. Definitions.net
4. Gingersoftware.com
5. Goodreads.com
6. Grammar-monster.com
7. Theidioms.com
8. Idiomsite.com
9. Merriam-webster.com
10. OxfordDictionary.com
11. Phrases.org.uk
12. Quoteinvestigator.com
13. Snopes.com
14. Stackexchange.com
15. Thefreedictionary.com
16. Urbandictionary.com
17. Word-detective.com
18. Youtube.com
19. https://www.gingersoftware.com/content/phrase-of-the-day/page23

Appendix

Some Helpful Hints

Types of Speech

There are three areas of speech, informal, semiformal and formal. Informal speech is defined as how you speak to family and friends. Semiformal speech is often used when talking to coworkers or in an office or professional environment. While formal speech is normally reserved for public speeches, official reports, essays, books, contracts and business letters. When you use idiomatic expressions, especially in a formal setting, it is very important that you understand the meaning and how it fits into the overall message that you want to deliver. Although metaphors are often helpful in conversation, using the wrong metaphor can seriously undermine your message.

Rhetoric and Oral Presentation

The Roman statesman Cicero was a master at rhetoric and many of his techniques are used today. The Greek statesman Demosthenes was a master of oratory whose work ethic serves as a model for those that aspire to improve their formal communication. If we dare to stand on the shoulders of these two ancient giants; we will gaze upon a landscape of language full of enchantment and linguistic beauty.

The following is a listing of some aspects of communication that could be used to augment the expressions in this book

How you deliver your message is just as important as what you say

- ➢ Using the correct inflection and amplitude (volume of your voice)- Speaking in a monotone becomes boring over time
- ➢ Place the right emphasis on words- Saying your words correctly and emphasizing certain parts of a phrase, helps to keep the listener engaged
- ➢ Pacing and pausing at the right time gives the listener an opportunity to digest what was said and perhaps applaud it or laugh at it
- ➢ Developing the rhythm and tone of your speech (the music of speech) – A popular technique is to use groups of threes. This is a powerful technique and helps to develop good rhythm and flow. Trios, triplets, and triads flourish in all aspects of the human endeavor. Our minds seem to be wired to be receptive to the power of three, e.g., *Friends, Romans, Countrymen; Duty, Honor, Country; Government of the people, by the people, for the people.* Blood, sweat and tears is more powerful than blood, toil, tears and sweat (a quote from a famous speech by Winston Churchill). In fact, toil is implied when you just mention the three.
- ➢ Proper use of directness and indirectness - Knowing when to be direct and when to be vague or indirect is an art and a science. Sometimes what is not said is just as important as what was said

> Feedback (responding to what has been said by others)- How others react to what you are saying and feeding back their response, is essential to keeping the dialogue moving in the right direction
> Framing (thinking about what you are saying and how it may be received) - It is a good idea to read what you intend to say out loud beforehand, especially if you are going to deliver it before a group of people
> As a rule of thumb, never mix your metaphors or use too many of them in one sentence (Although I have done so in this book; to illustrate certain points or to demonstrate how they could be used or how they relate to each other)
> Body Language:- Research shows that 60 to 90 percent of our communication with others is nonverbal, which means the body language we use is extremely important
>   - Smiling, laughter - Both smiling and laughter are signs of happiness and when used appropriately can relax the listener(s)
>   - Hand gestures - Using hand gestures while you speak not only helps others remember what you say, it also helps you to speak more quickly and effectively!
>   - Talking with your eyes (eye contact)- It is important to maintain good eye contact while speaking and not look down at the floor. If you are reading something, look up from time to time, particularly while addressing a group
>   - Posture - Posture is also a good indicator of the mood or inner feelings of a person. Therefore, good posture is always a plus and something that the speaker should be aware of

The Art of Communication

Writing and speaking have often been placed under the category of the arts. Yet both could be considered as science as well. To become a proficient writer or orator, one must study the rules and guidelines in the same way that a mathematician or a physicist must learn the rules of their disciplines. A person must have a methodical approach and be willing to experiment with different ideas available in their linguistic laboratory. Regardless of aptitude, practice and diligence are germane to improving your writing and speaking. Reading and research are essential ingredients to the final product.

Samuel Johnson once said: "One may have to read a complete library just to write one book of substance." We must be forever mindful that the kind of writing and speaking that we are exposed to is the kind of writing and speaking we will eventually develop. As far as writing is concerned, a person must have the diligence, patience and fortitude to rewrite a piece (sometimes several times) to achieve the desired result. Very seldom a piece of work is completed without the mind going through its period when thoughts are incubated, congealed and consolidated. Revisiting your work the next day and possibly rewriting it, is an integral part of the writing progression. This process often separates skillful writing from bad or mediocre writing. Hemmingway once commented that he rewrote the beginning of his novel The Sun Rises over fifty times. Authors such as F. Scott Fitzgerald not only kept copious notes on their subject matter, but logbooks of phrases to be used at a later date.

One significant way to improve your writing is to read good writers and to write as often as you can. These mental exercises keep your mind sharp and in shape. Just as a long-distance runner improves his endurance by running every day, instead of searching for words to use, the words will automatically come to you. When possible, add a personal touch or a sense of humor. Such techniques remind the reader that you are human and helps him or her identify with you subconsciously.

Although oral and written skills often go hand and hand, they are two separate beasts, each with their own set of idiosyncrasies and nuances that require specific skills. Statesmen such as Winston Churchill and Abraham Lincoln excelled at both. Although Thomas Jefferson was a highly skilled writer and a polymath, he was not a good orator.

- ➤ Three basic rules of writing and speaking are as follows:
  - Use enough detail to support your points
  - Follow a natural flow or order
  - Stick to your subject
- ➤ The order should be as follows:
  - Bait the reader by catching his or her attention or interest (The hook)
  - Introduce the general idea or background of your subject or topic
  - The main body of your writing or speech (tell the story)
  - The ending or conclusion of your argument or theme
  - Think of this process as making a sandwich for your reader to eat: with the beginning as one piece of bread on the top, the middle the meat; and the ending the bottom piece of bread
- ➤ Ideas: There are three popular ways of getting ideas
  - Those based on your own experiences and knowledge
  - Listening to the ideas of others that stimulate you
  - Or by reading and research (plagiarism is drawing from one source, research is drawing from many sources)
- ➤ Research
  - Your piece is only as good as the references that you use. In the age of the Internet, in which your facts and credibility can be easily checked, this is all the more important
  - Check your sources

- Keep good notes and references
- If possible, go to the place you are writing about

Books of the Old Testament

LAW	HISTORY	POETRY/WISDOM	MAJOR PROPHETS	MINOR PROPHETS
Genesis	Joshua	Job	Isaiah	Hosea
Exodus	Judges	Psalms	Jeremiah	Joel
Leviticus	Ruth	Proverbs	Laminations	Amos
Numbers	I Samuel	Ecclesiastes	Ezekiel	Obadiah
Deuteronomy	2 Samuel	Song Of Solomon	Daniel	Jonah
	I Kings			Micah
	2 Kings			Nahum
	1 Chronicles			Habakkuk
	Ezra			Zephaniah
	Nehemiah			Haggai
	Esther			Zechariah
				Malachi

Books of the New Testament

HISTORICAL BOOKS	PAULINE EPISTLES	NON-PAULINE EPISTLES	APOCALYPTIC LITERATURE	Color Codes
Matthew	Romans	Hebrews	Revelation	Synoptic Gospels
Mark	1 Corinthians	James		Catholic Epistles
Luke	2 Corinthians	1 Peter		Undisputed Epistles
Gospel of John	Galatians	2 Peter		First Attributed to Paul but now disputed
Acts	Ephesians	1 John		Pastoral Epistles
	Philippians	2 John		Deutero-Pauline Epistles
	Colossians	3 John		
	1 Thessalonians	Jude		
	2 Thessalonians			
	1 Timothy			
	2 Timothy			
	Titus			
	Philemon			

Greek and Roman Gods and Goddesses

Greek	Roman	Attribute
Aphrodite	Venus	Goddess of Love
Apollo Phoebus	Apollo	God of Light
Ares	Mars	God of War
Artemis	Diana	Virgin goddess of the hunt, wilderness, and childbirth
Asclepius	Asclepius	God of medicine and healing
Athena	Minerva	Goddess of Wisdom
Demeter	Ceres	Goddess of grain/crops
Dionysus	Bacchus	God of Wine
Eros	Cupid	God of Love
Hades	Pluto	God of Underworld
Hecate	Trivia	Goddess of witchcraft, crossroads, and justice
Helios	Sol	The sun God
Hephaestus	Vulcan	God of Fire
Hera	Juno	Queen of the Gods
Hermes	Mercury	Messenger of the Gods
Nike	Victoria	Goddess of Victory

Pan	Faunus	God of woods and pastures
Poseidon	Neptune	God of the Sea
Zeus	Jupiter	King of Gods

ACKNOWLEDGMENTS

The author is extremely grateful to the many family members and friends for giving him the fortitude to compile this book and to pursue a writing career. The author wishes to extend his acknowledgments to the following individuals: First and foremost, to my wife Jeanne Royal Singley of 35 plus years; whose patience and endearing support is written on each page in ink only visible to me. To my two sons: Bradford and Adrian, for putting up with their dad all these years and for making me so proud to be their father. To my loving parents, Lawson and Willie Mae Singley (both deceased); whose love, wisdom and guidance I will always cherish. To my uncles, particularly my Uncle Johnny (deceased) aunts, cousins and grandparents (Grandmother and Mommy Essie both deceased), many of them loss but not forgotten, whose perception is also compiled within the confines of this book.

To my sisters and brothers: Edward Singley (deceased), Margret Griggs (deceased), Brenda Wright (deceased), Robert Singley (deceased), Gloria Riley, Mary Crump (deceased), Linda McDaniel, David Singley and especially my older brother Amin Rasheed (Roger Singley) who was always there when I needed him and to their progeny. I would like to extend my appreciation to my Sister-in-laws: Helen Rasheed and Kitty Singley (deceased) and to the entire Singley family. Their support was not only vital to this book but to my life. Gratitude is also extended to my godparents, Sister Ruthie and Brother Chester, for their help in raising me. My appreciation is also extended to my wife's family, Lester McDaniel and Barbara Hughes and the McDaniel and Hughes siblings.

The number of individuals that helped me during my life is far too great to acknowledge without citing some and omitting others. However, there were some that had an enduring impact that warrant special recognition: From my college days: Steve Throne and James G. Spady, whose enlightening conversation and mentorship opened my eyes to a world hitherto unseen. Special thanks to my dearest friends, Jesse Brown, James Spigner, James Grant, Willie Dash, Bill Hart, Dr. Erasmus Feltus (deceased), Jimmy Martin and Charles Cook (deceased) who mentored me during my first job. A special thanks to Lynn Worthy, Alex Tatum, Jesse Brown, Steve Throne and Professor Joseph Kennedy for their review of my work and their faith in my abilities. To Mabel Elizabeth Singletary for her help in getting this book published. To the members of Mount Calvary Church of God in Elizabeth, NJ that prayed for me when I was sick and for providing me with a religious background.

To my team of doctors particularly: Dr. Frekko, Mrs. Frekko and their daughters, Dr. Bass, Dr. Lin, Dr. Juarbe, Dr. Baek, Dr. Lieberman and Dr. Melki. To the citizens of the town of Roselle, NJ (the first town in the world to have an electrical infrastructure). My appreciation is also extended to the following individuals: Mr. Frazier who kept on me about publishing my writing, Mrs. Roberts who gave me money for running errands as a child and families like the Sumners, Cooks, Simmons, etc., that formed a neighborhood that was the laboratory for my learning.

To my enduring friends and former coworkers, particularly my former secretary Alice Baker, former managers, John Bigelow, Alan Dunn, Randy Cline and longtime coworkers that supported me in this and

IN A NUTSHELL

other efforts: Mary Lott, Dick Alban, Laveer Jovel, Steve Becraft, Verna Wright, Jim Rader, Dave Epler, Steve Frinak, Jim Hanlon, Paul Gantz, Steve Williams, Stu Benner, Tim Bresnan, Douglas Smith (deceased), Bob McKay, Bob Peters, Dick Roberts, Scott Pettygrove, Zach Stern, Dale Mann, Dale Dahlke, Jeff Shires, Barry Constantine, Bahman Salamat, Jeff Dobek, Jim Burck, John Murphy, Bill Smith, Greg Kneer, Terry Fogle, Mark Mowen, Kevin Graul, Gary Bell, Brendan Regan, Mark and Cathy Flinchbaugh, Melvin Pierce, Pat Howley, Lee Lusby, Ralph Lee, Lenny Jacobs, John Sill, Rob Strain, Frank Hornbuckle, Wyatt Bell, Ken Grish, Jerry Carbone, Daun Green, Don Muller, Ed Kozlosky, Gordon Whitney, Rod Miller, Richard Mugg, Krista Ochlech, Ben Burt, Mike Zeher, Al Hughes, Don Eenigenburg, Wynn Aung, Carl Slutsky, Tim Malac, Stu Mullan, Tim Burns, Joe Colburn, R.T. Stokes, Mike Janes, Mark Beatson, Carmela Young and the employees at Fairchild Space and Defense, Orbital Sciences, Smith Industries, General Electric and so many others that have offered support and encouragement during this endeavor. To the many workers at Friends of the Library Montgomery County, MD and to the Sickles family long-time owners of the Book Alcove and relatives of the Civil War general Dan Sickles for providing me with inexpensive books and for encouraging me to continue to write.

Thanks, is also given to the following friends whose discussions helped in this endeavor. Gene Limb, Mark Edwards, Edward Fortney, Earl Spence, Earl Jenkins, Derrick Carr, Bristol Martin, Steve Cooper, Stephan Shin, Marcus (Doc) Coleman, Vince Coleman, Lenny Chornock, Dr. Gary Greenbaum (deceased) Robert White, Mike Slater, Joe Hasshen, Marcelo Flores, Stu Keeler, Grandville Smith, Earl Meadows, Tommy Arnold, Paul Kane, Kevin Kistler, Cameron Dryden, Reuben Smith, Calton Hall, Russ (40) Deshields, Greg Estep, Trenton Holmes, Cameron Simmons, Matt Fremin, Mike Wigal, Kevin Sinai, Heath Marshall, Kevin Correa, Leroy Gettinger, Mark Alan Hill, Kenny Jenkins, Lloyd McMillian, Jimmy McMillian, Steve Bender, Don Frost, Crispian Kirk, Chalk Dawson, Rashida Anderson, Kathy Amidon, Brian Hackett and Boyd Thomas. Gratitude is also extended to my fellow coworkers, staff and students at Rocky Hill Middle School, Clarksburg, Maryland. Specifically, Daphne Williams, Marion Martin, Olivia Reyes, Marc Cosby, Kimberly Wiltshire, Allen Ambush, the Montgomery County Public School (MCPS) staff at Clarksburg, Northwest and Watkins Mill High Schools; Martin Luther King Middle School and to Dr. Karl Reid of the National Society of Black Engineers (NSBE).

To the Washington Independent Review for helping to improve my writing skills and to Chris Matthews of MSNBC, David Maraniss Associate Editor of the Washington Post and Roger Williams of New England Publishing Associates, INC. for their comments on writing and the literary business. I also want to thank my classmates and teachers at Abraham Clark High School and Drexel University for providing me with intriguing dialogue and a good educational foundation. I would like to mention some of my Drexel colleagues specifically, Alton Knight, Colvin Bert, Gwen Evans, Derese Fisher, Alfred Taylor, Don Hinson, John Greene, David Adams (deceased) Mike Wright and Ray Gibson (deceased). Finally, I am grateful to my homeboys "the brothers": Lynn Worthy, Dr. Albert Ford, Kevin Williamson, Alex and Willis Tatum. Together we proved that little black boys who dare to dream can become doctors, lawyers, historians and engineers. The journey has been long, but it has also been joyous.

Let me end by saying that I know there are some that deserve personal recognition that I have failed to mention. To them I offer my sincere apology.

The Class of 1972, Abraham Clark High School, Roselle, New Jersey

Abate Marlene, Allen Arnella, Allen Mark Altobelli/Incannella Linda, Arneo/Himelman Maria, Augenstein/McMillan Elise, **Baldwin Donna, Ballin Gary**, Banker/Sheehy Dale, Baus John, Bertram Thomas, Bethel William, Beveridge Patty, Blades Steve, **Boggs Harold,** Bonner Larry, Bork Richard, Boryszewski Frank, Bragg Antionette, Brazaitis Linda, Breneiser Karen, Briddle/Albert Debra, **Briggs Nancy, Brody Evelyn**, Brody Diana, Brown Michael, Bukowski Paul, Burns Billy, Burns Vanessa, Burris Elliot, **Caldwell Lavorne, Carter Bernard,** Carter / Thomas Renee, Caruso Dan, Cascone Charles, **Chapka Mike**, Chrebet Clifford, Christian/Berry Nancy, **Chrusch Marc**, Coleman Harry, Crapanzano Joe, Crist Edward, Cullum/Chapka Jamie, **Curtis Jethro**, Daniels Jennifer, **Darby Ken**, DeCarlo Mike, Deczynski/Intile Chris, Deutschlander Janice, DiCillo Tony, Dittman/Daly Ginny, Dixon Paulette, Durham Marvin, Dutton Diane, Eirdosh John, Ellner/Blackwell Stephanie, Ferio Dave, Fernandez/Peyton Elaine, Finelli Bibiana, **Fish Justine**, Flanagan James, Flannery John, Flores/Tavares Irma, **Ford Albert,** Forgash/Ginsberg Sherri, Foucha Clarencelina, Foulkrod/Hoban Debbie, **Franklin Gary, Frieson Robin**, Fuchs Trudy, **Furtney Eric**, Galligan Veronica, Geczi, Mike, Gega Geoff, **George Robert**, Gigantino James, **Ginsberg Joel**, Gonzalez/Carew Rita, Gonzalez Raymond, **Gordon Chuck**, Gostyla Walter, Gray Jeffrey, Green Bruce, Green/Moll Nancy, Gregory Bruce, Grobstein Naomi, Hahn/McNulty Debbie, Hale/Wraith Ellen, Hall Dave, Hansen/Meseck Cynthia, Harsman/Kupcho Anita, Haskins Dave, Herman/Cooper Michele, Hoblick Michael, Hollerback Lee, Holliday Joe, Hunter Terry, Hura-Balog Thomas, Hyers/MacGregor Judy, Ilich Pete, Jacobs/Taylor Cynthia, **Jarvis Felice**, Jasones/Mahoney Nancy, Jervert Jan, **Johnson Ruth, Johnson Mike, Johnson Rudy, Johnson Pam, Johnson Evelyn**, Judd Steven, **Judkins Joe,** Kacerek, Frank Kaiser/Zurstsdt Wendy, Karlovich Dave, Kennedy Linda, **Kirschner Robert**, Klein/Drakeford Glynis, **Klem Debbie**, Klose Greg, Kornacki/Rubel Catherine, Kraft Ingrid, **Kraph Shirley**, Kuzma George, LaGrasso Angelo, LaPorte Kathy, Leffingwell Dan, Levy/Insalaco Brenda, Lockett John, **Longstreet Bruce**, Mackin Kathy, MacMillan Robin, Madersky Richard, Mahnken Richard, Marnick/Healey Linda, **Massey Vernon**, Matson Gary, Mauro Dennis, Maynor Bethenia, **McBride George**, McCain/Gonzalez Deborah, McKenna Pat, McKenzie Camile, **McMaster Duncan**, McNulty William, McSweeney Michelle, Meyers Wayne, Mildner/Santa, Maria Carol, **Mitchell Thadious,** Mitchell Richard, Monages Miriam, **Morton Veronica**, Mularz Stephen, **Muldrow Charlene**, Mundy/Davey Dolores, Musco Frank, Oehlke Paul, Orlando Robert, Ortuso Jim, Ostromecki Christopher, Peterson Brenda, Planin Harold, Piech Diane, Piercy Gwen, Piotrowski/Liatta Lydia Pisarski, Michael Pitchell, Jerry Puchalski/Newhardt Linda, **Pulley Mary, Rafte June, Ratcliff Debbie**, Rayner Nancy, Reuter James, Rice/Sawyer Cynthia, Richards/Howlett Audrae, Richlin Lisa, Roxbury Guy, Sachs/Laudon Robyn, Sainz Carlos, Sainz Rigoberto, Salermo, Mayda Samer, Gary **Saunders Brad**, Savick Edward, **Scales Jessica**, Schell Sandra, Schiff/Hakala Carol, Schleuter Walter, Schumann Lee, Schweitzer Frank, Scott

IN A NUTSHELL

Linda, **Sharkey Robert**, Shendell Mark, Shepard/Brodie Trudie, **Simmons Keith**, Simmons Walter, Simow Pat, **Sims Solomon**, **Singley Richard**, Sizemore James, Smith Douglas, **Smith Oliver**, Smith Kent, **Soltys/Banta Nancy**, Sommer/Colandrea, Veronica, **Spady Robert, Stamper Gregory, Stern Gary, Sumner Gary,** Svraka/Blagojevic Seka, Szczesny Ronald, Szuberla Casmir, **Tatum Willis, Tatum Alex,** Terpenning Frank, Terroni Darlene, Tilelli Christine, Todorovich Leopold, **Vaughan/Fowler Wanda,** Ventura Diane, Wactor Sandra, Waller Lewis, **Watkins June**, Watson Robert, Williams Ben, Williams Karen, Williams Adrienne, **Wilmore/Davis Pam**, Wilpiszeski Joe, **Wolf/Funk Cynthia, Worthy Lynn**, Yohannan John, **Zaccaro Richard**, Zarauskas Claire, Zelman Joseph

Bold represents people that I hung out with in High School

MY CHILDHOOD AND HIGH SCHOOL FRIENDS

From left to right: Lynn Worthy, Alex Tatum, me, Willis Tatum

About the Author

Richard Lawson Singley has worked in the Engineering field for over three decades. Richard spent many years employed as an Electrical Engineer, but never lost his passion for exploring the intricacies of the English language and historical events. He is the author of several forthcoming books and essays on various subjects including, religion, science, philosophy, history and politics. He has also worked as an educator and assistant in the Maryland Public School (MCPS) system. He is a graduate of Drexel University with a degree in Electrical Engineering. A native of Roselle, NJ; he is the father of two sons, Bradford and Adrian, and lives in the Washington, DC area with his life-long love and wife Jeanne. rich.singley5234@gmail.com

https://medium.com/@richardsingley

About Prometheus Educational and Business Consultants

Prometheus Educational and Business Consultants (PEBC) LLC is a company founded by Richard Lawson Singley for the purpose of preparing young students to meet the demanding challenges of the 21st century. Our goal is to help forge relationships between communities, educational institutions and businesses thereby creating career paths, opportunities and challenges for young students. Taking its name from the legendary Greek hero, Prometheus, that stole fire from the gods thereby bringing knowledge to humankind; PEBC is dedicated to improving the social, intellectual and personal skills required to interact with people of diverse backgrounds around the globe. The World Wide Web (WWW) has proven to be a conduit of information and at times it can appear to be overwhelming. It is our goal to streamline information by directing students to reliable sources and to expose students to a wide range of subjects and cultures. We believe that the aforementioned skills are vital to the success of the emerging global market centered around, but not exclusively limited to, the internet. It is our hope and intention to help create the next generation of polymaths and entrepreneurs eager to take on the challenges of the new millennium.

Made in the USA
Middletown, DE
15 December 2019

80860082R10186